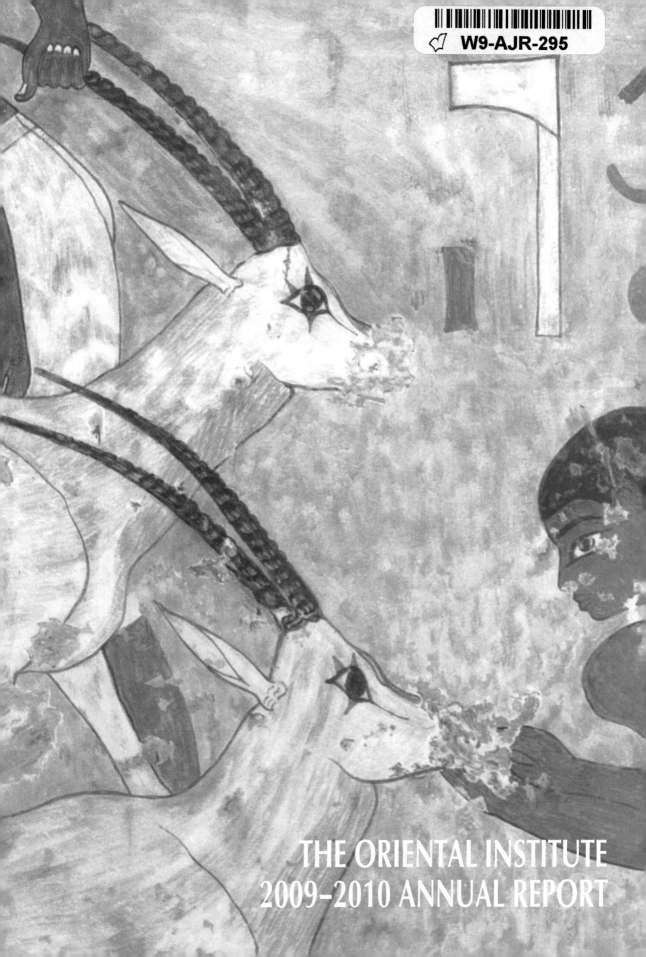

THE ORIENTAL INSTITUTE
2009–2010 ANNUAL REPORT

Cover illustration: Painted pottery sherd showing a procession of animals, including an ostrich. Figure 20 in Tell Zeidan report, below. Ubaid period. Tell Zeidan, Syria. Scale 1:1

The pages that divide the sections of this year's report feature images of animal paintings gathered from *Ancient Egyptian Paintings*, Volumes 1 and 2, by Nina M. Davies with Alan H. Gardiner (Chicago: University of Chicago Press, 1936).

Editor: Gil J. Stein

Production editor: Maeve Reed, with special thanks to Plamena Pehlivanova.

The Oriental Institute, Chicago

ISBN-13: 978-1-885923-77-6
ISBN-10: 1-885923-77-5

Printed by United Graphics Incorporated, Mattoon, Illinois, USA

The paper used in this publication meets the minimum requirements of American National Standard for Information Service — Permanence of Paper for Printed Library Materials, ANSI Z39.48-1984

∞

Overleaf: Feeding the oryxes. Detail from Ancient Egyptian Paintings, *Volume I, pl. 8*

CONTENTS

INTRODUCTION 5

   INTRODUCTION. *Gil J. Stein* 7

   IN MEMORIAM 9

RESEARCH 11

   PROJECT REPORTS 13

      ARCHAEOLOGY OF ISLAMIC CITIES. *Donald Whitcomb* 13

      CENTER FOR ANCIENT MIDDLE EASTERN LANDSCAPES (CAMEL). *Scott Branting* 16

      CHICAGO ASSYRIAN DICTIONARY (CAD). *Martha T. Roth* 21

      CHICAGO DEMOTIC DICTIONARY (CDD). *François Gaudard* and *Janet H. Johnson* 22

      CHICAGO HITTITE DICTIONARY (CHD AND *e*CHD). *Theo van den Hout* 25

      EPIGRAPHIC SURVEY. *W. Raymond Johnson* 29

      GIZA PLATEAU MAPPING PROJECT. *Mark Lehner* 40

      KERKENES DAĞ PROJECT. *Scott Branting* 65

      MARJ RABBA. *Yorke M. Rowan* 71

      MUMMY LABEL DATABASE (MLD). *François Gaudard, Raquel Martín Hernández,* and *Sofía Torallas Tovar* 79

      NIPPUR. *McGuire Gibson* 80

      PERSEPOLIS FORTIFICATION ARCHIVE PROJECT. *Matthew W. Stolper* 83

      SLAVES AND HOUSEHOLDS IN THE NEAR EAST. *Laura Culbertson* 92

      TELL EDFU. *Nadine Moeller* 94

      TELL ZEIDAN. *Gil J. Stein* 105

   INDIVIDUAL RESEARCH 119

   RESEARCH SUPPORT 140

      COMPUTER LABORATORY. *John C. Sanders* 140

      ELECTRONIC RESOURCES. *John C. Sanders* 143

      PUBLICATIONS OFFICE. *Thomas G. Urban* 151

      RESEARCH ARCHIVES. *Foy Scalf* 154

MUSEUM 161

   MUSEUM. *Geoff Emberling* 163

   SPECIAL EXHIBITS. *Emily Teeter* 166

   PUBLICITY AND MARKETING. *Emily Teeter* and *Thomas James* 169

   REGISTRATION. *Helen McDonald* and *Susan Allison* 173

   ARCHIVES. *John A. Larson* 176

   CONSERVATION. *Laura D'Alessandro* 179

   PREP SHOP. *Erik Lindahl* 181

   SUQ. *Denise Browning* 182

   PHOTOGRAPHY. *Anna R. Ressman* 183

PUBLIC EDUCATION 185

   PUBLIC EDUCATION. *Carole Krucoff* 187

   VOLUNTEER PROGRAM. *Catherine Dueñas* and *Terry Friedman* 205

DEVELOPMENT AND MEMBERSHIP 219

   DEVELOPMENT. *Steve Camp* and *Rebecca Silverman* 221

   VISITING COMMITTEE 224

   MEMBERSHIP. *Maeve Reed* 227

   SPECIAL EVENTS. *Meghan A. Winston* 231

   HONOR ROLL OF DONORS AND MEMBERS 236

CONTENTS

FACULTY AND STAFF 251

FACULTY AND STAFF OF THE ORIENTAL INSTITUTE 253

INFORMATION 264

INTRODUCTION

Overleaf: *Birds in acacia tree. Detail from* Ancient Egyptian Paintings, *Volume I, pl. 9*

INTRODUCTION

Gil J. Stein

I am honored to present you with this year's *Oriental Institute Annual Report 2009–2010*. As you can see from the impressive scope of activities by the faculty, researchers, and staff of the Oriental Institute this has been a highly productive year.

Our mission is to explore the ancient civilizations of the Near East through archaeological, textual, and art historical research, and to communicate the results of our work to both scholars and the broader public through our museum and programs of education and outreach.

The Oriental Institute is uniquely valuable in having scholars from complementary disciplines all under the same roof, sharing their insights and applying them toward a deeper, more holistic understanding of the world's earliest civilizations. This work of synthesis and integration of knowledge lies at the core of what we do — the creative work of turning "data" into "knowledge." As the famous French mathematician Henri Poincaré put it: "Science is built up of facts, as a house is with stones. But a collection of facts is no more a science than a heap of stones is a house." This synthetic goal animates the Institute's research in archaeology, textual studies, and public education.

The Oriental Institute now has eight archaeological excavations across the Near East — an unprecedented range of projects that testifies to the vitality of our research into the origins of Near Eastern civilizations. In parallel with our existing excavations at Edfu, Giza, Hamoukar, Kerkenes, Zeidan, and Zincirli, in 2009 the Institute conducted the first field season of the Galilee Prehistoric Project, directed by Yorke Rowan. This long-term project investigates the little-known fifth-millennium BC Chalcolithic period in Israel. In the first stage of this project, Yorke is excavating the village site of Marj Rabba to understand the organization of rural life and economy of the Galilee during the Chalcolithic. In a second exciting development, Donald Whitcomb secured the permit from the Palestinian National Authority in the West Bank to excavate at Khirbet el-Mafjar, the early Islamic portion of the fabled city of Jericho. Mafjar was the site of a palace and urban complex dating back to the earliest caliphs of the Umayyad dynasty and can help illuminate the workings of the early Islamic state.

In tandem with our excavations, the Oriental Institute's three dictionary projects — the Assyrian Dictionary edited by Martha Roth, the Demotic Dictionary edited by Janet Johnson, and the Hittite Dictionary co-edited by Harry Hoffner and Theo van den Hout — continue in their pathbreaking work of creating research tools for the entire discipline. We have reached a milestone in that the final volume of the Assyrian Dictionary should be published in the upcoming year.

The Epigraphic Survey under Ray Johnson has been making great strides, not just in the recording of the monuments at Luxor and Medinet Habu, but also in conservation and restoration of these monuments. The protection of cultural heritage has emerged as an important focus of the our work in Egypt. The Epigraphic Survey team has been working with the Egyptian Supreme Council of Antiquities and with USAID in a massive project to lower the water table in the area around the main monuments of western Thebes in order to protect and preserve the architecture.

The Oriental Institute is also breaking new ground in public education. In this past year, Carole Krucoff, Wendy Ennes, and numerous colleagues from the Institute and the Department of Near Eastern Languages and Civilizations completed a large-scale project funded by the National Endowment for the Humanities to create a Web-based curriculum that gives high-school teachers an extraordinary rich resource for teaching students about the ancient and modern Near East. In a parallel project this past year, the Museum opened a fascinating exhibit, Pioneers to the Past, which details the intertwined stories of the founding of the Oriental Institute in 1919, the beginnings of American scientific archaeology in the Fertile Crescent, and the origins of the countries of the modern Middle East. It has never been more important for Americans to understand this crucial region of the world, and the Museum and Public Education department have made major contributions toward that goal.

Finally, one of the most important and innovative accomplishments of the Oriental Institute in 2009–10 has been our progress toward the development of an Integrated Database (IDB). This long-term project seeks to link the many different computerized databases from our museum, archives, research archives (library), conservation section, dictionaries, and remote-sensing laboratory (CAMEL — the Center for the Ancient Middle Eastern Landscape). With the help of a large capital-budget grant from the University of Chicago, the Institute has been able to purchase the complex software that will form the heart of our integrative data structure. We are now moving ahead with a pilot project to incorporate the first of our many, formerly independent, databases into a unified structure. When this effort is completed, researchers and the public will be able to search through our collections for artifacts of a certain type, learn about their conservation status, then find and read publications about those artifacts, while also examining maps, plans, and photographs of the sites where they were found. This ability to move seamlessly from one archive of information to another has never been possible before, and it will revolutionize the way we do our research.

Overall, in 2009–2010, the Oriental Institute has made major strides in its work of discovery, while at the same time building new and innovative frameworks for research and the communication of that research to the world at large. I want to thank all the members of the Oriental Institute's community of scholars, staff, and supporters for the role they have played in this effort.

IN MEMORIAM
Rita Tallent Picken

This past year, we were greatly saddened by the death of Rita Tallent Picken, a true friend and generous supporter of the Oriental Institute. Rita's warm-hearted, generous, and intellectually curious presence was felt across the Institute's many programs and projects. She showed her love for the Oriental Institute not only through her involvement with the docent program for thirty years but also through her sponsorship of the Robert F. Picken Family Nubia Gallery and special exhibit The Life of Meresamun: A Temple Singer in Ancient Egypt. This past spring at the Oriental Institute's 90th Anniversary Gala, the Institute honored Rita with the James Henry Breasted Medallion — the highest honor that we give our Members and supporters to recognize their commitment to our mission. Most importantly, Rita was a person whose sweetness, gentle wit, and sparkling eyes always brightened up the

room. The Oriental Institute was like a second family for her and we all will miss her greatly. In a beautifully fitting commemoration of Rita's lifetime of service, her daughter, Kitty Picken has established the Rita T. Picken Professorship in Ancient Near Eastern Art at the Oriental Institute.

Myrtle Nims

We also saw the passing of Myrtle Nims, widow of Oriental Institute professor and former Epigraphic Survey Director Charles F. Nims. After her marriage to him in 1931, Myrtle accompanied him over the many years that Charles participated in the Oriental Institute's Epigraphic Survey at Chicago House in Luxor, Egypt, as an epigrapher, photographer, and eventually as field director. When work resumed in the 1940s after World War II, Myrtle was a constant presence at Chicago House through Charles' retirement in 1972. She was an active participant in the work at

Chicago House, responsible for binding books for the library for many years. When Charles became field director, she managed the building by shopping, planning menus, and arranging teas for Chicago House visitors. In this way, she became an integral part of the running of the Chicago House facilities and maintaining Chicago House's position as an attraction for dignitaries, visitors, and scholars. Oriental Institute Members who visited Chicago House during those years will remember her as a gracious hostess and kind ambassador for the Oriental Institute's work in Egypt. Included in her legacy to the Oriental Institute are: the many hundreds of photographs Charles took in Egypt, his book collection on Egypt and the Near East, and a generous estate plan. Myrtle was the last of the Oriental Institute family who participated in the Institute's work in the Near East in the 1930s.

RESEARCH

PROJECT REPORTS

ARCHAEOLOGY OF ISLAMIC CITIES

Donald Whitcomb

I outlined the contribution of the Oriental Institute to this field of research in the last *Annual Report*. This year requires a shift of focus to the nature of these studies outside of the Institute.

The role of the International Congress for the Archaeology of the Ancient Near East (ICAANE) has become fundamental for Islamic as well as for earlier Near Eastern archaeology. During the introduction to the 2008 meetings, I was invited to give a plenary statement on the relationship of "Ancient and Islamic" in Near (or Middle) Eastern archaeology and those present in Rome formally voted to include Islamic archaeology as an integral part of ICAANE. Our Italian hosts have now published this congress; this address begins a separate volume of *Proceedings of the 6th International Congress of the Archaeology of the Ancient Near East (ICAANE)*, Volume 3: *Islamic Session* (edited by Paolo Matthiae, Lorenzo Nigro, and Nicolo Marchetti; Wiesbaden: Harrassowitz, 2010). The volume presents some seventeen papers, over half Italian contributions illustrating the variety and intensity of Islamic research. Likewise, over half of the subjects are found in the region of Bilad al-Sham (mainly Syria), followed by Iran and Afghanistan.

Happily, one paper, by Alison Gascoigne, adds an Egyptian study, an area not normally included in the ICAANE meetings. While many papers are very useful site reports, others specialized in material artifacts, particularly the common interest in ceramics.

The seventh ICAANE meetings were held in London, in April, at the British Museum and University College. A curious arrangement for papers meant that some Islamic subjects were transferred to main themes; nevertheless, thirty-one papers (almost twice as many) in Islamic archaeology were given compared to the ones in Rome. This time, about two-thirds of the subject dealt with studies in Bilad al-Sham, but many more from Turkey and a good representation of the Red Sea and Persian Gulf regions. The Icelandic ash clouds prolonged the meetings, and conversations shifted from purely academic archaeology to tactical information on getting back (renting cars, flying to Madrid, etc.). Prompted by my Israeli colleagues, we visited the Victoria & Albert Museum to examine the new exhibitions of the ceramics department. The entire sixth floor, endowed with splendid natural light (even during the ash emergency),

Figure 1. Exhibition case of Islamic ceramics in the Victoria & Albert Museum in 1983

Figure 2. Palestinian school group entering the palace structure at Khirbat al-Mafjar

is divided into halves, the one on technology and cultural juxtapositions throughout the world, and the other will be a truly amazing collection of Islamic ceramics (fig. 1). Mariam Rosser-Owen, the curator in charge, showed us the finished cases and new cabinets of study collections. I had visited this collection in 1983 and studied some materials from Aden; the old-fashioned walnut cases reminded one of the traditional displays in the Oriental Institute Museum. This extra week proved an unexpected opportunity for me to read, at some leisure, the doctoral dissertation of Dimitri Baramki; this rare work is an account of the excavations at Khirbat al-Mafjar by its principal archaeologist and his unpublished interpretations of that early Islamic site (fig. 2).

This year may be considered a special "moment" in the history of Islamic archaeology with the appearance of two monographs dedicated to the discipline. The first is Alan Walmsley's *Early Islamic Syria: An Archaeological Assessment* (London, 2007). This volume had not appeared in time for the previous ICAANE and has now been used in classrooms. Styled as part of the Duckworth Debates in Archaeology, Walmsley picks up themes under constant discussion: material culture and social change, settlement processes (especially "urban archaeology"), and the nature of Islamic archaeology and Islamic studies. Sometimes the "debate" is a little forced, but the balance and presentation is extraordinary. Coming from some six months in Jerusalem, I found the coverage of sites and materials in Israel/Palestine somewhat limited in view of the wealth of information becoming available. This would have required another, much larger book.

More recently, Marcus Milwright has published *An Introduction to Islamic Archaeology* (Edinburgh, 2010). This book is intended as a general text book, defining the nature of the discipline and then giving detailed descriptions of the Islamic world from a traditional culture historical approach. He includes a wide range of examples that produces a rather kaleidoscopic effect on the topic under discussion. However, this is not the place to review the book but only to bring it to the attention of the interested scholar and student.

Banbhore 1139

Figure 3. Sgraffiato ceramics from Banbhore, Pakistan (courtesy K. Lashari, 2006)

To these may be added, or in a sense will be augmented by, recent dissertations on Islamic archaeology (which came to my attention when I was asked to serve as an external reader). Denis Genequand is a Swiss archaeologist who in February took his doctorate from Lausanne and the Sorbonne (technically two degrees). He is well known to archaeologists working in Syria and Jordan for his numerous surveys and now excavations at Qasr al-Hayr al-Sharqi, al-Bakhra, and at Palmyra (Tadmor). In many years of field research, he has been fixated on one question — the nature of the early Islamic *qusur*, the so-called "desert castles" — or as he styles them, "aristocratic Umayyad residences." The number of these monuments that have been identified seems to grow every year and many of these discoveries, both important and additional examples, belong to Denis. He has further seriously considered the ecological and economic basis through field observations and testing. In sum, the dissertation brings a much needed synthesis to this important subject; it will not be a block-buster movie, but certainly a pleasing monograph.

The subject of the *qusur* leads back to the newest of the Oriental Institute projects, the site of Khirbet al-Mafjar, near Jericho. This project returns to an early excavation of the 1930s and 1940s with new ideas for archaeological discoveries. Another approach is the revelation of new archaeological regions for which there is little knowledge. Here, a second dissertation allows the addition of the Sind, the southern province of Pakistan, as a new lecture for the Introduction to Islamic Archaeology course. The dissertation is a thorough study of the Islamic ceramics (fig. 3) of the Sind by Annabelle Collinet, submitted to the Sorbonne and based on the extensive excavations and surveys of Monique Kervran. There are no doubt many other research products; and the sum of the information from professional meetings, publications, and dissertations — not to mention fieldwork — points to the growing need for a means of communication, probably the long dreamt Web site.

CAMEL
CENTER FOR ANCIENT MIDDLE EASTERN LANDSCAPES

http://oi.uchicago.edu/research/camel

Scott Branting

Last year marked the completion of a three-year project of scanning and georectifying thousands of maps from the map collections of the Research Archives. This created an opportunity for CAMEL to focus on expanding its outreach during 2009–2010. CAMEL's primary focus will always be on the acquisition and management of geospatial data pertaining to the ancient and modern Near East. However, the data are meaningless if they are not used by researchers, students, and others interested in exploring different aspects of the region. It's when the data can be easily combined to answer research questions and educate that they become truly important.

To expand its outreach, CAMEL partnered with Wendy Ennes in the Oriental Institute's Education Department in order to develop an innovative educational program for students in the Chicago Public Schools. Funded by a grant from the Chicago Public Schools' Museum Connection Program, the Science of Archaeology Program created a curriculum for the sixth-grade students at Claremont Academy on 64th Street. The curriculum combined hands-on archaeological excavations using the simulated excavation site in the Kipper Family Archaeology Discovery Center with hands-on analysis of the freshly excavated data using the tools of Geographic Information Systems (GIS) computer software and CAMEL data (fig. 1a–c). Students were challenged to analyze the spatial patterning of objects they had excavated in order to determine the location

Figure 1a. During the past year, sixty students in the sixth-grade class of Claremont Academy participated in the Science of Archaeology Program developed in partnership between CAMEL and Wendy Ennes of the Oriental Institute's Education Department. Here some of the students participate in hands-on excavations undertaken in the Kipper Family Archaeology Discovery Center

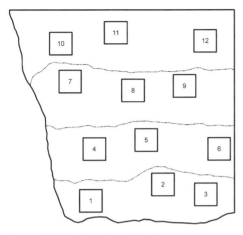

Figure 1b. The locations of artifacts they recovered were recorded using a scaled map of the simulated excavation site produced by CAMEL staff

Figure 1c. Both the map and the recorded data were then imported into GIS software on computers at the school. Students learned how to use the software to analyze the spatial distributions of the artifacts and then using clues contained in a fictitious ancient text they were able to draw hypotheses as to where a golden medallion might be uncovered

Figure 2. This British Survey map of the head of the Persian Gulf was produced in 1915 and is now a part of CAMEL's digital archive. Historical maps such as this one contain a great deal of information that had been lost by the time more modern imagery and maps were produced. For example, this map shows areas of marsh in southern Iraq that tragically no longer exist today. It also shows portions of canal systems, the reconstruction of which has been essential to understand more ancient landscapes of southern Mesopotamia

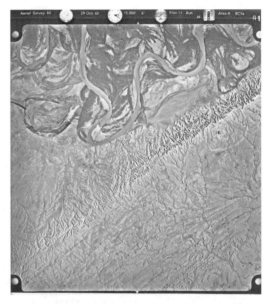

Figure 3. Donations of paper maps and aerial photographs pertaining to the Near East are always most welcomed by CAMEL. CAMEL can take these paper items and turn them into georectified digitial images that can be more easily used by researchers, students, and projects interested in the region. During 2009–2010 CAMEL received several such donations from people both in the Oriental Institute and around the world. This October 29, 1960, aerial photograph of the Dizful area in Iran was donated to CAMEL by Robert McC. Adams. Historical aerial photographs such as this one are extremely valuable as they provide a highly detailed view of the landscape at a certain point in time. In the case of Dizful, a major dam has since flooded the area covering all traces of the landscape seen in portions of this photograph

Figure 4. This is a section of an 1850 map produced during the expedition of a British officer, Lieutenant Colonel Chesney, which McGuire Gibson made available for CAMEL to digitize. Maps like this provide an invaluable glimpse of the landscape of the Near East well before the twentieth century. This section of this Chesney map shows the Strait of Hormuz and the coast of Oman.

of a particular artifact mentioned in a fictitious ancient text. This taught students about the interdisciplinary nature of archaeology, helped them understand specific challenges faced by Near Eastern archaeologists, and demonstrated the utility of using GIS software for spatial analysis just like CAMEL does. CAMEL's outreach was also enhanced through an article about its work, "Layers of the Past: Combining Data from Two Centuries' Worth of Images Creates a New View of the Ancient Near East," that appeared in the May/June issue of *Archaeology* magazine. This is the latest in a series of publicity and articles on the work of CAMEL, which continue to attract the attention of people around the world. While CAMEL has always provided data from its collections as freely as possible to hundreds of users who have contacted us, publicity like this increases the number of people interested in donating their own maps and data to CAMEL's collections and the number of people interested in putting these unique datasets to good use.

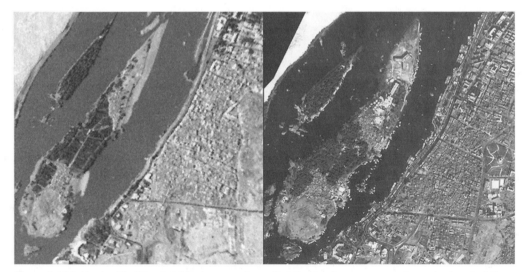

Figure 5. U.S. Declassified Spy Satellite images, also called Corona images, are an important part of the historical depth of CAMEL's holdings. These photos, taken largely in the 1960s and 1970s, were first declassified in the mid-1990s. An ongoing CAMEL project to georectify these images allows users to directly compare them digitally to more recent satellite imagery. Urban and agricultural development can then be analyzed to see how it has impacted archaeological sites in the intervening decades. These two images are of Elephantine in Egypt. On the left is a Corona image from July 19, 1963 and on the right is a DigitalGlobe Quickbird-2 satellite image taken on January 6, 2008. In the 2008 image, you can see new development such as the Movenpick Hotel and resort complex on the northern part of the island. On both images the archaeological site is visible on the southern part of the island, but with noticeably more encroachment from buildings today than in 1963

While extending its outreach, CAMEL was hard at work continuing to expand its core collections. In 2009–2010 CAMEL's digital collections increased by more than 3,000 to just over 13,000 geospatial datasets. This growth is expected to continue with donations and collaborative ventures such as the forthcoming digitization in 2011 of the map collections of the W. F. Albright Institute for Archaeological Research in Jerusalem and Chicago House in Luxor. Both of these centers along with several others are being funded under a four year U.S. Department of Education, Technological Innovation and Cooperation for Foreign Information Access (TICFIA) grant.

CAMEL also continued to make the data in its collections more readily available and useful. Work by volunteers and CAMEL staff progressed throughout the year on the georectification of the 1,100 U.S. Declassified Spy Satellite (Corona) images in the CAMEL collections. Georectification is a process by which images or maps of portions of the earth are encoded with their locational information so that they can be instantaneously overlayed in a GIS with other sources of data from that same area or adjacent areas. Georectifying these images will save individual users of these data the countless hours and expense of having to georectify the images themselves before they can be used. Three hundred of these images were sent last year to Jesse Casana at the University of Arkansas to be georectified as part of an ongoing National Endowment for the Humanities grant. The rest are being georectified by hand by CAMEL. One hundred of these images were georectified by CAMEL this past year.

Finally, CAMEL had a happy reminder this year of the role that it continues to play in the teaching and training of students at the University of Chicago. While CAMEL's data and facilities continue to be used throughout the year for teaching and research purposes, no event demonstrates that better than the graduation of one of our own. This year, Joshua Trampier, who has done an extraordinary job for numerous years as Assistant and then Associate Director of CAMEL, successfully completed his PhD in Egyptian Archaeology. His dissertation research, which incorporated a good deal of CAMEL data from the delta of Egypt along with archaeological survey,

Figure 6. This year CAMEL, on behalf of the Oriental Institute's Tell Zeidan Project, purchased a historical topographic map of Raqqa in Syria to aid the archaeological survey around Tell Zeidan. This map (on the right) is one of a large series of topographic maps of the Middle East created by the Soviet Union during the Cold War. The portion of the map right around Raqqa is compared here with a U.S. Declassified Spy Satellite (Corona) image taken on November 4, 1968 (on the left). Both the map and photo show the notable horseshoe-shaped wall of the Islamic-period city

provides an excellent example of the sort of research that CAMEL enables. While CAMEL will miss the important long-term contribution that Josh made to our team effort, we all wish him well in the years ahead.

CAMEL is as always indebted to all of those who give of their time and efforts. Without the dedicated staff and volunteers at CAMEL, nothing could be accomplished. During this year Joshua Trampier and Robert Tate served as Associate Directors and Elise MacArthur and Susan Penacho as Assistant Directors of CAMEL. William Kent was a Senior Supervisor. Bryan Kraemer served as a database administrator for our growing collections. Charlotte Simon worked with us, in her capacity as an intern in the Education Department, on the creation of the curriculum for the CPS Science of Archaeology Program. Matthew Cuda, Meg Swaney, Christopher Harvey, and Kevin Wilkerson were all Student Assistants. Our volunteers for 2009–2010 were: Marc Block, Jim Boves, Alexander Elwyn (who I inadvertently left off this list last year), Vincent van Exel, Debora Heard, and Larry Lissak. We always are happy to train new volunteers to work with us. In addition, I would like to thank all those who donated financially or in contributions of physical or digital geospatial data to CAMEL throughout this year.

Reference

Branting, Scott

1996   "The Alişar Regional Survey 1993–1994: A Preliminary Report." *Anatolica* 22: 145–58.

CHICAGO ASSYRIAN DICTIONARY (CAD)

Martha T. Roth

Preparing the final volume of the Chicago Assyrian Dictionary for publication occupied Editor-in-Charge Martha T. Roth, Research Assistants Jonathan Tenney (June and July) and Anna Steinhelper (since August 2009). All final galleys have been read, corrected, and returned to Eisenbrauns. By the end of June 2010, we were ready to begin sending back to Eisenbrauns corrected first pages, with the aim of seeing the volume published in academic year 2010–11.

Linda McLarnan, CAD Manuscript Editor since 1986, continues to lend her expert proof-reading skills even as she serves as Publications Expert in the Office of the President of the University.

————————

CHICAGO DEMOTIC DICTIONARY (CDD)

François Gaudard and Janet H. Johnson

During the past year, Janet Johnson, François Gaudard, Brittany Hayden, and Mary Szabady made progress in checking draft of entries for individual letters. Oriental Institute docent Larry Lissak assisted us by scanning photographs of various Demotic texts and also part of Wilhelm Spiegelberg's *Nachlasse* at a high resolution (1200 dpi). The latter will appear eventually on the Oriental Institute Web site. Letter files W, Ḥ, and Š have been posted online, and P and M will be posted soon, after a final style check. The last three letters, namely ʾI, T, and S, are currently being worked on, and the numbers' file is almost finished. On February 6, 2010, Jan gave a lecture entitled "What is Demotic and Why Write a Dictionary?" to the Chicago chapter of the American Research Center in Egypt, in which she discussed the range of texts found in Demotic and the purpose and status of the Chicago Demotic Dictionary. François attended the 6th Demotic Summer School, held in Heidelberg, from August 23 to 26, 2009, where he gave three presentations about the CDD "Problematic Entries" files. These meetings were extremely productive, and the Chicago Demotic Dictionary staff would like to thank Maren Schentuleit, the organizer, as well as all the meeting participants for their useful comments and suggestions. We are also grateful to all our colleagues, who regularly give us their input on the posted letter files, in particular, Joachim Friedrich Quack, Friedhelm Hoffmann, Eugene Cruz-Uribe, Jan Moje, and Andreas Winkler. Special thanks go to Marc Etienne, who kindly provided us with photographs of Demotic ostraca from the Louvre, as well as to Rodney Ast, Kim Ryholt, and Veena Elisabeth Frank Jørgensen for providing us with various references.

This year, as noted above, part of our effort focused on numbers. Usually numbers always followed the noun, which, as a general rule, was always singular: "five-hundred geese," for example, was written "goose five-hundred." This is frequently referred to as "book-keeping style" since it is in bookkeeping that this style is used in many modern languages. Numbers also had a feminine form indicated by the addition of a ‹ *.t* under the number, for example, **ꟼ** 2.*t*, or beside it, as is sometimes the case with number 9: **ꟼ** 9.*t*. The feminine form of number 1 was written identically with the feminine indefinite article ʾ *wˁ.t*. In year dates and in some other cases, however, the feminine *.t* was often omitted. Hundreds were recognizable by their long tails, as can be seen in the following selected examples: 100 ⸺, 200 ⸺, 300 ⸺, 800 ⸺.

Thousands, usually, had shorter tails: 1,000 **ꟼ**, 2,000 **ꟼ** or **ꟼ**, 3,000 **ꟼ**; 5,000 was written 3,000 (+) 2,000: **ꟼ ꟼ**, and 7,000 as 4,000 (+) 3,000: **ꟼ ꟼ**. Note that an entry for 9,000 **ꟼ**, which is missing in Erichsen's *Glossar*, has now been included in the CDD. In a number, thousands, hundreds, tens, and digits followed each other in sequence (right to left), but variants with the preposition *ḥnˁ* "(together) with," placed after the hundreds, are also attested. Such is for example the case with **ꟼ** 100 *ḥnˁ* 3 for 103, with ⸺ **ꟼ** 300 *ḥnˁ* 50 for 350, and with ⸺ **ꟼ** 1,900 *ḥnˁ* 50 for 1,950. Fractions were indicated by a diagonal stroke (**ꟼ** for the word **⟷** *rꜣ* "part") placed above the number. However, quite often the stroke in question was simply omitted. For example, 1/2 could be written **ꟼ** or **ꟼ**. Worth noting is the almost exclusive use of unit fractions (1 over any number). The only common exceptions are 2/3 **ꟼ** and 5/6 **ꟼ** (also written **ꟼ** or **ꟼ**), the latter originally being a ligature of 2/3 **ꟼ** + 1/6 **ꟼ** (also written **ꟼ** or **ꟼ**), as can be seen in the following early example from P. OI 17481, 1, where the two fractions are grouped but still written separately: **ꟼ**.

Numbers can be quite confusing to identify. Indeed, some occurrences of 20, written ⟨sign⟩ instead of the more common sign ⟨sign⟩, look like 1,000 ⟨sign⟩. Similarly, writings of 3 ⟨sign⟩ and 4 ⟨sign⟩ can look very much alike, and so can writings of 8 ⟨sign⟩ and 60 ⟨sign⟩, as well as those of 1/2 ⟨sign⟩, 50 ⟨sign⟩, 80 ⟨sign⟩, and 100,000 ⟨sign⟩. Also note that thousands sometimes had longer tails than expected, for instance, 3,000 ⟨sign⟩ and 8,000 ⟨sign⟩, which make them look very similar to hundreds, in the present case to 300 ⟨sign⟩ and 800 ⟨sign⟩. In general, however, the context helps telling them apart.

Interestingly, unlike for years and months, numbers indicating the day in dates were different from regular numbers, for example, 10 was written ⟨sign⟩ instead of ⟨sign⟩, ⟨sign⟩ was used for 20 instead of ⟨sign⟩, and ⟨sign⟩ for 8 instead of ⟨sign⟩. Such numbers were preceded by the word "day," namely, ⟨sign⟩ *sw*, also attested as ⟨signs⟩, and so on, which could be omitted.[1]

The Egyptian administrative/civil year consisted of 365 days. A solar year, however, lasts 365 ¼ days and as the Egyptians did not add an extra day every four years, as we do with leap years, little by little their civil calendar was no longer synchronized with the astronomical calendar; after a cycle of 1,460 years, the two calendars coincided again for a short time. The year was divided into three seasons: *ʒḥ.t* (*akhet*) "inundation" (mid-July to mid-November), *pr.t* (*peret*) "winter," literally "emergence" of crops (mid-November to mid-March), and *šmw* (*shemou*) "summer," literally "harvest" (mid-March to mid-July), each season being divided into four months of thirty days, for a total of 360 days, to which the ancient Egyptians added five extra days, called "epagomenal days" by Egyptologists, from the Greek αἱ ἐπαγόμεναι ἡμέραι "intercalated days." Each of them corresponded to the birthday of a particular god, namely, Osiris, Horus, Seth, Isis, and Nephthys. In Demotic, the fifth epagomenal day, for instance, could be referred to as *hrw ms(.t) Nb.t-Ḥ.t* "birthday of Nephthys," or *hrw 5 ḥb (sw)* 5 "five days of festival, day 5," or even, as in a date from P. Pavia 1120, 1: *ỉbt 4 šmw ʿrqy sw* 5 "fourth month of summer, day 30 (+) day 5." In 238 BC, as stated in the Canopus decree composed under the reign of Ptolemy III, there had been an attempt to add an extra epagomenal day every four years, in order to account for the missing quarter day in the Egyptian calendar. However, this idea did not take hold.

While in modern days a positive symbolism tends to be attached to the end of the year, in ancient Egypt the change of year was believed to be a very dangerous time. During that period, in particular during the five epagomenal days, the equilibrium, proper functioning, and order of the universe were threatened. Maat was endangered and the king was considered to be particularly vulnerable. Misfortune and disease could strike him at any time, and through him the people and entire land would be affected. The leontocephalic goddess Sekhmet and her emissaries bringing plagues and pestilences were held responsible for such troubles. For that reason, ritual texts, usually called litanies, were to be recited in order to protect the "living falcon," namely the king, from the so-called "seven arrows of the year," which was another way of referring to such evils. Amulets were also used by individuals for their own protection. At Edfu, this period, immediately preceding the inundation, was called *ỉʒd.t-rnp.t* (*iadet renpet*) "annual pestilence." Indeed, at this time of the year, certain conditions, such as the presence of stagnant water pools, combined with hot and dry weather, made it ideal for the development of sites of disease. The arrival of the flood would wipe them out.

A typical Egyptian date included the regnal year of the current pharaoh followed by the season, the month, and the day. For example, a text could be dated to "Year X of king Ptolemy X, Xth month of the summer, Xth day." Note that we know of at least one amusing example where the British also used a dating system based on regnal years, clearly imitating the ancient Egyptians. Indeed, a book entitled *The Gallery of Antiquities Selected from the British*

Museum, Part 2, *Egyptian Art*, by F. Arundale and J. Bonomi, was published in London "under the sanction of her Majesty the Queen Victoria and in the 6th year of her reign," which corresponds to 1842/1843.

Finally, the staff of the Chicago Demotic Dictionary would like to honor the memory of their dear friend and colleague Professor Traianos Gagos, who passed away tragically last April. Traianos was a fine gentleman and an eminent scholar who contributed enormously to the field of Greek and Byzantine papyrology in the United States and worldwide. He was Professor of Greek and Papyrology as well as Archivist of Papyrology at the University of Michigan; he served as President of the American Society of Papyrologists, editor of the *Bulletin of the American Society of Papyrologists* (*BASP*), co-editor of the Petra Papyri, and Director of the Advanced Papyrological Information System (APIS). His ties to the work and the people of the Oriental Institute were deepened during his sabbatical year among us in 1999. Traianos' generosity and enthusiasm were legendary. He helped us several times, answering our Greek papyrological questions, whether for the Chicago Demotic Dictionary or for various publications. We will sorely miss Traianos, his knowledge, his kindness, his gentleness, and above all his unfailing friendship.

Note

[1] It is only from the reign of Ptolemy VI (180–145 BC) onward that Demotic contracts started to include the day of the month on which they were drawn up.

CHICAGO HITTITE AND ELECTRONIC HITTITE DICTIONARY (CHD AND eCHD)

Theo van den Hout

Work on the words starting in *šu-* for what is going to be the last installment of the letter Š is well underway. Theo van den Hout and Harry Hoffner have finished work on all *ši-*words and the final batch was sent off to our outside consultants Gary Beckman (Ann Arbor), Craig Melchert (Los Angeles), and Gernot Wilhelm (Würzburg, Germany). We have already received back some of their comments that can then be incorporated into the final version. With the help of our junior editors Petra Goedegebuure, Richard Beal, and Oğuz Soysal, we should finish work on the Š in the coming year.

Among the *šu-*words there are as usual some important ones like, for instance, *šuppi-* and its many derivatives. *Šuppi-* is one of two Hittite words for "clean, pure." The other, *parkui-*, denotes that something is free of impurities: it can be used to describe gold and silver, undiluted drinks ("straight up"), a tablet can be called *parkui-* if it is "fair copy" of a text without major mistakes, clothes can be "clean," or somebody "innocent." But someone or something that is *parkui-* may not necessarily be fit to be in the presence of gods: that is the special range of *šuppi-*. *Šuppi-* has that higher degree of ritual purity that makes someone or something fit for a god and it can sometimes be rendered as "holy" or "sacred." According to his name the famous Hittite king Šuppiluliuma was so called after a town named "Holy Springs." As one can imagine, the Hittite texts with their emphasis on cult and ritual have a lot of *šuppi-* in them!

Kathleen Mineck and Oya Topcuoğlu continued to maintain the CHD word files. They are currently busy working on filing the *Keilschrifttexte aus Boghazköi* volumes 44, 45, and 50. A

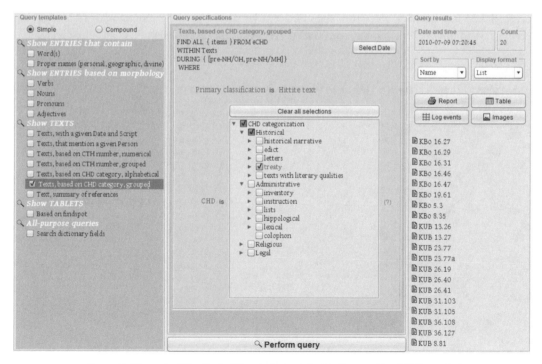

Figure 1. Query facility; find all treaty texts dated to the pre-Neo Hittite period

second project is the final cataloging and integration of old hand-written cards from the early excavations, many of which have already been used, when published, by the dictionary staff. Oya has done, moreover, a tremendous job in digitalizing a comprehensive Hittitological bibliography that Oğuz Soysal compiled over the years hand-written on cards. It contains many very rare items and will eventually be linked to our electronic dictionary project, the *e*CHD.

The *e*CHD is the realm of our programmers Sandra Schloen, Dennis Campbell, and student Seunghee Yie. Over the past year, the *e*CHD has seen several improvements, some in style, others in substance. The new style of the *e*CHD query facility provides a list of query templates, shown in the left pane (fig. 1). The query specification panel (center pane) allows the viewer to select various criteria to limit the search. The results of the query are shown in the rightmost pane. On the electronic front, the *e*CHD has seen several improvements, some in style, others in substance. The new style of the *e*CHD query facility provides a list of query templates, shown in the left pane in figure 1 below. The query specification panel (center pane) allows the viewer to select various criteria to limit the search. The results of the query are shown in the rightmost pane.

Dictionary articles can be searched for words based on string matches or based on morphological qualities. Texts can be selected based on dating, content or categorization. In the example above, only the texts that are designated as treaties are to be considered. Contextual scoping allows the viewer to restrict the range of the query; for example, to include only those texts from tablets found at Emar, or only those texts from Old Hittite and Middle Hittite periods.

The query facility is under ongoing development to make it more stable, substantial, and useful over time. New query templates and options for selection and scoping are added on a regular basis.

One of the challenges associated with the query system is the problem of finding words within the dictionary articles that are marked as being damaged, uncertain, omitted, erased, etc. That is, a string match for "peran" (or "pé-ra-an") is likely to miss "p]é-ra-an," "pé-]ra-an," "pé-ra-[an," "pé<-ra>-an," and other variations. To address this issue, each citation within the dictionary is being linked to a primary version of the cited text which extracts the indicators for damage, uncertainty, and the like, and which represents these conditions as metadata instead. The metadata is

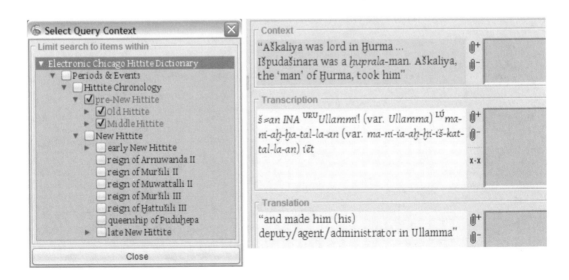

Figure 2. Screenshots of the eCHD search feature

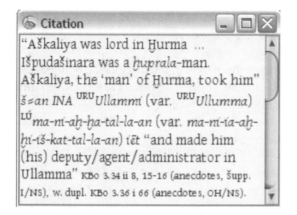

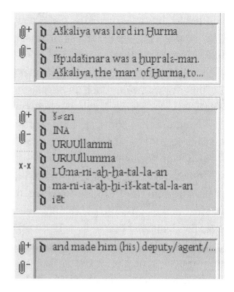

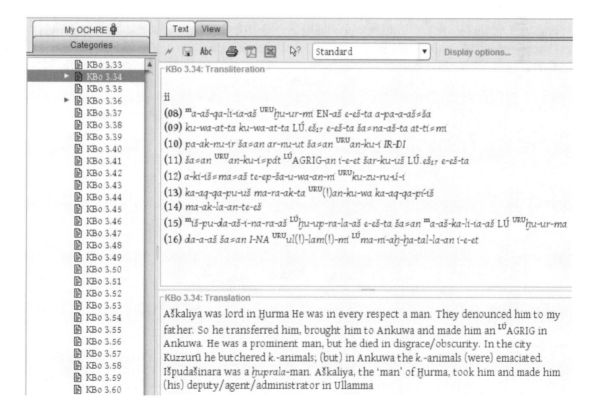

Figure 3. Screenshots of the eCHD

applied to the text when it is presented for display thus preserving the overall "look" of the text. This strategy allows the query mechanism to find string matches successfully while retaining the individual formatting characteristics of each specific reference.

To illustrate this approach, consider the following current form of the first citation of the article LÚ *maniyaḫḫatalla*. Each of the sections of the citation — the **Context, Transcription, and Translation** — were previously entered as explicitly formatted text.

Using the new strategy, each section of the citation is linked to the appropriate phrases of the text instead. The links may reference the translation of the text, or either of its word-by-word or sign-by-sign formats.

In both cases, the display of the Citation is the same.

A side benefit of linking to a pure form of the text is that access to the underlying structure of the text makes possible the display of sign-by-sign readings of each cited word as the cursor rolls over the displayed text.

While much of the textual content is referenced piecemeal in citations, the development of the master catalog of texts, in linkable units of both transliteration and translation, will greatly increase the substance and utility of the *e*CHD.

All of the textual content as well as the dictionary articles can now also be exported to PDF. This new feature, combined with the existing import utility, data entry interface, and display formats, completes the process from data entry to display and printing, paving the way for online composition and publication of new dictionary articles in the future.

As usual, we had several visitors. Craig Melchert (UCLA) came to our campus and gave a lecture that was sponsored among others by our Department of Near Eastern Languages and Civilizations. Anatolian archaeologist Ann Gunter (Northwestern University) delivered a lecture on the frontiers of the Hittite empire and paid the CHD a visit while here. Gary Beckman (University of Michigan), his student Ilgi Evrim, Ada Taggar-Cohen (Doshisha University, Kyoto, Japan), and again Willemijn Waal, now "Dr. Waal," consulted our files for their work.

EPIGRAPHIC SURVEY

W. Raymond Johnson

On April 15, 2010, the Epigraphic Survey, in cooperation with the Egyptian Supreme Council of Antiquities (SCA), completed its eighty-sixth, six-month field season in Luxor. Chicago House's activities included documentation work at Khonsu Temple at Karnak; documentation and conservation work at Medinet Habu; conservation, restoration, and an open-air museum at Luxor Temple; and the inauguration of a new program at the Theban Tomb (#107) of Nefersekheru.

Khonsu Temple, Karnak

Epigraphic Documentation

This year marked the second season of an Epigraphic Survey and American Research Center in Egypt (ARCE) collaboration at Khonsu Temple, Karnak. Chicago House senior epigrapher Brett McClain supervised the epigraphic team (epigrapher Jen Kimpton and artists Keli Alberts and Krisztián Vértes) in the recording of reused, inscribed stone-block material in the flooring, foundations, and

Figure 1. Brett, Jen, and Keli documenting foundation blocks in the Khonsu Temple court. Photo by Ray Johnson

western roof area of Ramesses III's Khonsu Temple (figs. 1–2). Photographer Yarko Kobylecky, assisted by Ellie Smith, provided large-format photography of selected blocks. ARCE's photographer Owen Murray provided additional photography of others. This documentation is necessary before ARCE's floor restoration work makes the reused material inaccessible. This season we recorded 226 reused, inscribed blocks and produced 167 drawings, of which 161 drawings were reviewed and cleared by the director. Jen Kimpton drew 62 isometric drawings of blocks with architectural details that will allow important analysis of the original structure(s). The material included loose fragments recovered from the floor fill in the 2008–2009 season, blocks reused in the first court and ramp leading to the porch, a small corpus of reused blocks from the western sanctuary roof, and reused blocks removed from the court during the 1970s and stored on platforms near the temple. A good number of the blocks that were reused in the court date to the time of Sety I. The documentation and preliminary analysis of the blocks and fragments — which appear to be part of an earlier, dismantled Khonsu Temple — will be completed next season. A preliminary report of this second season's work will appear in the *Journal of the American Research Center*. This

Figure 2. Keli tracing in the Khonsu court. Photo by Ray Johnson

project is funded by a grant from United States Agency for International Development (USAID) Egypt through ARCE.

Medinet Habu

Epigraphic Documentation and Publication

Epigraphic documentation supervised by Brett and senior artists Margaret De Jong and Susan Osgood continued in the small Amun temple of Hatshepsut and Thutmose III at Medinet Habu in the Thutmoside bark sanctuary ambulatory and its facade (*Medinet Habu* Volume X) and bark sanctuary (*Medinet Habu* Volume XII). Photography of the four, faceted Twenty-ninth Dynasty Akoris columns in the ambulatory (reused from the Twenty-fifth–Twenty-sixth–Dynasty gods' wives' chapels across the way) for *Medinet Habu* Volume XI was completed by photographer Yarko Kobylecky assisted by Ellie Smith, and the final drawing enlargements of the inscribed faces were produced for Sue. This season

Sue also recorded two Thutmoside pillars concealed by the Akoris doorway on the north side of the ambulatory by squeezing herself *inside* the hollow lintel and carefully tracing the upper parts of each pillar (fig. 3). Her tracings will be photographed by Yarko and used as the basis for reduced, facsimile drawings that will receive the standard collation procedure. Margaret concentrated her drawing on the ambulatory and facade of the Thutmoside temple and finished the well-preserved but extremely complex Ptolemy VIII recarved lintel on the facade. The facsimile drawings that were penciled, inked, and collated this season at Medinet Habu are as follows: penciling completed: 18; inking completed: 26; transfer check completed: 2; director's check: 3. We are very pleased to note here

Figure 3. Sue inside Akoris lintel at the Medinet Habu small Amun temple. Photo by Ray Johnson

that all Medinet Habu volumes as well as the latest — Oriental Institute Publications 136, *Medinet Habu* Volume IX, *The Eighteenth Dynasty Temple, Part 1: The Inner Sanctuaries* (Chicago 2009) — are now available for free PDF download from the Oriental Institute Publications Web site. Thanks to friends Lewis and Misty Gruber who funded the digital scanning, and Tom Urban and Leslie Schramer of the Oriental Institute Publications Office, all publications under the category "Egypt," including everything the Epigraphic Survey has ever published, are now available for download in the new digital format free of charge.

Figure 4. Margaret teaching a seminar on epigraphy for the archaeological field school. Photo by Ray Johnson

Medinet Habu Blockyard

The conservation team, supervised by Lotfi Hassan (Nahed Samir and Mohamed Abu el-Makarem), continued the moving of fragmentary material from the old Medinet Habu block-yard to the new blockyard facility we recently built against the inside southern Ramesses III enclosure wall (fig. 5). During February and March, Lotfi was assisted by Frank Helmholz and his team in the moving of the heavy blocks, about forty of them from a small Thutmoside temple of Sobek in Rizziqat, south of Esna, that had been dismantled and reused as a stone breeding tank for the sacred crocodiles in the Ptolemaic period. This material was brought to the Gurna

Figure 5. Lotfi and team moving material to the new blockyard. Photo by Nahed Samir

Inspectorate in the late 1960s and eventually made its way to Medinet Habu for storage. Some fragmentary material required consolidation before it could be moved, and some after moving in the covered area against the south wall designated for that purpose. Julia Schmied and Christian Greco continued to coordinate the inventorying and documentation of the miscellaneous fragmentary architectural and sculpture fragments prior to moving from the old blockyard, all entered on Julia's illustrated database, and they worked with the conservation team in the physical moving as well (fig. 6). Over two thousand blocks have now been transferred to the new blockyard. The transfer will be finished next season, as well as a small open-air–museum component in front of the new blockyard that has been constructed for appropriate joined fragmat and display groups. All of the conservation work at Medinet Habu and some of the epigraphic documentation are covered by a grant from USAID Egypt.

Figure 6. Julia working in the new blockyard. Photo by Ray Johnson

The Tomb of Nefersekheru (TT 107)

This winter the Epigraphic Survey initiated a condition study and preliminary, photographic documentation at the tomb of Nefersekheru (TT 107), west of el-Khokha, for which we have long held the concession. Initial investigation of the tomb and its courtyard was undertaken in early January by Ray, Brett, Boyo Ockinga, and Susanne Binder. Colleagues Boyo and Susanne (Macquarie University, Sydney) have had extensive experience working on private tombs in the area and have joined our team to help us with this one. Nefersekheru was Steward of Amenhotep III's sprawling jubilee palace complex south of Medinet Habu at Malkata, currently being surveyed and archaeologically investigated by the Metropolitan Museum of Art and Emory University with the SCA. Nefersekheru's tomb is one of the largest late Amenhotep III-period private tombs in Thebes. Instead of facing east, as do all the others (like Kheruef, Ramose, Amenemhet Surer, etc.), it faces south, toward Malkata and the setting sun. No complete plan has ever been made for the tomb, and it has never been cleared.

In January, we examined the courtyard and the portico in view of proposed archaeological, documentation, and conservation work to be undertaken on the exterior of the monument. We also removed the blocking stones from the entrance and explored the interior of the broad hall of the tomb — approximately 25 m wide — which is almost entirely filled with debris, to determine its condition. Our examinations included the unfinished sunken court and portico of the tomb, including the later (Dynasty 19) modifications to the court associated with the tomb of Paser (TT 106).

In February, the epigraphic team members Ray, Brett, Margaret, Sue, Yarko, and Ellie made a visit to the site to plan the documentation of the tomb portico, including the generation of negatives for photographic drawing enlargements. The scene divisions were laid out, and the scale of 1:3 was decided upon. Yarko and Ellie subsequently returned to the tomb over a period of ten days in order to complete the necessary photography. The negatives have now been prepared, and drawing enlargements will be made at the beginning of next season. Senior artists Margaret and Sue will undertake the penciling of the enlargements for the facade scenes (fig. 7) next year, supervised by Ray and Brett. On March 19, 2010, Chicago House's structural engineer Conor

Figure 7. Nefersekheru tomb facade. Photo by Ray Johnson

Figure 8. Restoration of Amenhotep III wall. Photo by Ray Johnson

Power inspected the tomb portico and court. He suggested that the poor condition of the limestone rock matrix around the tomb necessitates stabilization measures before drawing can begin next season (fig. 7). That will be the first course of action in October 2010, in consultation with Kent Weeks (who has offered to lend us pillar jacks and steel I-beams for that purpose) and the SCA. It is hoped that in the course of the 2010–2011 field season, considerable progress can be made on the initial copying of the very damaged but beautiful sunk relief scenes on the facade.

Luxor Temple

Conservation and Restoration Milestones...!

The Luxor Temple blockyard conservation program, coordinated by Hiroko Kariya and assisted by Tina Di Cerbo, conservator intern Siska Genbrugge, and Nan Ray, continued with preparations for the Luxor Temple blockyard open-air museum (figs. 9–10), supported by the World Monuments Fund (a Robert W. Wilson Challenge to Conserve Our Heritage grant). It is my great pleasure to announce that the open-air museum was completed and opened to the public on March 29, 2010. More than sixty-two fragment groups ranging in date from the Middle Kingdom through the present day were selected and reassembled in chronological order for display. Additional display platforms were designated for material recovered during the USAID-funded Luxor Temple dewatering program, trenching around the temple, conservation, and "rotating" exhibits. All displays are accompanied by educational signage in English and Arabic (thanks to Francis Amin and Mennat-Allah el-Dorry for their translation assistance). Sandstone pavement to guide the viewer, protective fencing, and lighting for night-time viewing are now in place to the east of the Luxor Temple sanctuary along the platforms that support fragment groups, reassembled over the last thirty years from the Middle Kingdom (Dynasty 12), New Kingdom (Dynasties 18, 19, 20), and later (Dynasties 21, 25, 26, 29, and 30), through the Ptolemaic, Roman, Christian, and Islamic periods. It is the only chronologically displayed — and labeled — open-air museum of its kind, and it represents a vital study collection that will educate and dazzle all visitors, scholars, and laymen alike. An online catalog is being prepared now.

Figure 9. Hiroko and workmen preparing Nectanebo II joined group. Photo by Ray Johnson

Figure 10. Luxor Temple blockyard open-air museum. Photo by Ray Johnson

We are excited to report yet another milestone. The restoration of 111 inscribed wall fragments to the original east interior wall of Amenhotep III's solar court at Luxor Temple was finished at the end of January by mason Frank Helmholz and the Chicago House workmen. The lime plaster surface between the stone fragments was applied by SCA conservators Salah Salim and Anwar Fouad Mahdi Jaama in early March, and missing details were added in paint on the plaster between the fragments by me in March and April. This project has been twenty-four years in the making and is very sweet to see completed. Restoration was begun under former director Lanny Bell and by conservator John Stewart, who between 1986 and 1988 restored twenty-seven fragments to the wall based on the reconstruction drawings of the present director. The work was interrupted and not resumed until 2007, when Hiroko began the treatment of each wall fragment in preparation for reassembly, after which Frank began the process. The 111 fragments were among the last quarried from the court of Amenhotep III (fig. 11) and complete the raised-relief depiction of the bark of the god Amun, followed by Amenhotep III and the royal *ka*, complete to the top of the king's *khepresh* crown. The whole bark scene preserves many painted details and has a wonderful and long history: it was carved by Amenhotep III, destroyed by Akhenaten, restored by Tutankhamun, appropriated by Horemheb, enlarged by Sety I, quarried and reused within the last few centuries, recovered during excavations between 1958 and 1962 that uncovered the Avenue of Sphinxes in front of Luxor Temple, recovered and recorded by Chicago House in the early 1980s, and now restored to its original wall in 2010. The final chapter of this fragment group will be written when the restored wall is included in the Epigraphic Survey's publication of the inscribed walls and architraves of the entire court.

Figure 11. Ray painting the missing bits on the Amenhotep III wall. Photo by Jay Heidel

Readers might remember that several hundred broken-up fragments of Nectanebo I sphinxes, originally from the Avenue of Sphinxes, were recovered during the clearance of the eastern tetrastyle and great Roman gate in 2006–2007. Chicago House helped recover the material and transport it into the Luxor Temple blockyard for storage and analysis. Shortly thereafter, in 2008, we initiated the reconstruction of sixteen sphinxes on three large mastabas, two small ones, and a section of the eastern blockyard south of the Abu el-Haggag mosque. Further reconstruction was carried out by SCA conservator Salah Salim this season, sponsored by Chicago House as a contribution to the SCA's current restoration efforts on the avenue. Salah is extremely adept at this work; by the middle of April, all the sphinxes and fragments had been transported to the recently cleared Avenue of Sphinxes area, north of Luxor Temple, and were reassembled on new pedestals, where they can now be seen.

Roman Wall and Thecla Church Projects

In another collaboration with the SCA and ARCE at Luxor Temple, the cleaning of remnants of the third-century AD Roman fortification wall — where it abuts the eastern pylon of Ramesses II — was begun in preparation for consolidation and restoration of the wall next season. The project was supervised by archaeologist Pamela Rose, with surveying done by architects Pieter Collet and Jay Heidel, and additional assistance by Andrew Bednarski (fig. 12). Cleaning revealed that the wall was made of mudbrick above baked-brick lower courses and foundations. While the baked brick is in good condition, the mudbrick wall surface above has eroded to the point where only the interior of the wall survives, like an apple core, and requires in-filling with new brick, scheduled for 2011. We are pleased to report that a gift from the Sawiris family in Egypt will allow the Epigraphic Survey to catalog, document, and survey the

Figure 12. Roman wall and bastion surveying by Jay and Pieter.
Photo by Ray Johnson

remains of the sixth-century AD Basilica of St. Thecla, which was built just north of the Roman wall and is the earliest-known church in Luxor. This exciting new program will allow us to integrate the church into the fortification-wall study and is expected to provide vital information about the transition period between the pagan and Christian religions, a hitherto little known chapter in the history of Luxor Temple. Over 150 blocks from the basilica sanctuary have already been located and entered into a special database by Nan Ray and will be moved to a special holding area for drawing and analysis next season. Future plans include studying the possibility of partial reconstruction of the sanctuary blocks in their original positions, as part of a comprehensive site management program for that area.

Epigraphic and Other Documentation

As part of the Epigraphic Survey's continuing study of Roman Luxor Temple, epigrapher Christian Greco continued to document and prepare full translations of the Latin and Greek inscriptions from Luxor Temple, inscribed on the walls and Roman monuments and fragments from the blockyard. He is studying the material firsthand and collating digital drawings made by Tina with a Wacom drawing tablet.

Educational signage for the temple proper was also initiated this season, designed by architect Jay Heidel, beginning with an orientation panel for the entire temple complex that will appear outside the main entrance (now on the east side of the temple), and in the fore area of the temple itself. Panels currently being designed include the Sphinx Avenue in front of the temple, the Ramesses II pylon entryway, the Ramesside Court, the great Colonnade Hall, the Amenhotep III court, the Roman Sanctuary, and the temple sanctuary.

Chicago House

The Chicago House Library

The Chicago House library opened on October 23, 2009, and closed on April 9, 2010. Access to the library was made somewhat challenging during the last half of the season, when the government of Egypt started installing a buried, reinforced concrete access tunnel for new water mains, electric cables, and telephone lines for the new Corniche (now under construction). But that did not deter our patrons. Librarian Marie Bryan, assisted by Anait Helmholz (during the latter part of the season) monitored accessions, oversaw the conversion of the library holdings to the Library of Congress system, and saw to the needs of the many library patrons, who totaled 808 this season. These included SCA officials and inspectors, Egyptian Egyptology students, foreign archaeological mission members, conservators, and this season the ARCE/SCA Archaeological Field School students who were working on the Luxor Temple medieval occupation mound from January into March. Occasionally, we would also see inspectors or engineers working on the USAID-funded dewatering project being implemented now in western Thebes, designed — like its counterpart on the east bank — to drain water away from the major west bank antiquities sites to reduce groundwater salt decay. Marie accessioned 180 new items to the library holdings, including sixty-eight monographs/books, eighty-two journals, and twenty-five series volumes (sixty-five of these items were gifts, some of them from Marie herself; thank you, Marie). Our CD publication collection grew by four, and 124 volumes were repaired by Anait. A total of 1,316 titles were completely converted to the Library of Congress classification system and reshelved accordingly. Foy Scalf of the Oriental Institute Research Archives and Vanessa Desclaux of the Institut français d'archéologie orientale library in Cairo kindly helped us out with scans of several articles for our users and to help us repair damaged volumes; special thanks to them both.

Photo Archives

Photo Archives registrar Ellie Smith registered 115 large-format negatives this season, and assisted photographer Yarko with block photography at Khonsu Temple (thirty-nine large-for-

mat negatives), in the Medinet Habu small Amun temple (eleven negatives), and at the Theban tomb (107) of Nefersekheru (thirty negatives). In addition to his site work, photographer Yarko (fig. 13) continued to take reference shots of fast-changing Luxor City and the west bank (particularly Gurnet Murai, south of Gurna, half of which was demolished this season), and the changing landscape around Chicago House, especially along the Corniche in front of our facility. Sue Lezon spent much of her time at Chicago House with Tina as they compiled and organized images for backup and external storage back home (thanks to a new grant for that program from ARCE's Antiquities Endowment Project). She also made time to document some of the changes in Luxor for the Photo Archives. It is my great pleasure to report that Sue received tenure from SUNY Plattsburgh this past summer and is now Associate Professor in Art, specializing in large-format folm and digital photography and photographic archiving. MABRUK, SUE!

Figure 13. Yarko photographing in the Nefersekheru portico. Photo by Ray Johnson

Alain and Emmanuelle Arnaudiès continued to coordinate the Chicago House Digital Archive Project, utilizing 4th Dimension Program and FileMaker Pro software. The ultimate goal of the project is to make a searchable database of everything the Epigraphic Survey has ever produced, including the entire large-format holdings of the Photo Archives (with Tina's and Sue's assistance), and eventually direct links from the Nelson Key Plans of all the sites in Luxor to picture files and published scenes produced by the Epigraphic Survey, as well as unpublished paleography and dictionary card files. To date, 1,785 bibliographical references have been entered in the database — 948 relating to Medinet Habu temple, 324 for Luxor Temple, 270 for Karnak Temple — eighty book review references have been recorded, and 481 PDF files have been downloaded and registered with bookmarks and page numbering. Bibliographies of the staff members have also been detailed.

Chicago House

Finance manager Safi Ouri and administrator Samir el-Guindy continued to ensure the smooth running of the Chicago House facility and our field operations in Luxor this year. With the help of Tina, who opens and closes the house for us each season with maximum efficiency (thank you, Tina!), Samir takes care of the day-to-day administration of the house and the Egyptian staff of temple workers and housemen. Safi keeps a watchful eye over the financial end of all our programs and in particular continues to manage our USAID, Antiquities Endowment Fund, and World Monuments Fund grants that cover work in Luxor Temple, Medinet Habu, the

Chicago House staff, 2009–2010. Photo by Yarko Kobylecky and Sue Lezon

Nefersekheru tomb, and the Photo Archives. Those grants are all expiring soon, so Safi and I are going to be very busy preparing new grant proposals this coming season. Our sincerest thanks go to Safi for her formidable accomplishments in the past, and the future!

In February, we were pleased to continue to house and lend the use of our Land Rover to the staff of the Joint Expedition to Malqata (JEM) for their second season of surveying work and archaeological investigations at the site of Amenhotep III's 5-kilometer-long palace complex south of Medinet Habu. Project directors Dr. Diana Craig Patch from the Metropolitan Museum of Art in New York and Dr. Peter Lacovara from the Michael C. Carlos Museum, Emory University in Atlanta, Georgia, coordinated the work in the Amun Temple and central workmens' village, with excellent results. The team also included Dr. Catharine H. Roehrig (MMA), Epigraphic Survey epigrapher Ginger Emery, surveyor Joel Paulson, and architect Charlie Evers†. I am pleased to report that the survey maps generated during the first season that delineate the area of Amenhotep III's palace complex have been used by the SCA in the planning and construction of an 11-kilometer protective wall around the site, 4 m in height, that is in the final stages of completion; I have seen it, and it is a wonder. It is a sad fact that measures like this are becoming necessary all over Egypt in the SCA's increasing efforts to protect archaeological sites from growing agricultural and residential expansion.

* * * * * * * * * *

This season, the Epigraphic Survey's professional staff, besides the director, consisted of J. Brett McClain as senior epigrapher, Jen Kimpton, Christina Di Cerbo, Ginger Emery, and Christian Greco as epigraphers; Boyo Ockinga and Susanne Binder as archaeologist/epigraphers; Margaret De Jong and Susan Osgood as senior artists; Krisztián Vértes and Keli Alberts as artists; Julia Schmied as blockyard and Archives Assistant; Pamela Rose as archaeologist; Jay Heidel and Pieter Collet as architect/surveyors; Yarko Kobylecky as staff photographer; Susan Lezon as photo archivist and photographer; Elinor Smith as photo archives registrar and photography assistant; Carlotta Maher as assistant to the director; Safinaz Ouri as finance manager; Samir el-Guindy as administrator; Marie Bryan as librarian; Anait Helmholz as librarian assistant; Frank Helmholz as master mason; Lotfi K. Hassan as conservation supervisor; Nahed Samir Andraus and Mohamed Abou el-Makarem as conservators at Medinet Habu; Hiroko Kariya as conservation supervisor at Luxor Temple, and conservator intern Siska Genbrugge, who worked with Hiroko. Nan Ray worked as Hiroko's assistant in the Luxor Temple blockyard; Alain and Emmanuelle Arnaudiès worked on the Digital Archives database, Louis Elia Louis Hanna worked as database architect, Conor Power worked as structural engineer, Helen Jacquet-Gordon and Jean Jacquet continued to consult with us from afar, and Girgis Samwell worked with us as chief engineer.

To the Egyptian Supreme Council of Antiquities we owe sincerest thanks for another, fruitful collaboration this season: especially to Dr. Zahi Hawass, secretary general of the SCA; Dr. Mohamed Ismael, general director of Foreign Missions; Dr. Sabry Abdel Aziz, head of the Pharaonic Sector for the SCA; Dr. Mansour Boraik, general director of Luxor; Mr. Mustafa Waziri, general director for the west bank of Luxor; Dr. Mohamed Assem, deputy director of Luxor; Mr. Ibrahim Suleiman, director of Karnak and Luxor Temples; Mr. Sultan Eid, director of Luxor Temple; and Mme. Sanaa, director of the Luxor Museum. Special thanks must go to our inspectors this season, at Luxor Temple: Mr. Gamal Mohamed Mostafa Hussein, Mr. Yehia Abdel Latif Abdel Rahim, and Mme. Hana Morsy Aldsoky; at Medinet Habu temple: Mr. Abu el-Haggag Taye Hussein Mahmoud, Mr. Abd el-Nasser Mohammed Ahmed, Mr. Imad Abdallah Abd el-Ghany, and Mr. Mohammed Ahmed Hussein; at Khonsu Temple: Mr. Ezzat Abou Bakr Saber, Mrs. Ghada Ibrahim Fouad, Mr. Omar Yousef Mahmoud, and Ms. Wafaa Jumaa Amin;

and at the tomb of Nefersekheru: Mr. Abd el-Ghani Abd el-Rahman Mohammed and Mr. Mostafa Mohammed Saleh. SCA conservators working with us included Salah Salim and Anwar Fouad Mahdi Jaama (at Luxor Temple) and Boghdady Abdel Hakam, El Tayeb abo el-Hagag, Abd el-Rahim Qenawy, and Iman Wasfy (at Medinet Habu). It was a pleasure working with them all.

Once again it is a pleasure to acknowledge the many friends of the Oriental Institute whose support allows Chicago House to maintain its documentation, conservation, and restoration work in Luxor. Special thanks must go to the American ambassador to Egypt, the Honorable Margaret Scobey; former American ambassador to Egypt Frank Ricciardone and Dr. Marie Ricciardone; former ambassador to Egypt David Welch and Gretchen Welch; Haynes Mahoney and Helen Lovejoy, Cultural Affairs Office of the U.S. Embassy; Hilda (Bambi) Arellano, director of the United States Agency for International Development in Egypt; Ken Ellis, former director of the USAID Egypt; Mr. Shafik Gabr, ARTOC Group, Cairo; Ahmed Ezz, EZZ Group, Cairo; David and Carlotta Maher; Nan Ray; Mark Rudkin; Dr. Barbara Mertz; Daniel Lindley and Lucia Woods Lindley; Dr. Marjorie M. Fisher; Eric and Andrea Colombel; Piers Litherland; Dr. Fred Giles; Tom Van Eynde; Helen and Jean Jacquet; Marjorie B. Kiewit; Nancy N. Lassalle; Julius Lewis; Tom and Linda Heagy; Misty and Lewis Gruber; O. J. and Angie Sopranos; Judge and Mrs. Warren Siegel; Barbara Breasted Whitesides and George Whitesides; Miriam Reitz Baer; Andrea Dudek; Khalil and Beth Noujaim; James Lichtenstein; Jack Josephson and Magda Saleh; the Secchia Family; Roger and Jane Hildebrand; Douglas and Nancy Abbey; Charles Michod Jr. and the Nuveen Benevolent Trust in memory of Marion Cowan; Gail Adèle; Karim and Janet Mostafa; Anna White; Emily Fine; Waheed and Christine Kamil; Kenneth and Theresa Williams; Thad and Diana Rasche; Louise Grunwald; Lowri Lee Sprung; Andrew Nourse and Patty Hardy; Kate Pitcairn; Drs. Francis and Lorna Straus; Michael and Mrs. Patricia Klowden; Donald Oster; Patrick and Shirley Ryan; Dr. William Kelly Simpson; Dr. Ben Harer; Dr. Roxie Walker; Tony and Lawrie Dean; Mr. Charles L. Michod, Jr.; Dr. Gerry Scott, Kathleen Scott, John Shearman, Mary Sadek, Amir Abdel Hamid, and Amira Khattab of the American Research Center in Egypt; Dr. Jarek Dobrolowski, and Janie Azziz of the Egyptian Antiquities Project; Dr. Michael Jones of the Egyptian Antiquities Conservation Project; and all of our friends and colleagues at the Oriental Institute. I must also express our gratitude to Nassef Sawiris and his family, British Petroleum, the Getty Grant Program of the J. Paul Getty Trust, LaSalle National Bank, Mobil Oil, Coca-Cola Egypt (Atlantic Industries), Vodafone Egypt, and the World Monuments Fund (and especially Robert Wilson) for their support of our work. Many, many thanks to you all!

* * * * * * * * * *

ADDRESSES OF THE EPIGRAPHIC SURVEY

October through March:	**April through September:**
Chicago House	The Oriental Institute
Luxor	1155 East 58th Street
Arab Republic of Egypt	Chicago, IL 60637
TEL: (011) (20) (95) 237-2525	TEL: (773) 702-9524
FAX: (011) (20) (95) 238-1620	FAX: (773) 702-9853

GIZA PLATEAU MAPPING PROJECT

Mark Lehner

Between January 31 and May 7, 2009, the Giza Plateau mapping project team worked at the flagship Heit el-Ghurab (HeG) site (aka Lost City site) and up on the Giza Plateau at the Khentkawes Town (KKT), the settlement attached to the monument of Queen Khentkawes I (fig. 1).[1] We embedded the Ancient Egypt Research Associates (AERA) Advanced Field School for Supreme Council of Antiquities (SCA) inspectors in our excavation program from February 7 to April 2, 2009. Co-field directors Mohsen Kamel and Ana Tavares oversaw the excavations.

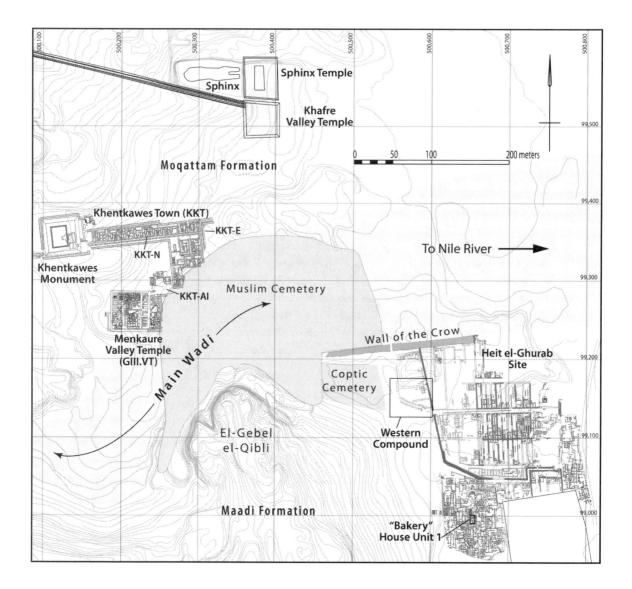

Figure 1. Topographic map showing the area around the Khentkawes Town and the HeG site. The contour lines are at 1-meter intervals

Heit el-Ghurab (HeG)

At the Lost City site (fig. 2), we investigated the Western Compound and, to the south in the Western Town, House Unit 1, possibly the residence and workplace of an administrator.

Exploring Terra Incognita: The Western Compound

Until now, the northwestern section of the site, which includes the Eastern and Western Compounds, has remained largely terra incognita, except for the fieldstone walls that we mapped in 2001. We targeted the Western Compound (fig. 3) for excavation in 2009 for two reasons. Lying immediately south of the Wall of the Crow and at a higher elevation than much of HeG,

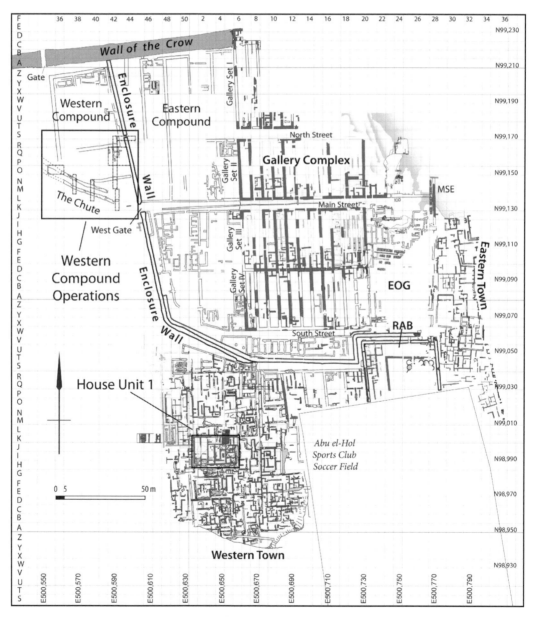

Figure 2. Plan of the Heit el-Ghurab (Lost City) site

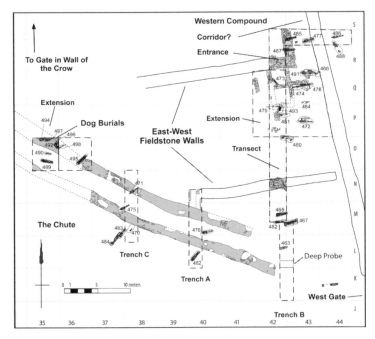

Figure 3. Plan of the Chute and Western Compound operations. The elongated oval features are burials (numbered 462–498)

the area remained dry in 2008 when a rising water table saturated other areas of the site. At that time, it was one of the few areas we could investigate without damaging the site. However, before we began excavations in 2009, the whole site dried out as a result of a program launched by the SCA to pump out groundwater at Giza. Nonetheless, we stuck to our decision to explore the Western Compound since we still knew nothing of it eight years after mapping the area.

Our goals in excavating the Western Compound were to establish the chronology, phasing, and function of the area and to explore a corridor of fieldstone walls, dubbed "the Chute," running northwest–southeast along the southern end of the compound. We began with questions. Was the Western Compound a provisional storage zone, like the water depot known from the entrance to the Workmen's Village at Amarna? Or did the Western Compound simply contain food-production facilities, especially bakeries? Did the occupants use the Western Compound as a holding area for the large numbers of animals consumed by people in the Lost City settlement, as indicated by Richard Redding's analysis of animal bone from our excavations over twenty years? Was the Chute used to funnel animals to slaughter, as suggested by the corridor configuration, which resembles a chute in an abattoir?

The Late Period Cemetery

Before we could explore the Old Kingdom deposits in the Western Compound, we had to wait for our osteo-archaeology team to excavate the dozens of Late Period burials that we encountered in our trenches. As a result, our fieldwork here was cut short, and we were unable to do as much as we had planned.

We expected to encounter some burials, but did not anticipate how much time they would require for proper excavation. The northwest section of the site is punctuated with thousands of burials dating from the Late Period (664–525 BC) into Roman times. In previous seasons, Jessica Kaiser and her osteo-archaeology team excavated close to 300 burials, producing systematic information on a corpus of 2,500-year-old human remains. In the Western Compound, the density of burials and their fragile, delicately painted mud coffins required careful excavation, consolidation, and lifting. Progress was frustratingly slow. During our 2009 season, the osteo team excavated seventeen burials within the Western Compound and nineteen in the Chute, as well as one in KKT.

Dog Burials

During our final days of excavation, we discovered a cache of eight dogs layered on top of one another in a burial pit (fig. 4). The two adults on the top showed signs of mummification. A black substance with imprints of linen wrappings enveloped their skeletons, while the bodies appear to have been tightly wrapped. The other dogs, young adults and puppies, were not tightly wrapped, but a gray powdery substance adhered to the bones, suggesting a possible inexpensive treatment for burial. Most likely the person who buried the dogs intended them as a votive offering. In the Late Period, people buried thousands of mummified ibis birds, falcons, baboons, cats, cows, bulls, shrews, small reptiles, amphibians, jackals, and dogs. Such animal cemeteries are large and numerous at Saqqara, but the only animal burials at Giza are a cache of ibis mummies and another of shrew mice. The burial of a hunting dog was recorded in a relief on a chapel block reused in tomb G 2188 (Reisner 1936), but its original context was never actually located.

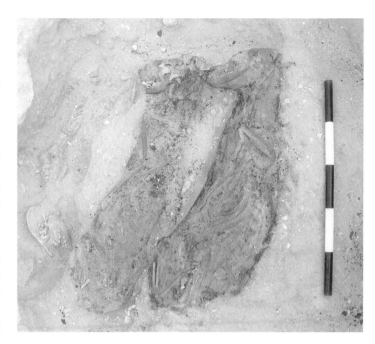

Figure 4. Dog burial at beginning of excavation.
Photo by Ayman Damarany

Old Kingdom Burials

Among scores of Late Period burials, we found two Old Kingdom graves dating close to the time people lived here. Lying under small chambers belonging to the later phases of Old Kingdom occupation (see below), these simple burials predate the limestone structures. They may have been poor people interred in free ground outside the Enclosure Wall. When builders expanded the settlement, they built their walls over the earlier graves. We must add these to three other Old Kingdom burials that we have found at the HeG settlement site. They could be outliers to the crowded "Workers' Cemetery" that Zahi Hawass and the Giza Inspectorate have excavated up the slope from our site.

Old Kingdom Landscaping, Compounds, and More Bakeries

We carried out the work in the Western Compound in two separate operations: the Western Compound and the Chute. The Advanced Field School students specializing in excavation techniques excavated the Western Compound, supervised by Freya Sadarangani, James Taylor, Essam Mohamed Shehab, and Rabee Eissa Mohamed. The plan was to clear down to the Old Kingdom floor level, along a transect beginning on the north in our grid square 3.S42, just where we saw a break through the Enclosure Wall (fig. 3). Because the break roughly aligns with North Street, 60 m (197 feet) to the east, we thought it might be a gate at the end of that street. The transect crossed two thick fieldstone walls that run east–west across the southern end of the Western

Compound and ended on the south at the eastern end of the Chute. We thought this trench would give us a section across all these Old Kingdom structures.

The team revealed another north–south wall, running parallel to the Enclosure Wall, possibly forming a corridor. This wall attached to the eastern end of one of the east–west fieldstone walls. Just where the two walls might connect in a 90-degree corner, a large dump of Old Kingdom pottery, disturbed by Late Period burials, obscured the possible intersection. However, the team was able to see an entrance that had been blocked by an enormous dump of sherds.

The entrance opened into the southeastern corner of a large space, extending 45 m to the north and 34 m to the east, taking up the northern two-thirds of the Western Compound, enclosed by thick walls. After the southern wall of this space had stood for a long while, people built thinner fieldstone walls up against it, forming small chambers, which were filled with dark ash and fragments of bread pots — yet more bakeries, which we can add to the dozens we have located elsewhere across the site (fig. 5).

Figure 5. Stone walls uncovered in the Western Compound. View to the northwest. The Wall of the Crow and its gate can be seen in the background. Photo by Jason Quinlan

As much as the numerous Late Period burials hindered a broader exposure of the Old Kingdom structures, the grave sections gave us valuable archaeological information. We could see in the burial cuts "tip lines" where baskets of fill had been dumped. This dumping raised the surface 2–3 m above the floor level of the Gallery Complex to the east.

From our work in the Western Compound, we learned that people began raising the surface in the northwestern area of the site before they built the Enclosure Wall. Sometime after they put up this wall, they built the structures in the Western Compound. People, rather than natural forces, continued to raise the area west of the Enclosure Wall by dumping sand. We also discovered that the opening in the Enclosure Wall was not an entrance or gate, but rather a gap that someone hacked through the wall.

The Puzzling Chute

The Chute starts 12 m west of West Gate and disappears on the northwest at the limit of our clearing (figs. 3, 6). Since uncovering and mapping the Chute in 2001, we have drawn a dashed line from its northwestern end to the gate in the Wall of the Crow, thinking it could be the principal conduit into the site. The fact that the passage between the walls is so restricted and then simply stops at an open area before West Gate led to the hypothesis that people used it to control, and perhaps count, animals brought to the site for slaughter, possibly in the open area.

Figure 6. The parallel stone walls of the Chute. In the background Main Street shows as a linear depression. View to the southeast. Photo by Mark Lehner

Ashraf Abd el-Aziz supervised Noha Hasan Bolbol, Amy McMahon, and May al-Haik. The goals of their excavation were to learn more about the date and purpose of the Chute, as well as to determine if it turns north to feed into the Gate in the Wall of the Crow.

The team excavated three trenches perpendicular to the Chute, Trenches A and C along its length and Trench B at the eastern end. Their stratigraphy established that the Chute walls are contemporary with the walls of the Western Compound.

The Chute consists of two parallel walls forming a passage 2.40 to 2.80 m wide. Each of the two walls, approximately 1.45 m wide, is built of uncoursed limestone blocks, with two "skin" walls holding a core of mixed material, including stone, sand, and broken pottery. The team excavated successive street surfaces inside the Chute, lying at approximately 18.08 m above sea level.

Trench B revealed that the space between the eastern end of the Chute and West Gate was an open area in which a series of trampled surfaces developed upon layers filled with large quantities of animal bone — from cattle and sheep in an upper layer and mostly from sheep in a lower one. The layers might indicate that people indeed butchered animals in front of West Gate. However, the walls of the Chute rest upon these trampled surfaces and thus postdate them. The results at best indicate that the inhabitants might have slaughtered animals in the area where people later built the eastern end of the Chute.

Where Goes the Road?

One of our goals was to determine whether the Chute turns north to the Gate in the Wall of the Crow (fig. 2) or continues to the northwest. To find out we cleared a thick sand overburden to the west as close as we could to the modern Coptic Cemetery. Here on line with the gate in the Wall of the Crow we found two very disturbed humps of stone, the remains of the Chute, indicating that it continues on its trajectory to the northwest. Perhaps this is already too far west-northwest to make a turn toward the Gate. Unfortunately, the end of digging was upon us before we could resolve this question.

Deep Probe and Ancient Landscaping

Could there have been an older Chute, remains of which lie underneath the walls we mapped? To assess this possibility, we excavated a deep probe trench 2 m below the base of the Chute walls in Trench B (fig. 3). The probe descended about 40 cm lower than the general floor level at the lower northern ends of the galleries. Below the animal bone layers (mentioned above), the probe showed thick dump deposits. People had intentionally filled and raised the area. This evidence for ancient landscaping is one of the most important results of our excavations in the northwest section of the site. The dumped layers of desert clay under the eastern end of the Chute and the dumped sand layers under the Western Compound show how massively people altered the terrain. We see similar extensive remodeling of the ancient landscape in other areas of the site, such as along the Wall of the Crow and in the Royal Administrative Building. We should not be surprised at the impressive scale of the artificial landscaping in a settlement of Giza Pyramid builders, for the pyramids and their quarries themselves represent human intervention on a geological scale.

Character of the Western Compound

The Western Compound appears to contain enormous dumps of pottery waste and ash. People built fieldstone walls and chambers, ad hoc, as they dumped, so that some of these structures rest upon already dumped waste, and such waste also covered the structures. In this respect, the Western Compound is similar to Area EOG, an industrial yard east of the galleries, with many bakeries (fig. 2). The Western Compound also resembles the Eastern Compound, with concentrated ashy dumps of pottery waste embedding fieldstone structures, one of which was a bakery Augusta McMahon excavated in 1991. Was the Western Compound a compounding, if you will, of the extensive production facilities, especially bread baking, that surrounded the central Gallery Complex?

The residents of the HeG settlement during its later years seem to have turned to bread baking on an industrial scale. It may be historically significant that the intensification of production, and the signs of its control, occurred in the later phase of occupation, not long before people abandoned this site.

House Unit 1

With great relief, by autumn 2008, we saw that the water table, which had been steadily rising and saturating the site since 2005, was falling as a result of the pumps installed by the SCA and Cairo University. We seized the opportunity to finish excavating House Unit 1 in the Western Town (fig. 2).

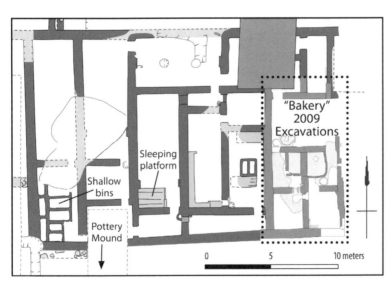

Figure 7. Plan of House Unit 1

House Unit 1 (fig. 7), the largest house we have so far found on the site, covers 400 sq. m, with approximately twenty rooms/spaces, including very large rooms, well-laid floors, traces of red and black paint on the base of the plastered walls, and a master bedroom with a sleeping platform for two.

Yukinori Kawae, assisted by Manami Yahata, continued the excavations of House Unit 1 that they had carried out over four seasons between 2004 and 2007. When Kawae had to

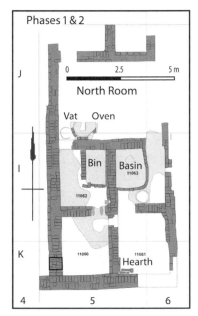

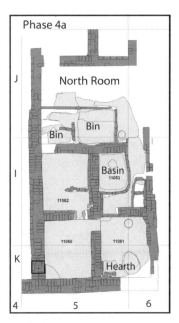

Figure 8. House Unit 1, phases in the "bakery"

leave unexpectedly mid-season, Freya Sadarangani took over. Advanced Field School students supplemented the team. They worked in the last unexcavated component within the house, the eastern end. We had dubbed it the "bakery" because, unlike the rest of the house with its well-laid floors, the chambers were buried in dark ashy fill that the residents allowed to accumulate over time, as we have seen in bakeries elsewhere on the site.

During its lifetime, the bakery went through a succession of renovations. The team identified at least four phases of remodeling and occupation (figs. 8–9), but they were unable to complete the excavations. The North Room initially included an oven and vat standing side by side. Later the residents built a rectangular bin around this area, followed by another, smaller bin. Over time ash accumulated, the floor rose, and the occupants built a small bin directly over the top of the oven, the vat, and the large bin. As a result of rebuilding and accumulation, the latest floors within the bakery are 60 cm higher than the other floors of House Unit 1.

Figure 9. House Unit 1 at the completion of excavations. View toward west. Photo by Jason Quinlan

In the two small chambers in the mid-section, the residents built more low bins. The one in the eastern room was a basin, with a sunken floor sloping down to a center hole where the occupants probably stuck a small pottery vat. Yet another vat and a smaller set of two bins were added later in the southeast corner.

The basin, vat socket, and small bins in this room are very similar to installations in the bakery we found east of the Pedestal Building during 2006 and 2007. They may have served the same function, which we speculated was malting. In this process emmer or barley grains are soaked in water and spread out on a cool, moist surface to sprout. Sprouting activates enzymes that convert the starches in the grain to sugar to support the growth of the emerging seedling. To halt sprouting before the seedling consumes the sugars, the grains are dried in warm air. In House Unit 1, workers might have used vats sunk into the floor of the basins for soaking grain, which they then spread out across the basin within the low rim, while excess water drained back to the socket or a vat.

Hearths in the southern rooms were probably used for baking and cooking. In the southeast chamber the hearth was lined with mud accretions against the southern and western walls. The structure is very similar to the hearths built against the southeastern corners of the bakeries we excavated in 1991. In the southwest chamber, ash with pottery and bone filled the southeast corner, which was scorched. In the northwestern corner, the team found a simple platform made of two pieces of limestone and one of granite.

Bakery or Brewery?

The preponderance of low bins and vats suggests that the "bakery" may have had as much to do with malting, hence brewing, as baking. Other evidence suggests that people might have devoted this complex to beer production. It connects via a long corridor to a room in the southwestern corner of the house with a set of eight shallow bins, like the ones we proposed were used for sprouting. Immediately south of this corridor, we found large quantities of beer-jar fragments in a massive dump we called "Pottery Mound."

Another possible connection to brewing may be a set of pedestals, similar to those we have found across the site, under Pottery Mound and in a court south of the "bakery." We hypothesize that jars and pedestals functioned together to effect evaporative cooling to keep grain cool and moist in a jar or other container, a stage preliminary to spreading out on a cool bin floor to allow continued sprouting.

If we could ascertain some degree of specialized work with brewing or malt production, it would be the first, and so far only, facilities for beer production that we have found across the site, whereas we have found dozens of bakeries. It will be interesting to see how this evidence of specialized beer production associated with House Unit 1 plays out in our continued excavations.

The Khentkawes Town (KKT) and the Menkaure Valley Temple (GIII.VT)

Expecting a wealth of information and new discoveries at the Khentkawes complex (fig. 10), where we have worked since 2005, we placed the core of the excavation team here. We were not disappointed. On the east we uncovered a striking arrangement of terraces, ramps, and stairways, and a very deep basin, which probably belong to Khentkawes' funerary complex. In the town, we completely excavated one of the houses and discovered that people may have abandoned the settlement for some time and then reoccupied it. To the south we pursued the elusive stratigraphic link between the Khentkawes Town and the Valley Temple of King Menkaure, possibly

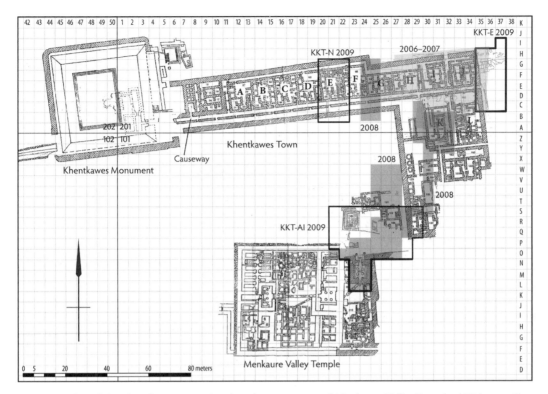

Figure 10. Plan of the Khentkawes Town (KKT) and Monument and Menkaure Valley Temple. AERA operations in 2009 are outlined in black, 2008 operations shown in gray, and 2006–2007 in light gray. The houses in KKT are indicated with letters. The KKT map is from Selim Hassan's original 1942 publication. The Menkaure Valley Temple map is from George Reisner's 1931 publication

Khentkawes' husband or father, and revealed a monumental approach ramp and another deep basin.

KKT-N: House E

For three seasons we have been gradually clearing and mapping the houses in the Khentkawes Town where Egyptologists have long thought priests lived. This season we seized the chance to excavate one of the better-preserved houses that remained after Selim Hassan's large-scale excavations in 1932 (Hassan 1943). We expanded our knowledge of the phasing and layout of this part of the town by dissecting a cross section of the causeway.

Khentkawes' town planners laid out eight houses along the north side the causeway. The western six houses (A–F) share the same general plan; the four houses on the east are smaller. Two larger houses (K–L) lay south of the causeway. We mapped the scant remains of the eastern houses in 2007. During 2007 and 2008, we progressively cleared southward across the foot of the town and westward along the causeway. In 2007 Lisa Yeomans and Pieter Collet recorded the meager traces of houses I–J, where many of the walls had been scoured down to bedrock. During our 2008 season, Collet continued clearing and mapping westward.

During 2009 Lisa Yeomans, assisted by Hanan Mahmoud, carried out the work in House E (figs. 11, 12). The structure covers approximately 189 sq. m (15.70 × 12.05 m), about mid-range between the area of the Eastern Town House (100 sq. m) and House Unit 1 (400 sq. m) at our HeG site (fig. 2). Yeomans and Mahmoud identified six discreet phases of occupation and

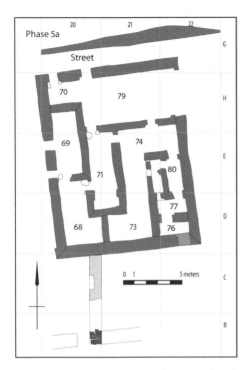

Figure 11. Plan of Building E, Phase 5a, Khentkawes Town, recorded by AERA excavators. The room numbers are those assigned by Hassan

structural modification (fig. 13). Originally the house had four elongated, north–south rooms, and one transversal room (74) opening from an open courtyard (79), which was shared with the neighboring house, House F to the east. A doorway on the north opened to a street along the town Enclosure Wall.

The main entrance, on the southeast, opens to a zigzag succession of small chambers (76, 77, 80), typical of Old Kingdom houses and shrines, which provided privacy from the street. These lead to a central room (74), a vestibule possibly left unroofed, from which doorways open north to the open courtyard (79) at the back of the house, another leading to a chamber that Hassan (1943) called a "kitchen" (73) and the third leading to an elongated room (71). The kitchen (73) showed substantial evidence of burning that left thick ash over the floor and damage to the western wall. The room may have been open or only partially covered with a light roof to allow smoke to escape.

Hassan designated Rooms 68 and 69 as bedrooms. However, we found a number of hearth features against the eastern wall of Room 69, opposite a doorway from Room 67 in House D, including pottery, bone, and burnt fish bone that suggest that Room 69 shared cooking facilities with people in House D. However, Room 68 could have been a bedroom, with a bed in an eastward niche. We have found bed platforms within niches that turn off a main room in the HeG site, and bed platforms within niches are known from ancient Egyptian houses at other sites.

Hassan described Room 71 as the "living room," but it might have served as another bedroom. At the southern end, pilasters define a niche, the width of the room. In House Unit 1 in the HeG site, the large central room was also configured with two pilasters defining a niche (fig. 7). A bed platform tucked in the niche suggests it was for sleeping.

In the first phase (5a) of House E, the builders framed two entrances to the street on the north. In the next phase (5b), they blocked the northern entrances of the house and partitioned off a small room (70) in the northwest corner (fig. 13). About this time, builders put up an east–west wall on the street to the south. This wall now formed the southern border

Figure 12. Building E, Khentkawes Town. Silos constructed in Phase 5c appear in the foreground. View to the southeast. Photo by Jason Quinlan

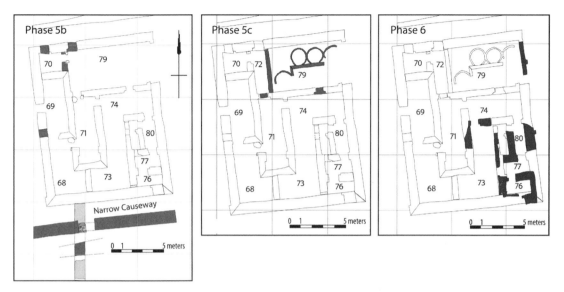

Figure 13. Phases of occupation and renovation in Building E, Khentkawes Town. Changes in the walls in Phases 5b through 6 are shown in dark gray

of a narrower causeway running straight from the doorway of Queen Khentkawes's chapel to the valley complex (see below).

Houses Intermingling

One of the most significant discoveries of our 2009 season is that what we perceive as separate house plans at some points in time were "intermingled" houses (figs. 13–14). These "separate" houses had rooms that were more easily accessible, or only accessible, from the house next door. Room 69, a "bedroom" in House E, could be more easily accessed through two open doorways from House D to the west. Room 79, Hassan's "reception hall" of House E, was completely open to the northern end of House F to the east during all but the last period (Phase 6) that people lived here. In fact Room 79 was for much of the time one very long court that continued east to span the entire width of House F. Hassan's map shows that the most direct access into this court was a doorway from the northern street into the part of the court spanning House F. At some point the occupants built walls to subdivide the western end of this court within House F into two small chambers, Rooms 83 and 84. We do not know when these walls went up since we have not yet excavated House F. But we suspect it was during Phase 6 of House E, when people made the thin north–south wall that closed Room 79, now with round silos, probably for storing grain, on the east. Even at this point, the most direct access into the granaries at the northern end of House E was through the doorway in the northern wall of House F. In fact, Lisa Yeomans' preliminary chronological

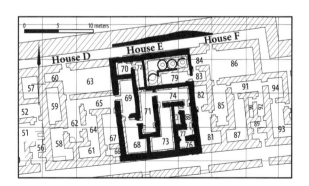

Figure 14. Khentkawes Town, Building E, phase 6 plan superimposed over a digitized version of Hassan's original map

phasing suggests that people blocked both of the two doorways through the northern wall of House E in Phase 5b, and then, in Phase 5c, they built the silos in Room 79. But they screened this storage off from the northwest corner of Building E with a thin wall (creating Room 72). Eventually they blocked the doorway through the southern wall of the silos court (Room 79) into the rest of House E via Room 74. If we correctly understand this sequence, people completely blocked access to the silos from inside House E, while making them fully accessible to House F. During Phase 6 they further limited access to the silos by erecting across the east end of the courtyard a thin wall with a door. The silos remained inaccessible to House E.

Hassan's map of the Khentkawes Town indicates no lateral access via doorways between Houses A, B, and C (fig. 10). However, doorways or openings allowed passage through four houses, D to G, without going into the northern street or causeway. Could what we perceive as four separate house plans have been occupied by one extended household at some period? Unfortunately, Hassan's map is not entirely reliable. We cannot be certain that the complex of rooms along the northern side of the Khentkawes causeway functioned as distinct structural and social units.

Abandonment and Reoccupation

Another significant discovery this season was that the Khentkawes Town may have been completely abandoned, perhaps for a considerable time. Evidence of abandonment has cropped up each of our three seasons of work, but it was particularly striking this season in House E and in the southern causeway and street during Phase 6 (fig. 13).

In House E people rebuilt and created walls using mudbricks different from those of the earlier building periods. The bricks are smaller and formed of brown sandy silt with a slight reddish tint, as though the soil had been burnt. Builders also used these small bricks to make a thin wall screening off the court with silos (Room 79). In this period the northwest corner of the house was now totally inaccessible, as all doorways had been blocked (in Phases 5b–c). The residents used the small brown bricks to repair major parts of the walls in the small chambers inside the southeast entrance, and the walls of Room 73, the kitchen, which might have suffered heat damage from long contact with cooking fires.

The causeway and street to the south were resurfaced at least three times. The original southern town Enclosure Wall was drastically cut down and its north side cut back, leaving only a patch of its characteristic large bricks of dark clay. It looks as though people robbed the bricks, as we know they did in much of the HeG site, for reuse elsewhere. People eventually rebuilt the wall over a thick layer of disintegrated brick and silt, perhaps generations later, on the same line as the earlier Enclosure Wall. They used small reddish brown bricks and small local limestone fragments as casing for a debris-filled core, a cheap way to fill out a 2.22-meter-thick wall.

Reoccupation of the town was not haphazard. Here and there throughout the settlement, masons rebuilt old walls that had been cut away and built new ones using the same small, reddish brown bricks and local limestone pieces. It is possible that a tax exemption or a re-endowment of the Khentkawes funerary cult encouraged people to move into the deserted town, as happened with the settlement inside the Menkaure Valley Temple to the south during the reign of the Sixth Dynasty pharaoh Pepi II.

KKT-E: Khentkawes Valley Complex

Queens of the pyramid age were buried in small pyramids and mastabas next to the large pyramid of the king. They usually did not have causeways leading from the chapels attached to their tombs or valley temples. Not only did Khentkawes I have a causeway, but we are also finding a valley complex with access ramps and quite possibly a harbor. She may have been one of those rare queens who, at the end of a dynasty, took the throne as king in her own right. Her titles can be read either "Mother of the Two Kings of Upper and Lower Egypt," or "Mother of the King of Upper and Lower Egypt, and King of Upper and Lower Egypt." Khentkawes I must have lived and ruled at the end of the Fourth Dynasty and built her tomb in the final years of our HeG site. She may have been Menkaure's daughter or a wife (or both).

Valley Complex for Khentkawes I

Until 2007 no one knew why the Khentkawes Town turned abruptly south forming an L-shape. During our 2007 season, we discovered a deep quarry cut that limited the

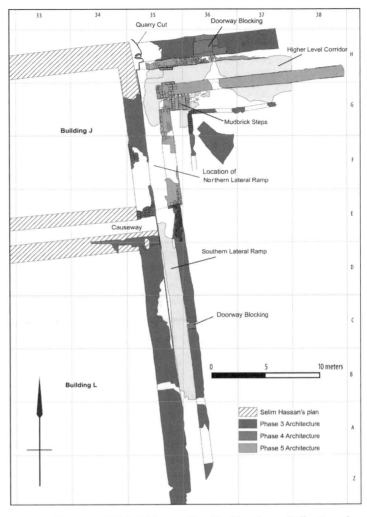

Figure 15. KKT-E 2009 operation. The Khentkawes Valley Complex, Phase 4–5. The Northern Lateral Ramp had not yet been built, but its future location is indicated

Figure 16. KKT-E 2009 operation. Clearing over two seasons revealed the Khentkawes Town Valley Complex. The Town sits above on a bedrock plane. Lateral ramps ascend the bedrock face to the threshold of the Khentkawes causeway. Photo by Mark Lehner

Figure 17. Isometric drawing of the east end of the Khentkawes Town and the Khentkawes Valley Complex. Drawing by Mark Lehner

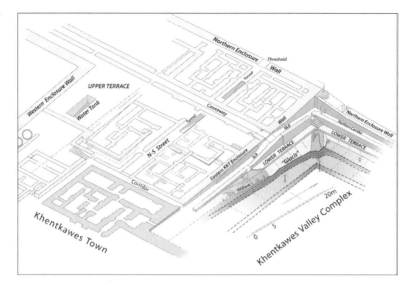

eastern extent of the town. The eastern Enclosure Wall ran flush along the edge of the cut. But, below, to the east, we found evidence of a large mudbrick complex buried deep under sand (figs. 15–17). In our 2009 season, we excavated 20 m along the north and 45 m along the west sides of this complex. We uncovered a lower terrace formed of crushed limestone over bedrock, retained by mudbrick walls. The open area in front of these walls drops 3 m to bedrock. We believe that this sand-filled depression is a basin that opens to the east.

From the depression, a stairway ramp leads up to the lower terrace, and from there another stairway leads to an upper corridor along the north and west sides of the basin. At the bottom of the stairs and in our excavation of the northern corridor, we found deposits of hundreds of votive miniature ceramics, similar to those archaeologists have found outside pyramid temples.

On the south, from the lower terrace a long north–south ramp ascends along the face of the bedrock ledge to the threshold of the queen's causeway at the east edge of the town. Builders later added a second ramp to the threshold from the north. We need to investigate this arrangement further, but we can suggest, based on its position, size, and layout, that it is the valley complex and harbor for the funerary monument of Queen Khentkawes.

KKT-E Excavations

Daniel Jones and Kasia Olchowska supervised the excavations in the area east of the Khentkawes Town (KKT-E). At the beginning of the 2009 season, they faced a mass of mudbrick tumble sloping to the south and east in the northwestern corner of the bedrock ledge. The thick eastern and northern Enclosure Walls had collapsed down to the southeast, better preserving the lower walls in this corner against forces of erosion that scoured the walls to the south.

In an early phase, builders made the Southern Lateral Ramp (SLR), rising between the eastern edge of the KKT-E town terrace and a parallel mudbrick wall (fig. 15). The builders filled the north–south corridor with crushed limestone to make a floor surface ascending to the causeway at an 11-degree slope. At the top of the Ramp, just south of the causeway threshold, a jamb projects from the corridor wall to make a restriction, possibly a doorway. Later the builders created a corridor raised above the level of the lower terrace and running north from the high end of SLR, then turning to run east for a distance of 12.40 m. The corridor is practically the same width as the Khentkawes causeway.

Still later the builders constructed the Northern Lateral Ramp (NLR) within the northern corridor, but because of the higher floor level of the corridor, its incline is half that of the SLR, rising at around 4 degrees over a length of 8.41 m. At the northern end of the NLR corridor, a doorway opens onto a stairway of six steps that descends to the lower terrace. The builders may have intended the northern corridor as a continuation of the causeway passage around the queen's valley complex, just as the Menkaure causeway corridor went around the king's valley temple on the west and south.

As we cleared the clean sand during our 2009 season, we realized that in order to create the lower terrace, the builders extended the remains of a bedrock quarry ledge with crushed limestone debris held in place by mudbrick retaining walls. The lateral ramps, the northern corridor, and the stairs rest on this lower terrace. From this level the bedrock drops again into a deeper depression.

The upper terrace on which the KKT is founded slopes down from north to south following the natural dip of the limestone bedrock strata, while the lower terrace is roughly level. Builders added the lateral ramps to bridge this difference in elevation.

We found a second stairway ramp embedded in the slope at the northwest corner of the terrace. The ramp descends at a slope of 20 degrees down into the clean, wet sand filling the basin at the base of the terrace. At the southern end of our clearing, we noted cuttings into the bedrock foundation of the terrace that might indicate where another stairway or ramp ascended as a complement to the one on the north.

Temple Harbor? The Very Deep Basin

In the depression below the complex, we cleared an area 30 m long (north–south) by 15 m wide (east–west) on the north, narrowing to 6 m wide on the south, where we were constrained by a road and the modern cemetery. It is hard to convey the immensity of the sand deposit that filled the KKT-E area and the great depth of the queen's valley complex. At the beginning of our 2009 season, the sand mounded up to around elevation 24.00 m above sea level. Our deepest probe reached 14.60 m above sea level, where we had to stop because of the water table. The drop of 9.4 m made this one of the deepest, most dramatic excavations we have ever undertaken at Giza.

At the bottom of our 2009 excavation, sand still filled the depression. Four drill cores that we made with a hand augur suggested that the bedrock bottom of the basin steps down toward the east. The core farthest out into the basin hit bedrock at about 12.50 m above sea level, which is our best estimate of the elevation of the Fourth Dynasty Nile Valley floodplain. Based on the erosion of the mudbrick retaining wall of the lower terrace, we estimated that water could have filled the basin to a total depth of 3.17 m.

The results from our previous seasons' work north of the Wall of the Crow (fig. 1) nearly 300 m due east of the Menkaure Valley Temple suggested that this temple could never have fronted directly onto Nile waters. Access to the Nile lay 700 to 800 m to the east across a terrace at 16.30 m above sea level, close to the level of the lower terrace in KKT-E, built on natural, desert wadi deposits. We found no evidence of Nile alluvium for up to 20 to 30 m north of the wall. Now, 50 to 100 m north of the Menkaure Valley Temple, we have evidence of a very deep cut into the bedrock reaching down to Old Kingdom floodplain levels. But our four cores so far show no silt that Nile floodwaters would have left at the bottom.

The artificial 90-degree cut into the bedrock at KKT-E, which drops the surface nearly 10 m, must continue at least 50 m farther east of our 2009 excavations. Exposed bedrock with rock-cut tombs continues much farther east just to the north of the open area east of KKT.

The stone Wall of the Crow forms the southern boundary of this open area, which takes in the mouth of the wadi between the Moqqatam Formation limestone outcrop on the north and the Maadi Formation knoll on the south. The 2500 BC surface 20 to 30 m north of the Wall of the Crow must have remained high and dry as an artificial terrace of limestone debris. We did not find the northern edge of that terrace. It is possible that farther north, we would find a large Fourth Dynasty cut that the builders made through the natural wadi sediments, and perhaps a wall they used to hold it in place. The edges might form the southern and northern sides of a basin that delivered water to the eastern foot of the terraced Khentkawes Town and perhaps to the town and valley temple of Menkaure.

Attached to the eastern front of the Menkaure Valley Temple (GIII.VT), we exposed the "glacis" of the eastern enclosure wall of the Ante-town as low as 16.00 m above sea level. Immediately beside the glacis, a broad ramp ascends to the Ante-town and temple. We have not seen the eastern ends of the broad ramp or the glacis, which disappear under the modern road and Muslim cemetery. If the depression or basin east of the Khentkawes Town extends 100 m south, it would reach the broad ramp. It is possible that the terrace we found in our 2004–2006 clearing north of the Wall of the Crow is the shoulder of a broad depression that delivered water to both the Khentkawes and Menkaure Valley complexes.

KKT-AI

One of our main reasons for working at KKT has been to determine how this town related to the settlement within the Menkaure Valley Temple (GIII.VT) just to the south. Reisner (1931) established with his excavations in 1908–1910 that people occupied the GIII.VT, and the Ante-town in front of it, until the end of the Sixth Dynasty. Hassan (1943) mentions houses of a later phase in the eastern part of KKT, but largely assumed that the queen's town dated to the late Fourth Dynasty. In 2005 we began work in the area between the KKT and the GIII.VT, the "interface" (KKT-AI), in order to establish the stratigraphic and chronological links between the two.

The only archaeological map known of the interface area, the one Hassan published in 1943, shows an empty area. But our 2005 clearing exposed a broad mud-paved ramp, which Hassan mentioned as a "causeway." Over three seasons we gathered a wealth of information on both settlements, but the stratigraphic link proved elusive. In 2008 we found the "Cut," a broad, irregular, west–east trench backfilled in ancient times with sandy limestone gravel. This deep, irregular canyon gouged out the northern side of the Ramp and removed the crucial deposits that link the settlements of Khentkawes and Menkaure. During 2008 we also cleared the second vestibule of the GIII.VT on the south side of the Ramp. Located at the northern front of the GIII. VT, Vestibule 2 opens north onto the upper end of the Ramp. In 2008, we left a large swath of post-1932 sandy overburden covering the northern upper end of the Ramp and filling a stone-lined basin, Water Tank 2, adjacent to the Ramp on the north.

In our 2009 operation, Mike House and James Taylor, assisted by Kate Liszka, Hanan Mahmoud, and Nagwan Bahaa Fayeza, removed the remaining post-1932 overburden and excavated strategically located trenches to resolve questions about chronology and stratigraphy.

The components of the interface comprise a truly monumental landscape, albeit built in limestone debris, mudbrick, and small-block limestone masonry (fig. 18). Below I describe the features that we cleared and mapped during the 2009 season: the southwestern corner of the

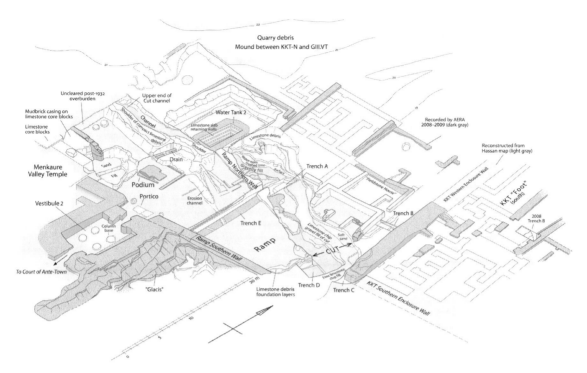

Figure 18. Isometric drawing of the Ramp area in the KKT-AI operation. View to the west. Drawing by Mark Lehner

Figure 19. Water Tank 2 and the KKT-AI operation. View to the south. Photo by Jason Quinlan

Figure 20. The Ramp area in the KKT-AI operation. View to the west. Photo by Jason Quinlan

southern end of the KKT "foot," the section of the settlement that runs to the south nearly touching the GIII.VT, the extramural houses, Water Tank 2, the Ramp, the Cut, and the Podium, a low platform at the top of the Ramp (figs. 18–20).

KKT Foot

In 2009 we cleared as far as we could south along the western Enclosure Wall (2.30 m thick) of the "foot" of the Khentkawes Town (KKT-F), exposing the very southwestern corner of the wall, where it turns to run east. According to Hassan's 1943 map, he followed the wall for about 13 m to the east, picking up the chambers and small magazines built into the interior of this corner of the KKT. We were able to trace the southern side of the corner for only 1.80 m because of the post-1932 overburden that supports the road around the modern cemetery.

In Trench C, we excavated a triangle, 1.86 × 2.18 × 2.52 m, along this stretch of the southern face of the KTT-F Enclosure Wall, taking in the modern embankment on the southeast and the Cut on the northwest. We found the Enclosure Wall preserved to a height of around 60 cm at the corner. In this short exposure, the Enclosure Wall shows a rectangular projection, or buttress, 52 cm (1 cubit) deep, about 87 cm wide, and only 35 cm from the corner. At some point in time, people filled in the southern face of the wall to the east of the projection so as to make the projection flush with the wall. But they left the corner notched, or rebated, by 52 cm.

It became apparent after our 2009 clearing and mapping that the KKT western Enclosure Wall strikes a near perfect perpendicular to the southern wall of the Ramp, which also functions as the northern wall of the Ante-town. This suggests that builders created the Ramp and the KKT-F along the same axes or orientation, with the same shift about 6 degrees west of true north that we see in the whole KKT. The general orientation slightly west of north is shared by the entire HeG settlement south of the Wall of the Crow. This orientation is noticeably different from that of the GIII.VT, which, like the Giza Pyramids and temples, is oriented closer to the true cardinal directions.

Extramural Houses

Hassan's 1943 map shows two house-like buildings between the KKT-F and Water Tank 2. We cleared and mapped the remains of most of the southeasterly unit, built of fieldstone, and part of the structure to the northwest, built of mudbrick. In the rectangular space between these units on the northeast in our grid squares UT26–27, we cleared and mapped ephemeral traces of mudbrick walls that might have made the two units a single complex. On Hassan's map more walls extend west of the northwestern unit and north of Water Tank 2. Farther west, Cairo University excavated in 1980 the deflated walls of a fieldstone building, about the size of these units. So the extramural settlement might have been fairly continuous along the entire northern side of the GIII.VT.

The easternmost fieldstone unit forms a street or corridor, 2.5 m wide, with the western Enclosure Wall of the KKT-F. We excavated Trench B, 1 m wide, in square R28, across this corridor and determined that the house was built sometime after the KKT western Enclosure Wall. The Cut truncated the eastern extramural house through the entire vertical height of its walls, up to 1 m high, as well as the floors and underlying layers, and obliterated the end of the corridor where a door might have opened onto the Ramp.

Water Tank 2

The builders set Water Tank 2[2] into the southeastern slope of limestone quarry debris piled between the GIII.VT and the northern part of KKT (figs. 18–19). They terraced the limestone quarry debris in four main levels, stepping the surface down into a masonry-lined basin for a total drop of 3.8 m. At the top of Level 1, remains of a mudbrick wall on the north and west sides and northeastern corner suggest that this wall may have once enclosed the entire upper perimeter.

Traces of another mudbrick wall remain on the northern, western, and eastern sides of the next level down. From Level 2, the surface drops about a meter to Level 3, a relatively flat surface, paved with gray Nile silt, around a masonry-lined tank. The slope between Levels 2 and 3 shows an irregular, steep edge with coarser limestone debris, possibly the result of erosion (from lapping water?) or simply the slipping and collapse of a fine crushed limestone render on the face of the slope.

A limestone drain (see below) emerges at Level 3 from under an embankment between the Ramp and Water Tank 2 (the "Partition Embankment," see below). The silt paving of Level 3 meets the back of the flagstones that form the upper perimeter of the masonry-lined tank. In the center of Level 3, the stone-lined tank opens, around 2×5 m. Level 4, the bottom of the tank, is a flat floor of compact crushed limestone. The total depth of the masonry-lined tank is 1.56 m. Masons set five stepped courses of limestone slabs in the sides.

Overall, Water Tank 2 narrows, funnel-like, from around 20×20 m at the upper perimeter, to about 1×4 m at the very bottom, and drops about 3.8 m from an upper rim elevation of around 20 m above sea level to 16.20 m above sea level. Why did its builders begin so wide, and drop so deep?

With the drain emerging from under the Partition Embankment at the edge of the masonry-lined tank, we take the impression that the builders intended the lowest level to be the main reservoir of water — assuming that water catchment and storage were its functions. The lowest masonry-lined tank could have held a little more than 6,100 liters of water. If water filled the tank up to the brim of Level 2, it would have comprised more than 31,300 liters, enough water for 400 people over 165 days if each consumed two liters a day.

If the inhabitants purposefully filled the tank with water from the Nile or canals to the east, they must have transported the water in pots and shoulder poles (or skins?). Or, did the builders intend that water would come from episodic, torrential rains and consequent desert wadi flooding, flowing in from the west? Any rainwater coming from the west would had to have run down a great mound of quarry debris that fills the area between the KKT and the GIII.VT. Then it would have to flow over an irregular ridge of limestone debris and hit the mudbrick wall along the west side of Level 1. A shallow gulley cuts through the southern low end of the ridge, indicating that at some point water might have flowed here. But any water pouring onto the terrace would flow to the south rather than east into the tank, because of the slope. Otherwise water from the west could enter the tank through the narrow channel through the Drain under the Partition Embankment after flowing east along the road between the embankment and the GIII.VT. But the small width of this channel does not match the immensity of Water Tank 2, and we see no evidence of major water flows in the surface around the southern end of the Drain.

The basin is oriented close to true north–south, like all pyramids and pyramid temples at Giza, and unlike KKT and the Ante-town, which are oriented slightly west of north, as noted above. Thus, Water Tank 2 most likely belongs to the GIII.VT layout rather than the KKT. Along with the Podium (see below), it may have served the cult and possibly the funeral of Menkaure.

The Partition Embankment

A wide embankment, a bar of quarry debris retained by fieldstone walls, separates the top of the Ramp from Level 2 of Water Tank 2. The builders cut back the southern side of the Partition Embankment to build an enclosure around the Podium (see below). The highest point on top of the embankment, as far as we cleared to the west, is about the same level as the terrace west of the Water Tank 2. The embankment narrows from 5.2 m wide at its east end to 4.3 m on the west. A shallow channel (see below) cuts longitudinally across the top of the embankment running east–west.

The Drain

The builders installed the Drain for a length of 6.70 m from the roadway to the water tank, under the Partition Embankment, as mentioned above. They laid a line of limestone pieces as the base, 26 cm wide, and cut a small channel, 9 cm wide, in the upper surface. The bottom of this little channel slopes 34 cm down from its southern end to its northern end, where the Drain emerges on Level 3 at the upper edge of the masonry-lined tank. Upon the base they laid broader limestone pieces, 35 to 41 cm wide, as a cover that they coated with gray alluvial silt. They then covered the Drain with the Partition Embankment. We see three meters of the length of the Drain exposed on its southern end at the bottom of a trench that someone, probably Selim Hassan's workers, cut through the Partition Embankment to follow the Drain. The slope of the Drain down to the north indicates that its builders intended for any water, or other fluids, to flow into Water Tank 2 away from the roadbed at the top of the Ramp behind the Podium. But, as noted above, the channel of the Drain is incongruously small compared to the immense capacity of the basin. Yet, the builders seem not to have created in the landscape any other option for water to flow into this great tank. The channel across the top of the Partition Embankment and the Cut leading down slope to the east from the southeastern corner of Water Tank 2 might suggest that water did flow through this alternative route, or that people created the channel and Cut as a conduit for such flow, albeit not one that corresponded to the original design and building.

The Cut

It appears that the Cut begins west of the limit of our clearing. We pick it up as a shallow channel, about 2 m wide, in the surface of the terrace west of the Water Tank 2 and the Partition Embankment. A subsidiary channel diverges on the Partition Embankment and carves a shallow erosion channel through the east end of the embankment and diagonally across the Ramp. The main channel turns to the northeast, where it cuts down through the southeast corner of Water Tank 2. To the east the Cut took away the northern shoulder wall of the Ramp, gouged out walls and floors of the extramural houses, and finally, toward the lower end of the Ramp, turned south and cut across and through the total thickness of the Ramp and its foundation. Trench D showed that the resulting canyon extends down 1.75 m, reaching 15.00 m above sea level.

It is worth noting that sides of the Cut channel are undercut, suggesting flowing water, as streams commonly undercut the outside of bends. However, where the Cut channel meets the western Enclosure Wall of the KKT, it turns south, sparing the wall. It is hard to imagine that, if flowing water created the Cut, it would have left the base of the mudbrick Enclosure Wall unscathed.

Whatever the source of the Cut, it appears that people late in the occupation tried to fix it by dumping large quantities of limestone gravel into the deep channel.

The Ramp

Hassan (1943: 53) referred to the Ramp between the KKT and the GIII.VT as a "broad causeway running westward from the valley." Low walls frame the roadbed of the Ramp on the north and south as it rises at a gentle slope of slightly more than 6 degrees. The Cut removed most of the northern shoulder wall of the Ramp, but the surviving length of 11.60 m stands about half a meter above the latest roadbed. The section in Trench A showed us that the wall is simply a molding in the top of the limestone debris forming the massive foundation of the Ramp. The southern shoulder wall has been scoured by erosion on its south side, but at the eastern end, where it is truncated by the Cut, it is at least 1.55 m wide. As preserved, the southern wall, like the northern one, rises about half a meter above the latest roadbed. On the west, the wall merges with the eastern wall of the Ante-town and may abut it. Trench E showed that the northern face of this wall is founded 1.94 m deeper than the top roadbed of the ramp; it extends down to elevation 15.92 m above sea level, indicating that it served from the beginning of the earliest phase of the Ramp as a retaining wall for the limestone debris of its foundation. Initially the Ramp may have been used to haul stone and other material up the plateau.

We do not know how far the Ramp originally extended east into the valley. It continues under the modern road around the modern cemetery, and possibly under the cemetery itself. We also lack the full width of the Ramp because the Cut took out the northern shoulder wall and edge of the roadbed and truncated the lower end. However, by projecting a line east from the surviving northern shoulder, we get a width of 7 m at the bottom of the Ramp. As the Ramp rises, it widens to 12.20 m at the top, between its northern shoulder wall and the Vestibule. At the top, the Ramp splits into a high road going up onto the Partition Embankment and a low road running from behind the Podium west along the northern side of the GIII.VT.

In constructing the Ramp, workers laid down a foundation consisting of a base layer, half a meter thick, of marl *(tafla)* and limestone debris. Next, a series of layers of dense marl and limestone raised the Ramp an additional 60 cm, followed by a sequence of make-up or leveling deposits capped with compacted silty surfaces. Trench E showed at least five alluvial silt or marl pavements of the roadbed, indicating continued maintenance of the road over an extended period.

The Podium

A low bench or podium, built of mudbricks, stands partially eroded at the top western end of the Ramp. The main section, 1.74×1.88 m, rises in the center about 30 cm. A projection extends like a miniature ramp to the east. On the north, east, and south, the Podium is surrounded by an enclosure of low, thin walls. The L-shaped northern and eastern walls, which survive to a height of only 2 to 10 cm, appear to be of a different phase — that is, they probably were built and functioned at a different time than the southern wall.

Hassan (1943) proposed that the Podium was part of the "washing tent" used to prepare Queen Khentkawes' body for burial. He believed that Vestibule 2 and the Ante-town were the queen's valley temple. More likely, they are late additions to the GIII.VT and its settlement. The Podium and its enclosure seem related to the Drain leading into Water Tank 2. These structures may have been built together as part of the GIII.VT and served the cult and possibly the funeral of Menkaure. However, we must also consider the possibility that people might have used these features to monitor and administer access to Water Tank 2, to the GIII.VT through Vestibule 2, and to the roadway continuing west behind the Podium.

Conclusions and Summary

Our work during the 2009 season produced the first detailed map of the interface between the KKT and GIII.VT. We revealed a truly monumental landscape, built of quarry debris, mudbrick, and small limestone blocks. The broad mud-paved ramp leading up to the plateau could have been a major portal to the Giza Necropolis, with the residents serving as gatekeepers. They might have used some of the features in the interface, such as the Podium, to monitor and administer movement in and out of the necropolis.

The area was occupied for over 300 years, to the end of the Old Kingdom, but with a hiatus at some point. The GIII.VT and Water Tank 2 were probably built as part of a single complex as they have the same orientation close to true north. The basin may have served in the funeral and cult of Menkaure. The Ramp, built with a very deep foundation, was used over a long period, perhaps starting as an incline for hauling stone and other building materials up to the plateau. The shoulder walls were constructed along the same orientation as the KKT foot, suggesting that it was intended as part of that layout, or that the KKT and GIII.VT Ante-town were planned and constructed together.

At some point, flash floods, or some other force, breached the wall around Water Tank 2, gouged a chasm (the Cut) across the northern side of the Ramp, and tore away part of the Extramural House complex. In slicing through the Ramp, the Cut destroyed much of the link between the GIII.VT and KKT. While flash floods were most likely responsible for the Cut, people may have contributed by attempting to channel the water. They may even have diverted floodwater into Water Tank 2. It seems that they tried to undo some of the Cut's damage by filling the deep canyon with limestone gravel.

At KKT we discovered that the structure off the eastern end of the town, which we had first glimpsed in 2007, was a complex of ramps and stairs leading from a deep basin up to the queen's causeway. We believe that this was the valley complex of Queen Khentkawes I, located on a harbor that may have been connected to the one in front of the Sphinx and Khafre Valley Temples to the northeast. Deposits of miniature votive ceramics suggest that the complex was used in ritual, probably for the queen's funeral and her cult.

In the KKT, our excavations of a "priest's house" in the "leg" of the town forces us to reconsider the history and function of the settlement. We found that over time Building E opened to the homes on either side, "intermingling," so to speak. Renovations diminished House E by sealing off the northern end, where the courtyard became accessible only to adjacent Building F. The causeway evolved over time as well. During an early phase of Building E, the builders erected a wall along the full length of the "leg" of the settlement inside the southern boundary wall, creating a narrow causeway. The residents of the houses could enter the causeway through doorways and proceed through adjacent openings into the wider corridor on the other side of the new wall. We found compelling evidence that people abandoned the settlement for some time and then reoccupied the town, probably in the Sixth Dynasty, when they rebuilt portions of House E and other areas of the community.

At our Heit el-Ghurab site, we found no evidence to support our theory that the Western Compound served as a holding and slaughter area for livestock. Nor did we find any evidence that the Chute corridor was the equivalent of an abattoir chute. We attempted to follow the path of this corridor to the west, believing that it might turn to the north and serve as a conduit leading into the town from the Gate in the Wall of the Crow to the West Gate in the Enclosure Wall at the western end of the main east–west street through the Gallery Complex. Alas, our season ended before we could excavate as far west as we hoped, but the stretch of the corridor that we exposed did not veer convincingly north and seemed to continue northwest, suggesting that the Chute was not a conduit from the Great Gate in Wall of the Crow.

In House Unit 1 in the Western Town, we were unable to excavate down to the earliest levels, but we identified at least four phases of remodeling and occupation in the five chambers that probably served as bakeries and kitchen areas, as we suspected. We found evidence that here the residents were also brewing. Three rooms included low basins and bins, and, similar to features we discovered elsewhere on the site, they may have been used for malting.

Acknowledgments for 2009 Season

For a successful 2009 season, we would like to thank Dr. Zahi Hawass, Undersecretary of State and Secretary General of the Supreme Council of Antiquities (SCA). We thank Sabry Abd al-Aziz, General Director of Pharaonic and Coptic Monuments; Mr. Atef Abu el-Dahab, General Director of the Central Department for Pharaonic and Coptic Monuments; Dr. Mahmoud Afifi, General Director of Giza; Mr. Kamal Waheed, General Director, Giza Pyramids; as well as Mr. Mohammed Shiha, Chief Inspector of Giza Pyramids. For help with the field school, we thank Shabaan Abd al-Gawad of the SCA administrative office. We thank Samy Dardir and Ahmed Eiz, for serving as SCA inspectors for the excavations and field school, and for work in the laboratory.

The AERA archaeological program would not be possible without the generous support of AERA's donors. For major support we thank the Ann and Robert H. Lurie Family Foundation, the David H. Koch Foundation, the Waitt Foundation, the Simonyi Fund for Arts and Sciences, Mr. and Mrs. Lee M. Bass, the Peter Norton Family Foundation, Ed and Kathy Fries, Glen Dash, Ann Thompswon, Marjorie Fisher, and our other dedicated donors. The field school was partly funded by a USAID grant administered by ARCE, for which we thank Gerry Scott, Michael Jones, and Janie Abdel Aziz.

We are grateful to Dr. Gil Stein, Director of the Oriental Institute, University of Chicago, for the Institute's support.

References

Arnold, F.

1998 "Die Priesterhäuser der Chentkaues in Giza." *Mitteilungen des Deutschen Archäologischen Instituts, Abteilung Kairo* 54: 1–18.

Hassan, S.

1943 *Excavations at Giza*. Volume 4: *1932–1933*. Cairo: Government Press.

Reisner, G.

1931 *Mycerinus, the Temples of the Third Pyramid at Giza*. Cambridge: Harvard University Press.

1936 "The Dog Which was Honored by the King of Upper and Lower Egypt." *Bulletin of the Museum of Fine Arts, Boston* 34/206: 96–99.

Notes

[1] A Khentkawes with the same titles was buried at Abusir during the Fifth Dynasty. She is designated II.

[2] We designated as Water Tank 1 a basin in the western side of the KKT-F.

KERKENES DAĞ PROJECT

Scott Branting

http://www.kerkenes.metu.edu.tr/

The 2009 season at Kerkenes Dağ laid the foundation for an extensive multi-year program of restoration within one of the key gates of this ancient Iron Age city. The Cappadocia Gate, so named by the project because the important region of Cappadocia lies fairly near in the southwesterly direction it leads, has been an area of intensive research since the beginning of the project (figs. 1–2). Its importance is inferred not only from the direction it leads to outside the walls, but also because of its size and its close proximity to the Palatial Complex within the city. Mapping of the gate from aerial photographs was undertaken as early as the second season of the project, in 1994. More detailed total station mapping was undertaken to recover the full plan of its walls, chamber, and towers starting in 1996.

Ten years ago, during the 1999 season, a large-scale clearance project was undertaken centered on the removal of the mass of fallen stone from the gate and from along the city wall for a significant area surrounding the gate. Work continued here on a yearly basis until 2003 and resulted in the removal of several meters of collapsed and broken stones from the gate and wall. This major effort was stopped in 2004, well above the original surfaces in the gate chamber, as it became apparent that the meters of freestanding walls of the towers and inner chamber of the gate had been burnt so heavily during the final destruction of the city so as to render them architecturally unsound. Further large-scale clearance, in the absence of an accompanying program of extensive restoration, was deemed too dangerous to continue. Limited work was undertaken within the gate and along the city wall when it was absolutely necessary to shore up a section or to check a specific part of the plan, but otherwise all work within this important gate ceased.

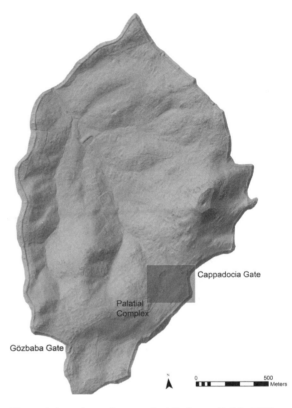

Figure 1. Locations of research at Kerkenes Dağ in 2009

Figure 2. The Cappadocia Gate with adjacent modern animal pens (foreground) and the view down toward Cappadocia beyond. On a clear day one can even see Mount Erciyes on the horizon near Kayseri in northern Cappadocia

This strategy changed in 2009 when funds were received from the U.S. Department of State's Ambassador's Fund for Cultural Preservation to begin a larger program of restoration within the Cappadocia Gate. Once again this important gate was the focus of extensive work, including an expansion of the geophysical survey in areas of the city adjacent to the gate and preliminary excavations within the gate that were necessary for submitting an application for restoration of the gate to the Turkish government.

Geophysical Investigations

Building upon the successful test area within the city next to the Cappadocia Gate in 2008 (see *2008–2009 Annual Report*, p. 89), a much larger area was surveyed adjacent to the gate in May of 2009 (fig. 3). A 56,800 sq. m area (5.5 ha) was covered by the resistivity survey successfully connecting this area with those surveyed in and around the Palatial Complex in 2006–2008 (fig. 4). Magnetometry survey conducted in this area in the mid-1990s revealed open areas delineated by freestanding walls, long narrow structures immediately opposite the gate that have been interpreted as

Figure 3. Workers collecting resistivity data during the May season

stables, the second-largest water storage pond in the city, and additional urban blocks up around the Palatial Complex. The resistivity survey in these areas confirmed this basic arrangement while providing additional details on secondary pools within the water storage system and more detailed information on the buildings within the additional urban blocks. Next year's resistivity survey is planned to continue working south and west of the area of the Cappadocia Gate and Palatial Complex back along the top of the ridge toward the Gözbaba Gate.

Figure 4. The results of the resistivity survey data in the area between the Cappadocia Gate and the Palatial Complex collected in 2009

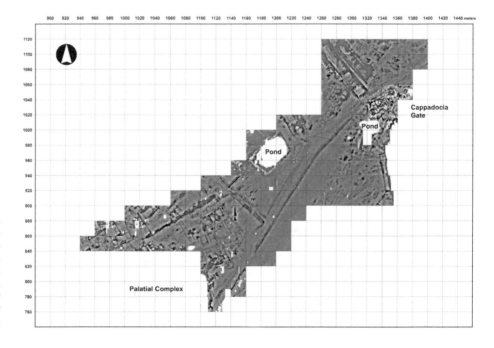

Excavations in the Cappadocia Gate

In preparation for reconstruction work within the Cappadocia Gate, excavations were conducted both inside and outside the gate (fig. 5). Outside of the gate, along its northeast side, the external wall was further exposed, and a pathway was constructed over the main city wall just to the east of the gate (fig. 6). The pathway provides a way for sheep, goats, and cows that graze the site to be rerouted around the main gate passage that they have been using to enter and leave the city. This was critical both for issues of safety as well as for the long-term sustainability of reconstructive work inside the gate.

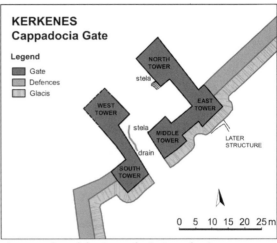

Figure 5. Plan of the Cappadocia Gate that incorporates the results of this year's excavations

Within the gate passage and gate chamber, excavation proceeded down through the last thick layers of collapsed stone and burnt debris (figs. 7–8). Stone paving was found underneath the debris throughout the gate passage and in the excavated portions of the gate chamber. This stone paving, like that in the entranceway to the Palatial Complex, shows some signs of wear from the people and animals that once used this gate to get into and out of the city. The pavement also incorporates a stone-lined drain, curving around the West Tower of the gate and then down into the lower passage, that would have helped direct the flow of water from rain or runoff down through the gate.

An impressive semi-aniconic stela had been uncovered within the gate passage adjacent to the North Tower of the gate in 2003 (see *2006–2007 Annual Report*, fig. 8). The high stepped platform upon which it had been placed was completely excavated this year down to the stone paving at its base. In addition, a second aniconic stela was uncovered set into the paving stones at the northwestern face of the western corner of the Middle Tower (fig. 9). Quite different in character and composition from the first stela, this second stela would have faced up the gate passage, past the downward-looking first stela, and on into the city.

However, a new stela was not the only thing found within the gate passage. Lying face down on the pavement to the western side of the gate passageway was the skeleton of a victim of the catastrophic destruction of the city around 547 BC (fig. 10). She was a healthy middle-aged woman who, from her positioning, apparently fell as she attempted to run out through the gate. Her left hand was raised up, protecting her face as she fell, while her right hand was off to her side as she reached out to break her fall. However, she died where she fell as immediately thereafter the heavy wooden beams

Figure 6. A view of the outside of the Cappadocia Gate showing the preserved sloping stone glacis that once stood at the base of the external walls and towers. The new walkway created to the east of the gate to divert animal traffic around the gate passage can be seen on the right of the photograph

of the gate structure, burning fiercely in the fire, fell directly upon her prone form.

No clues exist as to why this woman was still within the city as the fires raged and burned. While evidence for the horrible conflagration is found throughout the city, she is the first person that has been found who actually died as a result. This suggests perhaps that most of the population along with their belongings had been removed from the city prior to its destruction. Why was she not among them? Did she return to get a loved one or some treasured object? If so, that person apparently escaped her fate or that object was dropped before she fell. Was she perhaps hiding within the city while her fellow citizens were taken away

Figure 7. Excavations in the passage of the Cappadocia Gate undertaken to remove the fallen stone and debris before restoration work can begin

and the city set ablaze? We may never know the specific answers as to why her life ended so tragically here, but future excavations will eventually draw a better picture of the larger destruction of the city within which she perished.

Much more work remains to be done within the Cappadocia Gate over the next few seasons. Excavations will be undertaken to remove the remaining debris from the gate chamber, fully exposing the stone paved floors and precarious walls throughout this five-towered structure. Going hand in hand with the excavation will be a large program of restoration, replacing heavily burnt stones with new stone when necessary and shoring up the impressive walls to preserve them and make them safe for visitors for decades to come. One of the first visitors to see the results of the 2009 excavations in the Cappadocia Gate was the U.S. ambassador to Turkey, James Jeffrey (fig. 11). Without the generous funding for the start of the restoration project by the U.S. Department of State's Ambassador's Fund for Cultural Preservation, this work could not have commenced.

Figure 8. Photograph of the inside of the gate passage and chamber showing the extent of this year's excavation. Excavation will continue next year with the removal of the remaining portion of collapse in the gate chamber

Figure 9. The new aniconic stela discovered adjacent to the western corner of the Middle Tower

Figure 10. The right hand of the woman tragically killed within the Cappadocia Gate during the destruction of the city emerges from beneath the burning and collapse

Figure 11. Ambassador Jeffrey Stone visiting the excavations in the Cappadocia Gate and viewing the new stela uncovered there

Metallurgical Analysis

Ongoing laboratory analysis of the metals at Kerkenes Dağ by Joseph Lehner at UCLA continued during this year. Utilizing thin sections and isotopic analysis, he has been able to better understand both the manufacturing process of metal objects excavated at various locations within the city and the proveniences of their original ores. One of the more interesting results of this work so far is the identification of the practice of coating the surface of bronze sheet with a layer of tin, perhaps for decorative purposes. This is a practice that becomes common only centuries later.

Kerkenes Eco-center

A number of workshops and lectures focused on organic farming and food production were held in Şahmuratı throughout the year. With organic farming already having taken root in Şahmuratlı years ago through the early efforts of the Kerkenes Eco-center, these workshops provided a venue for local farmers to share their experiences with and learn from a growing community of organic farmers in villages across Turkey. Products from Şahmuratlı can be found in the excavation kitchens, in local stores, at local festivals, and even at events in Ankara. The Eco-center also has attracted a number of international visitors and participants, all eager to learn from its successes. One of those successes has been the development of solar-powered devices for cooking and drying food. The United Nations Development Programme's (UNDP) Global Environment Fund (GEF) recognized the success of an earlier grant they provided for this portion of the project, by generously awarding a second grant to build a second generation of several of these devices.

Acknowledgments

The Kerkenes Dağ Project is a joint project between the Oriental Institute and the British Institute of Archaeology in Ankara. It is co-directed by Dr. Geoffrey Summers of Middle East Technical University (METU). The Kerkenes Eco-center Project is directed by Françoise Summers of METU, who is also jointly directing the restoration work within the Cappadocia Gate with Geoffrey Summers and Dr. Nilüfer Yöney of Istanbul Technical University. Professor Dr. Yılmaz Erdal of Hacettepe University generously provided invaluable expertise in analyzing the skeletal remains found within the Cappadocia Gate.

Our thanks go to the director, Orhan Düzgün, and staff of the General Directorate of Cultural Assets and Museums, our official representative Şaban Kök, and the director, Hasan Şenyurt, and staff of the Yozgat Museum. Our principal sponsors this year were the Oriental Institute, the British Institute of Archaeology at Ankara, Middle East Technical University, the U.S. Department of State's Ambassador's Fund for Cultural Preservation, the United Nations Development Programme's Global Environment Fund, the Archeocommunity Foundation, the Charlotte Bonham-Carter Trust, the Erdoğan M. Akdağ Foundation, Toreador Turkey, Yozgat Çimento, MESA Mesken, Yenigün, Andante Travel, the Anglo-Turkish Society, the Binks Trust, Yozgat Çimento, AKG Gazbeton, the British Embassy, and anonymous donors. A full list of all participants and sponsors can be found on our Web site.

MARJ RABBA

Yorke M. Rowan

Our knowledge of life in the Galilee during the Chalcolithic period (ca. 4500–3600 BC), in contrast with that of regions such as the Negev, Golan, or Jordan Valley, is limited. The new research initiative launched by the Oriental Institute to explore the late prehistoric landscape of the Galilee is designed to examine the changing relationship of villages, ritual sites, and mortuary practices during this poorly understood time.

In the southern Levant, the late fifth to early fourth millennium BC (in this region, the Chalcolithic period, or the "Ghassulian" after the type site of Teleilat Ghassul) receives considerably less scholarly attention than does the Neolithic period or the later biblical ages. Not long after the fundamental changes of the "Neolithic Revolution," another transformation took place with ramifications that continue to the present day. Up until the development of pottery during the Late Neolithic and, later, copper smelting during the Chalcolithic, the essential items of life were made by reducing materials such as antler, bone, stone, and wood through carving, striking, pounding, and drilling. The alteration of matter such as clay and metallic ores from one state to another was a profound technological shift that wrought fundamental changes in society beyond simple improvements in efficiency. Before ceramic vessels were introduced, containers of wood and basketry existed. And as important as early smelted metals may have been, metal axes did not replace their flint equivalents, suggesting that the impact as a technological improvement was minimal. In contrast, the rarity and difficulty of producing copper items probably created a value that conferred prestige to those who possessed them.

At about the same time that smelted copper (and gold) first appears in the southern Levant, other fundamental changes provide evidence for new forms of political leadership, ritual centers, possible regional centers, and community cemeteries where novel mortuary practices indicate new perceptions of social identity. Distinctive Chalcolithic material culture includes not only various copper items (axes, awls, mace-heads, scepters, and "crowns"), but also diverse pottery forms made on a slow wheel; schematic "V-shaped" figurines, palettes, mace-heads, and pendants made of exotic rock; and long-distance materials such as shell, obsidian, and ivory. Despite their relative rarity, the increasing investment in such exotic items hints at an important shift in social relations and identity.

Most of this information derives from excavations of Chalcolithic sites located in the Negev, the Jordan Valley, or burial sites located along the Mediterranean coastal plain and low piedmont foothills. Yet in contrast, Chalcolithic settlements in the Golan offer very little evidence for metals or other exotic goods, suggesting different trajectories of change. In the region of the Upper and Lower Galilee, stretching from the Sea of Galilee to the Mediterranean, our limited knowledge of the period is based on preliminary reports of salvage excavations. With one important exception, these are small exposures of settlement sites that provide us with important glimpses of the material culture, but little else.

An important exception is the mortuary site of Peqi'in, a rich burial cave accidentally discovered during roadwork. Hundreds of secondary burials found along with elaborately decorated ossuaries (ceramic or stone boxes for human bones), pottery from different regions, and exotic items of ivory, copper, and basalt attest to the intensive use of this karstic cave. Burial of the dead is much more elaborate during the Chalcolithic than during preceding periods, and the secondary burial of selected skeletal elements (typically long bones and crania) in a new location is well known. At Peqi'in, however, ossuary decoration includes a range of modeled heads, beards, headgear, arms, and teeth, more complex and elaborate than any previously discovered, establishing a level of sophistication in the treatment of the dead previously unrecognized. Finds at Peqi'in indicate connections both local and distant. Were those who interred their loved ones here from the immediate region, or did they come from more distant areas? Given the dearth of excavated sites in the region, this question is difficult to answer and is just one of the many perplexing questions we hope to address through a multi-sited, multi-year investigation of the region.

In the summer of 2009, the first phase of this new investigation was launched at the previously unknown and unnamed site of Marj Rabba (Har ha-Sha'avi, west) in order to study the late fifth- to early fourth-millennium BC changes that occurred after the Neolithic period and prior to the appearance of walled towns and urbanism of the Bronze Age. Our goal is to examine material culture in the Galilee for comparison with other areas of the southern Levant in order to better understand the intra-regional and inter-regional connections of the inhabitants, and to obtain samples for botanical and faunal analyses that will allow interpretations of Galilean subsistence and economy during the Chalcolithic. In addition, no radiometric dates are available from a Chalcolithic settlement site in the Galilee, so we hope to obtain dates that will provide linkage to other regional chronological sequences.

With a small team of students, volunteers, and workers from the nearby town of Sakhnin, excavations at Marj Rabba were conducted from July 6 to August 5, 2009. The site, located about 1 km north of the Roman site of Yodfat, is situated on a saddle between two high points. No architecture was apparent on the site surface, but Chalcolithic material culture predominates, along with an occasional Roman sherd.

Two areas were selected for excavation (see fig. 1). The West Area, located in the forest planted by the Jewish National Fund, was selected to explore one of several large rock piles (cairns). In previous site visits, three or four cairns were identified; Chalcolithic pottery and occasional Roman/Byzantine sherds were found mixed in with the small limestone cobbles of the cairns. The cairn selected for test excavations had a north–south, double-row stone wall visible on the surface, with a possible perpendicular wall forming a corner on the north aspect. This is discussed below under "West Area."

The East Area, located in a strip of unplanted field, starts to the east of a high power line and continues to the east. This area was selected for initial examination because the land is not privately owned, the area was not plowed recently, and there are no olive trees. The extent of the site remains undetermined and will be more carefully surveyed during the 2011 field season.

East Area

Three and one half squares measuring 5 × 5 m were opened in the East Area. Squares C1 and D1 were separated by a 1-meter baulk, while square L1 is located 35 m to the east of square D1. In addition, the northern half of square D2 was excavated. Excavation in these areas recovered some modern debris and late Roman or Byzantine sherds in the highly compacted and disturbed upper layer, but below this, only Chalcolithic flint, pottery, and ground-stone finds are found.

Topsoil removal in square C1 quickly exposed large stones that proved to be part of wall foundations. This first wall (L.7) runs east–west in the northern section of the square, consists of large boulders and medium-sized fieldstones, and forms a corner with a north–south wall (L.6). A spindle whorl (B.012) was found while exposing wall L.6. In square D1, additional stone wall foundations continue the east–west line of wall L.7. The western area of the square recovered extremely large amounts of pottery, virtually all Chalcolithic; east of the center of the square,

Marj Rabba 2009

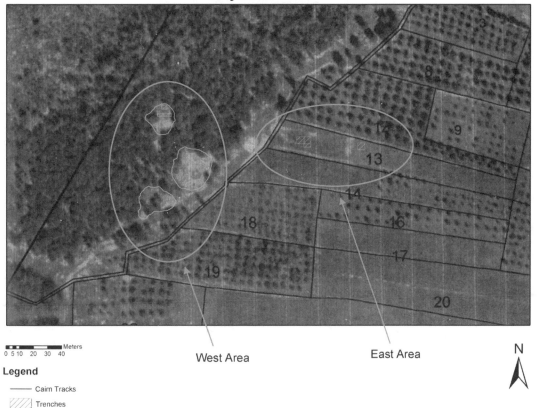

Figure 1. Aerial view of areas at Marj Rabba

another spindle whorl (B.041) was found. The northern half of square D2 was opened (L.14) in order to understand whether large stones exposed in the southern part of D1 are part of an installation, and in the southwest corner of D2, a paved area was constructed using flat mid-sized limestone cobbles (L.27; see fig. 2).

In squares D1 and D2, a curvilinear line of tightly packed smaller fieldstones (L.23) is bordered by a clear line of larger fieldstones (10–20 cm along the southwestern edge, 20–40 cm along the northern edge) extending to 1.7 m to the west from the eastern baulk (fig. 2). Near the eastern baulk of square D1, a fragment of a very large perforated flint disc (fig. 3; L.20, B.058) was recovered on top of the semi-circular feature; bifacially flaked to only 8 mm thick (maximum), the original was probably at least 15 cm long. In the continued exposure of the semi-circular feature (L.23), the fragment of a finely carved bone pendant (B.074), a bead, and a spindle whorl (B.073) were recovered. The large semi-circular feature (L.23; fig. 1) runs along the eastern baulk of squares D1–D2 4.10 m. The northern aspect appears to abut the southern face of wall L.7. Additional excavation of this feature during the 2010 field season, we hope, will determine if there is greater depth to the feature and whether it is circular.

In addition to this semi-circular stone feature, a number of other features were exposed at the interface just below topsoil. Along the southern edge of wall L.7, a small (ca. 68 × 90 cm), shallow (ca. 25 cm) pit probably postdates the wall. Along the western section of square D1, a small (ca. 1.0 m diameter), circular stone installation continues into the baulk. In the center of southern D1 and northern D2, a single course, roughly oval-shaped stone feature (L.26) was oriented

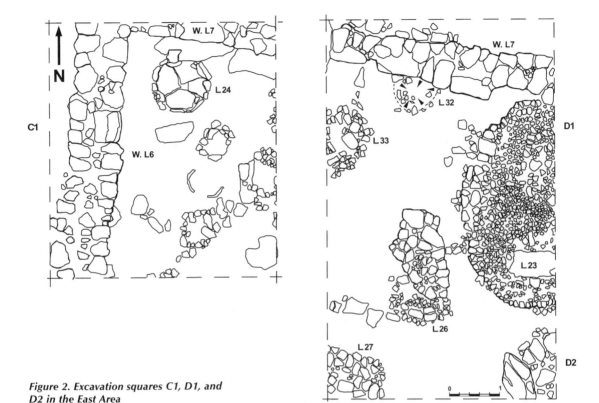

Figure 2. Excavation squares C1, D1, and D2 in the East Area

roughly north–south (1.8 m north–south; 1.0 m east–west). The eastern edge of the feature is well defined by six angular fieldstones, while the other edges of the feature are less definitive. We remain uncertain if we exposed the base of the feature at season's end and will continue to excavate it during the 2010 season.

Probably contemporaneous with L.26, a paved area (L.27) in the southwestern part of square D2 consisted of a single layer of flat limestone cobbles, which continues into the unexcavated area. Both this paved section (L.27) and the central feature (L.26) may be later than the stone arc feature (L.23); both appear to be only single-course features very near to the ground surface, while the bottom of L.23 is not yet exposed and may have greater depth. Addressing this problem will be of primary importance for the 2010 excavations. For the present, we assume that all are contemporaneous with walls L.7 and L.6.

An elliptical limestone slab-lined pit (L.24; see fig. 2) in square C1 measured 1.17 m (north–south) by 1.03 m (east–west) and was approximately 0.45 m in depth. The interior bottom of the pit was paved using four flat limestone slabs (top: 468.82; bottom: 468.54 above mean sea level). Stones used for the wall lining were between 10 and 36 cm and ranged from 3 to 15 cm in thickness, with small fieldstones wedged in between the larger slabs. The feature may have functioned as a silo; bags of sediment were kept for flotation. Although few artifacts were found inside the feature, at the top, a broken basalt grinding slab or handstone was found. The most completely preserved feature, this pit or silo is apparently built against the bedrock on which wall L.6 rests. Just to the south of it, a large flat limestone slab possibly served as a working surface. Farther to the southeast, in square C1, a feature appears to be the remains of a built surface, or possible hardened layer for a working surface L.26. The feature consisted of flat limestone slabs (ca. 15–20 cm) tightly packed together and lying flat (ca. north–south, 75 cm × east–west 60 cm). On top of

Figure 3. Perforated flint disc.
Scale 1:2

these stones, a very hard layer was constructed by pouring on a mudbrick-like material. Although it does not appear fired or even heat treated, the similarity to plaster is strong. The edges of this feature appear to be largely defined by rodent intrusions.

Summarizing the excavations in square C1, features L.24, L.25, L.30, and L.31 all appear to be contemporaneous. Based on the use of the bedrock for the construction of L.24, and the construction of wall L.7 on the bedrock, this suggests that these features were used at the same time as the structure defined by walls L.7 and L.6. Further excavation will be necessary in order to determine if additional surfaces or features predate these features. However, it seems clear that at least some of the features in squares D1–D2 must be later uses of the area (e.g., L.27, L.26).

Square L.1 (5 × 5 m) was located 35 m to the east of square D1 and opened in order to understand the depth and stratigraphic development of the site. A large amount of rock tumble was visible across the square below the topsoil. In the northeastern corner of the square, wall L.12 runs to the southwest. Constructed of a double row of stones, in a single spot, three courses remain. The wall is well built and abuts a later addition of a single row of stones (L.34) forming a curvilinear formation that runs into the southern baulk. L.34 was approximately 2.0 m in length and 0.50 m wide and appears to be a later addition to and reuse of wall L.12. To the north in the center of the square, a curvilinear wall fragment (L.5) consists of about seven stones and may have been the northern continuation of the structure. Bottom elevations of these two wall fragments are very similar (L.34, 468.08/. 10; L.5, 468.07/. 13 above mean sea level). In the center of the two curvilinear features (L.12, L.34), a cluster of stones (L.10) may have been a destroyed wall fragment or wall collapse. Abutting the western face of wall L.12, four carefully placed flat stones (L.35) remained in situ, where they were either the last traces of a paving, or, more likely, the remains of an interior bench. These extended 90 cm along the wall, to a width of 35 cm.

Below the stone line in the center of the square, an additional wall (L.18) running east–west was discovered. This wall, preserved as a single row (ca. 1.7 m long × 0.60 m wide) but three courses (at least), runs under wall L.12. By the end of the season, we remain uncertain whether the lowest course of the wall is exposed.

In the northern section of the square, a wall (L.22) was exposed in the northern profile running east–west to nearly 3 m, apparently parallel to wall L.18. Similar elevations would suggest that they are contemporaneous. Both walls will need further excavation, which necessitates opening a square to the north for wall L.22, in order to clarify their purpose and relationship to each other and the presumably later wall L.12.

At least three phases were exposed in square L.1. The single-row walls, L.34 and L.5, represent the latest phase with preserved architecture. The cluster of stones removed from the center of the square in L.10 may also belong to this phase. Below this phase, the more substantial well-built wall foundation L.12 and the associated "bench" feature (L.35) appear to be earlier and possibly reused by the later walls (L.34 and L.5). The earliest phase seems to be represented by the parallel walls L.18 and L.22. We have no exposed bedrock yet, so presumably the site continues below the foundations of these two walls.

West Area

In the area designated as Marj Rabba West (a series of three rock piles – cairns), two trenches were placed on cairn 1 (see fig. 1). Trenches 1 and 2 were placed adjacent to or straddling a north–south wall (designated L.501) visible on the surface of the cairn.

Trench 1

Two separate units were oriented perpendicular to the wall thus straddling the east and west faces of the wall (fig. 4). A 2×10 m trench was laid out, with one unit (2×3 m) to the east of the wall (L.500) and another (2×7 m) to the west of the wall (L.503) at the highest point of the cairn. Late Roman/Early Byzantine sherds were visible as well as flint and some fragments of basalt ground stone. Removal of the top layer of stone began on both sides of the wall (L.501). L.500 was assigned to the "topsoil" (a misnomer to describe the matrix because the matrix comprises mainly small stones and a minimal amount of sediment, about 5 percent) on the eastern side of the wall and L.503 on the western side of the wall. Very few finds were discovered at this level: modern metal was noted in L.500 to the east of the wall, and a basalt fragment and a Chalcolithic sickle blade were recovered from L.503 to the west of the wall. One piece of Chalcolithic pottery also was found at approximately the same elevation in southeast area, close to wall L.501.

On the east side of wall L.501, L.502 was assigned to the next stratigraphic change — which consisted of larger rocks and less soil. To the west of the wall, the stratigraphic change below the surface contained more dirt and fewer rocks (L.504). As work progressed it became evident that L.504 was the matrix sitting directly above the bedrock. Very few artifacts were found; a few lithics and three pieces of Chalcolithic pottery were recovered from the fill (L.504) directly above bedrock. A decision was made to excavate the remaining extent of the trench to the west in order to cover the entire east–west expanse of the cairn. The area was taken down in order to expose the entire cross section of the cairn and was assigned L.506 (same as L.503, approximately 85 percent rocks and the remainder soil).

East of wall L.501, a new layer with more earth and fewer rocks was noted below L.502 and designated L.505 (but rocks continue to constitute approximately 50 percent of the total matrix). Very few artifacts were recovered from this locus — a small number of chipped flint items and some very friable Chalcolithic pottery and a couple of late-era sherds were recovered. A Chalcolithic basalt fragment was recovered in this locus (505). This side of the wall L.501 is completely different from the east side (L.505). On the east side, the bedrock is underneath a hard-packed clay-rich sediment with pottery and flint. There were fewer rocks. In general there was a higher concentration of lithics in east side of wall L.501, while most of the pottery was recovered from the west side of locus, adjacent to wall L.501.

Trench 2

A second trench (3×4 m) was placed at the end of the northern end of wall L.501 in order to investigate a possible wall (L.511) running perpendicular (east–west) to the western face of wall L.501. The locus excavated across the top layer of T2 was assigned L.508, where three basalt fragments were recovered. Shortly after excavation started, bedrock began appearing at the bottom of this trench and indicated that this wall (L.511) rests directly on bedrock. T2 was expanded 1.0 m north in order to expose the corner of wall L.501 and wall L.511. Continued work in T2 on

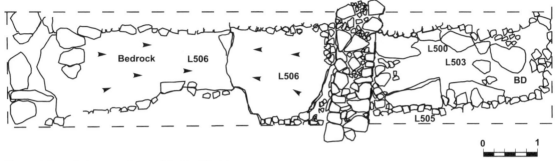

Figure 4. Trench 1, excavation unit in the West Area

the north side of the wall L.511 and in the corner where wall L.511 and wall L.501 meet exposed bedrock on the north side of wall L.511.

Walls L.511 and L.501

Wall L.511, which runs east–west and abuts the western face of wall L.501, is constructed of larger limestone blocks sitting directly on bedrock. The immediate corner of L.501 and L.511 also appears to sit on bedrock, but as wall L.501 progresses southward (toward T1), smaller stones and sediment are sandwiched between the bottom of the wall and bedrock.

Dating of the walls and their function remain obscure. Very few finds associated with the walls were recovered, making the determination of age difficult. Various visitors to the site posited differing opinions as to the date ranging from Hellenistic to Chalcolithic. The only sherds recovered were late Roman/Byzantine and Chalcolithic, while the basalt and flint artifacts all date to the Chalcolithic. A few faunal remains (in very poor condition) were recovered. The wall and the cairn remain enigmatic, and although the material culture remains allow a tentative Chalcolithic designation, the function is far from understood. With greater resources, more extensive excavations may be attempted in order to understand better the relationship between Areas East and West (if a relationship exists), to date the cairns, and to understand their function.

Conclusions and Plans for Future Research

The first field season at Marj Rabba confirmed the great potential of this site for investigations of the Galilee during the Chalcolithic period. The site, probably a small village with inhabitants who relied on crops such as wheat and possibly olive, as well as animal husbandry of goats, cows, and pigs, promises to establish the baseline for understanding the material culture of the Chalcolithic period in the Galilee. Our preliminary work demonstrates that preservation of architecture is good; material culture such as basalt and ceramic vessels, flint tools, and ground stone will also provide comparative analyses to complement the faunal study. At the same time, we may face tough problems, such as poor preservation of plant remains. Establishing absolute dates is an essential component of linking this village to the larger corpus of fifth- to early fourth-millennium sites in the southern Levant and is just one of the challenges we will face in future excavations.

Acknowledgments

My co-director, Dr. Morag Kersel, and I would like to take this opportunity to thank the Israel Antiquities Authority (IAA), in particular Shuka Dorfman (director), Dr. Gideon Avni (director of excavations and surveys), and the staff of the IAA for their support and assistance in granting us permission to initiate this new project. In addition, we would like to thank Keren Kayemeth L'Israel (Jewish National Fund) for permission to conduct excavations. For logistical support and advice, Dr. David Ilan, director of the Nelson Glueck School of Biblical Archaeology-Hebrew Union College was instrumental to a first season running so smoothly. For the logistical planning and day-to-day operations in the field, Dr. Dina Shalem was invaluable. Prof. Seymour Gitin provided advice and assistance and continues to help our efforts in the field. Also in Israel, our hosts at Moshav Shorashim generously welcomed us into their community. In Chicago, Steven Camp, Carla Hosein, and Mariana Perlinac provided guidance and administrative support that was greatly appreciated. I would also like to thank our dedicated field crew: Amanda Berman, Mark Dolynskyj, Chad Hill, Brittany Jackson, Natasha Jurko, and Stephanie Selover.

———————————

MUMMY LABEL DATABASE (MLD)

François Gaudard, Raquel Martín Hernández, and Sofía Torallas Tovar

During the past year, the editors of the Mummy Label Database, namely, Sofía Torallas Tovar, the instigator of the project, Raquel Martín Hernández, and François Gaudard, continued to make progress with the long task of completing the database. For details on this joint project of the Instituto de Lenguas y Culturas del Mediterráneo y Oriente Próximo, Centro de Ciencias Humanas y Sociales – CSIC, Madrid, and of the Oriental Institute of the University of Chicago, readers can consult the *2008–2009 Annual Report*.

New mummy labels, both published and unpublished, were entered into the database. In addition, as part of the project, the editors' activities also included several lectures and publications. For the conference Bridges between Life and Death: Dionysus, Mysteries and Magic in the Ancient Greek and Roman World, held at the University of Chicago Department of Classics, on April 23–24, 2009, Sofía delivered a lecture entitled "Expressions of Condolence and Farewell in the Mummy Labels of Roman Egypt." As for Raquel, she presented a paper on "El transporte de momias a través del Nilo. El testimonio de las etiquetas de momia," at the V Spanish Congress of Ancient Near East, in Toledo, on October 29, 2009. Raquel also delivered another paper on "El viaje de los muertos. Transporte fúnebre en los textos papiráceos y las etiquetas de momia," during the II Jornada d'Estudis Papirològics, held in Tarragona, on March 13, 2010, and she published "La catalogación de etiquetas de momia," in *Actas del XII Congreso de la Sociedad Española de Estudios Clásicos*, Vol. 1 (Madrid, 2009), pp. 249–55. François, together with Janet H. Johnson, published an article entitled "Six Stone Mummy Labels in the Oriental Institute Museum," in *Honi soit qui mal y pense: Studien zum pharaonischen, griechisch-römischen und spätantiken Ägypten zu Ehren von Heinz-Josef Thissen*, edited by Hermann Knuf, Christian Leitz, and Daniel von Recklinghausen, pp. 193–209 (Orientalia Lovaniensia Analecta 194; Leuven and Walpole: Peeters, 2010).

NIPPUR

McGuire Gibson

Although we cannot yet return to Nippur to excavate, we are digging into the old records of previous seasons, including those I directed, in order to publish the final reports. The Nippur Publication Project, funded by a grant from the National Endowment for the Humanities, is in its third year and is making steady progress. Although we are focusing first on the Inanna Temple, we are also addressing other areas of past excavation.

The Inanna Temple portion is the concern of Richard L. Zettler, from the University of Pennsylvania, who is currently working out the detailed stratigraphy below the Ur III level, which was the subject of his brilliant 1970s doctoral dissertation and subsequent book (fig. 1). Karen Wilson is dealing with the lowest part of that sequence, which she used as the basis for her 1985 dissertation. Jean Evans, an expert on Early Dynastic art, is working with them on the description and analysis of several classes of artifacts. Being the last student of Donald P. Hansen, who excavated much of the Inanna Temple, she brings to the work not only a fine analytical mind and a discerning eye, but also special insights derived from him. We expect to have in hand a manuscript on the entire Inanna Sequence within a year.

Since the project began, Jeremy Walker has been scanning thousands of records, drawings, photographs, and negatives from the Nippur excavations to give all the collaborators on the project, whether in Chicago, Pennsylvania, or Toronto, access to all the available data. More recently, we have had the good fortune to be joined by Karen Terras, who brings to the project an extraordinarily orderly mind and years of experience in handling a very similarly structured archaeological database on the Diyala Project. She is especially adept at enhancing the not-so-good-looking photographs in Photoshop.

Edward J. Keall in Toronto has started work, once again, on the Parthian remains at Nippur, which include the Parthian version of the Inanna Temple and the massive Fortress that sits upon and around the ancient ziggurat. Ed was brought onto the Nippur staff in 1966 because he was a specialist in Parthian and Sasanian periods, having worked for some years in Iran. He used the Parthian Nippur materials for his dissertation at the University of Michigan and then took on the responsibility for publishing the final reports. Like all of us, he subsequently took on other fieldwork, teaching, and curatorial responsibilities, and the Nippur book had to be put off. The project has hired a student at the University of Toronto to digitally re-draw the plans of those complex buildings, which will make them easier for analysis and description. We have also begun a computerized catalog of the objects from the seasons involved with the Parthian Fortress, a building that I know well, since it was the focus

Figure 1. Inanna Temple VIIA, late Early Dynastic III (ca. 2500 BC), with man standing in sanctuary, bathroom in foreground, 1958

Figure 2. Expert Sherqati pickman defining plasters on an altar of the Inanna Temple, 1961

Figure 3. Parthian-period bone handle showing nude female. Parthian level of the Inanna Temple, AD 100. Photo taken in 1958

Figure 5. View of north corner of Nippur E-kur ziggurat enclosed by very large mudbricks of the Parthian fortress; Pennsylvania dig house built of ancient baked bricks on top in the late 1890s. Photo taken in 1958

Figure 4. Plaque from doorjamb of Inanna Temple showing the "Master of Animals" motif. Early part of the Early Dynastic Period (ca. 2900–2800 BC). Photo taken in 1961

of my first field experience in Iraq as a student in 1964–65. For several months, I was usually the only person at the excavation supervising ninety workmen, as we removed a great mound of dirt that the University of Pennsylvania expedition had extracted from in front of the ziggurat and piled over part of the Parthian Fortress. That was a great introduction for someone new to Mesopotamian archaeology. From the dump we recovered more than a hundred artifacts that had been missed by the old expedition, and finally reached the Parthian building. Excavating Parthian structures is labor intensive, since they are so huge, but the articulating of the mudbricks is easy, since they are huge (20

Figure 6. Donald Hansen, on left, supervising the taking out of one of the statues of King Shulgi from a foundation deposit under the Ur III version of the Inanna Temple. James Knudsted, architect, on right. Photo taken 1958

× 40 × 20 cm) and are easy to see and define. I was alone on the mound because the then director, Jim Knudsted, was completing a new expedition house and Bob Biggs and Selma al-Radi were busy baking and otherwise conserving the hundred or so tablets that had been found earlier in the season at Abu Salabikh. Diane Taylor was also detained creating the object register for all the other artifacts that had been found at Abu Salabikh. From about January onwards, Jim and Diane were on the mound fairly often, but I still supervised much of the work, created the object catalog, cleaned and recorded about 200 coins that the workmen and our house steward, Abdullah Sultan, would find on the surface of the mound. I also did the photography of artifacts that year. The dig went on until June, and I stayed in Baghdad until July 14 photographing the Abu Salabikh tablets. Since I had gotten into Baghdad in September, it meant that I had an opportunity to witness all four seasons in the country, from unbelievable heat in September to balmy late October and early November to icy winter mornings and then to a short flower-filled spring, and yet another scorching summer.

While the rest of the current project team works on the seasons that had been dug under Carl Haines and Knudsted, I occasionally find time to deal with various aspects of the project, especially the WA and WG areas. WA is the location of the Gula Temple, or rather a stack of temples dedicated to that goddess of healing through at least a thousand years of Mesopotamian history. WG is situated at the highest point on the mound at Nippur, just to the west of WA, where we looked for and found a sequence of levels from the Parthian through the Sasanian to the Islamic period. The WG report should have been out several years ago, but we had problems with the way the pottery had been organized and we have to re-analyze and lay it out differently. That would take about two weeks to finish, and I am going to fit it into my schedule. I am also prodding Judith Franck to finish her report on the Old Babylonian houses at WB and James Armstrong to complete the revision of his study of Nippur from the time of the Kassites to the Chaldeans (ca. 1400–539 BC). Theirs were brilliant dissertations, which reflected incisive re-thinking of previously set schemes of thinking, and their work will not be well enough appreciated until the final reports appear.

PERSEPOLIS FORTIFICATION ARCHIVE PROJECT

Matthew W. Stolper

The Persepolis Fortification Archive is a treasury of information about the languages, society, institutions, religion, and art of the Achaemenid Persian Empire at its zenith, around 500 BC. Its value depends on a combination of complexity (the archive contains detailed information of many different kinds) and integrity (the archive is an excavated artifact, a single, coherent cache of tens of thousands of documents from a single time and place).

The legal crisis that puts the future of the many Persepolis Fortification tablets in doubt also endangers the integrity of the single Persepolis Fortification Archive. The suit is still before federal courts, and the threat remains grave and persistent, but while the law takes its stately course, the Persepolis Fortification Archive Project pursues its emergency priorities: to enable future research by making thorough records of the archive, and to enable current research by distributing the records freely and continuously.

During 2009–2010, Clinton Moyer (PhD 2009, Cornell), Joseph Lam (PhD candidate, NELC), Miller Prosser (PhD candidate, NELC), and John Walton (PhD candidate, NELC) continued to operate the two Polynomial Texture Mapping (PTM) domes and the BetterLight scanning camera,

Figure 1. Four BetterLight scans of a fragmentary Persepolis Fortification Aramaic tablet (PFAT 684). Clockwise from upper left: polarized light, infrared filter, negative tone scale, red filter

making very high-quality images of selected Fortification tablets and fragments (fig. 1). As of mid-2010, this phase of the project — a collaboration with the West Semitic Research Project (WSRP) at the University of Southern California — has captured images of about 2,600 items: more than 670 monolingual Aramaic tablets, more than 200 Aramaic epigraphs on tablets with Elamite cuneiform texts, about 1,500 sealed, uninscribed tablets, and about 200 Elamite tablets and fragments.

The range of imaging techniques, the range of detail that they reveal, and the rate of output from this phase of the project grow with experience. Making the images outruns processing them for display, so two PTM-image processing stations have been added at the Oriental Institute to supplement post-processing done at the University of

Figure 2. Wear and repair on one of the PTM domes

Southern California. Despite the duct-tape and baling-wire look of the PTM domes (fig. 2), their reliability is outstanding: the shutters of the cameras on the two PTM domes have tripped more than 1,000,000 times during the life of the project.

Manning the post-processing stations are some of the crew who are also making and editing conventional digital images of the largest component of the Persepolis Fortification Archive, the Elamite Fortification tablets and fragments. During the past year, this group included Lori Calabria, Jon Clindaniel, Gregory Hebda, Will Kent, Megaera Lorenz, Tytus Mikołajczak, and Lise Truex (all NELC), Joshua Skornik (Divinity School); Anastasia Chaplygina (MAPH); Nicholas Geller, Amy Genova, Erika Jeck, and Daniel Whittington (Classics); and returning Persepolis Fortification Archive Project alumnus Trevor Crowell (Catholic University). Three photography and editing stations are in use now, and so far this phase of the project has made about 50,000 images of about 4,000 tablets and fragments with Elamite cuneiform texts. Editing these pictures for display now runs ahead of taking them, so the backlog is shrinking. Older picture sets are being checked and reshot as necessary for completeness and to match the higher standards of the later sets that reflect the photographers' accumulated experience. Haphazard file names from earlier picture sets are being made consistent with later sets, to facilitate linked online display and to prepare metadata for long-term storage.

After two more extended visits to the Oriental Institute, Persepolis Fortification Archive Project editor Wouter Henkelman (Free University of Amsterdam and Collège de France) has finished revised, collated, and annotated editions of about 2,400 of the 2,600 Elamite texts known from preliminary editions by the late Richard Hallock (called NN texts). He expects to collate the remainder in the summer and autumn of 2010 and to furnish complete translations in preparation for online distribution and hard-copy publication. I have continued to make preliminary editions of new Elamite Fortification texts, concentrating on document types that are underrepresented in the published sample of the Persepolis Fortification Archive; as of mid-2010, I have recorded about 585 of these.

The second largest component of the Persepolis Fortification Archive consists of uninscribed (anepigraphic) tablets (PFUT or PFAnep), that is, tablets with seal impressions but without accompanying texts. Our first estimates of the number of useful pieces of this kind were too low. During nine trips to the Oriental Institute during the past year, Persepolis Fortification Archive Project editor Mark Garrison (Trinity University) systematically examined another 25 percent of the 2,600 boxes of Fortification tablets and fragments to select uninscribed tablets for cataloging and PTM imaging. Now that about half of the boxes of tablets have been sifted, more than 2,100 uninscribed tablets have been selected for study. Post-doctoral researcher Sabrina Maras (University of California–Berkeley) is cataloging this material under Garrison's direction, a process that involves identifying impressions of previously known seals, assigning numbers to new seals, and sketching impressions of them; during the summer of 2010, she is joined in this work by graduate student Jenn Finn (University of Michigan). The results continue to bear out the general observation that some seals used on uninscribed tablets were also used on Elamite or

Fort. 0276-101

 1 cm

Figure 3. Impression of a newly identified inscribed seal in Assyrian style accompanying a newly edited Elamite text of an underrepresented type

Aramaic Fortification tablets, but most — around ten times as many — were not: on 275 cataloged tablets, there are impressions of more than thirty seals previously known from tablets with Elamite texts, but there are also impressions of 300 new seals. Garrison also continues to read the seals on the NN tablets. As of mid-2010, he has identified seal impressions on almost half of the NN tablets, and about 1,250 tablets that have yielded impressions of another 465 previously unknown seals. Post-doctoral student Wu Xin (Institute for the Study of the Ancient World, New York) is documenting some of this material under Garrison's direction.

All told, impressions of about 2,500 distinct seals have been cataloged on Persepolis Fortification tablets so far, the markers of as many distinct individuals and offices. Even if new seals are identified at a slower rate as work continues, the Persepolis Fortification Archive is certain to yield one of the largest coherent sets of images from anywhere in the ancient world.

The third main component of the Persepolis Fortification Archive consists of tablets with texts in Aramaic, some 670 identified to date. Persepolis Fortification Archive Project editor Annalisa Azzoni (Vanderbilt University) made two extended trips to the Oriental Institute during the past year to work on them. She has examined, numbered, cataloged, and made preliminary editions of about 100 monolingual Aramaic tablets and about 110 of the 200 Aramaic epigraphs on Elamite tablets identified so far. She is developing a formal typology of the documents to allow consistency with work on the Elamite texts and to clarify functional connections among streams of data recorded in Aramaic and in Elamite. Graduate student Emily Wilson (Classics), working under the direction of Persepolis Fortification Archive Project editors Elspeth Dusinberre (University of Colorado) and Mark Garrison, has been completing Dusinberre's collated drawings of seals on the Aramaic tablets and entering new descriptive and cataloging data on the PFAT seals in the On-Line Cultural Heritage Research Environment (OCHRE, http://ochre.lib.uchicago.edu).

Figure 4. What the seals show that the texts do not: PTM views of altar scenes from seal impressions on four uninscribed fortification tablets

PF-NN 1478

Figure 5. What the seals tell about the seal users: among 2,500 seals identified so far in the PFA, only four show scenes of human warfare; here, a Persian archer shoots a Scythian warrior in the seal impression on an Elamite Fortification tablet

Persepolis Fortification Archive project manager Dennis Campbell (post-doctoral student, Oriental Institute) coordinates, connects, and smoothes data and images for presentation via OCHRE. Oriental Institute Internet data specialist Sandra Schloen has prepared a revised version of OCHRE's display of Persepolis Fortification Archive material that includes a range of options for viewing and combining texts, translations, glossaries, grammatical information, and seals, displayed with a new look and feel. Lying behind this display are improved tools for importing texts and glossing and parsing them, hotspotting images, and linking images to texts — all processes that are increasingly automated as the corpus of information in OCHRE grows. Graduate student Seunghee Yie (NELC) imports Elamite texts into OCHRE and prepares editions for export to other sites (notably the Cuneiform Digital Library Initiative [CDLI], http://cdli.ucla.edu); graduate student Wayne Munsch (Divinity School) tags and links photographs, transliterations, and grammatical parse of Elamite Fortification documents.

More than 20,000 conventional and high-quality digital images, more than 7,000 low-resolution PTM sets, more than 3,200 editions of Elamite texts, and 100 editions of Aramaic texts, drawings, and analytical information on more than 650 new seals and a catalog of about 1,100 previously known seals have been entered in OCHRE in preparation for public display. As of mid-2010, about 1,400 Fortification tablets are publicly available on OCHRE, including 1,250 Elamite tablets presented with transliterations, many with translations, and all with click-through glossary and morphological parsing, conventional photographs (many of them tagged and linked

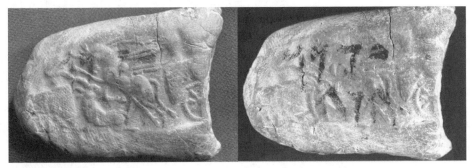

Figure 6. Two views of an Aramaic Fortification tablet: left, PTM image highlighting seal impression; right, BetterLight scan with red filter, highlighting inked text

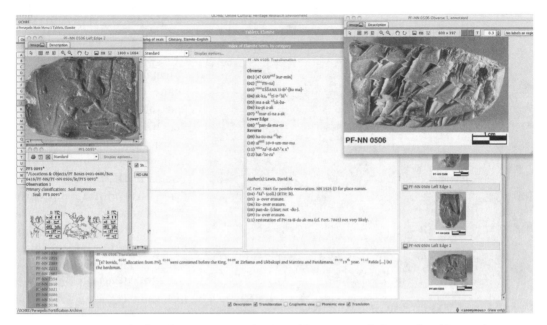

Figure 7. OCHRE display of an Elamite Fortification tablet, text, translation, and seal impression

to transliterations), seal analysis, and other options; 40 Aramaic tablets, presented with transliterations, translations, seal information, click-through glossary and parse, and high-quality images, including screen-resolution PTM images that allow the viewer to control the lighting on screen; and 110 uninscribed, sealed tablets with cataloging information, some collated drawings, and high-quality images, including live screen-resolution PTM imagery.

The West Semitic Research Project (WSRP) team at the University of Southern California presents images of Persepolis Fortification tablets via their online application InscriptiFact (http://www.inscriptifact.com). Publicly available there as of mid-2010 are about 15,000 images of about 525 Persepolis Fortification tablets, including 400 Aramaic and 100 uninscribed tablets. In the spring of 2010, InscriptiFact released a new version that incorporates a robust online viewer for high-resolution PTM imagery. This allows users to manipulate apparent lighting (direction,

Figure 8. Antiquity at Persepolis: three views of the seal impression and Aramaic epigraph on reverse of an Elamite Fortification tablet (PF 2026), displayed in Inscriptifact. Left: static views with polarized light and infrared filter; right, high-resolution PTM image. The Old Babylonian seal was more than 1,000 years old when it made this impression

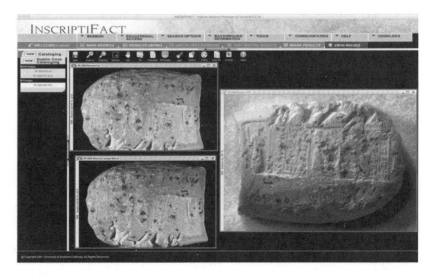

intensity, and focus of one light or two) and apparent surface reflectivity and to compare PTM views with one another and with high-resolution static images. The viewer and the PTM files can also be downloaded for local use.

Efforts to promote awareness of the plight of the Persepolis Fortification Archive, the unique qualities and value of the Persepolis Fortification Archive, and the aims, methods, and results of the Persepolis Fortification Archive Project included a panel at the annual meeting of the Archaeological Institute of America in January 2010, with presentations by me and by Persepolis Fortification Archive Project members Annalisa Azzoni, Dennis Campbell, Elspeth Dusinberre, and Mark Garrison, along with WSRP collaborators Marilyn Lundberg and Bruce Zuckerman (USC). A panel at the annual meeting of the American Oriental Society honoring the Achaemenid historian (and member of the Persepolis Fortification Archive Project's international advisory board) Amélie Kuhrt included papers by me and by project editors Garrison and Henkelman, and one by graduate student Persepolis Fortification Archive Project worker Tytus Mikołajczak. As *professeur invité* at the Collège de France in Paris in November 2009, Garrison gave four lectures on the glyptic art of the Persepolis Fortification Archive, drawing on recent project results. Azzoni lectured on the Persepolis Fortification Archive and the project at the Warren Center for the Humanities at Vanderbilt University, and at Baylor University. Dusinberre presented a talk on the Persepolis Fortification Archive at the Boulder, Colorado, Society of the Archaeological Institute of America. I talked about the Persepolis Fortification Archive and the project in and around Chicago at the Harvard Club, at the University of Chicago Humanities Day, at Wheaton College, at the Illinois Institute of Technology, at the Franke Institute for the Humanities, and at the Midwest Faculty Seminar; farther afield I talked at an event organized by Friends of the Persepolis Fortification Archive Project in Palo Alto (a video of the talk is available at

Figure 9. Athenian owl in Persepolis and California; title slide of PFA Project panel at 2010 meeting of the Archaeological Institute of America: an Athenian tetradrachm impressed on an uninscribed Fortification tablet, and the same image incorporated in the emblem of the AIA

http://www.youtube.com/watch?v=fv-o5qbwY8Q), at Berkeley, at the New York University Humanities Institute, at the University of Pennsylvania, at a symposium of the American Institute of Iranian Studies in New York, and at the British Museum. At Johns Hopkins University, I had the honor of devoting the annual W. F. Albright Memorial Lecture to the Persepolis Fortification Archive Project. At Oxford University, I described our methods and experience to the staff of an Oxford-Southampton pilot project using PTM imaging to record ancient artifacts.

For the worldwide online audience, the Persepolis Fortification Archive Project Weblog (http://persepolistablets.blogspot.com) provides access to articles from scholarly and news media about the archive, the lawsuit, and topics in Achaemenid archaeology and epigraphy: thirty-six entries were posted in the last year. Persepolis Fortification Archive Project editor Charles Jones (Institute for the Study of the Ancient World, New York) reports that the blog has been viewed more than 18,000 times in the last year, by more than 12,000 unique visitors, more than 1,800 of them repeat visitors. It has been viewed almost 70,000 times since it debuted in October 2006.

The University News Office released a new press release on the project's collaboration with WSRP in recording the Aramaic Fortification texts (http://news.uchicago.edu/news.php?asset_id=1732), with an accompanying video (http://www.youtube.com/watch?v=_iE0Pu-K0ss). Online journalistic accounts focus on the archive's legal situation and its broader implications for other cultural artifacts; examples are an article in the Phi Beta Kappa Society's Key Reporter by a lawyer working at Corcoran and Rowe, the firm representing Iran in the litigation (http://www.pbk.org/userfiles/file/flashversion/Spring2010/pageflip.html), and an article in the online journal of the U.S. State Department, America.gov (http://www.america.gov/st/peopleplace-english/2010/June/20100601093040cjnorab0.5233881.html).

Persepolis Fortification Archive Project editorial staff (Azzoni, Dusinberre, Garrison, Henkelman, Jones, and Stolper) prepared an entry for the *Encyclopaedia Iranica* on "Persepolis Administrative Archives," providing an authoritative description of the Persepolis Fortification and Treasury Archives and an extensive bibliography of current scholarship on them. Images, texts, analysis, and other current results also appear in a stream of publications by project staff and their collaborators, for example, "Seals Bearing Hieroglyphic Inscriptions from the Persepolis Fortification Archive" by Mark Garrison and Oriental Institute Egyptologist Robert Ritner, and "The First Achaemenid Administrative Document Discovered at Persepolis" by Charles E. Jones and Seunghee Yie, both in *ARTA: Achaemenid Research on Texts and Archaeology* (see http://www.achemenet.com/document/2010.002-Garrison&Ritner.pdf); "Archers at Persepolis," by Mark Garrison, in *The World of Achaemenid Persia*, edited by J. Curtis and St. John Simpson (London, 2010); and "New Observations on 'Greeks' in the Achaemenid Empire," by Wouter Henkelman and Robert Rollinger, and

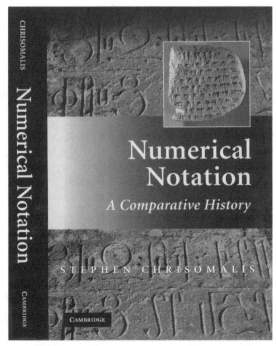

Figure 10. Old Persian tablet from the Persepolis Fortification Archive illustrated on the dust jacket of Numerical Notation: A Comparative History *(Cambridge, 2009)*

"Ethnic Identity and Ethnic Labelling at Persepolis," by Wouter Henkelman and me, both in *Organisation des pouvoirs et contacts culturels dans les pays de l'empire achéménide*, edited by P. Briant and M. Chauveau (Paris, 2009).

In last year's *Annual Report*, I mentioned that I was particularly pleased to have found a document of a new type, an example of the surprises that the Persepolis Fortification Archive still has to offer. Now I can report with even more delight that we have found four other examples of the same type. What began as an extraordinary sidelight has become a repeating feature of the Persepolis Fortification Archive's structure and function. This is a well-known phenomenon in work on ancient Near Eastern texts and objects: finding one clear example of something newly understood brings other examples out of the shadows. It is a reminder that the Persepolis Fortification Archive Project is not only producing emergency records of basic information; it is also making strides in our ability to interpret the information.

Gratifying in another sense is the citation of the unique Old Persian Fortification text in Stephen Chrisomalis's *Numerical Notation: A Comparative History*. The expected audience for the Persepolis Fortification Archive, students of the Achaemenid Persian empire as a whole or in its parts, is scattered among academic subdisciplines, but this citation testifies to the value of the Persepolis Fortification Archive for an unanticipated audience and unexpected research, and it vindicates the use of electronic techniques and media.

A sadder note in closing: July brought the startling news of the sudden death of John Melzian. John was an industrial designer by training and profession and key member of the InscriptiFact team by inclination and choice. He built and installed the Persepolis Fortification Archive Project's PTM domes, and he supported the work of the project with curiosity, perspicacity, realism, and grace.

———————————

SLAVES AND HOUSEHOLDS IN THE NEAR EAST

Laura Culbertson

This year's Oriental Institute Seminar centered on the topic of slavery in the ancient and pre-modern Near East. The event was held in Breasted Hall on March 5 and 6, 2010, and involved the participation of twelve scholars. The goal of the seminar was to explore new approaches to the study of slavery by considering the dynamics of slavery in the context of households. Slavery is of course a rather broad topic in history and anthropology, and consequently the purpose of this collaboration was to design and compare some specific approaches to slavery by examining a series of micro-historical contexts. It was noted throughout that the statuses, conditions, experiences, and realities of slaves differ widely according to historical contingencies and social contexts. Thus, the purpose of the collaboration was not to develop an essential definition of "Near Eastern" or "Oriental" slavery that can be extended to any Near Eastern context or data set, but rather to evaluate methodologies and compare key thematic and historical questions. Almost no comparison of ancient and pre-modern sources has been undertaken before this project, but the emphasis of the project on slaves in context allowed for some fascinating comparisons.

After introductions by Gil Stein and by me, the first session of the conference included four papers focusing on third-millennium states of Mesopotamia. Robert Englund spoke about "corporate" or institutional slaves, or groups of chattel slaves who were counted on rosters and lists in the same manner as animals or inanimate household items. Englund noted the difficulties of accessing linguistic and ethnographic information about institutional slaves. The following three papers focused on slaves of private households. Hans Neumann addressed some long-standing debates about the nature of private economy of early Mesopotamia, offering an important survey of the evidence for private slaves during this era. He made note of the types of labor activities conducted by private slaves and argued that private slavery did not constitute a significant part of the labor force in the economy of early Mesopotamia. In my own paper, I tracked the lives of private slaves in the third millennium and attempted to demonstrate the range of social possibilities and circumstances associated with private enslavement. I argued that many possible courses could result from enslavement to a private household, ranging from perpetual conflict to eventual freedom and status gain. Shifting the discussion to the second-millennium Old Babylonian period, Andrea Seri discussed the social life of female domestic slaves during this time and offered a new look at the close relationships and interactions between female slaves and their owners.

The Friday afternoon panel of the seminar included three stimulating papers on the medieval and pre-modern Middle East. Matthew Gordon's paper tracked two groups of slave elites in Abbasid-era sources, singers and soldiers, in order to compare patterns of social mobility. He demonstrated that, while both groups entered society as slaves and remained slaves, individuals belonging to these categories moved across social boundaries impenetrable to other members of society and played key roles in the highest households of the state, even forming their own households. Kathryn Babayan introduced fascinating sources called *majmu'a*s from Safavid-era Isfahan in Iran. Majmu'as are anthologies or collections of written entries and owned by elites and can be thought of as "archives of daily life." Among the entries included in these anthologies are formulas of manumission, and Babayan discussed how these declarations of freedom implicate the body parts of the slaves in the manumission process. The last speaker of the day, Ehud Toledano, discussed households of the seventeenth- to eighteenth-century Ottoman empire. He showed how enslavement was one means by which outsiders could be included in Ottoman society, avoiding social marginalization, and overviewed the types of bonds among members of Ottoman households, tracing transformations over the two centuries in question.

After the reception and dinner in Chinatown on Friday night, the symposium resumed Saturday morning with Jonathan Tenney's paper on families of institutional slaves from second-millennium Mesopotamia. Tenney introduced another important approach to the discussion, focusing on population dynamics of institutional slaves in fourteenth-century Nippur. Next, F. Rachel Magdalene discussed several interesting unpublished Neo-Babylonian documents that seem to mention four generations of Judeans living in Babylonia. Magdalene attempted to reconstruct a social-historical picture of exilic life of Judeans using these documents, showing that certain persons with Judean names owned slaves in Babylonia and were perhaps fairly well integrated into Babylonian society. Finally, Kristin Kleber finished the session with a useful discussion of temple personnel from Neo-Babylonian times called *širku*s. Kleber engaged debates about whether people who bore the designation *širku* should be considered slaves and argued that the role and position of these individuals are best understood by reconstructing the social dynamics among *širku*s and the people who surrounded them. In the final section of the event, Martha Roth and Indrani Chatterjee offered comments and engaging responses to the papers.

Overall, the event was a success both intellectually and logistically, and for this I am grateful to many people at the Oriental Institute. I thank Gil Stein for creating this post-doctoral program and for steering the project toward success with interest and enthusiasm, and I am grateful for the participants, some of whom traveled long distances to share their expertise. Chris Woods dedicated mentorship and much of his time to the project and also served as a chair for one of the panels; I also thank Matt Stolper and Fred Donner for serving as chairs. I am also very grateful to Mariana Perlinac and Meghan Winston for their logistical expertise and interest in the seminar series, and Tom Urban and Leslie Schramer for their work on the publication materials and for acting as a constant resource for the post-doctoral program. The publication of the papers should be available in the winter of 2011, just in time for the next seminar.

During my year in Chicago, I was able to make headway on a number of personal projects. With the help of the archives at the Oriental Institute and other fine resources at the university, I made considerable progress revising my dissertation for publication, and I prepared two articles for publication. I benefitted the most from the community of scholars to whom I had access, and from the academic and personal bonds that developed even during this short time.

TELL EDFU

Nadine Moeller

Introduction

The ongoing excavations at Tell Edfu have provided important new data for the study of early urban centers within Egypt. The discovery of the administrative quarters of this ancient town during the past four years has yielded several successive installations, which are characterized by a large granary court dating to the Second Intermediate Period (Dynasty Seventeen) and an earlier columned hall, which had been part of a substantial administrative complex dating to the late Middle Kingdom (Dynasties Twelve to Thirteen).

The fieldwork season at the settlement site of Tell Edfu took place from October 4 to November 12, 2009. The main objectives were finishing the full excavation of the eight silos, which had been discovered during the previous seasons, and exploring further elements of the columned hall underneath the silos as well as preparing a new excavation area farther to the northeast of the silo area that lies close to the Ptolemaic temple enclosure wall where Old Kingdom settlement remains have been located. Furthermore, the development of new digital image-capturing techniques reached its last stage of research. The new technique was carried out in collaboration with Lec Maj, former assistant director for research computing, University of Chicago, and has been funded by the Women's Board, of the University of Chicago, and the National Endowment for the Humanities in the form of a digital startup grant.

Excavation in the Silo Area

Last season, we received eagerly awaited official permission from the Supreme Council of Antiquities (SCA) to fully excavate and remove the walls that were built into the thick ash layer covering our excavation area (fig. 1). These walls lay above the granaries and were excavated in 1923. A photograph taken in 1928 from the top of the temple pylon clearly shows the ash layer and the small square silos that were built into it. A comparison with photos taken from the

Figure 1. Tell Edfu excavation area in 2009

pylon in 2008 shows that most of the walls that are lying above our excavation area were already excavated more than eighty years ago. Over the past three seasons at Tell Edfu, we recorded these walls in all their detail with drawings, descriptions, and photographs as well as an analysis of the few stratigraphic connections still preserved. Thus, we have now obtained the necessary information for the forthcoming publication in the first volume of the Edfu Reports series.

During the excavation of these wall remains, we have been able for the first time to provide a precise date for them. The few remains of in situ layers connected to these walls (since most of them were removed during the previous excavations) contained pottery that dates to the Late Period (Dynasties Twenty-five to Twenty-six). The walls belonged to larger domestic buildings, which seem to have been characterized by relatively thin walls of about 58 to 60 cm in width. They could have only been used for single-story houses since these walls are not strong enough to support additional floors above. Further elements of these houses were large open courtyards and numerous square magazines or cellars that had been built deeply into the ground and were used as storage space. These square magazines were about 1.2 m long and wide and about 2.5 m deep. Their walls were only one brick thick, about 14 cm, and bricks lined the pits that had been dug directly into the ground. Their floors were also paved with mudbricks. We have not been able to discover any original fill inside these magazines, which might have provided evidence for what exactly had been stored in them. The previous French excavations had already emptied them in the 1920s and refilled them with their own excavation rubbish, which contained modern straw and pieces of newspapers. In the western part of our excavation area, we excavated one of those square magazines, which had the western wall still preserved to its original height at 2.5 m above the floor level. Three small pieces of wooden beam fragments found on top of the wall indicated that these magazines were covered with mudbricks and wood. There must have been a trap door from above to access them, but no traces of the latter have been preserved. The general character of these Late Period houses seems to have been private, and no find has led us to believe otherwise.

New Kingdom Refuse Layers

The Late Period walls were built over very thick refuse layers, which have been dated to the first half of the New Kingdom. A clear hiatus in occupation can be seen between the abandonment of the Second Intermediate Period silos and the Late Period occupation. So far we have not discovered any evidence for Ramesside or Third Intermediate Period activities in this zone. A major change in the function of this town quarter from being an administrative, official area to being used as a refuse dump during the Eighteenth Dynasty until the installation of Late Period domestic buildings seems to have occurred. Apart from dumping large amounts of white ash (US 2013 in fig. 2) and discarded pottery mixed with occupation debris (US 2458 in fig. 2), there are few activities that can be observed here that date to the New Kingdom. The white ash might have been deposited from a nearby bakery since we did not find any traces of industrial activity such as unfired/vitrified pieces of pottery that would indicate pottery production or any metal slag that would be a sign for metal working. A large-scale baking facility somewhere nearby seems to be the most plausible explanation for the origins of the ash. The underlying sequence of a multitude of refuse layers (US 2458) containing a lot of pottery seems also to stem from some large-scale production activity nearby. Curious fragments of dried mud were found in large quantities in these layers; their function and origin are so far unknown. Among them were a large number of hieratic ostraca, which contain administrative lists. According to the context and paleography, they date from the late Second Intermediate Period to the early New Kingdom. Ostraca from

ash layer
US 2013

different fills of rubbish
US 2458

Figure 2. Refuse layers of the New Kingdom

reliable archaeological contexts are extremely rare, especially for the period in question.

A large quantity of animal bones was also excavated this year. Of particular note are the bones of several hippopotami. An entire upper skull (fig. 3) has been discovered in the area immediately east of Silos 405 and 303. Additionally, multiple pieces of jawbones, tusks, vertebrae, and leg bones have been found in different contexts in the silo area, some in the debris layers of the New Kingdom, others in earlier fill layers near the silos. The exact reason for them being deposited here and the puzzling fact that there is more than one occasion of dumping hippo bones are questions that we need to answer in the future.

Figure 3. Hippopotamus upper skull and vertebra discovered near the silos

The Silos of the Second Intermediate Period

The excavation of the Late Period walls and the refuse/ash layers underneath them allowed us for the first time to excavate the complete silos of which we had dug small parts in previous seasons (fig. 4). In the southern part, we completed the excavation of Silos 393 and 405 down to their original floor level. In the interior of Silo 393, we dug various fill layers and walking levels, which had accumulated above its original floor. Several small fireplaces visible on the surface of these walking levels indicate some sort of use after the actual function of the silo as granary had ceased. Two of those fill layers lying above the silo floor contained further hieratic ostraca that also date from the end of the Second Intermediate Period to the early New Kingdom (fig. 5). They must have been discarded after the silo had fallen out of use. They are very similar

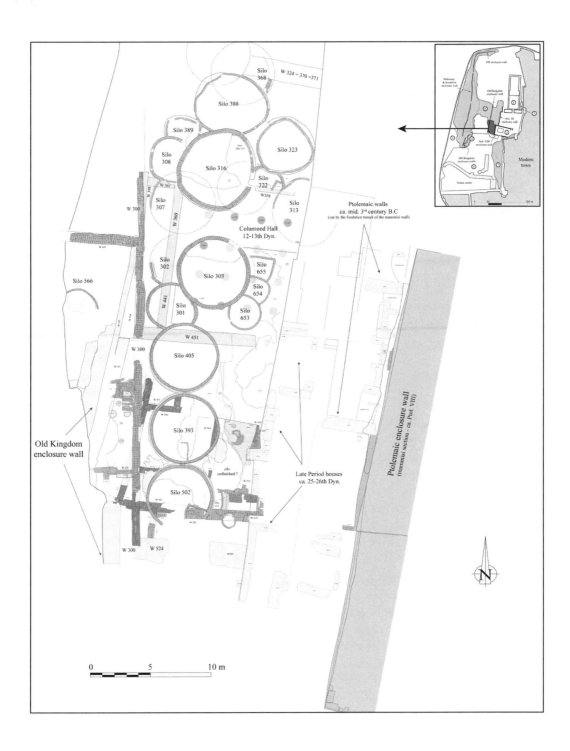

Figure 4. Plan of the silo area (2009)

Silo Si 393

US 2155
layer with ostraca

Figure 5. Layer with hieratic ostraca inside silo Si 393

to those found in the northern part of the site (layer US 2458) according to their paleography, suggesting that these pieces come from the same source and period, probably belonging to an archive that was discarded when the administrative buildings in this area were abandoned. Among the ostraca three shallow red bowls were found, broken into multiple pieces, which have been inscribed on the inside and outside in hieratic. These texts will be part of a detailed study by Kathryn Bandy (graduate student in the Department of Near Eastern Languages and Civilizations at the University of Chicago).

The large Silo 303 was also fully excavated (fig. 6). It has a diameter of 6 m, and its walls are preserved up to a height of 1.5 m. According to the stratigraphic evidence, this silo belongs to the first phase of silos built in the area and functioned at the same time as Silo 316. Inside Silo 303 we excavated all the layers down to the floor level of the older columned hall of the late Middle Kingdom, which lies underneath the silos. Against its eastern side we discovered three new silos (Silos 655, 654, and 653), which are abutting Silo 303 (fig. 7). They are much smaller in size and seem to have functioned as additional storage space. In the central one of the three, Silo 654, an intact female clay figurine was found (fig. 8). It was lying in the demolition layer of the silo, which also contained many mudbrick fragments. The figurine shows a woman carrying a baby on her back. A very similar figure has been discovered at Gebel Zeit in the sanctuary for Hathor. These figurines are typical for the Second Intermediate Period and have been interpreted as fertility figurines. In 2006 we found several such figurines in the demolition fill of Silo 316, though none of them with a baby.

It is now clear that Silo 316, together with Silo 303, form the first phase of grain silos in this area. They are characterized by large diameters (6.0–6.5 m), and their walls have a width of two bricks (30.6 cm). Other silos have been built against and around them. This year we uncovered Silo 388, which leans against Silo 316 on its northern side (fig. 9). The northwestern side of Silo

Figure 6. Excavation in progress inside Silo 303

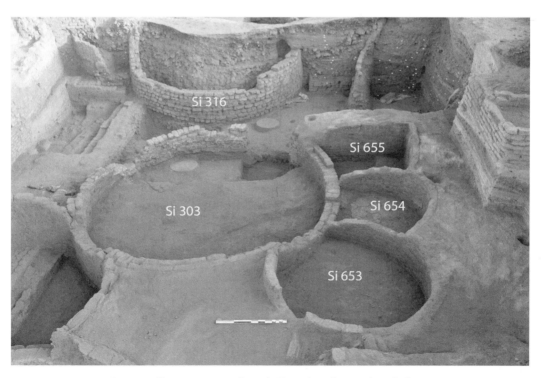

Figure 7. Silos 653, 654, and 655 built against the exterior of Silo 303

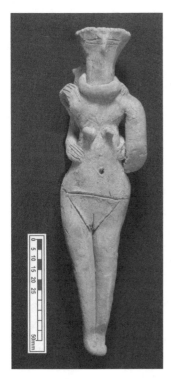

Figure 8. Clay fertility figurine found inside the silo demolition layer

388 is still preserved to a height of more than 3 m above floor level, and the curvature of the dome is easily visible, yet very fragile. This silo seems to have also been previously excavated, probably by the French in the 1920s or 1930s because it was filled with excavation debris.

Silo 388 could well be contemporary with the construction of the eastern Silo 323 and/or Silo 313. We cannot establish a precise relative chronology just yet since we are still missing some stratigraphic links in this area, which will be brought to light in excavation next season. Thus the floor of Silo 388 had not been reached by the end of this season, and it is one of the aims for 2010. This silo had been built at a time when the grain storage area was restructured. The main visible transformation was a considerable reduction of the size of the grain silos. In fact, in the north a 2.2 m high wall running east–west was constructed, reducing the extension of the silo court toward the north. A part of another silo wall can be seen that was integrated into this wall. This shows us not only that in its original layout the granary courtyard stretched farther in that direction but also that the latter silo could well have been contemporary to Silo 316 and Silo 303 since it shares identical architectural features.

Figure 9. Silos in the northern part of the excavation area

Columned Hall of the Middle Kingdom

Remains of a large columned hall were discovered underneath the silos, and this hall has been another focus of our excavations since its first discovery in 2005. We can reconstruct sixteen columns in total so far, but the eastern part of the building is still covered by later settlement layers, and thus the exact limits to the east are unknown. Last season we found new data in connection with the use of this late Middle Kingdom administrative building. Inside Silo 303 we excavated below the silo floors down to the thick mud floor of the columned hall. We found one more sandstone column base, which makes a total of six column bases in situ, while two other column bases were ripped out shortly after the building had fallen out of use and before the silos were built, leaving two large holes in the ground. The holes are clearly visible (fig. 10). On the mud floor we discovered a layer of abandonment, which corresponds to the exact moment when the columned hall was no longer used; only discarded pottery and various objects mixed with animal bones were left lying on the floor. Apart from many pieces of pottery, there were two interesting discoveries that merit mention here. We found numerous fired pottery weights, each of which has two holes and a deep groove running along the upper part that would have held a rope. Maybe they were used as net sinkers for weighing down fishing nets. Further analysis is planned in order to determine their precise function. Among the abundant pottery, a small group of sherds can be identified as Levantine Painted Ware. The sherds belong to at least one bichrome long-necked jug, the decoration of which includes a black crisscross zone with a red band above and below as well as an additional black band below (fig. 11). Fragments of the body are preserved, but the shoulder, neck, and handle are missing. Close parallels to these imports have also been found at Tell el-Dab'a during the late Middle Kingdom. This type of pottery has been found in the Levant and in Egypt and can be dated to the beginning of the Middle Bronze Age.

On and above the floor of the columned hall we also found numerous seal impressions indicating the opening and sealing of various commodities (boxes, baskets, letters) in this area.

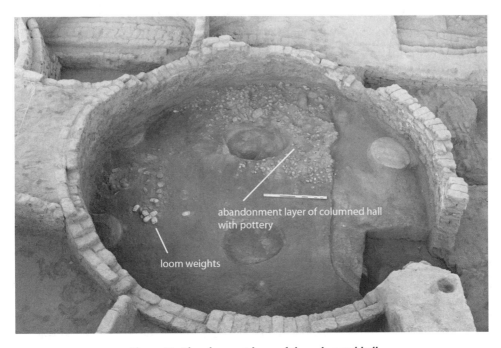

Figure 10. Abandonment layer of the columned hall

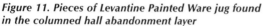

Figure 11. Pieces of Levantine Painted Ware jug found in the columned hall abandonment layer

Figure 12. Negative imprint of an octagonal column visible on a column base

The majority are scarab seals showing the typical decorative spiral motifs of the late Middle Kingdom; however, a few have personal names and titles. In 2007 we discovered several seal impressions showing the figure of a king wearing the crown of Upper and Lower Egypt with a tiny cartouche in front of his face that can be read as "Nimaatre," which is the throne name of Amenemhat III (see *News & Notes* 198).

Another new discovery in relation to the columned hall was made this season. On the surface of the newly excavated column base we were able for the first time to clearly see the negative imprint left by the removal of the actual column that had originally stood there. When removed, its negative imprint remained visible (fig. 12). We now have clear evidence that the columns were octagonal and most likely made of wood.

Preparation of New Excavation Layer with Old Kingdom Remains

In the north of the silo area, just behind the new mudbrick wall that was built by the SCA in 2002, we cleared several meters of sebbakh debris in order to access the underlying Old Kingdom layers (fig. 13). The cuts along the sides contained pottery dating to the Fourth and Sixth Dynasties, which would provide for the first time new information about the origins of the ancient town at Edfu. So far we know almost nothing about the provinces during the Fourth Dynasty since all the activity seems to have been concentrated in the Memphite region, Giza-Saqqara. We stopped the excavation here as soon as we reached in situ layers, which we will start to carefully excavate next season. This season's work was aimed at preparing the ground for the 2010 season. It seems that the sebbakhin had cut several large holes into the ground here, but there is enough material still in its original place that is worth excavating and studying. This would also be an ideal area to present our finished work to the tourists and visitors, since it can be seen from current ground level, and no access or climbing on the tell is required.

Digital Documentation of Archaeological Remains

A side project of the Tell Edfu Project focuses on the development of new digital image-capturing techniques for which research has been carried out in collaboration with Lec Maj. Work on site concentrated this year on the 3-D modeling aspect of this project using PhotoModeler Scanner software. As a study sample, we chose the digital recording of the lower part of a Ptolemaic house

Figure 13. Work in progress during preparation of new excavation area

that was excavated by the Franco-Polish mission in the 1930s and is still preserved in excellent condition (fig. 14). One of the challenges was to find the best possible reference markers, which are used for the automatic alignment of photographs to create a 3-D photo skeleton for extracting point-cloud data. In the field the local conditions such as strong sunlight created inevitable shadows, and the winds and the occasional roaming of wild dogs provided quite a few challenges. Another study sample was the female fertility figurine with the baby on her back. The processing of this data and the final generation of the 3-D models are currently in progress. Two other aspects of the project have been successfully completed. One is an adaptation of panoramic photography using a stationary tripod with a panoramic tripod head in order to capture general views of the excavations area. The other makes use of a photographic stitching program called Microsoft Photosynth, which is available online. The latter permits very detailed views of the archaeological remains that can be zoomed into, which are generated by numerous photos taken from many different angles with

Figure 14. Lower part of a Ptolemaic house showing reference markers used for 3-D modeling

different, overlapping reference points. First results can be seen on the Tell Edfu Project Web site at www.telledfu.org.

* * * * * * * * * *

I would like to thank Dr. Mohamed al-Bialy from the Aswan Inspectorate, and Mr. Mohamed Zenan Nubi as well as his colleagues from the inspectorate at Edfu for their ongoing support and help. A special thank you also goes to our inspector Dr. Sami es- Zeidan Osman for his collaboration and Ms. Faten Abd el-Halim Saleh for her help with the paperwork and its Arabic translation. The members of the Tell Edfu team were (in alphabetical order) Natasha Ayers (ceramics), Kathryn Bandy (ostraca and small finds), Georges Demidoff (Egyptology), Elise MacArthur (archaeology and photography), Lec Maj (computing and 3-D modelling), Gregory Marouard (archaeology), Virpi Perunka (ceramics), Foy Scalf (Demotic ostraca), Aurelie Schenk (archaeology), and Julia Schmied (photography).

Credit

All photos and drawings by the Tell Edfu Project 2009.

Web site: www.telledfu.org

————————

TELL ZEIDAN

Gil J. Stein

2009 Excavations and Laboratory Work

In the summer of 2009, the Oriental Institute conducted the second field season of excavations in the joint Syrian-American archaeological research project at Tell Zeidan in the Euphrates River Valley of north-central Syria (fig. 1). Gil Stein served as American co-director, while the Syrian co-director was Mr. Muhammad Sarhan, director of the Raqqa Museum. We gratefully acknowledge the support of the National Science Foundation (NSF) and the Oriental Institute, and the generosity of private donors in funding the 2009 fieldwork.

The Zeidan excavations explore the roots of urbanism in Upper Mesopotamia (modern-day northern Iraq, north Syria, and southeast Turkey) by excavating a large regional center or

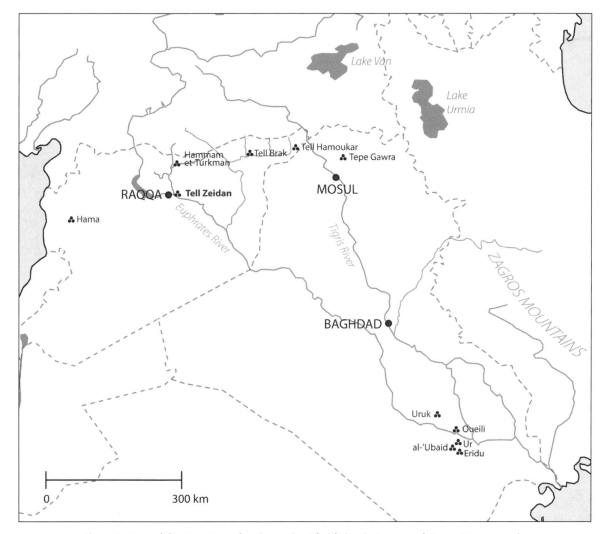

Figure 1. Map of the Near East, showing major Ubaid sites in Lower and Upper Mesopotamia

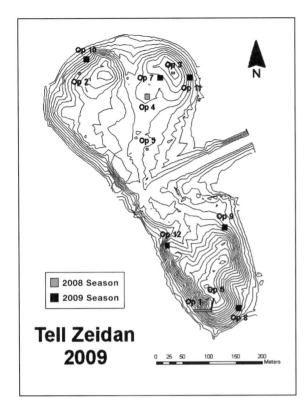

**Tell Zeidan
2009**

Legend:
- 2008 Season
- 2009 Season

0 25 50 100 150 200 Meters

*Figure 2. Topographic map of Tell Zeidan
showing the 2009 excavation areas*

town dating to the Halaf, Ubaid, and Late Chalcolithic 1 and 2 periods in a continuous sequence dating from 5800 to 4000 BC. Tell Zeidan is a large 12.5-hectare site consisting of three mounds enclosing a "lower town," located at the confluence of the Balikh River with the Euphrates River, 5 km east of the medieval and modern city of Raqqa. Because the site was abandoned around 4000 BC (with only a small ephemeral re-occupation in the early third millennium), Tell Zeidan provides an almost unique opportunity to make broad horizontal exposure of an Ubaid regional center in the sixth and fifth millennia BC, the time period that saw the first development of towns, political leadership, community temples, and social stratification. By studying the organization of society at Tell Zeidan in the Ubaid and Late Chalcolithic 1–2 periods, we hope to understand the ways in which these early towns gave rise to the earliest cities and urban civilization of the Near East.

Excavations

Excavations were conducted in eight trenches (called "operations") across the site: Operations 1, 6, 8, 9, and 12 on the south mound (the largest of Zeidan's three mounds); Operation 10 on the north slope of the northwest mound; and Operations 7 and 11 on the northeast mound (fig. 2).

The South Mound

Operation 1: Operation 1 is a 2 m wide step trench oriented east–west along the southwest slope of the southern high mound. The 2008 excavations had reached upper Halaf levels in the westernmost portion of the trench at the base of the mound. In 2009, excavations in the Halaf part of Operation 1 continued in a 2.0 × 2.5-meter-deep sounding, conducted by

Figure 3. The deep sounding into the Halaf deposits at the base of Operation 1

Figure 4. Spouted strainer jar with painted and impressed decoration. Operation 1 deep sounding, Halaf period

Figure 5. Hematite mace-head. Only half the mace-head was preserved. The pattern of the drill hole through the center shows that the mace-head was drilled from only one side. Operation 1 deep sounding, Halaf period

Michael Fisher (fig. 3). All deposits within the sounding appear to date to the Halaf, based on the ceramics. The deposits excavated in the deep sounding were a series of outdoor occupation surfaces (sometimes with hearths) alternating with trash deposits. The sounding yielded several complete Halaf ceramic vessels including a spouted strainer jar with impressed and painted decoration (fig. 4), and a secondary burial with a broken hematite polished mace-head (fig. 5). At a depth of 4.35 m beneath the present-day surface at the base of the mound, excavation was halted for safety reasons, due to the risks of working in such a narrow, deep trench. Excavation did not reach sterile deposits. In future seasons we hope to continue excavation in this area and discover whether any earlier occupations underlie the Halaf deposits at Zeidan.

Operation 6: Operation 6 consisted of two 2 × 3 m soundings (areas "A" and "B") laid out as part of a long trench extending from the top of the mound west-southwest toward the top of the Operation 1 step trench. Operation 1 had been placed 3.0 m below the top of the south mound, so it did not sample the uppermost deposits on the mound. The uppermost sampled deposits in Operation 1 dated to the Late Chalcolithic 1 period. Under the supervision of Abbas Alizadeh, Operation 6 was intended to document the missing uppermost 3.0 m of the south mound stratigraphic sequence.

The uppermost deposits in Operation 6 areas "A" and "B" consisted of a series of three infant burials (two jar burials and one inhumation) and five adult secondary burials consisting of stacked accumulations of disarticulated bone. It is highly unusual to have infants and adults interred together in the same burial area or cemetery inside the confines of a habitation site in the Late Chalcolithic 2 period. Instead, the usual pattern is one where infant jar burials were placed beneath house floors, while adults were buried off-site, presumably in a community cemetery. All the burials apparently date to a late phase of the Late Chalcolithic 2 period, based on the ceramics of the jar burials. The floor surface from which the pits were dug has apparently eroded away by the strong westerly winds that scour the site. The only grave goods associated with these burials were three stone labrets (fig. 6): ZD1879 (associated with adult secondary burial 5), ZD1859 (associated with infant jar burial 2), and ZD1887 (associated with the adult bone accumulation

Figure 6. Stone labrets or lip plugs, worn as an ornament, were found in association with Late Chalcolithic 2 burials (ca. 4200–4000 BC). Operation 6

Figure 7. Cache of 1,090 unbaked clay sling bullets found in trash deposits dating to the Ubaid period. Operation 8

Figure 8. Excavation of Ubaid-period pyrotechnic features — ovens and possibly kilns. Operation 8

in locus 8). The seven burials were all dug into earlier Late Chalcolithic 2 domestic architecture. Beneath the level with the Late Chalcolithic 2 domestic architecture were Late Chalcolithic 1 deposits with the characteristic flint-scraped beaded lip bowls. These deposits established the stratigraphic link to the adjacent Operation 1 and completed the sequence by demonstrating that the south mound at Tell Zeidan was apparently abandoned at the end of the Late Chalcolithic 2 period.

Operation 8: Operation 8 was excavated by Jean Evans and Lise Truex as a 10 × 10 m trench on the lower slope in the southeast corner of the south mound. We encountered Ubaid architecture along the western baulk immediately beneath the loose surface deposit on the mound slope. The architecture consisted of the eastern portion of a small mudbrick room, along with a corridor and a surrounding mudbrick enclosure wall with a doorway and door socket. All associated ceramics were Ubaid plain wares and painted wares, including well-painted fineware bowls. This architectural level overlay a thick ashy brown deposit of trash and wash with no associated buildings. Stratigraphy and associated ceramics securely date this trash and wash deposit to the Ubaid period. This deposit contained a cache of more than 1,090 unbaked clay sling bullets (fig. 7). The cache appears to have been discarded within the trash deposit and was not associated with any architecture or occupation surface.

The types of activities in Operation 8 changed over the course of the Ubaid period. The uppermost building level had the remains of a well-built house: walls 2, 3, 6, 7, 8, and 16. Beneath this architecture, a thick trash and ash layer (locus 28) sealed off an earlier occupation where this part of the site functioned as an industrial area. Excavations recovered a series of ten pyrotechnic features and associated ashy trash deposits (fig. 8). Eight of these features were excavated in 2009. The features are generally 1.5 × 1.0 m or 1.0 × 1.0 m and were excavated about 25 cm into the ground surface. The features often had three or four mudbricks arranged so as to support the floor of an aboveground superstructure. The features are sometimes plastered, and they always show evidence for intense heat — the inner part of the feature walls is generally vitrified to a crumbly pale green that grades into intense orange or reddish brown, and then to normal soil color. The features appear to be the firebox portion of an installation that originally had an aboveground superstructure — perhaps the heating chamber — that is no longer preserved. The features resemble kilns as known from other Ubaid village-sized sites in north Syria such as Tell el-Abr and Kozak Shamali. However, the features do not contain any artifacts or industrial debris that one might expect to see in a kiln or smelting furnace — there are no kiln wasters, no crucible fragments, and no copper slag, tuyeres (blowpipes used in smelting), or litharge (an industrial byproduct of refining silver). The features were not all in use at the same time, but instead seem to represent a series of outdoor surfaces and associated pyrotechnic features that were repaired, modified, or abandoned over an extended period.

Figure 9. Carved steatite stamp seal, heavily worn and re-used in a Late Chalcolithic 1 context (1,000 years after the end of the Halaf period). Operation 9, Halaf period

Operation 9: Operation 9 was excavated by Tate Paulette and Katharyn Hanson as a 10 × 10 m trench on the northeast slope of the south mound. Excavations in the southwest corner of the trench located a pit (locus 23) dating to the Late Chalcolithic 1 period. One surprising find in this context was a very worn Halaf-style incised and drilled steatite stamp seal with a loop on the back (fig. 9). The loop was broken, and its stubs were very worn. The Halaf seal must have been found 1,000 years later by Late Chalcolithic 1 inhabitants of the mound and kept as an ornament

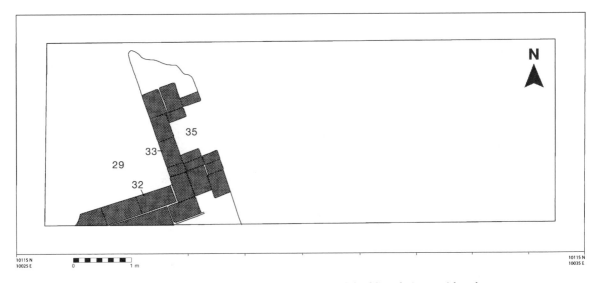

Figure 10. Partial exposure of a niched and buttressed mudbrick building dating to either the Late Chalcolithic 1 or the Ubaid–Late Chalcolithic 1 transitional phase. Niched- and buttressed-architectural style shows great continuity with earlier architectural styles of the Ubaid period. Operation 9

or talisman. Pit 23 cut into the uppermost preserved architecture in Operation 9 — a small portion of a niched and buttressed mudbrick building that apparently dates to the very beginning of the Ubaid–Late Chalcolithic 1 transitional phase (fig. 10). The wall of this building was three brick courses wide, with a 60 cm deep niche built into the outer face (35 in fig. 10). The niche was 90 cm wide. This appears to have been a public building, perhaps a temple similar to those at Tepe Gawra. Immediately to the east of this niched building, in mudbrick collapse deposit locus 27, excavation recovered more than fifteen pinched lumps of sealing clay, bearing finger impressions (fig. 11). This cache of sealing clays suggests that administrative or record-keeping activities might have been associated with this building. The niched building overlay a mudbrick building (walls 39, 40, and 51) that appears to have been built on a slope so that the walls had more brick courses to the north than they did to the south. An additional smaller room with walls only one course wide (walls 60, 62, 63, and 66) was added to the northwest of the original room (fig. 12). Based on ceramics, both rooms appear to date to the earliest stages of the Ubaid–Late Chalcolithic 1 transitional phase and to the very end of the Ubaid period. This is an extremely important result because it represents the first time that the Ubaid–Late Chalcolithic 1 transitional phase has been found in association with well-preserved, intact architecture. The deposits in this building also show a clear continuity between the Ubaid and the Late Chalcolithic 1 periods, rather than an abrupt transition.

Operation 12: Operation 12 was excavated by Abbas Alizadeh as an 8 m (east–west) × 10 m (north–south) trench on the northwest corner of the south mound. The trench was meant to explore and date a large area of mudbrick that had been visible on the mound slope in 2008. Surface ceramics in this area also appeared to be post-Chalcolithic. Excavations uncovered a large 6 × 6 m mudbrick platform built against the northwest slope of the south mound (fig. 13). The platform

Figure 11. Prepared lumps of unused sealing clay, bearing the finger impressions of the people who prepared the clay for use in sealing doors or containers such as jars or baskets. The sealing clay was found in association with the niched and buttressed walls, suggesting that this structure might have been an administrative building of some sort. Operation 9

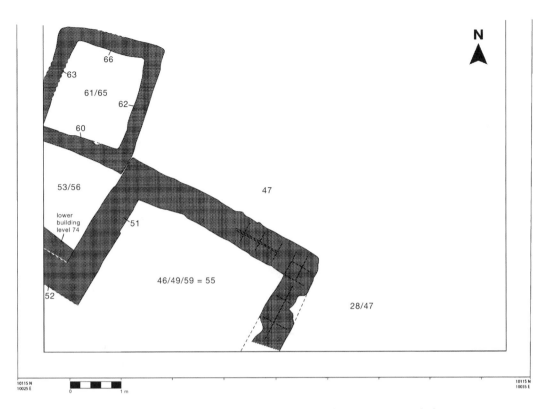

Figure 12. Mudbrick architecture dating to the Ubaid–Late Chalcolithic 1 transitional phase, and extending back into the end of the Ubaid period. Operation 9

Figure 13. 6 x 6 m stepped mudbrick platform with an access ramp on the northwest corner of the south mound. This platform appears to date to a small-scale later re-occupation of Tell Zeidan in the early third millennium BC. Operation 12

had two steps on its north side (loci 28 and 36) and was constructed of well-built mudbrick walls 14, 19, and 35 enclosing a core that was filled with mudbrick fragments (locus 8). The platform had an access ramp (locus 33) built up against the steps on its north face. After the construction of the platform, a second building phase added a room to the south of the platform (walls 16 and 32). Both phases share the same ceramic assemblage. This consists of wheel-made fine, medium, and coarse wares with either no visible temper or fine sand temper. The ceramics and the architecture are clearly post-Chalcolithic in date. The closest-published parallels to these ceramics that we were able to identify in the field derive from Hammam et-Turkman VI East, which the excavators date to the early third millennium BC. Although late ceramics occur sporadically across the site, Operation 12 is the only part of Tell Zeidan where this material has been found in stratigraphic context. It would therefore appear that Tell Zeidan was abandoned at the end of the Late Chalcolithic 2 period (ca. 3900 BC) for more than 1,000 years and then saw a brief partial reoccupation in the early third millennium BC.

The Northwest Mound

Operation 10: Operation 10 was opened as a 10 ×10 m trench on the northwest slope of the northwest mound, approximately 8 m below its highest point. The uppermost deposits in the trench dated to the Late Chalcolithic 1 period (fig. 14). Beneath a large clay-filled pit (perhaps used for brick manufacture?), excavations exposed a complex consisting of a small house and associated outdoor surface or courtyard (fig. 15) with a large bread oven/tannur. One large storage jar lay inside a room of the house. A complete baked clay "muller" (ZD2619) was found in room deposit 29 in this house (fig. 16). Mullers are a distinctive Ubaid artifact form in southern Mesopotamia, but their use in north Syria seems to have continued into the Late Chalcolithic 1 period. In the floor of the courtyard of the house, three very large storage jars had been buried so that only their mouths were visible at the level of the courtyard floor. One of the jars contained a flint-scraped, straight-sided "Coba bowl," apparently used as a scoop for the contents of the storage jar. In addition to the large storage jars, two infant jar burials (loci 45 and 54) had been dug into the courtyard floor.

Beneath the level of the courtyard and its large storage jars was a series of thick wash layers, which seem to indicate a period when most of Operation 10 was used as an open-air surface, probably adjacent to houses located in the area outside the limits of the trench. Ceramics from these wash layers (loci 58 and 62) dated to the Late Chalcolithic 1 period. These deposits sealed

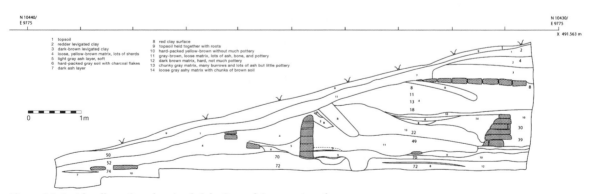

Figure 14. East baulk section showing brick pit overlying a series of houses dating to the Late Chalcolithic 1 period. Operation 10

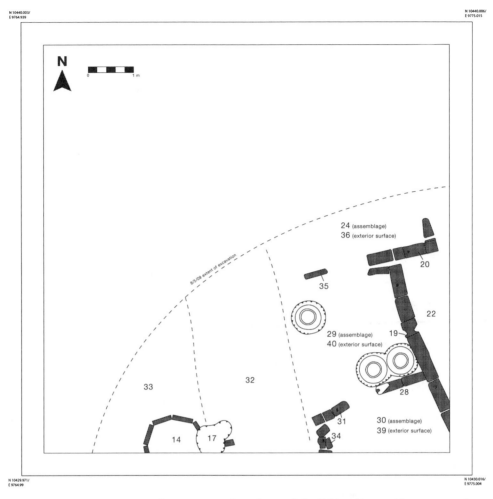

Figure 15. Top plan of Late Chalcolithic 1 house with an oven and two large grain-storage pithoi set into the courtyard floor. Operation 10

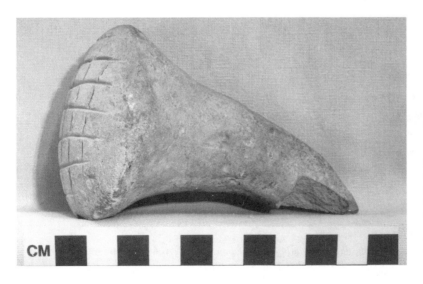

Figure 16. Baked clay "muller" found in the Late Chalcolithic 1 household deposits. The use of mullers in the Late Chalocolithic 1 period gives further evidence for strong continuities in material culture between the Ubaid and the immediately succeeding Late Chalocolithic 1 period. Operation 10

off two large pits, pit 57 (apparently a latrine) and pit 67, along with a mudbrick wall locus 65 — all set into wash layer 70. The pits were excavated, along with infant jar burial 71 (also set into wash layer 70). After the removal of the pits, wash layer 70 was excavated as well, revealing more of the face of wall 65. The presence and dating of these wash layers confirm that at least this part of the northwest mound saw long-term use as a domestic quarter during the Late Chalcolithic 1 period.

The Northeast Mound

Operation 7: Excavated by Khaled Jayyab and Nabil abu-l-Kheyr, Operation 7 was laid out as a 10 × 10 m trench along the southwest slope of the northeast mound (fig. 1). This trench aimed to recover Ubaid architecture and associated deposits. Initial excavations showed that the uppermost 50 cm consisted of a 50 cm thick deposit of wind-blown (Aeolian) fine silts, sealing off the final occupation of this part of the site. The underlying deposits were wash layers containing a mixture of Ubaid and Late Chalcolithic 1 and 2 ceramics. At this point, the size of the excavated area was reduced to a 2 × 9 m exposure along the north baulk. Excavations in this area located deposits of Ubaid midden and wash layers aligned along what appears to have been a drainage ditch dug by the Ubaid inhabitants of the site. Unfortunately, no architecture was located in association with these deposits. Excavation of Operation 7 was terminated after one week in order to focus our efforts on areas with architecture and associated remains. The trench was backfilled.

Operation 11: Excavated by Khaled Jayyab and Nabil abu-l-Kheyr, Operation 11 was laid out as a 10 × 10 m trench along the eastern slope of the northeast mound, after Operation 7 was closed. Except for a shallow deposit beneath the disturbed topsoil that dated to the Ubaid–Late Chalcolithic 1 transitional period (locus 4), all deposits in Operation 11 were Ubaid in date.

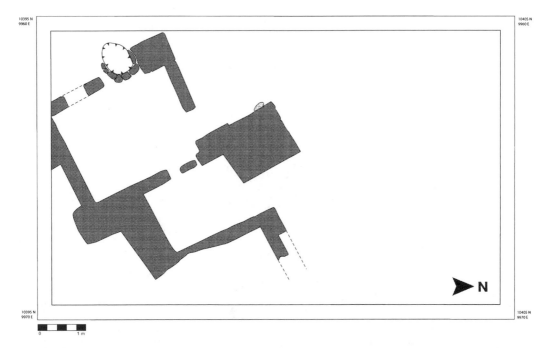

Figure 17. Partial exposure of a mudbrick house dating to the Ubaid period. Although modest in scale and construction, room deposits in this structure yielded remarkable imported prestige goods. Operation 11

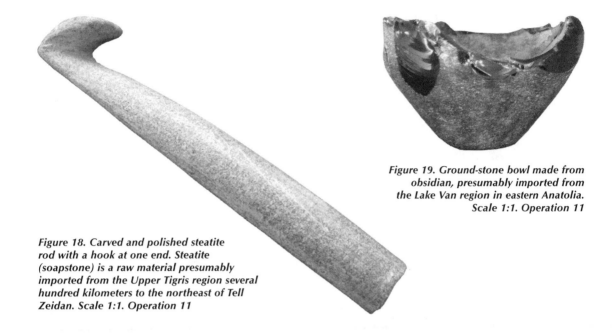

Figure 19. Ground-stone bowl made from obsidian, presumably imported from the Lake Van region in eastern Anatolia. Scale 1:1. Operation 11

Figure 18. Carved and polished steatite rod with a hook at one end. Steatite (soapstone) is a raw material presumably imported from the Upper Tigris region several hundred kilometers to the northeast of Tell Zeidan. Scale 1:1. Operation 11

The uppermost preserved Ubaid deposit was pit 5, which contained large amounts of ceramics, bone, five to six pieces of sealing clay, and a kiln waster. Beneath this were three architectural levels. The uppermost building level included the stub of a niched wall (locus 5) and a plastered surface (locus 15).

Beneath this level, wash layer 16 sealed off the second level of architecture, This consisted of a small Ubaid house with mudbrick walls one course wide — walls 18, 21, 22, 23, and 33, forming two rooms and a corridor (fig. 17). It was impossible to determine from the preserved portion whether or not this was part of a tripartite house plan. Although the house was simple in plan and construction, the floor (locus 31) of the northern room yielded two unusual finds made from carefully worked exotic raw materials — a beautiful rod with a hook at the end carved from steatite presumably imported from the Upper Tigris region in eastern Anatolia (fig. 18) and a fragmentary ground-stone cup made from obsidian presumably imported from the Lake Van area in eastern Anatolia (fig. 19). The combination of exotic, rare raw material and the high level of craftsmanship required to produce the bowl and the rod suggest that these would have been extremely valuable prestige goods or items of wealth in the Ubaid community at Zeidan. Kiln wasters from the manufacture of Ubaid ceramics (e.g., ZD2476) were also found in the rooms of this house. The house walls were built directly on top of the third and earliest building level documented in 2009. This consists of walls 38, 43, and 45. Each of these walls was at least three brick courses wide — much more substantial than the thin walls of the overlying architectural level. The tops of the walls of this earliest building level were reached in the final days of the 2009 season.

In-field Laboratory Analyses

Chipped Stone: Dr. Elizabeth Healey analyzed all the approximately 1,500 pieces of chipped stone recovered in 2008 from Operations 1–4. She examined two main aspects of the assemblage: lithic raw materials and retouched pieces. Roughly 75 percent of the chipped stone was cobbles gathered from the Balikh River. The cobbles were mainly used to manufacture casual flake tools.

About 20 percent of the chipped stone was a fine-grained brown nodular flint, most probably collected from the cliffs along the south bank of the Euphrates River, just a few kilometers to the south of the site. About 5 percent of the chipped stone was obsidian, predominantly the dark greenish black obsidian from the Bingöl and Nemrut Dağ sources in the Lake Van region of eastern Turkey. Almost all the blade tools were manufactured from either the Euphrates nodular flint or obsidian.

Retouched pieces were extremely common at Zeidan, ranging from 40 to 75 percent of the retouched pieces in the four operations. Most of the sickle elements showed traces of bitumen hafting and were oriented horizontally in the sickle. Other tools included denticulates, piercers, and drills. Scrapers were rare, and projectile points were (surprisingly) absent altogether.

Zooarchaeology: Kathryn Grossman began the analysis of faunal remains with bones recovered during the 2008 field season. To date, 3,000 bone fragments have been analyzed. Most of these are from Operation 1, with some remains from Operations 2, 3, and 4. The analysis so far shows a high proportion of the usual suite of Near Eastern domesticates (cattle, pigs, sheep, and goats), with a smaller amount of wild game (onagers, fallow deer, roe deer, gazelles, tortoises, and hares). The ratio of sheep to goats across the site is about 5:2, although as the analyzed sample increases, this ratio may show chronological variation. Relative proportions of the main domesticates are as follows: cattle 18.7 percent, sheep and goats 69.8 percent, pigs 11.5 percent. Kathryn also began to conduct a targeted study of faunal remains recovered from stratigraphically important Ubaid contexts of Operations 6, 7, 8, 9, 10, and 11 as part of the broader effort we are making to study intra-site differences in the distribution of ceramics, stone tools, animal bone remains, plant remains, and small finds in the different parts of the site.

Archaeobotany: Dr. Alexia Smith is in charge of archaeobotanical research for the Tell Zeidan excavations. During the 2009 season, fifty-four archaeobotanical samples were floated to recover the carbonized (burnt) remains of charcoal and seeds. By identifying these remains, we can reconstruct the environment and agricultural economy in the different occupational phases of Tell Zeidan. The samples consisted of material collected during both the 2008 and 2009 field seasons.

The light fractions from eight samples were analyzed. In general the samples appear to contain large quantities of wood and relatively few grains. This may be indicative of a wetter environment during the Ubaid period and/or a relatively low level of human impact on the landscape. From the samples examined so far, there appears to be little to no evidence for the use of dung fuel; wood appears to be the most commonly used fuel.

It is too early to talk securely about relative abundance of various crops, but from the samples analyzed so far, two-row hulled barley is the most numerous and frequently encountered grain. Emmer and einkorn wheat are found in much smaller proportions and tend to be more poorly preserved. Legumes are particularly poorly represented. This is typical at many Near Eastern sites and is often attributed to processing and preservation factors. Of the legumes identified so far, lentil and *Vicia* sp. are the most common. The abundance of wood and phytoliths is interesting and will be studied in greater depth in future seasons.

Ceramic Analysis: Philip Karsgaard and Khaled Jayyab worked on developing a ceramic typology and coding system for the Halaf, Ubaid, Late Chalcolithic 1 and 2 ceramics from Tell Zeidan. This typology focuses on vessel form, ware type, and decoration. We can already see that Tell Zeidan, as a site in the Balikh River Valley, had its own distinctively local forms, even though it shared similar ceramic forms with Ubaid and Late Chalcolithic 1–2 sites in the Euphrates Valley to the west, and the Upper Khabur River Valley to the east. Two aspects of the Ubaid ceramics at

Figure 20. Ubaid painted pottery sherd showing a procession of animals, including an ostrich. Naturalistic renderings of animals are a distinctive feature of Ubaid ceramics in north Syria and are very rarely found on ceramics in the southern Ubaid heartland. Scale 1:1

Zeidan are especially interesting and distinctively local in character. First, the Ubaid painted ceramics continue to use evolved forms of decoration that had been characteristic of painted pottery in the earlier Halaf period. Second, the Ubaid painted pottery of Tell Zeidan (and probably other north Syrian sites as well) differs from the Ubaid pottery of southern Mesopotamia in the use of animal motifs, often quite naturalistically rendered (fig. 20).

Overview of the 2009 Season

In 2009, we were able to build on and significantly expand our understanding of virtually all major occupation periods at Tell Zeidan. We now know that the Halaf occupation underlying the Ubaid was quite substantial and long lived. The Ubaid settlement seems to have been complex and differentiated, with some areas of public buildings, private houses, and craft or industrial areas. We can see evidence for the use of prestige goods or items of wealth made by highly skilled master craft specialists from rare imported raw materials. We can see that the Ubaid inhabitants of Zeidan had a distinctively local identity, despite their clear connections and affiliation with the broader context of the Ubaid world in southern Mesopotamia and other regions. Finally, in the architecture and use of mullers, we can see clear continuities and a gradual transition between the Ubaid and immediately succeeding Late Chalcolithic 1 period.

We hope to explore the complex tapestry of social and economic life at Tell Zeidan further in 2010.

Acknowledgments

We thank the Syrian General Directorate of Antiquities and Museums (DGAM), most notably Dr. Michel al-Maqdissi, Director of Excavations, and Dr. Bassam Jamous, General Director, for their support and assistance in this project. The project was supported by the National Science Foundation (NSF), the Oriental Institute, and the generosity of private donors. I also gratefully acknowledge Mr. Muhammad Sarhan, director of the Raqqa Museum and Syrian co-director of the joint Syrian-American excavation project. The entire team owes its deepest appreciation to Mahmoud al-Qaitab of the Raqqa Museum for his hospitality, friendship, and invaluable assistance in the day-to-day logistics of operating the excavation and maintaining our dig house. We thank the Raqqa branch of the Syrian Ministry of Education for allowing us to use the Zeki al-Arsouzi Primary School as our excavation field house in 2009. In Chicago, Steven Camp, Carla Hosein, D'Ann Condes, and Mariana Perlinac provided invaluable administrative support and assistance. Finally and most importantly, I want to express my deep gratitude to the Zeidan Project field staff: Abbas Alizadeh, Daniel Adler, Jean Evans, Michael Fisher, Kathryn Grossman, Katharyn Hanson, Al'a al-Hassani, Elizabeth Healey, Loujain Hetehet, Carrie Hritz, Khaled Abu-Jayyab, Philip Karsgaard, Nabil Abu-l Kheyr, Tate Paulette, Iman Saca, Jack Scott, Jennifer Smith, Stefan Smith, and Lise Truex.

———————————

INDIVIDUAL RESEARCH

Richard H. Beal

Richard H. Beal spent his time updating, reference checking, and copyediting articles for the third fascicle of the Š volume of the Chicago Hittite Dictionary. Outside of office time, he wrote the article "Hittite Anatolia: Political History" for the *Oxford Handbook of Ancient Anatolia*. Articles in the *Reallexikon der Assyriologie* on "Ships and Boats" and "Plague" are now in print. The article "Soldat (Hittite)" (Soldiers among the Hittites) is undergoing editing. An article has now been submitted for the same work on the Hittite port city of Ura, which is to be located somewhere on the Cilician coast. Although the Hittites were supposedly uncomfortable at sea or as merchants, it is only our lack of documentation in these areas that leads to this common opinion. However, a document from the Syrian port city of Ugarit finds the king of Ugarit complaining to the Hittite king that Hittite merchants from Ura were buying up all the real estate in Ugarit; in other words, Hittite merchants were not only engaged in, but also getting rich in, the sea trade with the Levant. In addition, the year has seen the appearance of the book he edited, along with Steven Holloway and JoAnn Scurlock, entitled *In the Wake of Tikva Frymer-Kensky*. This collects essays given at the 2007 Society of Biblical Literature meetings in honor of the late Tikva Frymer-Kensky, Assyriologist and Professor of Hebrew Bible at the University of Chicago.

Robert D. Biggs

Robert D. Biggs continued his work on the cuneiform inscriptions from the middle of the third millennium BC from the great temple of the goddess Inanna at Nippur, excavated by the Oriental Institute and other institutions some fifty years ago. Its final publication is being prepared by McGuire Gibson and his team. In his retirement he continues to study Babylonian liver and other omens, based on a diviner's inspection of other organs of the sheep, which is to further his research conducted during two weeks at the British Museum in 2009.

Scott Branting

Scott Branting continues to serve as the director of the Center for Ancient Middle Eastern Landscapes (CAMEL) and co-director of the Kerkenes Dağ archaeological project in central Turkey. Reports for both of these endeavors appear in separate sections of the *Annual Report*. He also remains involved in the publication phase of the MASS project, is co-director of the SHULGI project with Argonne National Laboratory, and continues to oversee the acquisition of the Integrated Database for the Oriental Institute. During this year, in partnership with Wendy Ennes of the Education Department, he developed the Science of Archaeology Outreach Program for the sixth-grade class of Claremont Academy in Chicago. He also served as a committee member for the Archaeological Institute of America (AIA) and as a delegate to the American Research Institute in Turkey (ARIT).

During the year, papers were presented at the seventh International Congress on the Archaeology of the Ancient Near East (ICAANE), Northwestern's Institute on Complex Systems (NICO), and the South Suburban Archaeological Society. Grants were received from the Chicago Public Schools Museum Connections Program and the U.S. Department of Education, in addition to a University of Chicago capital request awarded to the Institute to fund the purchase of the K EMu software that will run the Integrated Database. Two works appeared in publication: "Simulating Movement, Communication and Flows of Knowledge at Kerkenes Dağ" in *The Knowledge Economy and Technological Capabilities*, and "Kerkenes 2008" in *Kazı Sonuçları Toplantısı*. Several others are in the process of publication, including "Seven Solutions for Seven Problems with Least Cost Pathways" in *Archaeological Approaches to Least Cost Analysis*. Additionally, an article written by Eti Bonn-Muller entitled "Layers of the Past" that showcases the work of CAMEL appeared in the May/June issue of *Archaeology*.

Fred M. Donner

Fred M. Donner had an unusually hectic year. In August, he agreed to serve as the next director of the Center for Middle Eastern Studies (CMES), a position that dramatically increases his administrative responsibilities (and, incidentally, means that he spends much less time than before in his Oriental Institute office, and more in the offices of the CMES in Pick Hall — fortunately, not very far away). This was made more than usually exciting by the need to supervise writing of the federal Title VI grant application to the Department of Education, which provides the funding with which CMES helps underwrite the university's large staff of language lecturers for languages of the modern Middle East (Arabic, Persian, Turkish, Modern Hebrew, Armenian, Uzbek, etc.), as well as funding for an extensive outreach program for K–12 schools, two-year colleges, and the public at large, and support for symposia and conferences, including the annual Middle East History and Theory Conference, which this year drew several hundred people from around the country and abroad. It was also made more challenging by some unexpected staff turnover. By summer things had, thankfully, settled down, and we anticipate hearing soon about the application for the Title VI grant for the next four-year grant cycle.

Donner was engaged in his usual teaching duties; of particular note was a course in the spring, Arabic Palaeography and Epigraphy, during which a dozen students worked on Arabic papyri from the Oriental Institute's collection. Earlier generations of Arabic papyrologists, including the Oriental Institute's own famous Nabia Abbott (d. 1982), would positively be green with envy, seeing how today we can readily project a razor-sharp digital image of a papyrus document onto a large screen, so all in the classroom can study it from the comfort of their seats and call out possible readings for a troublesome passage; there is no doubt that the arduous task of reading these documents is greatly eased by having a dozen pairs of eyes, rather than merely one, gazing at the same thing and making suggestions.

Donner delivered a number of lectures during the year, including at the annual Middle East Studies Association meetings in Boston in November, another at St. Michael's College in Vermont in April, and a third to the graduating class of the Department of Near Eastern Studies at Berkeley in May. Most of these dealt with the question of Islam's beginnings and the way the terminology for institutions and practices in early Islam underwent a transformation to solidify Islam's ideological foundations.

Donner was also engaged in the normal chores of being external reviewer for tenure or promotion decision for several universities (including Princeton and Smith College), reviewing article drafts for journals and book drafts for publishers, and of course reading many, many dissertation chapters for some of the twenty students on whose dissertation committees he serves.

Donner's book *Muhammad and the Believers: At the Origins of Islam* (Harvard University Press) finally appeared in early May and has attracted a modicum of public notice, including a very favorable review in the *New York Times Book Review* (Sunday, June 27, 2010). After so many years working on this book, the positive response has been most gratifying. This year also saw the appearance of his article "Umayyad Efforts at Legitimation: The Umayyads' Silent Heritage," in *Umayyad Legacies/Heritages Omeyyades*, edited by A. Borrut and P. M. Cobb (Leiden: E. J. Brill).

François Gaudard

François Gaudard completed his fifteenth year in the Oriental Institute scholarly community, and he continued to work on the Chicago Demotic Dictionary (CDD; see separate report). He spent a very productive year, which included his participation in conferences and various publication projects.

On behalf of the Chicago Demotic Dictionary, François attended the sixth Demotic Summer School, held in Heidelberg, from August 23 to 26, 2009, where he gave three presentations about the CDD "Problematic Entries" files, in order to get input from international colleagues. François also continued to collaborate with Sofía Torallas Tovar and Raquel Martín Hernández as an editor of the Mummy Label Database (MLD; see separate report).

During the year, two of François' articles and one of his book reviews were published, namely, "Le P. Berlin 8278 et ses fragments: Un «nouveau» texte démotique comprenant des noms de lettres," in *Verba manent: Recueil d'études dédiées à Dimitri Meeks par ses collègues et amis*, edited by I. Régen and F. Servajean, pp. 165–69 (Two volumes; Cahiers Égypte Nilotique et Méditerranéenne 2; Montpellier: Université Paul Valéry, 2009); with Janet H. Johnson, "Six Stone Mummy Labels in the Oriental Institute Museum," in *Honi soit qui mal y pense: Studien zum pharaonischen, griechisch-römischen und spätantiken Ägypten zu Ehren von Heinz-Josef Thissen*, edited by H. Knuf, Chr. Leitz, and D. von Recklinghausen, pp. 193–209 (Orientalia Lovaniensia Analecta 194; Leuven and Walpole: Peeters, 2010); review of *Les Architraves du temple d'Esna: Paléographie*, by Dimitri Meeks, *Journal of Near Eastern Studies* 69/1 (2010): 133–34.

In the spring, François was asked to contribute two articles for the catalog of the next Oriental Institute's exhibition, curated by Christopher Woods, and whose theme deals with the origins of writing. The first article, entitled "Ptolemaic Hieroglyphs," describes the specificity and peculiarities of this script. The second consists of the edition of a still unpublished fragment of a funerary shroud from the Greco-Roman period, whose provenance has been identified by François as being Dendera. François will also publish two other related shroud fragments from the Oriental Institute's collections.

In addition, François is currently preparing an article to be published in a festschrift honoring a colleague. He also continued to work on several other publication projects such as a still unknown Late Ramesside letter (for details on this project, readers can consult the *2008–2009 Annual Report*), a Demotic priestly taxation list, a major copy of *The Book of the Dead* from the Ptolemaic period, and two fragments of *The Book of the Dead* from the Late Period, as well as various Coptic texts and mummy labels.

McGuire Gibson

Besides his involvement with the Nippur Publication Project, **McGuire Gibson** continued to work on another publication project with Dr. Mark Altaweel, a graduate of our Department of Near Eastern Languages and Civilizations. By Internet, Gibson and Altaweel keep in touch with a group of Iraqi archaeologists who are the authors of manuscripts on excavations carried out by Iraqis over the past forty years. Iraq has had a vibrant antiquities service since the 1920s, and Iraqis have administered it since 1932. While welcoming foreign expeditions, even during the period of the Sanctions of the 1990s, when other governments prevented most foreigners from working in the country, the Iraqis have carried out their own continuing program of excavations and salvage operations, which were routinely published in the official journal *Sumer*. The publication of *Sumer* was badly affected by the Sanctions, due not only to lack of funds but also to the fact that paper, ink, computer supplies, and other necessities for printing books were included on the absurd Sanctions list. The journal fell far behind and could be published only sporadically until recently. The looting of the Iraq Museum and the offices of the antiquities service, which are in the same building complex, resulted in the loss or partial destruction of manuscripts that were ready to go to press. The current project, which is now in its fourth and final year, allows the Iraqi authors to reconstruct their reports in Arabic so that Altaweel can translate them into English. Alexandra Witsell redraws the figures and enhances photographs, then formats the plates. Benjamin Studevent-Hickman reads any cuneiform inscriptions that occur. Gibson edits the manuscripts in consultation with the authors and Altaweel. Then the reports are published in international journals. With initial funding from the National Endowment for the Humanities, and another from the U.S. State Department, they have been able to set up collaborations with a total of six Iraqi colleagues. The result of the collaboration has been two articles published in the British journal *Iraq* on surface reconnaissance and soundings in the north of Iraq; one on an important prehistoric site south of ancient Assur, soon to appear as a chapter in a German book; one long report on Tell al-Wilaya, near Kut in southern Iraq, published in two issues of the Belgian journal *Akkadica*; and another important report in *Akkadica* concerning a newly excavated site near Amara, which can now be identified as the ancient city of Pashime. Gibson and Altaweel are meeting the Iraqi colleagues in Istanbul for a week in July 2010 to check the final manuscripts of a book-length report on Tell Asmar, ancient Eshnunna, a site that was previously excavated by the Oriental Institute in the 1930s; another manuscript on Tell Muqtadiya, which is also in the Diyala region north of Tell Asmar; and yet another on Tell Muhammad, a site within the southeastern part of modern Baghdad. They also have a manuscript on the site of Tell Shmid, one of the mounds in the south of Iraq that was the subject of a salvage operation in the years just before the 2003 war, but it has been difficult to bring this one to a close because the colleague involved is a Palestinian, long a resident in Baghdad, who has not been able to obtain a visa to meet with us in either Amman or Istanbul. As with all our colleagues, we have supplied him with Internet access, and we will try to finish the piece through that means. But nothing beats face-to-face contact, especially when trying to check on numerous details. There is one more manuscript, a book-length report on Iraqi work at Nimrud, ancient Calah, the Assyrian capital. This book will have, as its core, the Queens' Tombs, with their exquisite artifacts.

In addition to this work, Gibson has finally found the time to write up a report on a stratigraphic investigation on the Y Trench at Kish, which he carried out in 1978. This contribution will appear in a book on Kish, currently being completed by Karen Wilson. He also prepared for publication and read final proofs of an article on the Early Dynastic-Akkadian transition, a more developed presentation of material he first published in 1982. During the year, Gibson participated in three international conferences, one in London, which resulted in an unexpectedly long stay because of the Icelandic volcano. He still heads The American Academic Research Institute in Iraq (TAARII) and serves on the boards of the American Institute for Yemeni Studies and the Council of American Overseas Research Centers.

Petra M. Goedegebuure

In her study of the ancient languages of Anatolia, **Petra Goedegebuure** combines philology and the cultural background of texts with language typology and functional grammar. In doing so, Petra hopes to achieve two main goals. The first one is to describe Hittite and the other languages attested in ancient Anatolia at the level of pragmatics (how language is used in an interactive setting, as opposed to the study of meaning or form). Her second goal is to develop methods for applying modern linguistics to dead languages. Even though modern linguistic approaches are used in Hittitology and other extinct languages, they are usually not tested for their validity. This has led to the problem of linguists rejecting dead languages as an object of study and of philologists rejecting linguistics as a means of study.

In the presentation "The Pragmatic Function Focus in Hittite" (April 16, 2010, Workshop Linguistic Method and Theory and the Languages of the Ancient Near East, Oriental Institute), Petra suggested a framework for how to use functional linguistics for the description and better understanding of extinct languages. She concluded that general linguistic theories could be fruitfully applied to these languages if one uses an onomasiological approach (mapping forms on well-defined functions) based on contextual analysis. This approach is also exemplified in an article on Hittite question words ("Focus Structure and Q-word Questions in Hittite," *Linguistics* 47/4 [2009]: 945–69). Although the current opinion is that Hittite question words typically occur in clause-initial position, it turned out that Hittite question words could occur anywhere in the clause, depending on how much contrast the speaker wants to express.

Hattic, an isolate non-Indo-European language of Central Anatolia and typologically similar to Northwest Caucasian, was the language of the cult of the Old Hittite Kingdom (ca. 1650–1450). With only twenty bilinguals, some of which are very fragmentary, decipherment of this language proceeds slowly. Petra uses typology and language-contact studies to define the parameters for further grammatical analysis of this important but opaque language, as evidenced by a lecture "The Intricate Dance of Hittite and Hattian," November 13, 2009, Workshop Language Variation and Change, University of Chicago, and article "The Alignment of Hattian: An Active Language with an Ergative Base," in *Language in the Ancient Near East*, edited by L. Kogan,

N. Koslova, S. Loesov, and S. Tischenko, pp. 949–82 (Proceedings of the 53ᵉ Rencontre Assyriologique Internationale, Moscow; Babel and Bilbel 4; Orientalia et Classica 30; Winona Lake: Eisenbrauns, 2010).

Petra used philology combined with the comparative method to show that the final *-i* of one of the Hittite demonstratives is also present in several Luwian, Palaic, and Lydian demonstratives ("Deictic-emphatic -i and the Anatolian demonstratives," in a festschrift for a colleague [proof stage]).

Petra furthermore participated in the Chicago Hittite Dictionary Project as academic contributor (see separate report), continuing to write the lemma *ser* "on top, above, over, because of" (currently ninety pages).

During winter and spring, Petra taught Elementary Hittite (II and III) and two core classes, Language and the Human (winter, a writing class co-taught with four other faculty from the Department of Linguistics), and Anatolian History (spring).

Gene Gragg

The Mellon Foundation Emeritus Fellowship grant for the creation of COMA (Cushitic-Omotic Morphological Database) officially ended on March 1, 2010, and a final report was delivered on June 1. The grant's basic goal has been met. Although the archive is still being worked on, a provisional release of the whole application — data, scripts, and programs — is publicly available for downloading from our version control site http://bitbucket.org/gar/coma/overview/. (Click on the "get source ›› zip" menu to download a compressed file, coma.zip, of about 30 MB, which, unzipped, expands to a directory tree of data and application files taking up about 350 MB on a hard disk.) Until a stable release is produced, we will continue to use this site, which enables uploading (for collaborators with proper access) and downloading (for any interested party) of updates, corrections, and additions to a project, so that everyone working on it (or interested in it) has access to the most current version of the project. However, potential users need to keep in mind that, even though the data format and basic display modules are fairly stable, the data-query and data-manipulation software is still in a process of development, so that the contents of certain subdirectories in coma.zip can differ significantly, even from one day to the next.

The archive currently contains 5,444 verbal and pronominal paradigms in forty-five languages:

- Thirty-two Cushitic languages (4537 paradigms)
- Six Omotic languages (555 paradigms)
- Five Semitic languages (305 paradigms)
- Two Egyptian languages (Coptic, Middle Egyptian: 47 paradigms)

All of the data is currently undergoing proofreading and checking against sources. Although some additions are still to be made, the Cushitic and Omotic parts of the archive cover most of the published monographic morphological data in these languages. What will need to be added next are unpublished data, and data on less well-attested, older, and sometimes no longer spoken Cushitic and Omotic varieties, scattered in a wide variety of published sources.

In the course of the year, two papers were given centering on the project and its linguistic rationale and logical structure:

- Morphosyntax, Morphosemantics, and Homology: How to Query a Morphological Database, at the 38th North American Conference on Afroasatic Linguistics, Austin, Feburary 13–14
- What's in a Paradigm? Lessons from the Cushitic-Omotic Morphological Archive, at the conference Linguistic Method and Theory and the Languages of the Ancient Near East, Oriental Institute, April 16, 2010

Finally, by way of a new project, which in a sense complements and extends the work of COMA, Gragg has agreed to contribute to a survey volume *The Afroasiatic Languages* being edited by Zygmunt Frajzyngier for Cambridge University Press.

Rebecca Hasselbach

In the past academic year, **Rebecca Hasselbach** continued to work on her book project on the case system of the Semitic languages, which investigates the expression of grammatical roles and relations and their connection to parameters such as head- and dependent-marking and word order in Semitic. In this study, Hasselbach suggests an alternative reconstruction of both early Semitic case and alignment based on a typological approach. The manuscript of the book has been completed this spring and submitted to a publisher for review. Closely connected to the topic of her book manuscript is an article she is working on at the moment, which describes the connection of certain verbal markers, specifically markers expressing subordination and modal functions, and case markers. In this article she claims that the verbal endings -*u* and -*a* that are attested across Semitic can be etymologically and functionally derived from the nominative ending -*u* and the accusative in -*a*. In addition to these projects, Hasselbach wrote two entries for the *Encyclopedia of Hebrew Language and Linguistics*, including an article on "Canaanite and Hebrew" and one on "Demonstratives in Hebrew." Both have been accepted for publication and are now in press.

This year also saw the publication of an article on Old South Arabian by Hasselbach: "Altsüdarabisch," in *Sprachen aus der Welt des Alten Testaments*, edited by Holger Gzella, pp. 132–59 (Darmstadt: Wissenschaftliche Buchgesellschaft, 2009). In addition, several review articles written by Hasselbach appeared, including review of *Current Issues in the Analysis of Semitic Grammar and Lexicon* I, edited by Lutz Edzard and Jan Retsö, in *Zeitschrift der Deutschen Morgenländischen Gesellschaft* 159 (2009): 157–60; review of *Current Issues in the Analysis of Semitic Grammar and Lexicon* II, by the same editors, in *Zeitschrift der Deutschen Morgenländischen Gesellschaft* 159 (2009): 405–09; and review of *La formation des mots dans les langues sémitiques*, edited by Philippe Cassuto and Pierre Larcher, in *Zeitschrift der Deutschen Morgenländischen Gesellschaft* 160 (2010): 165–68.

Hasselbach further presented several papers at academic conferences in the past academic year. She talked about "The Function of Case Markers in Semitic" at the Annual Meeting of the North American Conference on Afroasiatic Linguistics in Austin, Texas, February 2010; on "Akkadian Demonstratives from a Comparative Perspective" at the meeting of the American Oriental Society in St. Louis, March; and on "The Application of Linguistic Typology to Semitic" at the conference on Linguistic Theory at the Oriental Institute, April 2010.

Hasselbach also continued her work as book-review editor for the departmental journal *Journal of Near Eastern Studies* throughout the academic year and served on various committees.

Harry A. Hoffner

In addition to periodic duties in editing articles for the Hittite Dictionary Project, **Harry A. Hoffner** had several articles published in the *Reallexikon der Assyriologie* this past year. They included "Schöpfungsmythen," "Sexualität," and "Strafe."

In addition, the following articles appeared in festschrifts:

- "The Institutional 'Poverty' of Hurrian Diviners and *entanni*-Women," in *Pax Hethitica: Studies on the Hittites and Their Neighbours in Honour of Itamar Singer*, edited by Yoram Cohen, Amir Gilan, and Jared L. Miller, pp. 214–25 (Studien zu den Boğazköy Texten 51; Wiesbaden: Harrassowitz, 2010). This work deals with an unpublished Hittite fragment, which gives for the first time a glimpse of an ancient equivalent of "poverty vows" applying to two classes of Hittite cult personnel.

- "A Grammatical Profile of the Middle Hittite Maşat Texts," in *Gedenkschrift für Erich Neu*, edited by Jörg Klinger and Elisabeth Rieken (Wiesbaden: Harrassowitz, 2010).

- "A Tribute to Erich Neu," in *Gedenkschrift für Erich Neu*, edited by Jörg Klinger and Elisabeth Rieken (Wiesbaden: Harrassowitz, 2010).

Harry continues to do research on a commentary on First and Second Samuel for a new biblical commentary series to be published both as print volumes and as computer software.

Janet Johnson

Janet Johnson spent much of the year working on the Chicago Demotic Dictionary (see separate report). She gave several lectures — "Cleopatra as CEO" to different groups throughout California and "What Is Demotic and Why Write a Dictionary?" to the Chicago chapter of the American Research Center in Egypt (ARCE) — and participated in the Oriental Institute's Museum Education Symposium Women in the Middle East, Past and Present, talking on "Women in Pharaonic and Hellenistic Egypt." She attended the Annual Meeting of ARCE as the Oriental Institute representative to the Research Supporting Members (RSM) Council and was elected by that council to the ARCE Board of Governors. She participated in a small way (writing catalog entries) for the upcoming exhibit on the Invention of Writing. In the spring, she team-taught a new course on Abydos with Nadine Moeller, looking at both the archaeological and textual records dealing with this important religious center. She was pleased to serve again as sponsor for Julie Stauder-Porchet and for Andréas Stauder, both of whom have research grants from the National Science Foundation of Switzerland to work on Egyptological topics.

W. Raymond Johnson

This year, **W. Raymond Johnson** completed his thirty-second year working in Egypt, his thirty-first full year working for the Epigraphic Survey in Luxor, and his thirteenth season as Field Director. He participated in two colloquia in Egypt this fall and winter. On November 5, 2009, he presented a paper entitled "An Hungarian/American Collaboration in Luxor. Recent Work of the Epigraphic Survey, Oriental Institute, University of Chicago at Khonsu Temple, Karnak" at the colloquium "Hungarian Excavations in the Theban Necropolis: A Celebration of 102 Years of Fieldwork in Egypt," Supreme Council of Antiquities, Zamalek, Cairo. On January 5, 2010, he presented a paper entitled "The New Digital Publication Program of the Oriental Institute and Epigraphic Survey, University of Chicago, at Medinet Habu" at the colloquium, "The Temples of Millions of Years and the Royal Power at Thebes in the New Kingdom," Supreme Council of Antiquities, Luxor. He is preparing articles for both colloquia now, as well as several secret festschrift articles that he is not at liberty to name at this time. This spring and summer Ray also published articles on the battle reliefs of Tutankhamun and their possible historical bearing on the recent re-examination of the young king's mummy in *KMT* magazine, *Archaeology* magazine, and a special issue of *U.S. News and World Report: Mysteries of History*. On June 30th Ray spoke at the opening of the exhibition "Das geheimnisvolle Grab 63: Die neueste Entdeckung im Tal der Könige – Archäologie und Kunst von Susan Osgood" in the Museum August Kestner, Hannover, Germany, that featured the epigraphic art work of Chicago House artist Sue Osgood and the publications of the Epigraphic Survey. Ray also wrote a chapter on the work of the Epigraphic Survey for the exhibition catalog edited by Eberhard Dziobek and Christian Loeben.

Walter E. Kaegi

Walter Kaegi was on leave of absence in Fall Quarter 2009 and Winter Quarter 2010. He prepared his book manuscript "Muslim Expansion and Byzantine Collapse in North Africa" for publication by Cambridge University Press — designing maps, selecting illustrations of coins, updating references, and developing an index. He published a joint article with Paul M. Cobb (University of Pennsylvania), "Heraclius, Shahrbarāz, and al-Tabarī," in the collective volume *Al-Tabarī: A Medieval Muslim Historian and His Work*, edited by Hugh N. Kennedy, pp. 95–112 (Studies in Late Antiquity and Early Islam 15; Princeton: Darwin Press, 2008). He completed an article entitled "Carl Hermann Kraeling: A Reminiscence" that includes recollections of an earlier director of the Oriental Institute, Carl H. Kraeling. He completed his contribution for the Oriental Institute's National Endowment for the Humanities project on "Teaching the Middle East: A Resource for High School Educators" (in press, 2010). It covers the period from 323 BC to AD 622, that is, approximately from Alexander the Great to Muhammad. He wrote and read the paper "Reassessing Seventh-Century Identities," for the International Congress Visions of Community: Ethnicity, Religion and Power in the Early Medieval West, Byzantium and the Islamic World, Akademie der Wissenschaften, Phil.-Hist. Kl., Vienna, Austria, June 17, 2009. He spoke on "Arnold J. Toynbee the Byzantine Historian" at the Byzantine Studies Conference (Byzantine Studies Association North America) Annual Meeting, Florida State University, Sarasota, November 8, 2009. He delivered an invited lecture "The Muslim Conquest of Byzantine North Africa" at the Center for Middle Eastern and North African Studies, University of Michigan, Ann Arbor, on November 16, 2009. He read a paper "The Face of Protracted War" at the Dumbarton

Oaks (Harvard) Symposium on Warfare in the Byzantine World, Washington, D.C., on May 2, 2010. He published four book reviews: review of *Being Byzantine*, by Gill Page, in *Journal of Interdisciplinary History* 40 (2010): 586–88; review of *The Crusades and the Christian World of the East*, by Christopher MacEvitt, in *Journal of Religion* 89 (2009): 591–93; review of *Muhammad: Islam's First Great General*, by R. A. Gabriel, in *Journal of Late Antiquity* 2/2(2009): 392–93; and review of *Basil II and the Governance of Empire*, by Catherine Holmes, *Speculum* 84 (2009): 734–36. He continued to serve as president of the U.S. National Committee for Byzantine Studies. At the University of Chicago, he served as a member of the Executive Committee of the local Phi Beta Kappa chapter and as chair of the Nominations Committee for the History Department for selection of a chair for the department. He continued to act as history bibliographer for *Byzantinische Zeitschrift* and as co-director of the Workshop on Late Antiquity and Byzantium. On April 10, 2010, historian William Palmer interviewed him at length via telephone concerning the history of the University of Chicago History Department.

Carol Meyer

Carol Meyer completed her analysis of the ground-stone artifacts from the Tell Hamoukar 2005 and 2006 seasons, barring only some long-awaited locus information. The work includes a working typology of the various ground-stone artifacts, an illustrated checklist for excavators, a draft report of the material, and a new database table with descriptive information, itself linked to other tables with drawings or photographs. Meyer also wrote a report on a Late Chalcolithic deposit of stone artifacts. Judging from the types of stone, the odd assortment of artifacts, and a unique two-foot-tall gypsum "fang," the deposit may be labeled "ritual." Work resumed on the final report on the Bir Umm Fawkhir 1999 excavations and the 2001 study seasons. To date, five chapters out of a projected ten are drafted, including the key chapter on the excavations with all top plans, sections, and matrices. The next major chapter, pottery, is in progress. Meyer also completed a review of *Antinoupolis I* for *Bulletin of the American Society of Papyrologists* and an article on "The Wadi Hammamat" for the new *Encyclopedia of Ancient History*.

Nadine Moeller

In October and November 2009, **Nadine Moeller** directed the annual field season at Tell Edfu in southern Egypt (see separate report). In March she participated at the international conference on Radiocarbon Dating and Egyptian Chronology, which was held in the University of Oxford. The main objective of this colloquium was to advance the synchronization of absolute scientific dating and Egyptian historical chronology. In this regard, the great potential for acquiring new and reliable radiocarbon dates by analyzing samples from Tell Edfu was outlined. The stratified layers at the site extensively cover the transitional and much-disputed periods from the late Middle Kingdom to the Second Intermediate Period, which was the focus of Nadine Moeller's paper. It will be published as part of the forthcoming conference proceedings. The latest discoveries at Tell Edfu were presented at the Annual Meeting of the American Research Center in Egypt, which was held in Oakland, California, at the end of April.

In May, she was invited to give a talk about Tell Edfu to the Visiting Committee, which was well received. At the end of May, the much awaited results of her National Endowment for the Humanities collaborative grant proposal were announced: the Tell Edfu Project was awarded $250,000 for three years, which will allow the pursuit of several research objectives at the site. Meanwhile, the first volume of the Tell Edfu Reports is currently being prepared for publication as well as an article that focuses on the analysis of the data from the 2009 season. These field-work results will be contextualized within the wider perspective of settlement archaeology and will be submitted by September 2010 to the peer-reviewed *Journal of the American Research Center in Egypt*. Moeller published two articles during the past year, one in the festschrift for Barry Kemp edited by Salima Ikram and Aidan Dodson, entitled "The Archaeological Evidence for Town Administration," and one in the French journal *Cahiers de Recherches de l'Institut de Papyrologie et d'Égyptologie de Lille* 28, with the title "The Influence of Royal Power on Ancient Egyptian Settlements from an Archaeological Perspective." Moeller also started new research for her book project entitled *The Settlements of Ancient Egypt*, whose aim is to bring together all the available archeological evidence for towns and cities in ancient Egypt and to provide a wide-ranging analysis of different types of settlements, offering a viable model for urbanism that will explain the role of towns and cities in ancient Egyptian civilization.

Further work also continues on the Mendes archives, which was given to the Oriental Institute last year. The entire collection of site plans and drawings was scanned and is now stored in the archives of the Oriental Institute. The scanning of the numerous slides from the excavation was also started and continues with the help of Jessica Henderson, a graduate student in the Department of Near Eastern Languages and Civilizations.

Dennis Pardee

Since last reporting in these pages, **Dennis Pardee** has for the first time become a productive member of one of the Oriental Institute's own projects — his principal area of research being texts from Ras Shamra, a Syro-French excavation. The text of the inscribed stela dating to the eighth century BC discovered during the Oriental Institute expedition to Zincirli was entrusted to him for publication, and the article appeared in late 2009 ("A New Aramaic Inscription from Zincirli," *Bulletin of the American Schools of Oriental Research* 356: 51–71). The text is important for multiple reasons (religious, historical, social, etc.). Pardee chose to concentrate on the linguistic, identifying the language as a previously unattested dialect of Aramaic situated typologically between the "Samalian" inscriptions left by two kings of the city at the nearby cult site of Gercin and the more-or-less standard Old Aramaic adopted by King Barrakib, plausibly for political reasons in the age of Assyrian hegemony.

An English version of the *Manuel d'ougaritique* (published in 2004 and co-authored with P. Bordreuil) also appeared late in 2009. It contains a brief introduction to the history and culture of ancient Ugarit, a *précis* of Ugaritic grammar, and, like the French version, fifty-five Ugaritic texts representing all the major literary genres, from mythological to school texts. The authors consider this selection of texts to be the principal novelty of the manual, because they are presented in the following forms: new color photographs, new hand copies, transliterations into Roman script, and translation with brief notes. All words represented in the texts are listed in a glossary. The editor, Eisenbrauns, decided to publish this *Manual of Ugaritic* simultaneously in print and electronic versions; the electronic version features hypertext passage from photograph to copy to transliteration/translation.

The discovery of the scribe Thabilu has also continued apace. In his last report, Pardee described the similarities between a text discovered in 1955 at Ras Shamra (RS 19.039) and one discovered forty-three years later at the nearby site of Ras Ibn Hani (RIH 98/02). The text from Ras Shamra bears what Pardee considers to be the "signature" of the scribe (literally, "of Thabilu"), while the identification of that scribe with the text from Ras Ibn Hani is based on palaeographic features. The claim for identity has appeared as "Deux tablettes ougaritiques de la main d'un même scribe, trouvées sur deux sites distincts: RS 19.039 et RIH 98/02" in the new journal coming out of Paris, *Semitica et Classica* 1 (2008): 9–38. While wrapping up loose ends in the study of the Ugaritic texts kept in the Louvre, Pardee moved from the larger and better-preserved mythological texts inscribed by the famous scribe Ilimilku to a series of smaller fragments in different hands. In the process, he became convinced that two of these fragments were also inscribed by Thabilu and that one of these also bears the scribe's signature, an identification previously recognized only by the great Otto Eissfeldt. The reading on the tablet RS 5.229 is ambiguous because only the last sign of the name is well preserved, but the restoration is epigraphically unexceptional, and the scribal hand matches that of the two tablets studied earlier. The other fragment, RS 5.559, even more poorly preserved, bears a sign form absolutely typical of Thabilu and is thus added to this scribe's *œuvre* for palaeographic reasons. The study of these two fragments will appear under the title "RS 5.229: Restitution d'une nouvelle signature du scribe *Thabilu*." Several scholars had remarked the palaeographic similarity between some of these texts and one of the more famous texts — more famous because better preserved — the text that goes under the name of "The Marriage of Nikkal" according to which the West Semitic lunar god Yarihu takes in marriage the Mesopotamian lunar goddess Nikkal. This tablet bears the excavation number RS 5.194, having been discovered very near to the two fragmentary texts just discussed. The palaeographic similarities and the proximity of findspot led Pardee to undertake a full epigraphic study of RS 5.194, and he has concluded that Thabilu is in all likelihood the author of this text as well — though the text bears none of the forms most typical of that scribe, the general *ductus* of the hand is identical to Thabilu's (this study is to appear under the title "RS 5.194 (CTA 24): Nouvelle étude épigraphique suivie de remarques philologiques et littéraires" in *Semitica et Classica* as a follow-up to the first article). The likely existence of three texts from the same area set down by the same scribe led former University of Chicago student Robert Hawley (now with the Centre National de la Recherche Scientifique in Paris) to study the three texts from that same area that are in the Akkadian language but Ugaritic script, and the one in Ugaritic script that bears texts in both Akkadian and Ugaritic. There are good palaeographic reasons to identify these texts also as from the hand of Thabilu, and the same might be said of some of the Hurrian texts in Ugaritic script from that area of the mound. Because the text from Ras Ibn Hani should date to some years before those signed by Ilimilku, it appears plausible that Thabilu was Ilimilku's senior, by as much as half a century or as little as a decade in the time span 1250 to 1200 BC, depending on when the career of each began and ended. Thabilu's work was typically set down on single tablets, while Ilimilku inscribed large multi-columned tablets that fit into series (at least six for the Baal story, three for Kirta, and three for Aqhat). All but one of Ilimilku's tablets were discovered on the Acropolis of Ras Shamra, while the findspots of Thabilu's works are more diverse: the neighboring site of Ras Ibn Hani, the royal palace at Ugarit, and the area on the west side of the Acropolis that was excavated during the fifth campaign in 1933. It appears likely that Thabilu inscribed texts in Ugaritic, Akkadian, and Hurrian, but all in Ugaritic script. It is debated whether the Ilimilku who signed several Ugaritic tablets may be identified with one of the scribes by the same name known to have worked in Akkadian, but if the identification of Thabilu as the scribe of these multiple documents is correct, then this scribe was not only bilingual but also "biscriptal," for his Akkadian works would all be in the syllabic cuneiform script that was at home in Mesopotamia. It would also appear that Thabilu's interests were broader: he inscribed not only Akkadian and Hurrian religious texts, but also mythological, lyric, and divinatory texts in Ugaritic.

Seth Richardson

Seth Richardson saw several long-term projects come to fruition this past year, including the publication of an edited volume on rebellions and political life in the cuneiform world, a study of Old Babylonian divinatory literature, and an update to his online database of personal names from seventeenth-century BC documents. His volume of late Old Babylonian texts is now in preparation for publication, as well as a number of other small notes and reviews. He enjoyed meeting with colleagues and speaking in Los Angeles, Cambridge, St. Louis, and New Orleans, and he looks forward to a new year busy with new book and article projects, as well as panels he has organized in Atlanta and Boston at the American Schools of Oriental Research and American Historical Association meetings.

Robert K. Ritner

In late October, **Robert Ritner**'s volume *The Libyan Anarchy: Inscriptions from Egypt's Third Intermediate Period* was published by the Society of Biblical Literature and Brill for the series Writings from the Ancient World. The volume provides translations, transliterations, and textual commentary for the primary documents of Egyptian history, society, and religion from approximately 1100 to 650 BC, when Egypt was ruled by Libyan and Nubian dynasties and had occasional relations with Judah and the encroaching Assyrian empire. The 176 texts collected in the volume include first editions as well as re-edited inscriptions and chronicle the collapse of a unified Egypt into multiple, local states with titular "pharaohs" and ruling princes of Libyan ancestry (Dynasties Twenty-one to Twenty-four), the relatively superficial control of Nubian imperialism (Dynasty Twenty-five), and the ultimate reunification of the state by rulers of Sais (Dynasty Twenty-six). A significant underlying feature of the collapse and recovery is the intrusion and later suppression of Libyan tribal features; see Ritner's contributions in *Annual Report*s for 2007–2008 and 2008–2009.

Ritner's further publications during the year include an analysis of a Pyramid Text spell that likely inspired a critical episode in Demotic literature: "Setna's Spell of Taking Security (Setna I, col. IV/31–34)," published in *Honi soit qui mal y pense: Studien zum pharaonischen, griechisch-römischen und spätantiken Ägypten zu Ehren von Heinz-Josef Thissen*, edited by Hermann Knuf, Christian Leitz, and Daniel von Recklinghausen, pp. 425–28 (Orientalia Lovaniensia Analecta 194; Leuven and Walpole: Peeters, 2010). His study of "Two Third Intermediate Period Books of the Dead: P. Houston 31.72 and P. Brooklyn 37.1801E," published in *Millions of Jubilees: Studies in Honor of David P. Silverman*, edited by Zahi Hawass and Jennifer Wegner, pp. 591–608 (Cahiers 2; Cairo: Supreme Counsel of Antiquities of Égypte, 2010), examined two funerary texts prepared for women engaged as chantresses in the cults of the Theban gods Amon, Mut, and Khonsu. The publication of the Houston papyrus marks the beginning of Ritner's fuller study and complete catalog of the Egyptian collection of the Museum of Fine Arts, Houston.

The issue of chantresses of the Third Intermediate Period was again treated by Ritner in an online response to the Oriental Institute's recent exhibit on Meresamun. His "Reading the Coffin of Meresamun" provides critical, but overlooked, information regarding the text and decoration of Meresamun's coffin, yielding both the name of her father and, far more importantly, the name of the "universalist" deity that she invoked and presumably served: "Ra-Horachty-Atum, Lord of the Two Lands, the Heliopolitan, Ptah-Sokar-Osiris, Lord of the Sanctuary of Sokar, Onnophrios ('The Perfect Being'), Lord of the Sacred Land, the Great God, Lord of Heaven." This composite name, uniting two trinities of solar and underworld gods, is strikingly addressed by the singular "he" and represents a further example of a theological statement of "one unified god" securely linked to the little temple of Medinet Habu. Meresamun's coffin is significant in providing the only example of a woman associated with this theological development. The article appears on the Oriental Institute's Web site: http://oi.uchicago.edu/research/is/reading_coffin_meresamun. html.

Ritner was particularly active on the lecture circuit, speaking on "The Nubian Pharaohs and Their Rule in Egypt" at the Clay Center in Charleston, West Virginia, in conjunction with the exhibit Lost Kingdoms of the Nile: Treasures from the Museum of Fine Arts, Boston (January 20). In Philadelphia on March 12, he delivered the keynote address "Aspects of Cushite 'Egyptianization': Piety, Prestige and Propaganda" for the Center for Ancient Studies at the University of Pennsylvania's second annual graduate student conference The Sincerest Form of Flattery: Emulation and Imitation in the Ancient World. On April 9, he spoke in Ann Arbor at the Midwest Consortium in Ancient Religions session on "The Hymns of Isidorus from Medinet Madi," explaining the pantheistic nature of Isis "The One" in "Thiouis at Medinet Madi." On April 16, he concluded the seventh annual Legacy of Egypt lecture series at the University of Memphis, with a discussion of "Curses and Love Charms in Ancient Egypt." On May 13, for the Classical Art Society of the Art Institute of Chicago, he contrasted the differing artistic traditions of Egypt and Greece and their exceptional interactions in "The Legacy of Thoth-Hermes: Cross-cultural Interactions in Hellenistic Egypt." In late May, he was an invited participant at the conference Problems of Canonicity and Identity Formation in Ancient Egypt and Mesopotamia, held at the University of Copenhagen, where he provided a discussion of "'King Petemenekh': New Kingdom Royal Sarcophagi Texts on a Private Coffin" (May 27).

In addition to research, he taught courses on Coptic and hieroglyphic texts and grammar and served on multiple committees for the Oriental Institute and the Department of Near Eastern Languages and Civilizations.

———————————

Yorke M. Rowan

In July–August 2009, **Yorke M. Rowan** began a new field project in Israel, excavations at Marj Rabba (see separate report). Marj Rabba is a prehistoric site roughly dating to the mid-fifth to early fourth millennium BC, commonly termed the Chalcolithic period. These excavations seek to understand how the people in the Galilee differed in terms of social, political, and economic organization in contrast to other regions such as the Golan, Jordan Valley, and Negev, where most excavations of Chalcolithic sites have taken place. This initial season indicates that the site is well preserved and possibly more extensive than originally projected.

Yorke participated in a number of national and international conferences during the academic year. In August, he attended the World Archaeology Inter-congress meetings held in Ramallah, for which he served on the organizing committee and co-organized (with Morag Kersel) the session Looting, Landscape and Law. In September, he and David Ilan presented the paper "Reconstituting the Dead: Ossuaries in the Chalcolithic of the Southern Levant" at the Annual Meetings of the European Association of Archaeologists in Riva del Garda, Italy. In November, he presented "Between Household and Landscape: Searching for Chalcolithic Communities" in the session Archaeology of Prehistoric Communities, Theoretical Concerns: The Placing and Spacing of Prehistoric Communities, which he co-organized with Meredith Chesson for the Annual Meetings of the American Schools of Oriental Research held in New Orleans. With Morag Kersel, he presented "It's a Small World After All: Tourism and Representation of the Past at Mini-Israel" for a session on Tourism, Archaeology and Development at the Annual Meetings of the American Anthropological Association held in Philadelphia in December.

In January 2010, Yorke was invited to participate in the Centre national de la recherche scientifique–sponsored workshop Electronic Publications and Knowledge Bases: Grinding Material as a Case Study, held at the Institut National d'Histoire de l'Art in Paris, where he presented a lecture entitled "Diachronic Change in Late Prehistoric Ground Stone Assemblage from the Southern Levant." Also related to his interest in analyses of ground-stone artifacts, Yorke was invited to serve as a discussant for the session Understanding the Uses of Ground Stone Tools: New Directions and Developments held on April 17 at the Annual Meetings of the Society for American Archaeology held in St. Louis. In March, he was invited to present his ideas concerning prehistoric interactions between the Levant and Egypt at a brown-bag lunch at the Joukowsky Institute for Archaeology and the Ancient World at Brown University, where he gave the lecture "Crossing the Nile: Early Evidence for Levantine and Egyptian Interaction."

During February, Yorke hosted Ofer Marder, head of the Prehistory Branch of the Israel Antiquities Authority, who was visiting the Oriental Institute in order to study the Megiddo flint assemblage as part of the Megiddo Stages Publication Project directed by Eliot Braun. Yorke also acted as a moderator for Israelite Archaeology and Contemporary Israeli Identity: Reconstructions of Modern Antiquity in Modern Israel, a conference organized by David Schloen and Josef Stern (director, Center for Jewish Studies), held at the Oriental Institute on April 30.

With co-editor Jaimie Lovell, Yorke submitted the manuscript for "Culture, Chronology and the Chalcolithic: Theory and Transition" to the copy editor. Yorke also has published his review of *Stone Vessels in the Levant*, by Rachael T. Sparks, in *Bulletin of the American Schools of Oriental Research* 358: 76–77, and his co-authored chapter (with J. Forsen) "Ground Stone and Small Artifacts from Area C" appeared in the volume *Khirbat Iskandar: Final Report on the Early Bronze IV Area C "Gateway" and Cemeteries*, edited by Suzanne Richard, Jesse Lang, Paul Holsdorf, and Glen Peterman, pp. 145–58 (Archaeological Reports 14; Boston: American Schools for Oriental Research, 2010).

Foy Scalf

Foy Scalf and project co-founder Jackie Jay were pleased to officially launch the Oriental Institute Demotic Ostraca Online (OIDOO) project during the academic year of 2009–2010 (http://oi.uchicago.edu/research/projects/oidoo/). Now, full editions and Museum registry information for nearly 300 Demotic ostraca from the Oriental Institute collection are accessible through this online database, which provides researchers with exciting new methods for manipulating the data from these texts, including complex searching and sorting functions. Foy and Jackie will continue to edit new material and update the database periodically until the Oriental Institute's collection of nearly 900 Demotic ostraca is completed.

In November, Foy arrived in Edfu for the final weeks of Nadine Moeller's excavation in order to examine Demotic ostraca that Moeller's team discovered during the season. These constitute a growing corpus of administrative material, which, combined with the Demotic ostraca excavated during previous seasons, offers interesting insights into the local administration of Edfu during the Ptolemaic period. Following the excavation, Foy assisted Moeller as she escorted an exceptional group of travelers with the Splendors of the Nile Tour on behalf of the Oriental Institute. In addition to reading Egyptian inscriptions in answering passengers' questions, Foy edited a blog for the tour members to record their trip while sharing photos and memories (http://oisplendorsofthenile.blogspot.com/).

During the Winter Quarter, Foy taught an eight-week continuing-education class for the Oriental Institute, Temples of Greco-Roman Egypt. Several dedicated students from that class continued their introduction to Greco-Roman Egypt during the Spring Quarter in Foy's course, History of Ptolemaic and Roman Egypt. Proving surprisingly popular, the history course attracted a large class of eager students who left with a new understanding and appreciation of the "later" periods of Egyptian history.

Foy gave several lectures in the fall. On October 14, he spoke at Wheaton College on "The Mechanics of the Ptolemaic Economy in Egypt" as a part of a class on ancient Mediterranean economies, which included fellow Oriental Institute scholars Dennis Pardee, Matthew Stolper, and post-doctoral seminar alum Seth Sanders. On October 17, Foy presented "The Process of Creation according to the Ancient Egyptians" at the Oriental Institute as part of a mini-series on creation myths in the ancient Near East, complemented by the lectures of Andrea Seri, Theo van den Hout, and Margaret Mitchell.

Foy's article "Magical Bricks in the Oriental Institute Museum of the University of Chicago" appeared in *Studien zur altägyptischen Kultur* 38 (2009): 275–95, and "Is That a Rhetorical Question? Shipwrecked Sailor (pHermitage 1115), 150 Reconsidered" appeared in *Zeitschrift für Ägyptische Sprache und Altertumskunde* 136/2 (2009): 155–59. Foy's review of *Cleopatra Beyond the Myth*, by M. Chaveau, and review of *Cleopatra: A Sourcebook*, by Prudence Jones, appeared in *Journal of Near Eastern Studies* 69 (2010): 108–09.

Andrea Seri

Andrea Seri presented a paper entitled "On Female Domestic Slaves during the Old Babylonian Period" at the sixth annual University of Chicago Oriental Institute Seminar dealing with Slaves and Households in the Ancient Near East that took place March 5–6, 2010. She was also invited to give a lecture on "Intertextuality in *Enūma eliš*" at the University of Notre Dame on

March 31, 2010. Between March 24 and 26, Andrea participated in the Berkeley Prosopography Project workshop, hosted by the University of California at Berkeley, where she worked with scholars from Berkeley, Philadelphia, Germany, and the Netherlands on Mesopotamian prosopographies.

Andrea reviewed volume 14 of *Altbabylonische Briefe* for the journal *Bibliotheca Orientalis*. She submitted an article entitled "Borrowings to Create Anew: Intertextuality in the Babylonian Poem of Creation," to be published in an anniversary volume. She wrote a paper on "The Adaptation of Cuneiform to Write Akkadian" that will appear in the catalog of the Oriental Institute forthcoming exhibit on first writing systems. During the academic year, Andrea finished the draft of her second book *The House of Prisoners: State and Slavery in Uruk During the Revolt against Samsu-iluna*, which she plans to submit for publication at the end of the summer. Andrea has also reviewed articles for the *Journal of Near Eastern Studies*, she evaluated a research project for the Universidad de Buenos Aires, and in January 2010 she became a member of the Oriental Institute publications committee.

Oğuz Soysal

Oğuz Soysal continued his job with the Chicago Hittite Dictionary (CHD) Project. Much of his time was spent writing articles on words beginning with *tu* and preparing the transliterations of the recent cuneiform editions, *Keilschrifttexte aus Boğazköi* volumes 47 and 58, for the CHD files. His personal research has continued to focus on Hittite history/culture and the Hattian language. Soysal published the following articles in 2009/2010: "Zu den Trinkgefäßen bei den Hethitern auch in Verbindung mit Kulttrinken," in *Festschrift für Gernot Wilhelm anlässlich seines 65. Geburtstages am 28. Januar 2010*, edited by Jeanette Fincke, pp. 335–54 (Dresden: Islet, 2009), and "Zum Namen der Göttin Kataḫzipuri mit besonderer Berücksichtigung des Kasussystems des Hattischen," in *Language in the Ancient Near East*, edited by L. Kogan, N. Koslova, S. Loesov, and S. Tischenko, pp. 1041–58 (Proceedings of the 53[e] Rencontre Assyriologique Internationale; Babel and Bibel 4; Orientalia et Classica 30; Winona Lake: Eisenbrauns, 2010). He also published an extensive review article of *Keilschrifttexte aus Boghazköi* volume 53, by J. L. Miller, with the title "On Recent Cuneiform Editions of Hittite Fragments (I)," *Journal of the American Oriental Society* 129 (2009): 295–306, and two entries "Šanku" and "Šarmaššu" in the German series *Reallexikon der Assyriologie* volume 12, part 1/2 (2009): 24, 69.

Furthermore, five articles including three contributions for a festschrift and for *Reallexikon der Assyriologie*, as well as a book review to be submitted to the *Journal of the Near Eastern Studies*, have been prepared and are awaiting publication.

In addition, Soysal, in cooperation with Rukiye Akdoğan and Tom Urban, has made the final corrections to the cuneiform publication entitled *Ankara Arkeoloji Müzesinde Bulunan Boğazköy Tabletleri* II, which is to be published by the Oriental Institute in early 2011.

Gil J. Stein

In July–August 2009, **Gil J. Stein** conducted the second field season as American co-director of the Joint Syrian-American excavations at Tell Zeidan. Located 5 km east of the modern city of Raqqa in the Euphrates River valley at its juncture with the Balikh River, Tell Zeidan is a 12.5 hectare regional center dating to the Halaf, Ubaid, and Late Chalcolithic 1–2 periods (ca. 5800–4000 BC). A fuller description of the excavations is presented in the Tell Zeidan report (this volume).

Gil has also continued with the work toward publication of his 1992–1997 excavations at Hacınebi, a fourth-millennium BC Uruk Mesopotamian colony in the Euphrates valley of southeast Turkey. Oriental Institute volunteer Iren Glasner has been scanning slides and inked object drawings, while Dr. Belinda Monahan has been refining our typology of local Anatolian and Mesopotamian Uruk ceramic types, and identifying parallels at contemporaneous sites in Turkey, Syria, and Iraq. With over 71,000 coded diagnostics (rims, handles, bases, decorated sherds), Hacınebi has one of the largest stratigraphically excavated ceramic data sets currently available for this time period in the Near East. Once published, we hope that the Hacınebi ceramic sequence can make a significant contribution to our understanding of Uruk Mesopotamia and the world's earliest-known colonial network.

Gil has given a series of lectures and presentations over the past year. In October 2009, he spoke to the University of Chicago Womens' Board on the topic "Archaeology in the Heartland of Cities: The Oriental Institute's current work in Mesopotamia and the Near East." In November 2009 Gil gave a lecture at the Arts Club of Chicago on "Cities of the Plain: The Two Urbanizations of Mesopotamia." In December 2009, he presented a lecture at the Carsten Niebuhr Institute at the University of Copenhagen on the topic "The Ubaid Period in Upper Mesopotamia: Complexity, Social Identity and Inter-regional Interaction." In April 2010, Gil presented a paper at the 7th International Congress on the Archaeology of the Ancient Near East (ICAANE) at the British Museum, London, titled "The Joint Syrian-American Excavations at Tell Zeidan: Investigations of the Ubaid and Late Chalcolithic 1–2 in North Syria."

In 2010, Gil published one book chapter "Local Identities and Interaction Spheres: Modeling Regional Variation in the 'Ubaid Horizon" in the volume *Beyond the Ubaid: Transformation and Integration in the Late Prehistoric Societies of the Middle East*, edited by Robert Carter and Graham Philip (Studies in Ancient Oriental Civilization 63; Chicago: The Oriental Institute of the University of Chicago, 2010).

Emily Teeter

With the delivery of manuscripts on the baked clay figurines from Medinet Habu and on religious cults in Egypt to their respective publishers, **Emily Teeter** has turned to several other projects — a source book of readings on Egyptian religion to appear in the Cambridge Companion to Ancient Mediterranean Religions and another source-book project for the Society of Biblical Literature. She also contributed two chapters to the catalog for the Pioneers to the Past exhibit, an entry to the UCLA online Encyclopedia of Egyptology, and a book review to the *Journal of Near Eastern Studies*.

She gave innumerable tours and talks about Meresamun, including one to the International Women's Association and another (with Michael Vannier and Josh Harker) for the University of

Chicago Humanities Day. Emily also spoke in the Works of the Mind Series on "Egyptomania! James Henry Breasted and the Birth of America Egyptology" in conjunction with the Pioneers to the Past exhibit.

Emily attended several meetings of the Board of the American Research Center as well as the Annual Meeting held in Oakland. In April she escorted a group from the University of Toronto and the Art Institute of Chicago to Egypt and Jordan, with a few spare days to meet with American Research Center in Egypt staff in Cairo.

Theo van den Hout

Besides his work as chair of the Department of Near Eastern Languages and Civilizations (NELC), on the Chicago Hittite Dictionary, and his classes, **Theo van den Hout** submitted several manuscripts for articles. Two of these were in connection with conferences he attended: one on administration in the Hittite Empire held in Pavia, Italy (see last year's report), the other in Leiden in December of 2009 on palaeography and the origins of the Hittite cuneiform script. A shorter German version of the latter was delivered late in January 2010 in Berlin, while a somewhat more popularized version will appear in the catalog for the upcoming special exhibit Visible Language: Inventions of Writing in the Ancient Middle East and Beyond here at the Oriental Institute. It has long been unclear from whom the Hittites borrowed their cuneiform script. It looks Babylonian but cannot have been adopted straight from there, both from the point of view of specific sign shapes and for historical reasons. The much closer north Syrian area and especially the town of Alalakh have been mentioned as a possible source, but the script of the latter settlement, although quite similar, also seems to show some deviations that always stood in the way of an easy identification. Now, a careful palaeographic analysis of the Alalakh cuneiform variant and some traits of the oldest Hittite texts that had been largely ignored in the past make Alalakh and the north Syrian area a very likely candidate as the direct source of the Hittite script. Historically, it fits well since the Old Hittite kings Hattusili I and his grandson Mursili I campaigned actively in that part of the ancient Near East in the second half of the seventeenth century BC.

Other manuscripts submitted by Theo in the past year included a contribution to a festschrift for a colleague (on so-called wood scribes), one on Hittite historiography, and one for a volume on Anatolia for Oxford University Press. Theo also submitted to Cambridge University Press the final manuscript of his textbook *The Elements of Hittite*, due out this year. Apart from the conferences already mentioned in Leiden and Berlin in the winter, Theo was one of the speakers at the Oriental Institute mini-series on Creation Stories in October.

Since the previous *Annual Report,* the following publications have appeared in print: "A Century of Hittite Text Dating and the Origins of the Hittite Cuneiform Script," *Incontri Linguistici* 32 (2009): 11–35; "Reflections on the Origins and Development of the Hittite Tablet Collections in Ḫattuša and Their Consequences for the Rise of Hittite Literacy," in *Central-north Anatolia in the Hittite Period: New Perspectives in Light of Recent Research*, edited by F. Pecchioli Daddi, G. Torri, and C. Corti, pp. 71–96 (Acts of the International Conference Held at the University of Florence, February 7–9, 2007; Studi Asiana 5; Rome: Herder, 2009); "Randnotizen zu einigen Briefen aus Maşat Höyük," in *Festschrift für Gernot Wilhelm anlässlich seines 65. Geburtstages am 28. Januar 2010*, edited by Jeanette Fincke, pp. 394–402 (Dresden: Islet,

2009); "A Note on Hittite Envelopes and HKM 86" (with Cem Karasu), in *Pax Hethitica: Studies on the Hittites and Their Neighbours in Honour of Itamar Singer*, edited by Yoram Cohen, Amir Gilan, and Jared L. Miller, pp. 372–77 (Studien zu den Boğazköy Texten 51; Wiesbaden: Harrassowitz, 2010), 372–77. Two long entries came out in the *Reallexikon der Assyriologie* volume 12: "Schaf. B. Bei den Hethitern," pp. 121–26, and "Schreiber. D. Bei den Hethitern," pp. 273–80. Finally, Theo wrote a brief article for children on the Luwian Hieroglyphic script entitled "Let's Talk Luwian," in *Dig*, February 2010, p. 22.

Donald Whitcomb

Donald Whitcomb left the last account of the individual research happily engaged in archaeological visits and research based at Hebrew University in Jerusalem. With the end of the school year, Donald's wife Janet Johnson was able to make her first visit to Israel. Of course this meant tours, but with a difference: Gideon Avni generously showed both around Jerusalem, including some places Don had not seen before; then they went to Caesarea with Ken Holum, its long-time excavator (and Yael Arnon, who engaged them in lively debates on multitudes of archaeological problems for the Islamic periods — more than Jan wished to hear). Next, they participated in an impromptu workshop organized by Edna Stern and Katherine Burke on Islamic ceramics. Then he took a trip south for a conference at Ben Gurion University in Beersheva, but mainly an excuse to visit a few of the sites in the Negev (Donald did try his hand at "gender archaeology" with a paper on the "Ladies of Quseir").

Jan returned to Chicago in early July, just before Don participated in the "From Jahiliyya to Islam" conference; this is a very prestigious event at Hebrew University, which included a day of archaeological papers this year. He revised some old ideas on the origins of the mosque before a very knowledgeable and critical audience. In the last few weeks, Don wrapped up some long-standing papers on Islamic archaeology of Caesarea and Jerusalem. He was able to visit Rafi Greenberg's excavations at Khirbat Kerak (Beit Yerach), a site well known to the Oriental Institute. This year Rafi was working with a talented archaeologist, Taufik Dea'dle, on the Islamic component hoping to confirm Don's ideas on its medieval importance as Sinnabra. Both Rafi and Taufik are actively engaged in Community Archaeology, the involvement of local populations both Arab and Jewish in their understanding and appreciation of their archaeological heritage, in what Rafi calls "multivocular" approaches.

Finally, just before leaving Israel, Donald was able to attend a conference by the World Archaeological Congress in Ramallah. This was a wonderful opportunity to renew his acquaintance and meet many Palestinian archaeologists and hear about progress on the

West Bank. Don spoke with Hamdan Taha, director of the Palestinian Department of Archaeology, about his hopes for the site of Khirbat al-Mafjar. With the strong encouragement of Gil Stein, this led to a special visit to Ramallah, in March, for detailed plans for this site. Thus, the spring presentation of archaeological projects of the Oriental Institute included its newest, and very prestigeous, excavation plans for the site of Khirbat al-Mafjar. The site is a magnificent early Islamic palace com-

Hamdan Taha at the place entrance of Khirbat al-Mafjar

Gideon Avni and Taufik Dea'dle examine plans of Kkirbat Kerak

plex filled with magnificent mosaics, stuccos, and — well, this will be the subject of a special report next year (*Inshallah*).

Karen L. Wilson

During the past year, **Karen L. Wilson** continued to work on the final publication of the Oriental Institute excavations at the sites of Nippur and Abu Salabikh in Iraq during the late 1950s and early 1960s. This project is sponsored by a grant awarded to McGuire Gibson by the National Endowment for the Humanities and is a joint endeavor undertaken with Robert Biggs, Jean Evans, McGuire Gibson (University of Chicago), and Richard Zettler (University of Pennsylvania). The project so far has included the preparation of a digital catalog of finds linked with images of the objects, plus the scanning of all negatives and drawings as well as the field records generated by work on the sites. A draft of a final publication covering the results of the excavation of the Inanna Temple at Nippur is planned to be completed by the end of 2010.

Karen also continued to serve as Kish Project Coordinator at the Field Museum, preparing the final publication of the results of the Joint Field Museum and Oxford University Expedition to Kish in 1923–1933. That publication will include papers presented at a symposium in November 2008 focusing on current research and excavations at the site. Contributions will include studies of the human remains, textual evidence, lithics, animal figurines, and stucco as well as a catalog of the Field Museum holdings from the site.

Karen's book, *Bismaya: Recovering the Lost City of Adab*, which chronicles and presents the results of the University of Chicago's first expedition to Iraq in 1903–1905, is currently in press at the Oriental Institute Publications Office.

Christopher Woods

Christopher Woods devoted this past year to several projects involving Sumerian literature, language, and writing. Finally, Chris's article "At the Edge of the World: Cosmological Conceptions of the Eastern Horizon in Mesopotamia" appeared in print in the *Journal of Near Eastern Religions* (2009). Another article, "Grammar and Context: Enki and Ninhursag ll. 1–3 and a Curious Sumerian Construction," completed this year and slated for a festschrift, offers a new grammatical understanding and interpretation of the problematic first lines of the famous Sumerian creation myth, Enki and Ninhursag. Also completed this year are an article for the Cambridge History of Linguistics that concerns indigenous traditions of grammatical thought in Mesopotamia, an article ("New Light on the Sumerian Language") for the Canadian Society for Mesopotamian Studies, which is based on a lecture Chris gave before that society last year, and a note on subordinate clauses to appear in Cornell University Studies in Assyriology and Sumerology 6.

In April Chris organized, with Andréas Stauder, a conference, "Linguistic Method and Theory and the Languages of the Ancient Near East," where Chris gave the paper "The Morphographic Basis of Sumerian Writing." Chris and Andréas plan to publish the proceedings of the conference, which focused on the research currently conducted in this area by Oriental Institute faculty and graduate students. A great deal of time was devoted to curating our special exhibit, Visible Language: Inventions of Writing in the Ancient Middle East and Beyond, set to open in late September. The catalog Chris edited includes two of his articles "Visible Language: The Earliest Writing Systems" and "The Earliest Mesopotamian Writing."

RESEARCH SUPPORT
COMPUTER LABORATORY
John C. Sanders

Projects

Integrated Database

It always takes longer than one initially thinks! Twenty years after proposing a merger of all the Oriental Institute's records, documents, photographs, and field records into a single integrated computer database (IDB), and after months of our people talking to their people, dotting all the I's and crossing all the T's, we signed the contract with KE Software on July 13, 2010, for the purchase and installation of their EMu (Electronic Museum) database system! Yes, technically, this date is two weeks into this new fiscal year, but I could not wait until next year's *Annual Report* to announce the good news.

Many people within the Institute and in the university's Information Technology Services (ITS) unit worked hard over the past few years to help us reach this point. And, of course, now the work really begins anew for many of the same cast of characters as the integrated database system is installed and starts to operate for the faculty, staff, and general public. While not meaning to leave anyone's participation out, which I am sure I will, let me thank by name the following individuals: former Oriental Institute directors William Sumner and Gene Gragg, and current director Gil Stein; faculty and staff members Steve Camp, Scott Branting, Geoff Emberling, Thomas James, Carole Krucoff, Wendy Ennes, Helen McDonald, Susan Allison, Ray Tindel, John Larson, Laura D'Alessandro, Alison Whyte, Thomas Urban, Foy Scalf, and Charles Jones; and from ITS, Edward Jakubas, Kaylea Champion, Robert Griffith, and John Gronke. And special recognition is due our database volunteer over the past decade, George Sundell. Thank you all; it wouldn't have happened without your over-the-top efforts!

Software installation and training will start in November 2010, with data migration to follow over the winter, and we should be up and running the new integrated database in the spring of 2011. I will report on all these stages in next year's *Annual Report*.

Although we will start this year with only our Museum Registration database and our Research Archives (Library) Catalog moved to the new IDB system, if I might be permitted to gaze into a crystal ball for future predictions, the IDB in perhaps five to ten years will contain the following Institute records and data:

- Museum Registration: paper records and various computer database files; 180,000 registered objects, 150,000 unregistered objects. Annual expansion is uneven, but 5,000 to 10,000 unregistered objects are registered.

- Museum Conservation: paper records and various computer database files; 75,000 analysis and treatment records, and images. Annual expansion circa 2,000–8,000 records and images.

- Museum Archives: paper documents, field records, and photographic negatives and prints. 10,000,000 paper documents, 200,000 images and prints. Annual expansion circa 20,000 records, images, and prints.

- Research Archives (Library): paper records and online catalog; 250,000 records in our current online library catalog, 400,000 cards from the Institute's former library card catalog, 40,000 additional records to finish retrospective cataloging. Annual expansion circa 10,000 records.

- Research Archives (Library): ancient Near Eastern map collections; 4,000 paper maps. Annual expansion circa 50 maps.

- Satellite and aerial photographic imagery (both rectified and non-rectified images); 7,500 image files at present. Annual expansion circa 10,000 images per year for the next three years.

- Oriental Institute publications; 500 publications in Adobe PDF files. Annual expansion circa 10 Adobe PDF files.

Electronic Publications Initiative

Once again, this past year saw major progress with the Institute's Electronic Publications Initiative. Fifty-two electronic versions of current or past Institute publications, in Adobe Portable Document Format (PDF), were made available for free download on the Institute's Web site. The vast majority of these new downloadable publications pertain to ancient Egypt, and now all of the Institute's Egyptian-related publications are available electronically. As in previous years, the costs for their electronic preparation were offset by a most generous gift from Misty and Lewis Gruber. Their support of our Egyptological research is greatly appreciated.

Additionally, three new letter volumes (Ḥ, W, and Š) for the Chicago Demotic Dictionary project were finished this past year, converted to PDF, and were made available for free download on the Institute's Web site.

The Institute's Electronic Publications Initiative dictates that current and future print publications produced by the Oriental Institute Publications Office are also made available electronically through the Institute's Web site. I encourage everyone to read that portion of the Publications Office section of this *Annual Report* regarding the status of the Institute's Electronic Publications Initiative, then visit the Catalog of Publications page on our Web site, where you can download these past and current titles of our publications in electronic form:

http://oi.uchicago.edu/research/pubs/catalog/

A list of the volume titles, which were processed into digital format and made available to the public on the Institute's Web site during this past year, can be found in the Electronic Resources section of this *Annual Report*.

Currently, 273 Oriental Institute publications are available as PDFs. When fully implemented, our Electronic Publications Initiative will make accessible all 400+ titles in our Publications Office catalog.

The Oriental Institute Web Site

A major, and important, backlog of electronic publications on our Web site was eliminated this year with the addition of all Institute *News & Notes* newsletters from the current Spring 2010 issue back through 2002, now available as PDFs. Select lead articles in *News & Notes* published between 1990 and 2001 remain available on the Web site, but in HTML format. As time permits over the next year or two, these editions will be converted to the Adobe PDF format, along with as many pre-1990 *News & Notes* publications as we can find in our archives.

Dr. Seth Richardson's "Late Old Babylonian Personal Names Index" was added to the Philology Research Projects component of the Web site. This searchable file of personal names derives from cuneiform texts chiefly dating to the reigns of the last three kings of the First Dynasty of Babylon, 1683–1595 B.C. Version 1 indexes 13,573 unique attestations of personal names from almost 3,000 texts, including 4,678 entries from around 700 unpublished texts.

Audio tours of the Oriental Institute Museum galleries were made available for free download from the Web site this past year, so that you can use your own iPod or other MP3 player to take any or all of our special tours. Current tours are "Highlights of the Collection of the Oriental Institute," a tour of "The Ancient Near East in the Time of Tutankhamun," and a special "Ancient Egypt for Kids" tour.

A new photographic exhibit, "Breasted's 1919–1920 Expedition to the Near East," was added to the Museum component of the Web site in May. These 1,875 photographs chronicle Illinois native James Henry Breasted's daring travels through Egypt and Mesopotamia in the unstable aftermath of World War I. Breasted, a leading Egyptologist, was the founder of the Oriental Institute at the University of Chicago, and this journey was the first Oriental Institute project. The goals of his ambitious expedition were to acquire artifacts for the new Institute and to select sites for later excavation.

Persepolis Fortification Archive

The Computer Lab continued to assist the ongoing collaboration of scholars, support staff in the university's Humanities Computing Department and Regenstein Library, and a small army of graduate students from the University of Chicago who are imaging and recording the Persepolis Fortification Archive (PFA) tablets. Two additional computers for image capture and processing were set up in the project's third-floor facilities, and I stayed abreast of the scanning operations as they progressed throughout the year.

For additional information regarding this project, please read the Persepolis Fortification Archive section of this *Annual Report,* where project director Matthew Stolper outlines in detail the current progress of the scanning and cataloging of these most important ancient texts. Also, up-to-date information about the project's work is available in the Persepolis Fortification Archive component on the Oriental Institute Web site.

* * * * * * * * * *

For further information concerning the above-mentioned research projects and other electronic resources in general, refer to the What's New page on the Oriental Institute's Web site, at

http://oi.uchicago.edu/news/

See the Electronic Resources section of this *Annual Report* for the complete URL to each of the Web site resources mentioned in this article.

ELECTRONIC RESOURCES

John C. Sanders

Oriental Institute World-Wide Web Site

Several Oriental Institute units and projects either updated existing pages or became a new presence on the Institute's Web site during the past year.

ARCHAEOLOGY: Nubian Expedition

The Oriental Institute's return to Nubia in 2006 and 2007 for archaeological field work is detailed on our new Nubian Expedition pages. Between January and March 2007, the Oriental Institute joined international teams in the 4th Cataract region in archaeological investigation of the area, an area that had, prior to the salvage project, received virtually no attention.

> http://oi.uchicago.edu/research/projects/oine/

ARCHAEOLOGY: Adopt-a-Dig Program

The Oriental Institute is launching its Adopt-a-Dig program, which creates a new partnership of discovery between you, our supporters, and the field researchers whose projects are rewriting the history of the rise of civilization. With seven active digs in Egypt, Israel, Syria, and Turkey, you now have the opportunity to partner with field projects that closely match your own interests.

> https://oi.uchicago.edu/getinvolved/donate/adoptadig/

PHILOLOGY: Chicago Demotic Dictionary

Chicago Demotic Dictionary publishes letter Ḥ.

> http://oi.uchicago.edu/research/pubs/catalog/cdd/

Chicago Demotic Dictionary publishes letter W.

> http://oi.uchicago.edu/research/pubs/catalog/cdd/

Chicago Demotic Dictionary publishes letter Š.

> http://oi.uchicago.edu/research/pubs/catalog/cdd/

PHILOLOGY: Chicago Hittite Dictionary

A new brochure, The Oriental Institute Chicago Hittite Dictionary Project, describing the project's on-going work on the Chicago Hittite Dictionary and its *e*CHD component is now available for electronic download in the Adobe PDF format.

> http://oi.uchicago.edu/pdf/chd_brochure_2010.pdf

MUSEUM: Audio Tours

Audio tours of the Oriental Institute Museum galleries are now available for free download so that you can use your own iPod or other MP3 player to take any or all of our special tours. Current tours are Highlights of the Collection of the Oriental Institute, a tour of The Ancient Near East in the Time of Tutankhamun, and a special Ancient Egypt for Kids tour.

> http://oi.uchicago.edu/museum/tours/audio.html

MUSEUM: Special Exhibits

A brief description and several images from the Oriental Institute Museum's upcoming special exhibit, Visible Language: Inventions of Writing in the Ancient Middle East and Beyond, to run from September 27, 2010, through March 6, 2011.

http://oi.uchicago.edu/museum/special/writing/

MUSEUM: Egyptian Highlights from the Collection

The Highlights from the Collection Web page for Ancient Egypt has been updated. Thirteen objects from the Oriental Institute Museum's collection are described in detail, accompanied by twenty-two photographs.

http://oi.uchicago.edu/museum/highlights/egypt.html

MUSEUM: Photographic Database

The Oriental Institute Museum Archives Photographic Database is now available for public access. As of February 2010, there are more than 70,000 entries from our photo catalog in the database, 35,000 of which have an image scanned and attached. At the login page, click the Guest Account radio button and then click Login. Use the left and right hand buttons on the screen to scroll through the database, or use the magnifying glass to search.

http://babylon-orinst.uchicago.edu/fmi/iwp/res/iwp_home.html

In the online publication of *Breasted's 1919–1920 Expedition to the Near East*, 1,875 photographs chronicle Illinois native James Henry Breasted's daring travels through Egypt and Mesopotamia in the unstable aftermath of World War I. Breasted, a leading Egyptologist, was the founder of the Oriental Institute at the University of Chicago, and this journey was the first Oriental Institute project. The goals of his ambitious expedition were to acquire artifacts for the new Institute and to select sites for later excavation.

http://oi.uchicago.edu/museum/collections/pa/pioneer/

PUBLICATIONS OFFICE: Electronic Publications

OIDA 1. *Letters from James Henry Breasted to His Family, August 1919–July 1920*. Edited by John A. Larson. 2010.

http://oi.uchicago.edu/research/pubs/catalog/oida/oida1.html

OIMP 23. *Ancient Egypt: Treasures from the Collection of the Oriental Institute*. By Emily Teeter. Originally published in 2003.

http://oi.uchicago.edu/research/pubs/catalog/oimp/oimp23.html

OIMP 30. *Pioneers to the Past: American Archaeologists in the Middle East, 1919–1920*. Edited by Geoff Emberling. Published in 2010.

http://oi.uchicago.edu/research/pubs/catalog/oimp/oimp30.html

OINE 1. *The Beit el-Wali Temple of Ramesses* II. By Herbert Ricke, George R. Hughes, and Edward F. Wente. Originally published in 1967.

http://oi.uchicago.edu/research/pubs/catalog/oine/oine1.html

OINE 3. *Excavations between Abu Simbel and the Sudan Frontier*, Part 1: *The A-Group Royal Cemetery at Qustul, Cemetery* L. By B. B. Williams. Originally published in 1986.

http://oi.uchicago.edu/research/pubs/catalog/oine/oine3.html

OINE 4. *Excavations between Abu Simbel and the Sudan Frontier*, Parts 2, 3, and 4: *Neolithic, A-Group, and Post A-Group Remains from Cemeteries W, V, S, Q, T, and a Cave East of Cemetery K*. By B. B. Williams. Originally published in 1989.

http://oi.uchicago.edu/research/pubs/catalog/oine/oine4.html

OINE 5. *Excavations between Abu Simbel and the Sudan Frontier*, Part 5: *C-Group, Pan Grave, and Kerma Remains at Adindan Cemeteries T, K, U, and J*. By B. B. Williams. Originally published in 1983.

http://oi.uchicago.edu/research/pubs/catalog/oine/oine5.html

OINE 7. *Excavations between Abu Simbel and the Sudan Frontier*, Part 7: *Twenty-fifth Dynasty and Napatan Remains at Qustul Cemeteries W and V*. By B. B. Williams. Originally published in 1990.

http://oi.uchicago.edu/research/pubs/catalog/oine/oine7.html

OINE 8. *Excavations between Abu Simbel and the Sudan Frontier*, Part 8: *Meroitic Remains from Qustul Cemetery Q, Ballana Cemetery B, and a Ballana Settlement*. By B. B. Williams et. al. Originally published in 1991.

http://oi.uchicago.edu/research/pubs/catalog/oine/oine8.html

OINE 9. *Excavations between Abu Simbel and the Sudan Frontier*, Part 9: *Noubadian X-Group Remains from Royal Complexes in Cemeteries Q and 219 and Private Cemeteries Q, R, V, W, B, J, and M at Qustul and Ballana*. By B. B. Williams. Originally published in 1991.

http://oi.uchicago.edu/research/pubs/catalog/oine/oine9.html

OINE 10. *Excavations at Serra East*, Parts 1–5: *A-Group, C-Group, Pan Grave, New Kingdom, and X-Group Remains from Cemeteries A-G and Rock Shelters*. By B. B. Williams. Originally published in 1993.

http://oi.uchicago.edu/research/pubs/catalog/oine/oine10.html

OIP 8. *Medinet Habu*, Volume I: *Earlier Historical Records of Ramses III*. The Epigraphic Survey. Originally published in 1930.

http://oi.uchicago.edu/research/pubs/catalog/oip/oip8.html

OIP 9. *Medinet Habu*, Volume II: *The Later Historical Records of Ramses III*. The Epigraphic Survey. Originally published in 1932.

http://oi.uchicago.edu/research/pubs/catalog/oip/oip9.html

OIP 23. *Medinet Habu*, Volume III: *The Calendar, the "Slaughterhouse," and Minor Records of Ramses III*. The Epigraphic Survey. Originally published in 1934.

http://oi.uchicago.edu/research/pubs/catalog/oip/oip23.html

OIP 25. *Reliefs and Inscriptions at Karnak*, Volume I: *Ramses III's Temple with the Great Inclosure of Amon*, Part I. The Epigraphic Survey. Originally published in 1936.

http://oi.uchicago.edu/research/pubs/catalog/oip/oip25.html

OIP 31. *The Mastaba of Mereruka*, Part I: *Chambers A 1-10*. The Sakkara Expedition. Originally published in 1938.

http://oi.uchicago.edu/research/pubs/catalog/oip/oip31.html

OIP 35. *Reliefs and Inscriptions at Karnak*, Volume II: *Ramses III's Temple within the Great Inclosure of Amon*, Part II; and *Ramses III's Temple in the Precinct of Mut*. The Epigraphic Survey. Originally published in 1936.

http://oi.uchicago.edu/research/pubs/catalog/oip/oip35.html

OIP 36. *Medinet Habu Graffiti: Facsimiles*. Edited by William F. Edgerton. Originally published in 1937.

http://oi.uchicago.edu/research/pubs/catalog/oip/oip36.html

OIP 39. *The Mastaba of Mereruka*, Part II: *Chamber A 11-13, Doorjambs and Inscriptions of Chambers A 1-21, Tomb Chamber, and Exterior*. The Sakkarah Expedition. Originally published in 1938.

http://oi.uchicago.edu/research/pubs/catalog/oip/oip39.html

OIP 48. *Mounds in the Plain of Antioch: An Archeological Survey*. Robert J. Braidwood. Originally published in 1937.

http://oi.uchicago.edu/research/pubs/catalog/oip/oip48.html

OIP 51. *Medinet Habu*, Volume 4: *Festival Scenes of Ramses III*. The Epigraphic Survey. Originally published in 1940.

http://oi.uchicago.edu/research/pubs/catalog/oip/oip51.html

OIP 55. *The Excavation of Medinet Habu*, Volume VI: *The Mortuary Temple of Ramses III*, Part II. By Uvo Hölscher. With contributions by Rudolf Anthes. Originally published in 1951.

http://oi.uchicago.edu/research/pubs/catalog/oip/oip55.html

OIP 56. *Key Plans Showing Locations of Theban Temple Decorations*. By Harold Hayden Nelson. Originally published in 1941.

http://oi.uchicago.edu/research/pubs/catalog/oip/oip56.html

OIP 74. *Reliefs and Inscriptions at Karnak*, Volume III: *The Bubastite Portal*. The Epigraphic Survey. Originally published in 1954.

http://oi.uchicago.edu/research/pubs/catalog/oip/oip74.html

OIP 83. *Medinet Habu*, Volume V: *The Temple Proper*, Part I: *The Portico, the Treasury, and Chapels Adjoining the First Hypostyle Hall with Marginal Material from the Forecourts*. The Epigraphic Survey. Originally published in 1957.

http://oi.uchicago.edu/research/pubs/catalog/oip/oip83.html

OIP 84. *Medinet Habu*, Volume IV: *The Temple Proper*, Part II: *The Re Chapel, the Royal Mortuary Complex, and Adjacent Rooms with Miscellaneous Material from the Pylons, the Forecourts, and the First Hypostyle Hall*. The Epigraphic Survey. Originally published in 1963.

http://oi.uchicago.edu/research/pubs/catalog/oip/oip84.html

OIP 93. *Medinet Habu*, Volume VII: *The Temple Proper*, Part III: *The Third Hypostyle Hall and All Rooms Accessible from It with Friezes of Scenes from the Roof Terraces and Exterior Walls of the Temple*. The Epigraphic Survey. Originally published in 1964.

> http://oi.uchicago.edu/research/pubs/catalog/oip/oip93.html

OIP 100. *The Temple of Khonsu*, Volume I: *Scenes of King Herihor in the Court*. The Epigraphic Survey. Originally published in 1979.

> http://oi.uchicago.edu/research/pubs/catalog/oip/oip100.html

OIP 103. *The Temple of Khonsu*, Volume 2: *Scenes and Inscriptions in the Court and the First Hypostyle Hall*. The Epigraphic Survey. Originally published in 1981.

> http://oi.uchicago.edu/research/pubs/catalog/oip/oip103.html

OIP 107. *Reliefs and Inscriptions at Karnak*, Volume IV: *The Battle Reliefs of King Sety I*. The Epigraphic Survey. Originally published in 1986.

> http://oi.uchicago.edu/research/pubs/catalog/oip/oip107.html

OIP 112. *Reliefs and Inscriptions at Luxor Temple*, Volume 1: *The Festival Procession of Opet in the Colonnade Hall*. The Epigraphic Survey. Originally published in 1994.

> http://oi.uchicago.edu/research/pubs/catalog/oip/oip112.html

OIP 116. *Reliefs and Inscriptions at Luxor Temple*, Volume 2: *The Facade, Portals, Upper Register Scenes, Columns, Marginalia, and Statuary in the Colonnade Hall*. The Epigraphic Survey. Originally published in 1998.

> http://oi.uchicago.edu/research/pubs/catalog/oip/oip116.html

OIP 136. *Medinet Habu*, Volume IX: *The Eighteenth Dynasty Temple*, Part I: *The Inner Sanctuaries*. The Epigraphic Survey. 2009.

> http://oi.uchicago.edu/research/pubs/catalog/oip/oip136.html

OIS 6. *Divination and Interpretation of Signs in the Ancient World*. Edited by Amar Annus. 2010.

> http://oi.uchicago.edu/research/pubs/catalog/ois/ois6.html

SAOC 42. *The Road to Kadesh: A Historical Interpretation of the Battle Reliefs of King Sety I at Karnak*. By W. J. Murnane. Originally published in 1985.

> http://oi.uchicago.edu/research/pubs/catalog/oip/saoc42.html

SAOC 53. *Glass from Quseir al-Qadim and the Indian Ocean Trade*. By Carol Meyer. Originally published in 1992.

> http://oi.uchicago.edu/research/pubs/catalog/oip/saoc53.html

SAOC 54. *The Mechanics of Ancient Egyptian Magical Practice*. By R. K. Ritner. Originally published in 1993.

> http://oi.uchicago.edu/research/pubs/catalog/oip/saoc54.html

SAOC 63. *Beyond the Ubaid: Transformation and Integration in the Late Prehistoric Societies of the Middle East*. Edited by Robert A. Carter and Graham Philip. 2010.

> http://oi.uchicago.edu/research/pubs/catalog/oip/saoc63.html

Ancient Egyptian Paintings Selected, Copied, and Described, Volume I: *Descriptive Text.* By Nina M. Davies with the editorial assistance of Alan H. Gardiner. Originally published in 1936.

http://oi.uchicago.edu/research/pubs/catalog/misc/paintings1.html

Ancient Egyptian Paintings Selected, Copied, and Described, Volume II: *Descriptive Text.* By Nina M. Davies with the editorial assistance of Alan H. Gardiner. Originally published in 1936.

http://oi.uchicago.edu/research/pubs/catalog/misc/paintings2.html

Egypt through the Stereoscope: A Journey through the Land of the Pharaohs. By James Henry Breasted. Originally published in 1908. Electronic publication in 2010.

http://oi.uchicago.edu/research/pubs/catalog/misc/stereoscope.html

Lost Egypt, Volume I: *A Limited Edition Portfolio Series of Photographic Images from Egypt's Past.* The Epigraphic Survey. Originally published in 1992.

http://oi.uchicago.edu/research/pubs/catalog/le/

Lost Egypt, Volumes II: *A Limited Edition Portfolio Series of Photographic Images from Egypt's Past.* The Epigraphic Survey. Originally published in 1992.

http://oi.uchicago.edu/research/pubs/catalog/le/

Lost Egypt, Volume III: *A Limited Edition Portfolio Series of Photographic Images from Egypt's Past.* The Epigraphic Survey. Originally published in 1992.

http://oi.uchicago.edu/research/pubs/catalog/le/

Pioneer to the Past: The Story of James Henry Breasted, Archaeologist, Told by His Son Charles Breasted. By Charles Breasted. Reprint of the Charles Scribner's Sons 1943 edition. Published in 2009.

http://oi.uchicago.edu/research/pubs/catalog/misc/pioneer.html

The Temple of King Sethos I at Abydos, Volume I: *The Chapels of Osiris, Isis and Horus.* Copied by Amice M. Calverley, with the assistance of Myrtle F. Broome, and edited by Alan H. Gardiner. Originally published in 1933.

http://oi.uchicago.edu/research/pubs/catalog/misc/sethos1.html

The Temple of King Sethos I at Abydos, Volume II: *The Chapels of Amen-Re', Re'-Harakhti, Ptah, and King Sethos.* Copied by Amice M. Calverley, with the assistance of Myrtle F. Broome, and edited by Alan H. Gardiner. Originally published in 1935.

http://oi.uchicago.edu/research/pubs/catalog/misc/sethos2.html

The Temple of King Sethos I at Abydos, Volume III: *The Osiris Complex.* Copied by Amice M. Calverley, with the assistance of Myrtle F. Broome, and edited by Alan H. Gardiner. Originally published in 1938.

http://oi.uchicago.edu/research/pubs/catalog/misc/sethos3.html

The Temple of King Sethos I at Abydos, Volume IV: *The Second Hypostyle Hall.* Copied by Amice M. Calverley, with the assistance of Myrtle F. Broome, and edited by Alan H. Gardiner. Originally published in 1958.

http://oi.uchicago.edu/research/pubs/catalog/misc/sethos4.html

PUBLICATIONS OFFICE: Oriental Institute Annual Reports

Annual Report 2008–2009

> http://oi.uchicago.edu/research/pubs/ar/08-09/

PUBLICATIONS OFFICE: Oriental Institute *News & Notes*

The Oriental Institute Publications Office announces the electronic publication, in Adobe Acrobat (pdf) format, of all Institute News & Notes newsletters from the current Spring 2010 issue back through 2002.

> http://oi.uchicago.edu/research/pubs/nn/

RESEARCH ARCHIVES

An Introduction and Guide to the Oriental Institute Research Archives

> http://oi.uchicago.edu/pdf/research_archives_introduction&guide.pdf

The Oriental Institute's online catalog of the Research Archives has significantly increased the retrospective cataloging of material from before 1990. The total number of records stands at 322,000+.

> http://oilib.uchicago.edu

Oriental Institute Research Archives Acquisitions Lists

> http://oi.uchicago.edu/pdf/AcquisitionsList-June2009.pdf
> http://oi.uchicago.edu/pdf/AcquisitionsList-July2009.pdf
> http://oi.uchicago.edu/pdf/AcquisitionsList-August2009.pdf
> http://oi.uchicago.edu/pdf/AcquisitionsList-September2009.pdf
> http://oi.uchicago.edu/pdf/AcquisitionsList-October2009.pdf
> http://oi.uchicago.edu/pdf/AcquisitionsList-November2009.pdf
> http://oi.uchicago.edu/pdf/AcquisitionsList-December2009.pdf
> http://oi.uchicago.edu/pdf/AcquisitionsList-January2010.pdf
> http://oi.uchicago.edu/pdf/AcquisitionsList-February2010.pdf
> http://oi.uchicago.edu/pdf/AcquisitionsList-March2010.pdf
> http://oi.uchicago.edu/pdf/AcquisitionsList-April2010.pdf
> http://oi.uchicago.edu/pdf/AcquisitionsList-May2010.pdf

RESEARCH ARCHIVES: Adopt-a-Journal Campaign

> http://oi.uchicago.edu/research/library/adopt-a-journal.html

SYMPOSIA

Slaves and Households in the Near East

> http://oi.uchicago.edu/research/symposia/2009.html

INDIVIDUAL SCHOLARSHIP: Norman Golb

The Autograph Memoirs of Obadiah the Proselyte of Oppido Lucano

> http://oi.uchicago.edu/research/is/autograph_memoirs_obadiah.html

The Messianic Pretender Solomon Ibn Al Ruji and His Son Menahem (The So-Called "David Alroy")

> http://oi.uchicago.edu/research/is/false_messiah.html

Observations on the Bipolar Theory of So-Called "Qumran Spellings" (Revised and Expanded Edition)

> http://oi.uchicago.edu/research/is/bipolar_theory.html

A review of the current Dead Sea Scrolls Exhibit at the Milwaukee Public Museum

> http://oi.uchicago.edu/pdf/milwaukee_dss_exhibit_2010.pdf

Expanding on a previous article: "Further Evidence Concerning Judah b. Solomon and the 'Tower of Las Metamis' Mentioned in MS de Rossi 1105"

> http://oi.uchicago.edu/pdf/metamis.pdf

A French-language version of Professor Norman Golb's 2008 article, "A New Wrinkle in the Qumran 'Yahad' Theory"

> http://oi.uchicago.edu/pdf/new_wrinkle_in_yahad_claim_french.pdf

INDIVIDUAL SCHOLARSHIP: Robert K. Ritner

Reading the Coffin of Meresamun

> http://oi.uchicago.edu/research/is/reading_coffin_meresamun.html

----

Although Charles Jones is no longer in charge of the Oriental Institute's Research Archives, he still actively maintains several vital electronic resources for ancient Near Eastern studies just as he had done during his tenure in Chicago. Thank you, Chuck, for your continuing service to the field, and our faculty, staff, and students.

ABZU: Guide to Resources for the Study of the Ancient Near East Available on the Internet

> http://www.etana.org/abzu

ETANA: Electronic Tools and Ancient Near Eastern Archives – Core Texts

A substantial selection of digitized titles from the collections of the Research Archives has been added to the ETANA Core Texts this year.

> http://www.etana.org/coretexts.shtml

IRAQCRISIS

A moderated list for communicating substantive information on cultural property damaged, destroyed or lost from libraries and museums in Iraq during and after the war in April 2003, and on the world-wide response to the crisis. A component of the Oriental Institute's response to the cultural heritage crisis in the aftermath of the war in Iraq, this list provides a moderated forum for the distribution of information.

> https://listhost.uchicago.edu/mailman/listinfo/iraqcrisis

PUBLICATIONS OFFICE

Thomas G. Urban

The full-time staff of the Publications Office remains Thomas G. Urban and Leslie Schramer. Sabahat Adil, Aliya Bagewadi, and Felicia Whitcomb, after a very productive year, moved on to other pursuits. We are very fortunate to welcome new staff members Rebecca Cain, Plamena Pehlivanova, and Natalie Whiting.

The Publications Office continues to assist the Membership and Development Offices with the publication of *News & Notes*, *Annual Report*, and miscellaneous postcards, brochures, and posters. While the print publication of this year's Annual Report is once again in black and white, we will post a color PDF version online. View the report at the Oriental Institute Web site: http://oi.uchicago.edu/research/pubs/ar/. Also, we very much enjoyed working with this year's post-doctoral scholar Laura Culbertson.

Sales

The David Brown Book Company and Oxbow Books, Ltd., U.K., continue to represent the Institute for its book distribution. Although a limited number of titles are available for in-house sales in the Suq shop, please note that all external orders for Institute publications should be addressed to: The David Brown Book Company, P.O. Box 511, Oakville, CT 06779; Telephone Toll Free: 1-800-791-9354; Fax: 1-860-945-9468; E-mail: david.brown.bk.co@snet.net; Web site: www.oxbowbooks.com.

Information related to the sales and distribution of Oriental Institute titles may be obtained via e-mail:

> oi-publications@uchicago.edu

Electronic Publications

As part of the Oriental Institute's Electronic Initiative, all new titles are simultaneously issued in print and as Adobe Acrobat PDF (Portable Document Format) files delivered through the Internet. Older titles are scanned, saved as .tif and .pdf files, with the latter being posted on-line, as time and funds permit. This year the Oriental Institute was very fortunate to expend the generous support from Misty and Lewis Gruber that has allowed the remaining titles of every Egyptological title published by the Institute — 124 books — since its inception to be scanned and distributed on the Internet at no cost to the end user; please see the Electronic Resources report (above) for a complete list of titles distributed through the Internet.

The scanning of the older titles has been done by Northern MicroGraphics (NMT Corporation, http://normicro.com), located in La Crosse, Wisconsin.

The Electronic Initiative has already proved to be very successful. The posted pdfs are available wherever the Internet reaches, and our older titles, as well as new titles, are especially appreciated in countries that do not have our books on their library shelves.

An additional benefit to the scanning and uploading of all titles to the Internet is that we can very easily have out-of-print titles reprinted and once again made available in print. We were very fortunate during last year to begin working with the HF Group (North Manchester, Indiana), which is able to reprint our older, over-sized titles (such as Erich Schmidt's *Persepolis* 2 [OIP 69]).

Volumes Printed in Print and Online

1. *The Assyrian Dictionary of the Oriental Institute of the University of Chicago*, Volume 6, Letter Ḫ. 1956. Digital reprint. CAD H

2. *Beyond the Ubaid: Transformation and Integration in the Late Prehistoric Societies of the Middle East*. Edited by Robert A. Carter and Graham Philip. SAOC 63

3. *Divination and Interpretation of Signs in the Ancient World*. Edited by Amar Annus. OIS 6

4. *Lost Nubia*. John A. Larson. Digital reprint. 2006. OIMP 24

5. *Medinet Habu*, Volume IX: *The Eighteenth Dynasty Temple*, Part 1: *The Inner Sanctuaries*. The Epigraphic Survey. OIP 136

6. *Persepolis* II: *Contents of the Treasury and Other Discoveries*. Erich F. Schmidt. 1957. Digital reprint. OIP 69

7. *Pioneer to the Past: The Story of James Henry Breasted, Archaeologist, Told by His Son Charles Breasted*. Charles Breasted. Reprint of the Charles Scribner's Sons 1943 Edition with New Foreword and Photographs. Miscellaneous Publication

8. *Pioneers to the Past: American Archaeologists in the Middle East, 1919–1920*. Edited by Geoff Emberling. OIMP 30

9. *Sacred Space and Sacred Function in Ancient Thebes*. Edited byPeter F. Dorman and Betsy M. Bryan. Digital reprint. SAOC 61

Volumes Distributed Online

1. *The Demotic Dictionary of the Oriental Institute of the University of Chicago*, Letter W. Edited by Janet H. Johnson. CDD W

2. *The Demotic Dictionary of the Oriental Institute of the University of Chicago*, Letter Ḥ. Edited by Janet H. Johnson. CDD H2

3. *The Demotic Dictionary of the Oriental Institute of the University of Chicago*, Letter Š. Edited by Janet H. Johnson. CDD Sh

4. *Egypt through the Stereoscope: A Journey through the Land of the Pharaohs*. By James Henry Breasted. Re-issue. Miscellaneous Publication

5. *Letters from James Henry Breasted to His Family, August 1919–July 1920*. Edited by John A. Larson. OIDA 1

6–37. Thirty-two issues of *News & Notes*, Nos. 172–204, from Winter 2002 to Winter 2010

38–100. Sixty-three older Egyptological titles, scanned, prepared, and uploaded to the Internet with the generous support of Misty and Lewis Gruber. See Electronic Resources (separate report)

Volumes in Preparation

1. *Ancient Israel: Cultural Crossroads of the Ancient Near East.* Gabrielle Novacek. OIMP 31

2. *Ankara Arkeoloji Müzesinde bulunan Boğazköy Tabletleri,* Volume 2: *Boğazköy Tablets in the Archaeological Museum of Ankara.* ABoT 2. Rukiye Ozdoğan and Oğuz Soysal. AS 28

3. *The Assyrian Dictionary of the Oriental Institute of the University of Chicago,* Volume U/W. CAD U/W

4. *Baked Clay Figurines and Votive Beds from Medinet Habu.* Emily Teeter. OIP 133

5. *Bismaya: Recovering the Lost City of Adab.* Karen L. Wilson. OIP 137

6. *European Cartographers and the Ottoman World, 1500–1750: Maps from the Collection of O. J. Sopranos.* By Ian Manners. Digital reprint. OIMP 27

7. *Grammatical Case in the Languages of the Middle East and Europe* (Acts of the International Colloquium: Variations, Concurrence et Evolution des Cas dans divers Domains Linguistiques, Paris, April 2–4, 2007). Edited by Michèle Fruyt, Dennis Pardee, and Michel Mazoyer. SAOC 64

8. *Hamoukar,* Volume 1: *Urbanism and Cultural Landscapes in Northeastern Syria: The Tell Hamoukar Survey, 1999–2001.* Jason A. Ur. OIP 138

9. *The Monumental Complex of King Ahmose at Abydos,* Volume 1: *The Pyramid Temple of Ahmose and Its Environs: Architecture and Decoration.* Stephen P. Harvey. OIP 139

10. *The 1996–1997 Survey Seasons at Bir Umm Fawakhir.* Carol A. Meyer. OIC 30

11. *Perspectives on Ptolemaic Thebes.* Edited by Peter F. Dorman and Betsy M. Bryan. SAOC 65

12. *Pesher Nahum: Texts and Studies in Jewish History and Literature from Antiquity through the Middle Ages Presented to Norman Golb.* Edited by Joel L. Kraemer and Michael G. Wechsler, with Fred Donner, Joshua Holo, and Dennis Pardee. SAOC 66

RESEARCH ARCHIVES

Foy Scalf

Introduction[1]

When you think of the Oriental Institute, our world-class museum collections and archaeological excavation projects probably come immediately to mind. What may be less apparent is the significant role of the Research Archives. The Research Archives (fig. 1), formerly known as the Oriental Institute Library, is at the very heart of the Oriental Institute and is fundamental to its mission.[2] With over 50,000 volumes, we are a unique scholarly resource that is essential for every research project within the building. In fact, it is the one place within the Oriental Institute where all our researchers come together on a regular basis.[3] We are the metaphorical crossroads of the intellectual study of the ancient Near East, where ideas are shared and debated, championed or destroyed. In our reading room and in our stacks, on a daily basis, discoveries are being made, hypotheses are being born, and even archaeology — the archaeology of ideas — is being conducted.

In addition to our internal service, we are continuously supplying an international web of scholars with a flow of information unimaginable only ten years ago. Oriental Institute research associates working with projects across the globe, archaeologists in the field, and graduate students right here at home rely on the one-of-a-kind scholarly resource that our collections provide. Many research associates working in the United States, the Middle East, and abroad, without access to the Research Archives, call upon us to deliver copies of publications necessary for their work, but unavailable to them. When an Oriental Institute archaeologist uncovers some enigmatic object in the field, we are often their first point of contact, and we can scan and send publications to them right in the field. At the very mention of a new publication overlapping with their dissertation topic, scrambling graduate students routinely inquire about the latest scholarship. New discoveries do not only happen in the field; they are happening every day inside the minds of our patrons. Many of our greatest publications, the Oriental Institute Publication volumes we know and love, were born, raised, and disciplined in our reading room.

In that regard, the Oriental Institute has been and continues to be at the forefront of studying the ancient Middle East on its own terms, not as some exotic other that is somehow inherently different from us, but as the foundation of the urban society we take for granted all around us.[4]

---

[1] Portions of the introduction were presented at the Oriental Institute for the Research Endowment Campaign Completion Event, March 27, 2010.

[2] The original designation for the in-house collection of scholarly reference materials was the Oriental Institute Library, referred to as such by James H. Breasted, *The Oriental Institute* (Chicago: University of Chicago Press, 1933), p. 122, and Shirley A. Lyon in *Oriental Institute Annual Report 1969/70*, p. 29. The *Oriental Institute Annual Report 1972/73*, pp. 48–49 listed under "Needs of the Oriental Institute" $950,000 for the "[e]ndowment for an Oriental Institute Library." The designation "Research Archives" was announced in *Oriental Institute Annual Report 1973/74*, pp. 56–58, in order to distinguish the Institute's collection from that of the University of Chicago library system.

[3] I like to think of the Oriental Institute as a country club for ancient Near East studies, in the same vein as the Princeton Mathematics department had been described as "a country club for math" in Sylvia Nasar, *A Beautiful Mind* (New York: Simon and Schuster, 1998), p. 50.

[4] For Western views of the Middle East as Other, see, e.g., the fundamental work of Edward Said, *Orientalism* (New York: Pantheon Books, 1978). Oriental Institute founder James H. Breasted continuously emphasized the role of the ancient Near East in shaping civilization. As Edith W. Ware stated in her introduction to the revised edition of Breasted's *The Conquest of Civilization* (New York: Harper and Brothers, 1938), p. iii, his work "struck a new logical balance in which the Orient occupied its appropriate place." Such feelings were enshrined in the tympanum above the Oriental Institute doors, showing what Breasted described as "the transition of civilization from the ancient Orient to

Figure 1. Research Archives Reading Room circa 1963

Their pots and pans have more than abstract museal qualities as art objects; they are the reflections of past lives lived, past challenges faced, and past discoveries forged. These challenges cannot be accomplished in a vacuum. All our projects rely on the foundation laid by past generations of scholars and the records they have left us in the form of scholarship, that is, published research in print form. From identifying sites on a satellite image to describing museum items in a database, from a new study of religious ritual papyri to determining the definition of an unrecognized word, every project within the Oriental Institute depends upon the Research Archives for its vast treasure of ideas, knowledge, and data.

This interactive collaboration of scholars, both within and without the Research Archives, exemplifies the important steps taken during 2009–2010 to fulfill our mission:

> ... to make its resources available and useful to the faculty, staff, and projects of the Oriental Institute and to sustain and preserve for future generations a universe of knowledge and creativity relating to the languages and cultures of the ancient Near East and to the ancient and modern scholarly traditions associated with the ancient Near East.[5]

As described below, we continue striving to maintain our position as a premier scholarly resource for studying the ancient Near East in acquisitions, bibliographic data, online tools, and open-access publications for Oriental Institute faculty, staff, students, Members, and the scholarly community. I believe that the essential value of the Research Archives is reflected in the breadth, depth, and quality of recent work produced by Oriental Institute scholars.

the West" in *The Oriental Institute* (Chicago: University of Chicago Press, 1933), p. 103. The tympanum was featured in Emily Teeter and Leslie Schramer, "Some Decorative Motifs of the Oriental Institute Building," *Oriental Institute News & Notes* 199 (Fall 2008), p. 17.

[5] As stated by Charles E. Jones, *Oriental Institute Annual Report 2003–2004*, p. 161.

Acquisitions

Acquisitions for 2009–2010 remained near 1,200 volumes, maintaining the 15 percent increase witnessed in 2008–2009 (table 1). During my tenure thus far as head of Research Archives, acquisitions have been top priority, for Oriental Institute researchers need access to such materials in order to continue fulfilling the mission of the Oriental Institute: gather, interpret, and disseminate knowledge about the cultures of the ancient Near East. The rate of publication in the fields of ancient Near East studies continues to increase, demonstrating the growth and vitality of our fields. Supporting the research of scholars within the Oriental Institute is the basic mission of the Research Archives. To that end, our efficient use of funds and low infrastructure expenditures are essential to maintain our elite level of scholarly resources.

Table 1. Research Archives acquisitions, May 2009–April 2010

Month	Monographs, Series, Pamphlets	Journals	Total
July 2009	122	66	188
August 2009	154	38	192
September 2009	92	25	117
October 2009	111	36	147
November 2009	33	32	65
December 2009	20	34	54
January 2010	43	40	83
February 2010	37	43	80
March 2010	27	44	71
April 2010	27	18	45
May 2010	38	55	93
June 2010	47	15	62
Totals	751	446	1,197

Online Catalog

From July 1, 2009, to June 30, 2010, the Research Archives online catalog has grown by 35,000 records, from 330,000 to 365,000 analytic records (table 2). During the last four years, we have made a serious attempt to revolutionize the online catalog. Complete coverage of the collection within the Research Archives is our primary goal. The retrospective cataloging of the monographs has been completed, and we have turned our attention to the journals. The pamphlet files will be completed last. However, our secondary goal is to create a serious bibliographic research tool. At present, the Research Archives online catalog is one of the largest publicly accessible online databases for ancient Near East studies, and it is one of the few resources scholars can consult in order to search complete analytic records for individually authored journal articles, chapters, papers, and books.

Table 2. Catalog records

Year	Number of Catalog Records Added	Total Number of Catalog Records
2009–2010	35,000	365,000
2008–2009	63,000	330,000
2007–2008	62,000	257,000
2006–2007	28,000	195,000
—	—	—
2003–2004	10,000	130,000

For the online catalog, academic year 2010–2011 is shaping up to be one of the most exciting for the Research Archives since the launch of the electronic catalog and its publication online. Our major goal this year is migration to a new database software which will improve the usability and functionality of the database as well as expanding the realm of possibilities for what we can do. Over the next eight months, we will begin the arduous task of database design, data cleanup, and data migration. Once complete, users will experience a revolution in functionality, enabling complex searching and sorting along with a variety of new, internally linked data sets, increasing the already immense value of our database.

In addition, we have furthered our project of adding links to individual catalog entries. In the past year, we have added links for *Académie des inscriptions et belles-lettres*, *Comptes rendus des séances de l'année* (J/CRAIBL), *Antiquity* (J/ANT), *Catholic Biblical Quarterly* (J/CBQ), and *Palestine Exploration Quarterly* (J/PEQ). We also continue to add links to all online material for newly acquired volumes. As more volumes become available online, our backlist of links to be added grows steadily. Currently, there are over 90,000 links to online material in the catalog (table 3).

Table 3. Links to online records in the catalog

Call Number	Journal	Journal	Access
JAOS	Journal of the American Oriental Society	14,385	JSTOR
CBQ	Catholic Biblical Quarterly	11,222	Ebsco
ANT	Antiquity	11,034	Antiquity
AJA	American Journal of Archaeology	10,988	JSTOR/AJA
ZQE	Zeitschrift für Papyrologie und Epigraphik	7,336	JSTOR
Syria	Syria	5,351	JSTOR
JNES	Journal of Near Eastern Studies	4,854	JSTOR/JNES
JEA	Journal of Egyptian Archaeology	3,950	JSTOR
BASOR	Bulletin of the American School of Oriental Research	3,646	JSTOR
ZDMG	Zeitschrift der Deutschen Morgenländischen Gesellschaft	2,835	Open
CRAIBL	Académie des inscriptions et belles-lettres. Comptes rendus	2,254	Open
BIAR	Near Eastern Archaeology (formerly Biblical Archaeologist)	2,006	JSTOR
PEQ	Palestine Exploration Quarterly	1,651	Ebsco
ZA	Zeitschrift für Assyriologie	1,476	Open
JESHO	Journal of the Economic and Social History of the Orient	1,444	JSTOR
BIFAO	Bulletin de l'Institut Français d'Archéologie Orientale	1,133	Open

Table 3. Links to online records in the catalog (cont.)

Call Number	Journal	Journal	Access
JARCE	*Journal of the American Research Center in Egypt*	1,132	JSTOR
RBL	*Review of Biblical Literature*	925	Open
JCS	*Journal of Cuneiform Studies*	970	JSTOR
IRQ	*Iraq*	876	JSTOR
ANS	*Anatolian Studies*	683	JSTOR
FUB	*Forschungen und Berichte*	673	JSTOR
IRN	*Iran*	601	JSTOR
JANES	*Journal of the Ancient Near Eastern Society*	322	Open
Orj	*Orient: Report of the Society for Near Eastern Studies in Japan*	299	Open
Bib	*Biblica*	286	Open
ARO	*Ars Orientalis*	206	JSTOR
BSEG	*Bulletin: Society d'Egyptologie Geneve*	135	Open
BMSEAS	*British Museum Studies in Ancient Egypt and Sudan*	52	Open
LingAeg	*Lingua Aegyptia*	46	Open
StOr	*Studia Orontica*	32	Open
ARTA	*Achaemenid Research on Texts and Archaeology*	29	Open
CDLJ	*Cuneiform Digital Library Journal*	25	Open
CDLB	*Cuneiform Digital Library Bulletin*	18	Open
ENiM	*Égypte Nilotique et Méditerranéenne*	6	Open
CDLN	*Cuneiform Digital Library Notes*	8	Open
	Total	92,889	

Resources on the Web

In addition to the online catalog, the Research Archives maintains a series of open-access online resources.

Introduction and Guide

http://oi.uchicago.edu/pdf/research_archives_introduction&guide.pdf

An updated introduction and guide to the Research Archives contains a brief history, a guide to the Research Archives collection, and instructions for using the online catalog.

Dissertations

http://oi.uchicago.edu/research/library/dissertation/

With the permission of the authors, the Research Archives provides access to Adobe Portable Document Format (PDF) copies of dissertations completed in the Department of Near Eastern Languages and Civilizations of the University of Chicago. The following were added during the 2009–2010 academic year:

A. Asa Eger. The Spaces between the Teeth: Environment, Settlement, and Interaction on the Islamic-Byzantine Frontier. PhD dissertation. Chicago, 2008.

http://oi.uchicago.edu/research/library/dissertation/eger.html

Dissertation Proposals

http://oi.uchicago.edu/research/library/dissertation/proposals/

With the permission of the authors, the Research Archives provides access to Adobe Portable Document Format (PDF) copies of dissertation proposals completed in the Department of Near Eastern Languages and Civilizations of the University of Chicago. Access to dissertation proposals provides PhD candidates the opportunity to promote their work while simultaneously sharing current research with colleagues and interested scholars. Although dormant for several years, we have now revived this project with the hope of fostering increased participation.

Acquisitions Lists

http://oi.uchicago.edu/research/library/acquisitions.html

The acquisitions lists of the Research Archives are distributed in Adobe Portable Document Format (PDF) on a monthly basis. This process has been active and continuative since September 2007.

Annual Reports

http://oi.uchicago.edu/research/library/annualreports.html

Annual Reports for the Research Archives are available from 1991 to 2009.

Monographs

http://oilib.uchicago.edu

Copies of out-of-copyright monographs have been scanned and are made available in Adobe Portable Document Format (PDF) through links in the online catalog of the Research Archives. As of June 2010, the Research Archives provides access to over 150 volumes. A selection of recent additions follows:

Edwyn Bevan. *Jerusalem under the High-priests: Five Lectures on the Period between Nehemiah and the New Testament.* London: Edward Arnold, 1930.

Margaret A. Murray. *Egyptian Temples.* London: Sampson Low, Marston, 1931.

N. Reich. *Demotische und griechische Texte auf Mumientäfelchen in der Sammlung der Papyrus Erzherzog Rainer.* Leipzig: Verlag von Eduard Avenarius, 1908.

Claude F. A. Schaeffer. *The Cuneiform Texts of Ras Shamra-Ugarit.* London: Oxford University Press, 1939.

Siegfried Schott. *Mythe und Mythenbildung im alten Ägypten.* Leipzig: J. C. Hinrichs Verlag, 1945.

Adopt-a-Journal

http://oi.uchicago.edu/research/library/adopt-a-journal.html

The Research Archives has launched an "Adopt-a-Journal" campaign in order to increase support for the Research Archives. Donors are recognized through personalized book plates made in their honor and placed in volumes of their choosing.

Visitors

The Research Archives is a popular place for visiting scholars, and we have had the pleasure to accommodate the research trips of many individuals, including (in alphabetical order): Richard Averbeck, Nicole Brisch, Arthur L. George, Jonathan Price, Daniel Justel, Isaac Kalimi, Adam Miglio, Brian Muhs, Rune Nyord, Ryan Perry, Joshua Roberson, Seth Sanders, Julie Stauder-Porchet, Andréas Stauder, Maren Schentuleit, Jonathan Tenney, and Irene Winter.

Acknowledgments

The Research Archives continues to receive generous support from a variety of sources, including faculty, staff, volunteers, and employees. Our exchange program could not function without the help of Leslie Schramer and Tom Urban in the Oriental Institute Publications Department; Chris Woods, Kathy Mineck, and Drew Baumann of the *Journal of Near Eastern Studies*; and Seth Sanders of the *Journal of Ancient Near Eastern Religions*. I would like to further acknowledge here the generous donations and help from the following (in alphabetical order): Abbas Alizadeh, Fred Donner, Andrea Dudek, Geoff Emberling, Mary Louise Jackowicz, James Tillanpaugh, Emily Teeter, Donald Whitcomb, and Bruce Williams.

I have been fortunate to have exceptional library staff, the very blood and sweat behind our achievements, and they deserve a hearty thank you. Laura Holzweg, NELC graduate student studying Islamic archaeology, completed the cataloging of the monographs and is currently assisting with new acquisitions. Lori Calabria, NELC graduate student studying Egyptology, has focused on cataloging new acquisitions. NELC graduate student in Near Eastern archaeology Monique Vincent and University of Chicago undergraduate Jill Waller focused on retrospective cataloging of the journal collection. I would like to thank them for their hard work, which is crucial to our mission.

Our steadfast team of volunteers continues to help the Research Archives in tremendous ways. When on break from volunteering in the Suq and collecting stamps, Ray Broms is the driving force behind our scanning project, scanning several volumes every week. Stephanie Duran participated in our retrospective cataloging of the journals, taking on the monumental task of cataloging early volumes of *Archaeology* magazine. Through the leadership of Andrea Dudek, and her recruitment of volunteer Mary Louise Jackowicz, we have begun a comprehensive inventory of our journal collection. Tireless Oriental Institute volunteer James Tillanpaugh aided in our scanning and cataloging processes. All their help contributes a great deal to what the Research Archives offers.

MUSEUM

Geoff Emberling

The Museum has been an active, productive, engaged place in the past year — it is a theme that echoes through the contributions of Museum staff in the pages that follow, and one that accurately reflects the pace and efficiency of work throughout the Museum. It is truly a pleasure to work in such a collegial and productive environment.

Among the most widely visible results of our work has been continuing activity in our special exhibits program. Exhibits provide a regular opportunity for us in the Institute to convey the excitement of discovery, ongoing research, and new insights into the ancient Middle Eastern past. It is also a way for us to explore ways in which these histories (and prehistories) remain relevant and interesting to us today. Understanding the ways in which civilizations rise and fall is one of the themes of continuing interest, and our collections also have the capacity to inspire curiosity and wonder and to transport visitors to other cultures, times, and places.

Our current exhibit, Pioneers to the Past: American Archaeologists in the Middle East, 1919–1920 (fig. 1), tells the story of a great archaeological adventure, as the Institute's founder James Henry Breasted traveled across a war-torn Middle East in the aftermath of World War I, purchasing antiquities, identifying sites for excavation, and making contact with local and colonial officials. As noted below, it has had great publicity, public interest, and associated programs.

However, in many ways, most of the work that we do in the Museum goes on behind the locked doors of the collections areas. As noted below, many scholars have worked with our object and archival collections in the past year. One project that I found particularly exciting was organized by Wayne Pitard, Director of the Spurlock Museum at the University of Illinois. He and his team came to the Museum to take 360-degree photographs of cylinder seals, and they are absolutely beautiful, showing details of carving and relationship of carving to patterns in the stone that one cannot see on a regular impression in modeling clay (fig. 2).

We are also undertaking major improvements to Museum infrastructure, in keeping with museum standards and best practices.

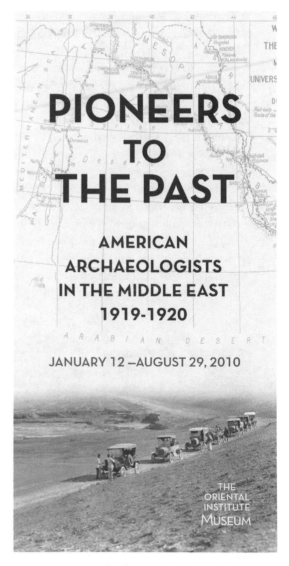

Figure 1. Banner for the Pioneers to the Past exhibit

We are continuing to re-house our collection in modern storage cabinets and materials due to the generous support of the Institute of Museum and Library Services (the "Conservation Project Support" program), and will begin an additional and important project that will re-house and document our metals collection with support of the National Endowment for the Humanities (NEH; "Sustaining Cultural Heritage Collections"). This project contains funds to purchase some additional photographic equipment as we work to upgrade our photo studio. We continue to document and register the collection in order to provide greater access to researchers both in the Institute and beyond, this year continuing our project of registering fragments of Neo-Assyrian reliefs from Khorsabad (with the help of Oriental Institute Research Associate Eleanor Guralnick). In addition, we have significantly increased the rate of cataloging and scanning photographs from the Archives. And we have moved the entire Archives collection out of storage, installed a compact storage system, and moved the entire collection back in, funded by the University of Chicago's Capital Projects budgets.

All this work is going to be increasingly accessible in the year to come because of an Institute-wide project to install a modern database system that will link Museum registration records to archival documents to publications and photographs. This project, called the Integrated Database, was proposed by John Sanders in 1993. As detailed in his report in this volume, its realization, due to begin this coming year, is truly a group effort led by Gil Stein and Steve Camp in their successful request for funding from the University of Chicago. We are excited also to report that an additional grant from IMLS ("Museums for America") will support the implementation of the database program across the Institute.

None of this work — exhibits and behind-the-scenes collections care and management — would be possible without the funding support noted above, and the dedication and hard work of our interns and volunteers, too many to thank individually here (although they are all named below!). The Oriental Institute had the foresight to develop a volunteer program more than forty years ago now. More recently, through a collaboration with Professor Morris Fred, who teaches a course on anthropology of museums in the University of Chicago and also teaches in MAPSS (Master of Arts Program in the Social Sciences), we have developed a semi-formal internship program over the past three years. This year, for the first time, the number of interns exceeded the number of Museum staff. We will not be able to expand the program any further because of limits of space and supervision, but all the Museum staff have learned how to make the intern

Figure 2. (Left) Photo of a cylinder seal (A12687) from Chatal Höyük in the Amuq Plain along with (right) a roll-out photograph of the seal's surface taken by Wayne Pitard and his team

experience more interesting and more useful all around. We look forward to continuing this program in the future.

I will not attempt to summarize all the activity in the pages that follow here, but would like to mention a few projects that I have been particularly involved in myself. Working with graduate student Katharyn Hanson and volunteers Sue Geshwender and Mari Terman, as well as Museum staff, I have worked to add labels to the Edgar and Deborah Jannotta Mesopotamian Gallery to enhance information about the archaeological context and date of objects on display. This is important given our standing as a research collection. This project, generously funded by Oriental Institute docents, is a major undertaking that has involved wrestling with a range of different sources of information about objects, some outdated, to develop new labels. Putting labels in cases has inevitably meant moving some objects, and the need to reinterpret some of the objects in their new context within the case. Particular thanks to Sue for the long hours and enthusiasm she has devoted to this project. By the time this volume is printed, we will have finished about half the labels in the gallery and will hope to sustain our momentum over the next year. This is one type of project that will be greatly facilitated in the future by the Integrated Database.

Another project is our audiotour program, which we started in the fall of 2008 with the generous support of Joyce and Roger Isaacs. We have continued to add to our offerings — this year, adding our first special-exhibit tour and a tour on the ancient Middle Eastern context of the Bible. With further support from Joyce and Roger, and the help of Karina Chavarria and docent Siwei Wang, we have just finished translations of our highlights tour into Mandarin Chinese and Spanish, as well as our kids' tour of ancient Egypt into Spanish. Our tours were rented nearly a thousand times last year, and we expect that number to continue to grow.

We have seen attendance decline in the Museum over the past two years, with a 5 percent decrease from the last fiscal year. We find this difficult to explain, given the press attention and awards our exhibits have received, and given news reports that many museums are experiencing increased attendance. In the coming year, we will be conducting formal audience research with Slover-Linett, a Chicago audience-research firm with broad experience in museums, thanks to a grant from the Arts Engagement Exchange, in an attempt to identify ways in which we can build our audience. We are also hoping that budgets will allow some funds for advertising. We are fortunate that, as a university museum we are not entirely dependent on attendance and revenue in order to present exhibits and programs and to maintain the collection. But with declining attendance, we miss opportunities to reach broader audiences and to generate interest and support for the research work that is the mission of the Oriental Institute.

Finally, I would note that we have reorganized departments within the Institute this past year. In recognition of the many accomplishments of the Education Department led by Carole Krucoff, Oriental Institute Director Gil Stein has made Education (now Public Education) a separate department within the Institute. Museum staff, while maintaining an interest in education, now focus more on exhibits and collections. We wish Carole and her staff well in their new position and fully expect to continue and develop further our many collaborations.

The year to come promises to be interesting and productive, as always. We will install two exciting exhibits — Visible Language: Inventions of Writing in the Ancient Middle East and Beyond (opens September 28, 2010), curated by Christopher Woods, Associate Professor of Sumerology; and The First Pharaohs (opens March 29, 2011), curated by Emily Teeter.

Preparations for the Visible Language show are in full swing, with catalog writing, exhibit design, arrangements for loans (including an exciting loan of the earliest Mesopotamian cuneiform tablets from Berlin that have never been exhibited in the United States), and a fascinating CT-scanning project we are doing in collaboration with Dr. Michael Vannier at the University

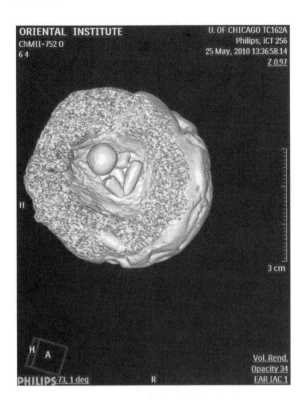

ORIENTAL INSTITUTE U. OF CHICAGO TC162A
ChMII-752 0 Philips, iCT 256
6 4 25 May, 2010 13:36:58.14
Z 0.97
H
3 cm
H A
Vol. Rend.
Opacity 34
PHILIPS 73, 1 deg R FAR IAC 1

Figure 3. Rendering of a token ball from Chogha Mish, Iran, ca. 3400 BC. The token ball was scanned in a CT scanner at the University of Chicago Hospitals by Dr. Michael Vannier. The resulting images were processed by Monica Witczak, so that the tokens inside the clay ball are visible. The next stage of visualization will be to extract each token individually

of Chicago Hospitals. We have scanned a collection of "token balls" — hollow clay balls that contain small geometric clay tokens — that are a precursor to the invention of writing, and we hope this will be a research contribution in addition to an exciting element in the exhibit (fig. 3).

Fundraising for these exhibits is going quite well, thanks to Exelon Corporation, the Women's Board of the University of Chicago, the Antiquities Endowment Fund of the American Research Center in Egypt, and a number of generous private donors. A word to any potential donors who may be reading: our fundraising is not over, and there are still opportunities to contribute.

We will also begin publication of additional volumes in the Museum Highlights series begun by Emily Teeter's book on ancient Egypt with publication of a book on ancient Israel by Gabrielle Novacek. Two other manuscripts (Mesopotamia and Nubia) have been written, and others are in preparation. We aim to have seven volumes published within the next few years.

The coming year will also see development of further exhibits and audiotours, marketing efforts, and collections projects. Go team!

SPECIAL EXHIBITS

Emily Teeter

The interval for this report covers two exhibits: The Life of Meresamun: A Temple Singer in Ancient Egypt (closed on December 6, 2009), and Pioneers to the Past: American Archaeologists in the Middle East, 1919–1920 (opened on January 11, 2010). Details about the Meresamun exhibit can be found in the 2008–2009 *Annual Report*, pp. 194–97. The show generated a tremendous amount of publicity, including a cover article in *Archaeology* magazine. Even after the show closed, Meresamun has been featured in the press, and she continues to gain friends on her Facebook page (more than 1,500 to date). After the exhibit closed, Meresamun was returned to her location in the Joseph and Mary Grimshaw Egyptian Gallery. We re-wrote the label to incorporate some of the information that had been in the show, and we installed the video kiosk near the mummy. We would like to again thank Exelon and Philips Healthcare for their support of the exhibit.

The Pioneers to the Past show was a good example of how collaboration can advance an initial idea. At one point, it was considered that images from the 1919–1920 expedition would be published as a book to commemorate the ninetieth anniversary of the founding of the Oriental Institute. That gradually developed into the photos being the subject of an exhibit, which under the guidance of Geoff Emberling took further form as images and extracts from

Figure 1. View of the exhibit Pioneers to the Past with objects acquired by Breasted in cases that imitate vintage shipping crates

Breasted's letters provided the framework for an extended discussion of the historical context of the trip, as a commentary on the intellectual ownership of the past, and the connections between politics and archaeology and how they have changed in the last ninety years. It was due to input from our community focus group that the show was told in two "voices" — Breasted's own and modern commentary.

The show is divided into an introduction; sections on travels in Egypt, Mesopotamia, and the Arab State; and finally an appraisal of the impact of the expedition on the later activities of the Oriental Institute.

Pioneers to the Past proved to be an ideal overall introduction to the Oriental Institute. For example, in the introductory section, we exhibited a copy of *Ancient Times*, a book that made an important and lasting connection between John D. Rockefeller Jr. and Breasted; the letter from Rockefeller giving Breasted $50,000 to found the Oriental Institute; and Breasted's passport, which is full of interesting stamps and endorsements that document his travels.

In order to give the show more presence and variety, we included a selection of objects that Breasted acquired in Paris and Egypt. Working with material supplied by Peggy Grant, I wrote labels that are primarily excerpts from Breasted's letters, including comments about the dealers from whom he acquired the objects or the object itself. For example, the label for Papyrus Ryerson read,

> Among Breasted's greatest purchases was a perfectly preserved Book of the Dead. Breasted wrote:
>
> "And then I could hardly believe my eyes ... a beautiful brown roll of papyrus, as fresh and uninjured as if it had been a roll of wall paper just arrived from the shop!... Tano laid it down on the table, put his finger on the unrolled inch or two and giving the roll a fillip, he sent it gliding across the table, exposing a perfectly intact bare surface before the beginning of the writing.... And then came the writing! An exquisitely written hieroglyphic copy of the Book of the Dead with wonderfully wrought vignettes, the finest copy of the Book of the Dead which has left Egypt for many years!"

Our design team, led by Brian Zimerle and Erik Lindahl with very valuable advice from Dianne Hanau-Strain, graphically separated the voices — Breasted's images and letters are located on a dark band above slanted ramps that are mounted with the modern commentary. We ended

Figure 2. Membership Coordinator Maeve Reed tends the Oriental Institute information table at "Spotlight on Chicago"

up with a lot of fun and effective design features. Working from the photos, Brian designed striking silhouettes (steamship, biplane, Model T Ford, and "arabanah" [horse-drawn cart]) that echoed the different forms of transportation the expedition employed. Dianne laboriously reworked a vintage map to trace Breasted's travels and to also give a sense of the era. Erik came up with the inspired idea to build exhibit cases in imitation of packing crates, complete with stencils (themselves vintage) with the address "Oriental Institute, Chicago." Through the generosity of Richard Martin of Archeophone Records of Champaign, Illinois, we were able to play music from 1919–1920 in the gallery, which again helped give the visitor a sense of the era. We are very proud that exhibit was voted "Best Museum Exhibit of 2010" in a poll conducted by the *Chicago Reader*.

This was the first exhibit to have its own audiotour, a feature that has proven to be popular with our visitors. The audiotour was an ideal way for us to share more-extended excerpts from the letters with our visitors. The tour was recorded and edited by Tiffany Salone of the university's Media Initiatives Group and includes vintage music provided by Archeophone Records. Tom James designed a program mounted in a kiosk that allows visitors to view all the photography from the expedition as well as to scroll through all of Breasted's letters home from a kiosk in the gallery. This material was also posted on our Web site. Our positive experience with the Meresamun Facebook page motivated us to construct one for Breasted, but rather than anyone "channeling" him (as was the case with Meresamun), we let Breasted "speak" to his more than 1,000 Facebook friends through his letters. Intern Adrienne Frie undertook a massive project editing the letters and posting them so that "friends" could follow what the expedition was doing that week ninety years ago (see also "Publicity and Marketing," below). Adrienne was an important part of the exhibit team — she also edited and proofread the text for the catalog, worked on the object labels, and attended installation meetings.

We brought the rest of our galleries into the theme of the show by marking every object that was acquired by the expedition with a special graphic designed by Tom James. This was an effective way of producing interest in the special exhibit among visitors who may not have heard about it, and the special labels gave a very clear idea of the breadth of Breasted's acquisitions.

The Members' opening for the exhibit on January 11 continued the theme of the show, complete with cookies in the form of pith helmets made with a cookie cutter custom made by Erik, and Denise stocked the Suq with real pith helmets and books that related to the theme of the exhibit. We were honored to have Breasted's grandchildren and great-grandchildren visit the exhibit on February 17.

We would like to thank Exelon Corporation, as well as Barbara Breasted Whitesides and Robert and Peggy Grant, for their support of the Pioneers to the Past show.

We also thank our community focus group, who helped us with the Pioneers to the Past show and who have been giving us good advice about the writing exhibit and other upcoming shows. The group consists of Randy Adamsick, Nathan Mason, Christine Carrino, Angela Adams, Molly

Woulfe, Dianne Hanau-Strain, and Patty McNamara. The group meets with Geoff, Emily, Carole, Wendy, and interns who are working on the exhibits.

We are now immersed in finalizing the exhibit Visible Language: Inventions of Writing in the Ancient Middle East and Beyond, curated by Chris Woods, which will open to Members on September 27. I am also well ahead on the planning for Earliest Egypt: The First Pharaohs (tentative title) show that opens March 29, 2011.

We continue our practice of issuing a catalog for each exhibit, and thanks to Tom Urban and Leslie Schramer of our Publications Department, these handsome and useful volumes appear in time for the opening (a feat that even some of the larger museums cannot always manage). The catalogs continue to be in demand even after the presentation of the show, and two of them, *Lost Nubia* (2006) and *European Cartographers and the Ottoman World, 1500–1750* (2007), have been reprinted (see report under "Publications"). We also issued a reprint of Charles Breasted's biography of his father, *Pioneer to the Past,* with a new selection of photographs made available by archivist John Larson.

Upcoming Exhibits (*some titles and dates are tentative*)

Visible Language: Inventions of Writing in the Ancient Middle East and Beyond
(Members' reception, September 27)
September 28, 2010–March 6, 2011

Earliest Egypt: The First Pharaohs
March 29–October 23, 2011

Ceramic Arts of the Ancient Middle East
November 15, 2011–April 29, 2012

Birds in Ancient Egypt
May 29–October 21, 2012

PUBLICITY AND MARKETING
Emily Teeter and Thomas James

This was an incredibly busy year for marketing and publicity. We collaborated with new organizations and more fully incorporated new media into our strategies. The Oriental Institute does not have a dedicated marketing specialist or publicist. Rather, our efforts are shared among units of the Institute. Among the many people involved are Jessica Caracci, Maeve Reed, Wendy Ennes, Carole Krucoff, Geoff Emberling, interns Amanda Sorensen and Adrienne Frie, the authors of this report, and of course William Harms of the University's News Office, who shows us how the professionals do it.

Our main goals are to raise awareness of the mission and work of the Oriental Institute and its Museum and to increase Museum visitorship. The overall strategy is that visitors to the Museum have the potential to become Members, volunteers, and donors. The Museum and its programs are a unique and powerful marketing tool. This trickle-down effect is very evident in the most current visitor's guide (developed in 2009 under a grant from the Chicago Community Trust) that incorporates a Museum plan with information about the *E-Tablet* and becoming a Member or a volunteer. As a result, some of our efforts are aimed at publicizing special exhibits, others at specific programs, and yet others at promoting the Oriental Institute as a whole.

This year saw a new level of collaboration with the Department of Cultural Affairs of the city of Chicago. The city offers very diverse programs that, over the years, thanks largely to Carole Krucoff's ingenuity, we have been able to tap into. This year we took a more proactive stance, meeting with Dorothy Coyle, the director of the Department of Cultural Affairs. She had many good ideas about expanding our audience that coincided with the new emphasis that the city is placing on neighbor attractions. One outgrowth of this meeting was collaboration with the city's World Kitchen program. In June, Carole and Emily, working with Judith Dunbar Hines, director of the city's Culinary Arts and Events, produced a two-session program based on ancient Egyptian food. On June 3, about 100 people (90 percent of whom were not Oriental Institute Members) attended a lecture and then toured the Joseph and Mary Grimshaw Egyptian Gallery, where many representations of food can be found.

We were very fortunate to have Amanda Sorensen as an intern for six months. We assigned her many of our promotion projects. She monitored the city's explorechicago.com site to ensure that our listing was up to date, and she also followed up on other recommendations by Dorothy Coyle such as pursuing city-related tourism possibilities. Amanda organized receptions here at the Institute for Chicago Greeters (February 17), the Chicago Tour-Guide Professionals Association (April 7), and hotel concierges (May 4). Through Nathan Mason, a member of our community focus group, we also had discussions with the city's Department of Aviation, exploring the possibility of placing a version of some of our shows (Catastrophe and Pioneers) in O'Hare Airport Terminal 5 departure areas. Conversations are ongoing.

Amanda also oversaw our relations with the Chicago Convention and Tourism Bureau (CCTB). This group deals with inbound group travel, especially conventions. We joined the CCTB for the year to assess how effective their offerings might be for generating more Museum attendance. Amanda's primary assignment was to be the contact with CCTB and to take advantage of as many of their programs as was applicable to our mission. One of Geoff's main goals is to have the Oriental Institute incorporated into bus tours of the city, and CCTB seemed to be a good conduit to that clientele. Amanda was tireless in following up every lead, going to orientations at McCormick Place, and calling destination-management companies (who work with inbound traffic). She attended a CCTB-sponsored Webinar on March 10 on "The Essentials of Search Engine Optimization," and she monitored and updated the CCTB Web listings. Emily and Jessica also attended a showcase for new CCTB members. Although it became apparent that CCTB is primarily designed to assist people in the hospitality business (hotels and restaurants), there were some opportunities for us as well. Amanda organized a reception for principal staff members of the CCTB, who in turn gave us valuable advice about attracting and marketing to groups. Jacquie Brave, of Accenting Chicago!, a destination-management company, met with a group of us to give further advice about increasing traffic.

We also attempted to attract new audiences through e-mail and mail solicitation of special-interest groups such as retirement centers and social clubs. Using the list of upcoming conventions supplied through our membership in CCTB, Amanda sent messages to organizations whose mission seemed to be in keeping with ours. She edited the press release for the Pioneers to the Past show for in-flight and travel magazines, playing up the aspects of "trip from hell," and she wrote the clever press release "A Passion for Fashion" for women's media highlighting how much information on the history of fashion is contained in our exhibits. Amanda also began to send announcements of our new Bible audiotour to churches and religious groups. She also paid visits to downtown hotels to ensure that concierges had information about the Oriental Institute. In the effort to attract more visitors from the immediate area, Amanda, working with Maeve, arranged for special discounts to Oriental Institute Members in local restaurants.

Another market that we are exploring is the GLBT community. Volunteer Sue Geshwender researched statistics about education, income levels, and spending, all of which indicate that it is potentially a good market for us. Sue and Emily talked with staff of the Center on Halsted to explore programs, and Emily contacted the Chicago History Museum to see what their experience has been with the "Out at the CHM" lecture series. Sue and Emily also met with Ben Beadles, who has had a great deal of experience working with non-profit arts communities.

Those involved with marketing spent a lot of time attending seminars and training sessions. Amanda attended CCTB orientation in November, a Marketing and Technology Seminar led by Adam Thurman in January 2010, and a workshop on Immersive Experiences in marketing in February 24. Maeve attended a two-week Arts Engagement Learning Circle on Branding in March, and Maeve and Emily attended the annual Spotlight (a showcase for the city's cultural offerings). We hope to report in the future that these efforts have resulted in a rise in Museum and event attendance.

The Oriental Institute and its projects received important media coverage in the last year, including a story on the Persepolis Tablet Project in *Payvand Iran News*, the Henrietta Herbolsheimer Syro-Anatolian Gallery mentioned in *Near Eastern Archaeology* magazine, the Iraqi training program in the *University of Chicago Magazine*, Gil Stein's work at Tell Zeidan in the *New York Times*, the work of the CAMEL lab in *Archaeology* magazine, and a general article on the Museum in the in-flight magazine of Etihad Airlines (the national magazine of the United Arab Emirates).

Publicity for special exhibits is driven by a comprehensive plan that identifies a variety of target audiences and how we might reach them. After each exhibit, the marketing plan is reviewed to assess its effectiveness. There is a great amount of variability in each plan because each exhibit is different. For example, the Meresamun show had a science component that included the medical community as a target audience, while Pioneers to the Past has appealed to those with an interest in history. Further, for some shows, we have a modest marketing budget, while for others, we have virtually no funds for promotion. The two exhibits presented during the interval of this report, The Life of Meresamun: A Temple Singer in Ancient Egypt, and Pioneers to the Past: American Archaeologists in the Middle East, 1919–1920, generated a huge amount of publicity. Thanks to the subject matter and Philips Healthcare publicists, Meresamun was in the news throughout the world (see further details in the 2008–2009 *Annual Report*, pp. 200–01). Since the time of that report, Meresamun has been featured in *National Geographic* and in a multiple-page (and cover) color spread in *Illustrerad Vetenskap* (a Danish popular-science magazine), and *KMT* magazine. The show received positive critical reviews in *Near Eastern Archaeology* magazine and the *American Journal of Archaeology*.

We promoted the Pioneers to the Past exhibit with spots on NPR radio and banners at the entrance of the Institute. We were thrilled that the show was voted "Best Museum Exhibit of 2010" in a poll conducted by the *Chicago Reader*. The exhibit was featured in the *Wall Street Journal*, the *Chicago Tribune*, *Time Out Chicago*, *Archaeology* magazine (twice), the *Biblical Archaeologist*, the *Hyde Park Herald*, and the alumni magazine of North Central College (which Breasted attended).

New Media

Over the past couple of years, we have been experimenting with an increasing number of ways in which we can directly interact with the world over the Internet. These "new media" outlets have become too big to ignore — in March 2010 Facebook edged out Google to become the most visited site on the Internet, accounting for more than 7 percent of all Internet traffic. The interactive Web has blossomed into a place where it is easy to follow people or institutions on Twitter, subscribe to blogs, or become a friend or fan on Facebook. Over the past year, the Oriental Institute began to try and expand the way we communicate with our Membership and the world at large through Facebook, Twitter, and blogging.

Our Facebook efforts, which began a few years ago when "Meresamun" (http://bit.ly/Meresamun) joined Facebook to promote her special exhibit and with the creation of the Oriental Institute Facebook fan page, intensified this year when "James Henry Breasted" (http://bit.ly/JHBreasted) signed up to promote the Pioneers to the Past show. Tom has been posting photos and letters documenting the trip that our show follows.

The main Oriental Institute presence on Facebook is in the form of our institutional Facebook page (http://bit.ly/OI-Facebook). If you haven't seen it, we hope you'll visit soon. You can visit whether you're a member of Facebook or not — but if you are, we'd love it if you became a fan! We're using Facebook to pose questions, announce events, share photographs, and compile links to news stories about work that our researchers are doing. The Research Archives also have a fan page on Facebook (http://bit.ly/OI-Archives), and we encourage you to check it out as well.

The Oriental Institute Twitter page (http://twitter.com/oimuseum/) is a little newer, and a little less developed. The vision we have for it is not only as a place where we can share the things that we're doing here at the Institute, but also as a place to share all news of interest to those who are interested in Near Eastern studies. All of our Facebook status updates also automatically update over Twitter. Let us know if you think we're doing okay. Follow us and send us an @ message over Twitter with suggestions on how to improve.

One last thing we're trying out for the first time is blogging. As a tie-in with Pioneers to the Past, we are publishing Breasted's letters home to his family. It's completely unintentional, but the dates from Breasted's 1919–1920 trip through the Middle East happen to coincide exactly with our calendar this year. Letters that he wrote on Monday, May 17, 1920, will show up on the blog on Monday, May 17, 2010. We're also putting a selection of photographs from the same days as the letters onto the blog, so that you can get Breasted's vivid descriptions of what he was seeing and doing and also see exactly what he saw. The Breasted Blog is located at: https://blogs.uchicago.edu/oi/ — if you use an RSS (really simple syndication) feed reader, you can also add Breasted's RSS feed to your reader and get automatic updates every time he makes a new post. These things all tie in together. All Facebook statuses automatically go out as tweets not long afterward. Breasted Blog posts are automatically announced on Facebook and Twitter.

In the future we may branch out into other forms of new media. We'd love to have a YouTube channel, but we just don't produce enough new video content at the moment. We're working on a Flickr account, where we'll be able to show people a lot more of what we have in our photographic collection. The new big thing seems to be Foursquare, and we haven't yet decided how or if we're going to move into that market. Be sure though, that as new communication services come to market, we'll look into them and see if they fit our mission.

REGISTRATION

Helen McDonald and Susan Allison

We have begun the registration and re-housing of another section of material for a new Institute of Museum and Library Services (IMLS) cabinet grant awarded in 2009 and due to run until 2011. We received the first cabinet delivery relating to this grant in February 2010 and will get the second and final delivery before the end of the year. This grant includes material from Nubian sites in the area of Bab Kalabsha (several sites of the X-Group and Christian periods) and Qasr el-Wizz (a church and monastery site of the Nubian Christian period). The Bab Kalabsha material includes both ceramics (from settlements and cemeteries) and stone architectural fragments from temples of the X-Group period. The Qasr el-Wizz material is more extensive and mostly ceramic, though there are also some objects such as clay sealings. With the help of Master of Arts Program in the Social Sciences (MAPPS) students and volunteers, the Bab Kalabsha material is now registered and re-housed (550 pieces). Most of the Wizz material is also re-housed (2,000 pieces so far). A total of 2,750 digital images have been taken of the re-housed material. We are also committed to re-housing a variety of large pots and the rest of the registered stone objects that are still in temporary storage boxes.

During the summers of 2009 and 2010, we embarked on a systematic inventory of our Egyptian cabinets, containing mostly stone and ceramic objects. This useful and necessary task was undertaken in the summer of 2009 by Courtney Jacobson and Aleksandra Hallman and in summer 2010 by Maggie Geoga and Junli Song. So far some fifty cabinets containing nearly 13,000 objects have been inventoried. New labels have been printed where necessary and Museum numbers marked on objects where unclear or non-existent. Lists have been made of all the un-numbered pieces lurking among the registered material. The last stage will be to put details of all of the "no-number items" in a spreadsheet and then take digital images of them for comparison with records of missing objects.

In the summer of 2009, we also conducted an inventory of the metals room in preparation for a National Endowment for the Humanities application that Laura D'Alessandro was writing for new cabinets and the re-housing of our metal collection. Elizabeth Wolfson, Becky Caroli, and Susan Allison inventoried the approximately 11,000 objects in the metals room. Problem objects were noted and will be researched in the future. In July we heard that the application was successful, and a contract conservator will be hired later in the year to work on this project for two years.

We have begun to re-assemble a selection of sherds to form the basis of a teaching collection for members of faculty to use. So far over 3,300 sherds have been identified and moved, most of them newly registered. Several of our volunteers have worked on the registration of small groups of sherds collected from the surfaces of a variety of sites. We expect to continue to add to this collection until we have a reasonably representative selection and then consult with members of faculty as to what else might be added.

The project of photographing and updating our records of the Egyptian Predynastic collection undertaken by Susan Allison has continued. This work is in preparation for a planned exhibit on early Egypt. Almost all of the 3,000 early Egyptian objects have now been photographed and their records updated. Registration has continued to play its part in those projects that have included the rest of the collections staff such as the Khorsabad relief project and the object movements relating to the installation of the Pioneers to the Past exhibit (both described in more detail elsewhere). We have kept track of objects relating to the forthcoming Visible Language exhibit that is due to open in September of this year.

In preparation for our move to new database software, and with the assistance of George Sundell, we have been looking critically at the structure of our current database and asking ourselves what extra fields or tables we might like to have in the new one. We have also begun the time-consuming process of cleaning up our data. This has involved looking at all the different terms used in certain fields and working toward a more rigorous standardization of terms and editing records accordingly. Contracts with a vendor of museum-specific database software are on the verge of being signed, and we hope to begin the changeover later this year.

As to loans, we lent two small, inscribed Egyptian bowls from the Tutankhamun embalming cache to the Metropolitan Museum of Art in New York for an exhibit on the funeral of Tutankhamen. It runs until September. We recently renewed a loan of two Egyptian objects for a further two years to the Du Sable Museum of African American History. These are a Nubian A-Group pot and an ushebti of Nitocris.

On October 2, Registration hosted a visit by the Grolier Club. We turned our office space into a display of Islamic manuscripts and book bindings. The club members also visited the Special Collections of the Regenstein Library.

In April alterations were made to the source of chilled water that is so important to our climate-control system. Now instead of having just the Pick Hall chillers as our source, we are plugged into a university-wide system that links all the chilled water sources, including that of the Regenstein Library, into one big loop. The changeover took a week, during which our system was hooked up to a temporary chiller parked out on University Avenue. This change has been beneficial, with fewer problems with the supply of chilled water since the changeover.

The Registration Department has moved or inventoried just over 48,000 objects this year. Nearly 5,750 were the subject of research of all kinds, and 330 objects were used in teaching and training. Nearly 950 objects were moved for either photography or drawing. Just over 36,000 were inventoried or had their locations updated. Over 4,700 objects were registered, mostly relating to the current re-housing grant and the development of the teaching collection. A further thousand objects were re-housed. Over 10,000 bag labels were printed for newly registered objects or inventoried objects whose labels were inadequate. Over 300 objects were moved for temporary exhibits that were installed, dismantled, or in preparation this year, and 1,800 were moved that relate to preparations for the Earliest Egypt exhibit. Almost 100 objects were moved relating to loans or while being considered for loans of various sorts.

It has been a busy year for visiting researchers.

- The Amuq publication project has continued to be a main focus of activity, as our three researchers Lynn Swartz Dodd (Tell Judaidah), Marina Pucci (Chatal Höyük), and Heather Snow (Tell Tayinat) continued to work on final publications of the later levels at those sites. We have hosted visits from two of the Amuq researchers this year (Marina Pucci and Lynn Swartz Dodd). Fiona Haughey (the Tayinat draughtsperson) visited for a month this spring to draw some 300 Tayinat objects for publication. Both Marina and Lynn have recruited Near Eastern Languages and Civilizations students to assist with digital imaging and sherd recording and drawing (Natasha Ayers and Dan Mahoney have worked from time to time on Judaidah sherds, and Courtney Jacobson has drawn sherds from Chatal Höyük). Once again the Amuq office in the Archaeology Labs has been a hive of activity.

- In July of 2009, Wayne Pitard of the Spurlock Museum visited with a team to photograph all of the Amuq cylinder seals. They used a set-up that includes a spool on which to place the cylinder seal and rotate it as it is photographed. This gives a sort of a "roll out" of the seal, though of course it is backwards compared to an actual rolling of the seal. As a follow-up to this project, we then lent the Spurlock modern rollings of all the Amuq cylinder seals, so that those could also be photographed for comparison with the seal photographs.

- In February we lent fifty-five Iron Age arrowheads made of bronze from the Amuq sites, Megiddo, and Persepolis to Argonne for x-ray fluorescence and x-ray diffraction analysis with high-energy synchrotron radiation. The principal investigators of this project are Lynn Dodd, Heather Snow, and Liz Friedman.

- Helen Taylor visited for three weeks in September to study Bakun-period sherds from William Sumner's Kur River Basin survey. This is part of her PhD research.

- Also in September, Philip Stockhammer came and studied sixty Mycenean sherds from Megiddo.

- In the autumn, Ann Gunter of Northwestern University came over to look at ceramic, metal, and faience objects from Khorsabad.

- Ryan Perry (PhD student from University College London) visited to work on the Fakhariyah material in December.

- Pedro Azara visited in December to look at a variety of Diyala objects with a view to borrowing some for an exhibit in Barcelona and Madrid on Sumerian art.

- Sandra Knudsen from the Toledo Art Museum visited in January to look at objects that may be available for loan to the Toledo Art Museum.

- Daniela Rosenow visited in January to research our material from Bubastis.

- Ofer Marder of the Israel Antiquities Authority visited in February to study the flint from the "Early Stages" at Megiddo as part of Eliot Braun's re-appraisal of all of the "Early Stages" material.

- In March, Catherine Marro came and studied a selection of Amuq phase F sherds.

- In April, Tine Bagh researched some Egyptian objects that we acquired from W. F. Petrie.

- Natasha Ayers has recently completed detailed descriptions and drawings of the 237 pots from the tombs at Assasif. This is part of Christine Lilyquist's publication of the Assasif material, which was excavated by the Metropolitan Museum of Art in the 1920s.

The Museum collections continue to be used for teaching and research by Oriental Institute staff and Near Eastern Languages and Civilizations faculty and students. Users include the following:

- Kate Grossman used a selection of flints and sherds for her evening class on early Mesopotamia in November.

- Donald Whitcomb used Islamic sherds from Tell Fakhariyah, Rayy, Samarra, Hama, and Fustat for a class held in the Spring Quarter.

- Jan Johnson used one of our Demotic annuity contracts for a class in the spring.

- Robert Ritner used a number of heart scarabs for the exam of the Beginning Hieroglyphs class.

- Fred Donner used a selection of early Arabic papyri for his Palaeography and Epigraphy class, with the students each choosing a papyrus to translate.

- Karen Wilson has continued working on a publication of the pottery from the Inanna Temple sounding at Nippur with McGuire Gibson, Richard Zettler, Jean Evans, and others.

- Angela Altenhofen has continued to draw seal impressions for the Diyala project, objects for Marina Pucci's forthcoming Chatal Höyük publication, and for Eliot Braun's publication of the Early Bronze Age "Early Stages" at Megiddo.

- Clemens Reichel visited and photographed a selection of Diyala sealings and tablets. Larry Lissak has begun to photograph a variety of Diyala objects for the Diyala online database project.

- Bruce Williams has recommenced work on the Serra material for a forthcoming Oriental Institute Nubian Expedition volume (it will be volume 11). Fortunately we have registered and re-housed all of the Serra ceramics as part of the previous IMLS re-housing grant, so it is now readily accessible. Bruce's work will enable us to improve the information in the database.

- François Gaudard researched our Egyptian inscribed linen.

- During summer 2009, Elise MacArthur researched our inscribed early Egyptian objects. Her work will be applied to her thesis as well as our future Earliest Egypt temporary exhibit.

- At the beginning of this summer, Rozenn Bailleul-Lesuer began research for her planned temporary exhibit on birds in Egypt.

These accomplishments have been made possible by the capable and efficient efforts of our Museum Assistant, Courtney Jacobson, and with the assistance of a wonderful group of volunteers and interns, including Cassandra Callewaert, Becky Caroli, Gretel Braidwood, Joe Diamond, Maggie Geoga, Aleksandra Hallman, Janet Helman, Ila Patlogan, Andrew Rutledge, Matthew Sawina, Daila Shefner, Toni Smith, Junli Song, Jim Sopranos, George Sundell, Raymond Tindel, and Elizabeth Wolfson. The volunteers have together contributed well over a thousand hours of their time to Museum Registration, and we are grateful for all their help.

ARCHIVES

John A. Larson

As of December 2009, John Larson has served as Museum Archivist for twenty-nine years.

Photographic Services

The income from photographic image sales and reproduction fees enables us to purchase archival supplies and equipment for the Archives and for photography. Between July 1, 2009, and June 30, 2010, we experienced a decrease in the number of requests and, consequently, in the amount of income. This can be attributed to the state of the world-wide economy and a decline in the number of new book titles being published. Thomas R. James and Michael Camp prepared the paperwork and handled all the other details that are involved in processing the requests that we received for Oriental Institute proprietary images and reproduction permissions during the past year.

On the positive side, this was a banner year in the ongoing effort to transfer the information from the existing photographic-image card catalogs into a Filemaker Server database of Oriental Institute photographs (available as a working document online at http://oi.uchicago.edu/museum/

collections/pa/database.html). At the beginning of the fiscal year, the photo database contained approximately 57,800 records. Currently, we have 80,600 records in the photo database, and that number continues to increase. The interns who have worked under the supervision of Tom James — Eric Beckman, Michael Camp, Christine Efta, Shaheen Gutierrez, Adam Hemmings, Margaret Moline, Miranda Pettengill, James Pike, Daniel Sarosta, Charley Spence, and Jennifer Ziermann — have entered the data from roughly 23,000 card-catalog records into the photo database.

The records that are currently in the photo database derive from several sources. Some of the records in the photo database are from new photography that is being generated for forthcoming publications and other projects, some are from archival records, and some are from previously unregistered field photography. The lion's share of the records is from the card catalogs for previously registered photographs, negatives, and slides. In the card catalogs, there are 68,470 photograph cards, 46,299 negative cards, and 12,250 slide cards. Currently we are working through the photograph catalog cards — 47,815 photograph cards have been entered to date, representing 70 percent of the total number of photograph cards. Happily, there is substantial overlap among the card-catalog systems for the different types of photographic media. In the process of entering the data from the photo catalog cards, we have also entered the data for 31,014 negative catalog cards (67 percent of the total), and 4,534 slide catalog cards (37 percent of the total). So far, 35,954 of the records in the database have thumbnail images attached, either archival material that has been scanned, or new photography that is being generated weekly.

Archives

Visiting scholars during fiscal year 2009/2010 included Lindsay Allen, Lindsay Ambridge, Gwenda Blair, Joe Bonno, Peter Brand, Eliot Braun, James H. Breasted III, John Breasted, Azra Dawood, Lynn Schwarz Dodd, James Goode, Robert Hawley, Daniel Meyer, Ivan Moreno, Dennis O'Connor, Marina Pucci, Carole Roche, Bernd Schipper, and Julie Stauder-Porchet. From within our own Oriental Institute community, Geoff Emberling, Robert Ritner, Emily Teeter, Karen L. Wilson, and Jonathan Winnerman have conducted research using Archives materials. We would especially like to thank Tom James for his tireless assistance in the ongoing operation of the Archives.

Recent Acquisitions

In November 2009, Charlotte Otten presented to the Oriental Institute Archives a small personal collection of her photographs and correspondence, relating to her field season at the site of Jarmo in Iraqi Kurdistan with Robert and Linda Braidwood. This is a most welcome addition to the Archives and includes a series of ethnographic photographs taken by Dr. Otten while she was in Iraq in the 1950s.

Volunteers and Student Assistants

The following people have contributed their time as Archives volunteers during fiscal year 2009/2010 and have made it possible for us to continue a number of projects in the Oriental Institute Archives that would not have been possible without their generous assistance: Jean Fincher, Peggy Grant, Sandra Jacobsohn, Roberta Kovitz, Robert Wagner, and Carole Yoshida. We are grateful to have benefited from the help of these dedicated volunteers, and we thank them here for all of their efforts on behalf of the Archives.

Archivist John Larson has also been assisted in the Oriental Institute Archives during this fiscal year by student intern Betsy Giles (summer 2009), and Masters of Arts Program in Social Sciences (MAPSS) graduate-student volunteer Daniel Kovacs (Fall Quarter 2009). Manuel Alex Moya (academic year 2009/2010) and Stephanie O'Brien (Winter/Spring Quarters 2010), both MAPSS graduate students, have worked on a variety of projects in the Archives and have been assigned to the Archives compact-storage project since January 2010. Elizabeth Wolfson, who has worked past summers for John Larson in the Archives (2008) and Helen McDonald in Museum Registration (2009), returned in June to work on the Archives compact-storage project for the summer of 2010.

Figure 1. Before the installation of the collapsible archival shelving

Figure 2. After the installation of the collapsible archival shelving

Archives Compact-Storage Project

Lastly, we would like to report on a project designed to maximize the use of space in our climate-controlled Archives storage room. On Tuesday, January 19, 2010, the Oriental Institute Archives was closed for research appointments in order to begin preparing for the installation of compact-storage shelving, which took place throughout the months of April and May. Beginning in June, we started moving the archives collections back into our newly remodeled space. This process is expected to continue until the end of August 2010, and we expect to reopen the Oriental Institute Archives for research appointments after Labor Day, on Tuesday, September 7, 2010.

The overall appearance of the Oriental Institute Archives storage room has changed dramatically during the past six months. We now have more than 1,050 new shelves and 50 additional map-case drawers for oversize materials. The compact-storage shelves are mounted on carriages set on tracks, which enable us to take the greatest possible advantage of our available floor space. Our previously existing installation of 65 shelves for our collection of boxed black-and-white large-format negatives has been moved to a new location, and we have also moved four mapcase cabinets, which contain a total of 160 drawers.

The successful implementation of the Oriental Institute Archives compact-storage project would not have been possible without the hard work and cooperation of a large number of individuals and teams. On behalf of the Archives, John Larson would like to record our thanks to Gil Stein and Steve Camp for submitting the original proposal to the University of Chicago's Capital Projects Committee; to the members of the Capital Projects Committee for approving and funding the project; to the Capital Project Delivery section of the Facilities Services department, especially Denise Davis and Richard Bumstead; to Andy Cobb of the Facilities Services department; to Mark Cheng and Jonathan Estanislao of MDC Architects, P.C., Streamwood, Illinois; to Mike Dawson, Rick Dasko, and their installation team at Bradford Systems Corporation, Bensenville, Illinois; to Thomas Fawcett, Shaun Gray, and their team at 360 Contractors; to Carlos and the guys at Hogan and Son Movers and Storage, Chicago; to Geoff Emberling, Susan Allison, Laura D'Alessandro, Brian Zimerle, Thomas James, Erik Lindahl, Helen McDonald, and Alison Whyte, all of the Oriental Institute Museum staff; and to Carla Hosein and D'Ann Condes of Oriental Institute Administration.

CONSERVATION

Laura D'Alessandro

This past year, Conservation staff kept busy with a variety of projects. Alison Whyte, Assistant Conservator, was the lead conservator in the Museum's two exhibits: Pioneers to the Past and Visible Language. Alison also attended the American Institute for Conservators' annual meeting in Milwaukee, where she presented a poster that she produced: "Bastiani and Beyond: Restorers at the Oriental Institute, 1930–1970." This overview of the work of Donatello Bastiani and his team of restorers beautifully details the accomplishments of Bastiani over a forty-year period in a pre-conservation world. There are plans to have the poster — or a version of the contents — on display in the Museum for visitors to enjoy and appreciate. Alison finished up the year with a brief stint at Scott Branting's site of Kerkenes, where she focused on the stabilization and long-term storage needs of two large iron bands and the treatment and installation of two stone sculptures at the nearby museum in Yozgat.

Conservation staff also played a modest role in the Chicago-based training of Iraqi conservators. The group, jointly sponsored by the US State Department and the Field Museum of Natural History, spent two weeks in the Conservation Laboratory, where we provided workshops on unbaked clays and copper-alloy conservation to six Iraqi colleagues. We very much enjoyed our short time with our Iraqi visitors as they generously shared their experiences with us and provided presentations on some of their more interesting projects from the Baghdad National Museum and historical and archaeological sites from all around Iraq. It was a wonderful opportunity to share experiences and learn from each other. We'll have another opportunity next year to meet more of our Iraqi colleagues when the last group of Iraqis from this program visits Chicago.

This past year saw the departure of the laboratory's two contract conservators: Monica Hudak, whose work on the Persepolis Fortification Project tablets was instrumental in keeping a flow of cleaned and stabilized tablets prepared for the critical imaging portion of the project, and Jeanne Mandel, an area conservator who worked part time with Monica on the conservation of the Persepolis tablets.

Last summer we were helped in the laboratory by two volunteers, Claire Barker, an intern from George Washington University, and Lillian Rosner, a Lab School junior and daughter of Professor Martha Roth. Their assistance with the cleaning of Khorsabad stone fragments under the supervision of conservation staff was very helpful. Lillian was also instrumental in assisting with the completion of another important project: the Institute of Museum and Library Sciences (IMLS) funded re-housing of a portion of the Nubian organic collection. With a little direction, her amazing (and unsuspected) box- and tray-construction talents provided custom storage containers for a variety of artifacts in materials ranging from leather and wood to bone and textiles.

This summer we are being assisted in the Conservation Laboratory by Kristen Gillette, a recent Wheaton College graduate, and Nicole Pizzini, a 2009 graduate of Illinois Wesleyan University. Both young women are working on completing their prerequisite experience for application to a graduate art-conservation training program. Their patience and care while working on the Khorsabad stone fragments has been very much appreciated.

The Museum was fortunate to once again receive an IMLS 2009 Conservation Project Support grant that is generously funding the re-housing of over 2,000 objects from Nubia and Megiddo. And thanks to the National Endowment for the Humanities (NEH) and a new funding category, Sustaining Cultural Heritage Collections, the Museum has received a grant that will allow us to re-house the entire metals collection of over 10,000 artifacts. The NEH grant will support a contract conservator's position to oversee the two-year project. In addition to new customized cabinets, the grant activities will support conservation time on the Department of Geophysical Sciences' scanning electron microscope and allow for the proper identification of some of the metals in the collection that had been misidentified in the past.

Conservation staff has also taken part in a variety of interesting and varied research projects over the past year. One of the collaborative projects that began last year involved working with researchers from the University of Southern California and Argonne National Laboratories on identifying the original composition of copper alloys used in the Amuq region, Megiddo, and Persepolis using non-destructive techniques. This project is ongoing; we hope to have some exciting results by next summer.

Closer to home, another project that we are working on involves Dr. Michael Vannier, radiology professor in the University of Chicago Hospitals. After working on Lady Meresamun's CT-scanning project, Dr. Vannier became interested in another project involving ancient materials — using their unique attenuation value as a means of identification. Using the hospital's state-of-the-art Dual CT-scanning device, Dr. Vannier and his team are scanning a variety of ancient materials at four different energies. Our role in the Conservation Lab is to determine the density and elemental analysis of the materials that can be tied to their attenuation values in order to establish a database of materials that can be identified, sight unseen, by CT scanning.

As a wonderful conclusion to the year, Conservation hosted a small group from the University of Chicago Women's Board for a tour of the Conservation Laboratory. The Women's Board has been very supportive of conservation at the Oriental Institute going back to the lab's inception in the early 1970s. We were very pleased when Gil Stein told us that he had arranged a tour and provided us with an opportunity to thank representatives of the Women's Board for their most recent grant to the laboratory. The focus of the visit was the lab's latest addition, the Compact Phoenix, a laser cleaning system that was funded by a generous grant from the Women's Board. It was exciting to finally be able to show this state-of-the-art equipment to the Women's Board and talk about its myriad uses. While we could not demonstrate the laser during the tour, due to safety issues, we were able to show a brief video of the laser in action that the university's radiation safety officer, Donald Samaan, had graciously filmed for us for this event. We really appreciated the enthusiasm of the participants as they took time out of their busy schedules to learn about a few of our ongoing projects and see what their funding has supported and encouraged over the years.

PREP SHOP

Erik Lindahl

The Oriental Institute Museum Preparation Shop has been a busy place over the last year. We have returned Meresamun to her home in the Joseph and Mary Grimshaw Egyptian Gallery, embarked on an exciting journey with James Henry Breasted, and started to explore the origins of writing. We have packed up and moved the contents of the Museum Archives, and they are in the process of being moved back in, and the Museum has been made compliant with the Americans with Disabilities Act. Meanwhile, past projects continue, particularly the registration of our collection of Neo-Assyrian reliefs, updating Museum labels and displays, and continuing to improve lighting in the galleries.

The year began and has ended with the uncrating, cleaning, photography, and re-housing of previously unregistered Khorsabad fragments. New pallet racking was also installed in heavy-object storage to help make the collection more accessible for the long term.

Throughout the year we have been working toward the long-term goal of updating the labels in the galleries. We are also taking this opportunity to refine the exhibits. This year we have been working on the Edgar and Deborah Jannotta Mesopotamian Gallery. Geoff Embering has been the main force behind this project with curatorial help from Kathryn Hanson and Sue Geshwender. Brian Zimerle has been handling any graphic-design issues.

As a result of a university-wide movement toward compliance with the Americans with Disabilities Act, the entire campus was surveyed and the Museum was asked to make certain modifications to the galleries in order to comply. Most of these requested modifications were to make the galleries friendlier to people with low vision. Stanchions were installed around sculpture in the Robert and Deborah Aliber Persian Gallery, and cane rails were installed between the legs of the display cases. We also took this opportunity to upgrade the existing Museum stanchions.

The special-exhibits program continued with Meresamun being returned to her home in the Joseph and Mary Grimshaw Egyptian Gallery. The Breasted exhibit opened in January. It was rewarding to go on Breasted's journey while designing the exhibit. Brian Zimerle did an excellent job with the graphics and photographs. To try and evoke the aesthetic of the time and place, we designed and constructed shipping-crate–like display cases and a gallery wall that suggests a temporary military-like structure. Since the opening of Pioneers to the Past, we have been working on Visible Language: Inventions of Writing in the Ancient Middle East and Beyond.

Another Museum project that demanded a substantial amount of the Prep Shop's time over the last year was the installation of compact storage in the Museum Archives. To create space for the Archives material that needed to be removed during construction, we emptied the Prep Shop, condensed as much of the material in heavy-object storage as possible, and moved all of our unused display cases to our off-site storage warehouse. We also took this opportunity to have the floors in the shop thoroughly cleaned and sealed. This project is nearing completion — all but a few carts of Archives material have been returned.

The year ended with the production of the Visible Language exhibit in full swing. There are so many talented people involved with this exhibit; it is bound to be a success.

SUQ

Denise Browning

This was a year of many changes for the Suq in relationship to its staff and volunteers. Jennifer Westerfeld, who has worked for us for over ten years, left for an internship at Dumbarton Oaks. Jo Ellen Urban, who fell ill and died unexpectedly, will be missed. And three of our Suq student employees graduated this year; congratulations to Ashley Stanton, Maureen Hsia, and Kristen Smart. We also lost volunteer James Tillpaugh, who opened a new coffee house in Wicker Park, but we gained Erin Mukwaya, a delightful new student volunteer.

We were pleased to help with the note-card development for the annual Members' event, Passport to the Middle East: Check Out Our Digs!, and with the opening of the Pioneers to the Past exhibit.

We also participated this June in the Arabesque Festival, which was held downtown in Daley Plaza. We had a booth filled with our merchandise and volunteers from the Museum and the Suq. We handed out hundreds of brochures informing everyone about the Oriental Institute. Special thanks to Andrea Dudek and her niece, Erin Flynn, as well as Semra Prescott, Judy Bell-Qualls,

Ray Broms, Carole Krucoff, and Jennifer Westerfeld.

Unfortunately, the Suq felt the recession like most museum stores, with net sales down 10 percent this year. We did develop two lovely new limestone coaster sets, one of our Egyptian stela and one of our lamassu.

We had two major donations to the Suq this year, from the sculpture collection of Dr. Charles Ray and the textile collection of Barbara Watson. Many thanks!

This year the Suq was the target of a shoplifter. With the quick and coordinated action of Ashley Stanton, James Tillapaugh, the Oriental Institute security's personnel and

Suq booth at the Arabesque Festival

cameras, and the University Police, we were able to catch him on his second attempt.

A special thanks to Florence Ovadia, who does our beautiful displays on Monday, and to Norma van der Meulen, who designs jewelry for us as well as volunteering on Wednesdays in the Suq. In addition, recently Jane Meloy has started helping us on Mondays to restock and design some of our wall and shelf displays.

PHOTOGRAPHY

Anna R. Ressman

The 2009–2010 year has been an intense and productive year for the Photography Department. Much of what has been accomplished was done with the help of excellent assistants and summer interns. Colin Halverson and Katherine Weber, both students in the Masters of Arts Program in Social Sciences (MAPSS), worked as digital photography assistants from the Fall 2009 Quarter through the end of the Spring 2010 Quarter. Kevin Duong, also a MAPSS student, began working as a digital photography assistant in the Fall 2009 Quarter and will continue to work as my assistant through the end of the Summer 2010 Quarter. Finally, we have had the pleasure of welcoming Summer 2010 interns Clare Brody, a 2010 graduate of the Laboratory Schools, and Matthew Carville, a senior in the college. Craig Tews served as a volunteer photographer during the winter of 2010. Ian Randall, a 2009 graduate of the MAPSS program, worked as a digital photography assistant through the end of the Summer 2009 Quarter. And Claire Barker, then a graduate student at George Washington University, was our summer 2009 intern.

The Photography Department has now been operating for almost three years as an exclusively digital imaging studio that is capable of producing professional images at today's technological standards. Throughout the last year, we have been modernizing our equipment and supplementing our equipment with new tools to increase productivity and to help streamline the workflow. The studio and processing spaces are being cleaned and reorganized as time allows. This spring the

Photography Department offices underwent a major cleaning and reorganization project that was accomplished thanks to many long, tedious hours of work by digital photography assistants Kevin Duong, Colin Halverson, and Katherine Weber. A large number of old filing cabinets, which housed documents from past decades, were sifted through. Ian Randall inventoried all of the old darkroom and studio equipment, photographic papers, film, cameras, and accessories (several hundred pieces in total). And the 2010 digital photography assistants spent many hours researching specifications and monetary values for all inventory items. The photography studio underwent additional reorganization to streamline the work process.

In the spring of 2010, the Photography Department acquired a new state-of-the-art Canon 5D Mark II as well as a new macro lens that offers magnification up to five times the size of the subject. A new tripod and other small-equipment purchases have allowed the studio to operate as a more flexible and efficient workspace. Finally, the processing end of our workflow has increased in efficiency and productivity thanks to a new desktop computer for the digital photography assistants, which was purchased in the fall of 2009, and a cutting-edge computer monitor, which enables professional-grade strict color management, purchased in the spring of 2010.

New photography of Museum artifacts has been extensive. The summer of 2009 through September witnessed photographing of additional Khorsabad large relief fragments. Claire Barker completed extensive processing and clipping of these large object photographs, and the clipped objects were placed on line drawings of the north and south walls of the royal palace of the Assyrian king Sargon II. We have begun work on the large Robert F. Picken Family Nubia Gallery highlights book; twenty-seven objects have been photographed so far. The catalog *Pioneers to the Past* was completed in September and October 2009. This catalog included photos of the passport James Henry Breasted traveled with throughout Mesopotamia and Egypt as well as the American flag he carried during his travels. The photographs of his passport have been published online at *Archaeology* magazine (http://www.archaeology.org/online/features/breasted/). New photography was completed for the *Visible Language* special-exhibit catalog, our largest and most extensive photographic assignment for a special-exhibit catalog to date. A total of 103 objects were photographed, and 99 of those images are included in the catalog.

We have also completed work on several other projects over the year. Photographs from the CT scans of selected objects in the Visible Language exhibition were taken at the University of Chicago Hospitals in September of 2009. We documented and photographed important research done at Argonne National Laboratory on some of our Amuq arrowheads in February of 2010. Many outside requests for new photography were also fulfilled.

We are also preparing to expand into social-media outlets. The department will shortly have a Flickr page that will provide some photographs of selected objects from recent and current book projects and will be accompanied by brief curatorial information. Such a page will provide a valuable educational resource for classroom instructors, encourage increased visibility for many of the exhibits here at the Museum, and allow visitors to engage with the exciting developments at the Institute more generally.

Overall the Photography Department has had an exciting and demanding year. Major improvements in efficiency were made, several important projects were completed including work for three separate books or catalogs, and new photography of Museum objects was included in multiple national and international publications, which brought the Oriental Institute to a wide and diverse audience. The 2009–2010 period has been another fruitful and exciting year working with everyone at the Oriental Institute.

———————————

PUBLIC EDUCATION

PUBLIC EDUCATION

Carole Krucoff

This *Annual Report* marks the beginning of a new era for public programs and community engagement at the Oriental Institute. Because of the great success in reaching new audiences that Museum Education and the Volunteer Program have had over the years, we have now been made our own unit within the Oriental Institute. Working together as the Public Education Department, the Education and Volunteer Program staff will be joining with Oriental Institute faculty, staff, and students, as well as the wider university community, to develop innovative and exciting new educational services on site and online that will share the work of the Institute and its Museum with new audiences locally, regionally, and around the world.

While much of this past year was dedicated to thoughtful discussions and strategic planning for ways our reorganized department would be structured and function, we also continued to offer a rich array of programs that attracted thousands of visitors to the Oriental Institute. Read on to find reports that describe how public and grant-funded programs and the services offered by the Volunteer Program brought the ancient world and the work of the Institute to life for audiences ranging from K–12 students and teachers to youth and families from throughout the metropolitan area to adult learners of all ages and backgrounds who were eager to broaden their understanding of the ancient Middle East and its connection to the modern world.

Public and Grant-funded Programs

Public programs this past year brought 6,774 participants to the Oriental Institute, an increase of more than 23 percent over last year. This increase is largely due to a wide range of collaborations with long-time and new partners on campus, throughout the community, and even across the nation. Partnerships ranged from remarkable musical performances supported by the Hyde Park Jazz Festival (fig. 1) to media campaigns with area library systems, to local and nationally supported events highlighting special exhibits. These collaborations helped us expand our horizons and attract new adult and family audiences, many of whom had never before visited the Oriental Institute.

Grant-funded support from the Harper Court Arts Council and the Chicago Public Schools and a major award from the Polk Bros. Foundation are helping us provide in-depth learning experiences for Chicago-area teachers and their students. And a multi-year award from the National Endowment for the Humanities is supporting a ground-breaking online initiative that will provide high school educators nationwide with unique resources to help build student understanding of the ancient and contemporary Middle East.

Figure 1. The lammasu in the Yelda Khorsabad Court smiles down on jazz violinist Samuel "Savoir Faire" Williams during his Hyde Park Jazz Festival performance at the Oriental Institute. Photo by Marc Monaghan

Major Initiatives for Teachers and Students

Empowering teachers to enrich student learning through meaningful study of ancient civilizations is central to the mission of the Education Department. The prime way for us to reach this goal is to draw upon the scholarly expertise, renowned collections, and online capabilities of the Oriental Institute. This past year, well over a million visitors were attracted to the online education outreach programs that have already been developed for the Oriental Institute Web site. These include Ancient Mesopotamia: This History, Our History; the Teacher Resource Center; and Kids Corner, which features a unique interactive on ways in which the ancient Egyptians prepared mummies for burial. This year, the four major initiatives described below are helping us reach even more teachers and students, both on site and online, in ways that will be meaningful and beneficial today and well into the future.

Teaching the Middle East: A Resource for High School Educators

Since 2007, the Oriental Institute and two on-campus partners — the Center for Middle Eastern Studies (CMES) and the eCUIP Digital Library in Regenstein Library — have been working together to create Teaching the Middle East: A Resource for High School Educators, an online education initiative supported by the National Endowment for the Humanities. The goal of this multi-year project, due to be launched in the fall of 2010, is to provide high school world-history teachers across the nation with online resources that draw upon the best in humanities scholarship to help build student understanding of the ancient and contemporary Middle East.

Teaching the Middle East contains eighteen academic essays, or modules, which focus on various aspects of ancient and contemporary Middle Eastern archaeology, history, and culture. These modules have been created by fourteen University of Chicago scholars, including the following:

- Orit Bashkin, Assistant Professor of Modern Middle Eastern History
- Fred M. Donner, Professor of Near Eastern History
- Geoff Emberling, Chief Curator, Oriental Institute Museum
- Janet H. Johnson, Morton D. Hull Distinguished Service Professor of Egyptology
- Wadad Kadi, The Avalon Foundation Distinguished Service Professor Emerita of Islamic Studies
- Walter E. Kaegi, Professor of History
- Jenny Myers, Oriental Institute Research Associate
- Michael Sells, John Henry Barrows Professor of Islamic History and Literature
- Holly Shissler, Associate Professor of Ottoman and Turkish History
- Gil J. Stein, Professor of Near Eastern Archaeology and Director of the Oriental Institute
- Martin Stokes, Fellow of St. John's College, Oxford University
- Matthew W. Stolper, John A. Wilson Professor of Assyriology
- Christopher Woods, Associate Professor of Sumerology
- John E. Woods, Professor of Iranian and Central Asian History and of Near Eastern Languages and Civilizations

Orit Bashkin, Geoff Emberling, and Gil Stein served as the project's Faculty Review Committee. Leslie Schramer of the Institute's Publications Office copyedited each module with great care and precision.

Eight high-school educators from the Chicago area have served as the advisory board. These educators, whose feedback and ideas were invaluable, created the discussion questions and thirty-six classroom lesson plans that are key teaching and learning tools for each module. Advisors include Farhat Khan, manager of cultural diversity, Office of Strategic Initiatives, Chicago Public Schools; Maryhelen Matejevic, Assistant Principal for Curriculum and Instruction, Mount Carmel High School; Blake Noel, social studies teacher, Bronzeville Scholastic Institute; Lisa Perez, Area Library Coordinator, Department of Libraries and Information Services for Chicago Public Schools; Peter Scheidler, advanced placement economics and social studies teacher, and Mike Shea, Social Studies Department chair and world studies teacher, both of Kenwood Academy; Laura Wangerin, history teacher, Latin School of Chicago; and Howard Wright, world studies/history teacher, Hinsdale South High School.

Figure 2. Historic Perspectives Web page from the NEH Teaching the Middle East: A Resource for High School Educators Web site

Wendy Ennes, Associate Head of Public Education, Technology, and Innovation, has been the manager and driving force of the Teaching the Middle East project. She developed the grant proposal, created and managed the timetable for the entire project, facilitated meetings with faculty and teacher advisors, provided photography for images used in the project, handled all budgetary concerns and reports, and served as liaison to the National Endowment for the Humanities.

Wendy also supervised the work of nine Department of Near Eastern Languages and Civilizations (NELC) and Center for Middle Eastern Studies (CMES) graduate students, who provided the links to Web resources — including images, video, and sound recordings — that expand and enrich each module, and she supervised five student interns who provided additional crucial support. Kendra Grimmet, a student in the University of Chicago's Department of Fine Art, helped edit and format essays and image captions and also researched and fact-checked Web resources and links. Charlotte Simon, a graduate student enrolled in the University of Chicago's Master of Arts Program in the Social Sciences (MAPPS), provided major assistance with editing and formatting essays and captions, as well as researching Web resources and dictionary terminology. She also provided key editorial support for the lesson plans created by the Teacher Advisory Board. Interns Clare Brody, Lauren Horn, and Caitlin Wyler, offered additional research and editorial support.

Wendy also worked closely with colleagues from our partner organizations on campus. Alex Barna, Outreach Coordinator for CMES, played a key role by facilitating the completion of faculty essays; Steven Lane is the designer of the project's Web site (fig. 2); and Julia Brazas, Director of the University of Chicago's WebDocent project, served as professional evaluator.

Teaching the Middle East's extraordinary partnership, which combines the expertise of scholars, teachers, public-programs specialists, and technology professionals, is already attracting attention from educational organizations across the county. The project's unique resources will soon be available nationwide to enrich teaching and learning about the Middle East for many years to come.

Interactive Learning and the Middle East: Serving Schools and the Latino Community

Over the past several years, the generosity of the Polk Bros. Foundation has enabled us to reach underserved school and family audiences in a wide variety of significant ways, including development of award-winning curriculum materials on the ancient Middle East for classroom use, the creation of Family Activity Cards in English and Spanish, and the interactive computer kiosks that are now available throughout the galleries of the Oriental Institute Museum. Most recently, the foundation awarded us support for Interactive Learning and the Middle East: Serving Schools and the Latino Community. This initiative is allowing us to develop a Spanish-language version of the interactive learning experiences on the Museum's computer kiosks. Once this process is complete, we will transform these bilingual computer experiences into interactive DVDs that also contain curriculum-related lesson plans for use in school classrooms. Created by an advisory board of six Chicago Public School educators, the lesson plans, combined with the computer interactives, will make these DVDs vital enrichment resources for state-mandated study of ancient civilizations as well as for technology instruction.

The herculean task of creating a Spanish-language version for all the materials that accompany each computer interactive was finalized last year, thanks to the dedicated translation efforts of Maria Theresa Chagñon, University of Chicago graduate in Romance languages; Ninfa Flores, bilingual education teacher for the Chicago Public Schools; Catherine Dueñas, Volunteer Programs Associate whose fluency in Spanish has been crucial to the entire project; and Karina Chavarria, a former MAPPS intern and now a part-time staff member whose fluency in Spanish has made her an ideal editor. Karina also helped create the Spanish-language recordings for the interactives, a process that was begun by recording-consultant Teresa Vazquez.

This year, Wendy Ennes, who has served as art director and liaison to the project's Teacher Advisory Board, also assumed the role of computer programmer and multimedia architect. Wendy completed this intricate and highly labor-intensive aspect of the project and is now involved in the mechanics of publishing the interactives for the Museum's kiosks and developing the DVD. Due to her efforts, we envision all of the Museum's computer kiosks will be fully bilingual this summer. These activities will join the bilingual Family Activity Cards as well as new Spanish-language audiotours currently being developed by Karina Chavarria and Catherine Dueñas, to provide exciting and ongoing learning experiences for all Spanish- and English-speaking visitors.

In anticipation of all these learning experiences being implemented, we have developed two major marketing campaigns. The first is entitled "Every Day Is Family Day at the Oriental Institute." Working in concert with community organizations in Chicago's Pilsen neighborhood, as well as colleagues at the city's National Museum of Mexican Art, Karina Chavarria and Jessica Caracci, Education Programs Associate, are preparing bilingual advertising materials, contacting Spanish-language media, and seeking venues for outreach activities in the Latino community. This campaign, which will also include promotion to city-wide media as well as public libraries, is due to be underway by late summer and will continue into the fall of 2010.

Plans are also underway for widespread distribution of the interactive DVDs. This fall we will host a series of grant-funded teacher workshops to introduce the Museum and the new DVD resources to area schools, and we will provide each teacher with complimentary copies for their classrooms and school libraries. Support from the Polk Bros. Foundation is also enabling us to produce several thousand additional DVDS, so that we can promote these unique resources to teachers locally and nationally, and to educators in Spanish-speaking countries around the world.

The Kipper Family Archaeology Discovery Center

Our third special initiative is the Kipper Family Archaeology Discovery Center (KADC), a simulated archaeological dig that re-creates an ancient Near Eastern excavation site. The KADC engages students in thinking like scientists as they uncover, record, and analyze their finds in the simulated excavation site. They then discover how ancient artifacts excavated by Oriental Institute archaeologists go "from ground to gallery" on a Docent-led tour of the Museum. The KADC celebrated its second season by serving 730 middle-school students and their teachers, nearly double the number who took part in the center's first year of operation. Participants came from the city and suburbs and ranged from gifted students to those with special needs. Support from the Harper Court Arts Council enabled us to provide a program entitled "Young Archaeologists" for four Hyde Park Chicago Public Schools who rarely visit the Oriental Institute. Ten teachers and administrators and 266 sixth-grade students from Ariel Community Academy, Bret Harte Elementary School, Kozminski Community Academy, and Shoesmith Elementary School took part in this program, which included the following:

- Outreach visits to each school to provide curriculum resources and pre-visit materials
- A workshop to introduce teachers to the Museum and the KADC experience
- Funding for bus transportation
- Funding for the complete KADC experience

At the end of the program, each student received a certificate recognizing them as a "Junior Archaeologist" (fig. 3), and all were invited to return to the Institute with their families. All students and teachers who took part in this program were asked to complete evaluation forms. Teacher comments ranged from "I love this program; the students were engaged at all times," to "Students talked about the program for weeks. They want to come back." When responding to an evaluation question on what about the program could be improved, one student summarized the thoughts of many when she said, "I don't think anything should be improved. The KADC program was amazing!!!"

Jessica Caracci, Education Programs Associate, is coordinator of the KADC program. Along with scheduling all school visits to the KADC, she recruited, trained, and supervised four graduate-student interns from the MAPSS program — Sarah Brophy, Allison Drtina, Stephanie O'Brien, and Agnes Sohn — to serve as the main KADC facilitators this past year. Geoff Emberling provided special insights on archaeology and the reproduction of artifacts in the KADC during the facilitators' training.

Lauren Wojnarowski, a graduate student in museum studies at Eastern Illinois who interned with us and worked on a wide variety of educational projects, served as a KADC facilitator and assistant trainer, as did Kendra Grimmett, from the University of Chicago's Art Department. MAPSS interns Melanna Kallionakis and Kent Navalesi assisted with office management as well as facilitation for the Young Archaeologists program. Melanna,

CERTIFICATE OF TRAINING

This award is presented to

_____

for completion of training as a

JUNIOR ARCHAEOLOGIST

in the KADC Archaeological Dig
program at the Oriental Institute.

_____

CAROLE KRUCOFF
Head of Public Education

THIS PROGRAM MADE POSSIBLE BY A GRANT FROM THE HARPER COURT ARTS COUNCIL.

Figure 3. Students who took part in the Kipper Family Archaeology Discovery Center program supported by the Harper Court Arts Council had their name inscribed on this award certifying them as a Junior Archaeologist

Figure 4. Adult-education course instructor Kate Grossman (standing) prepares the students in her "Digging Deeper: An Introduction to Archaeology" course for their excavation experience in the Kipper Family Archaeology Center. Photo by Carole Krucoff

along with Kendra and Owen Berliner, a MAPSS student and archaeologist, also joined with Jessica to develop and pilot new KADC programs, using our second season as a testing ground to reach out to new audiences.

Owen saw the simulated dig experience as the perfect vehicle for scout groups to earn their Archaeology Badge. When a Boy Scout troop during the summer asked to visit the KADC, he created a special PowerPoint program and variety of badge-related activities for them. The program was a great success, and we now have a model we can use to serve this new audience.

Kate Grossman, PhD candidate in NELC, introduced another new audience to the KADC. As an instructor for an adult-education course called "Digging Deeper: An Introduction to Archeology," she made lectures and textbook descriptions come alive when she brought all her students to the KADC for a day of hands-on excavation experiences (fig. 4). Kate was so pleased with the outcome that she has offered to help us develop weekend "archaeology fantasy camps" for adults.

Jessica proved how successful KADC programming can be for families when a weekend program she called "Dig It" filled to capacity with parents and children eager to find out if Indiana Jones was a typical archaeologist. She also included excavation sessions during our annual children's summer day camps offered with the Lill Street Art Center. And a special pilot program showed us that the KADC is the perfect place for fun and learning even for six- and seven-year-olds celebrating a child's birthday.

At last year's Oriental Institute Gala, a KADC birthday-party event was part of the silent auction. The winner was Nancy Baum, a Member and Volunteer Docent, who arranged for her granddaughter to celebrate her seventh birthday with us. The birthday girl and fourteen of her friends were thrilled with the dig experience (fig. 5), and they enjoyed their visit to the Museum to see objects actually found by Oriental Institute archaeologists. A hands-on craft activity and a birthday cake decorated with the pyramids at Giza (fig. 6) ended the festive afternoon. Meghan Winston, Development Associate for Special Events, provided the cake, which was a special gift donated by Visiting Committee member Kitty Picken. Jessica encouraged interns Melanna Kallionakis and Kendra Grimmett to develop this successful birthday-party pilot, which will become a feature of the Education Department's special programming for Oriental Institute Family Members this coming fall.

All of this year's pilot programs validate Jessica's vision for the KADC. Along with its central role for schools, she sees the center as a springboard for development of a diverse array of programs that can provide exciting and rewarding learning experiences for adults, youth, families, and the special-needs community.

Figure 6. A birthday cake decorated with the pyramids at Giza was a highlight for the young girl pictured here who celebrated her seventh birthday during a party at the KADC. Kitty Picken, Oriental Institute Visiting Committee member, donated the cake as a special gift for this party. Photo by Nancy Baum

Figure 5. Celebrating her seventh birthday at the KADC, the birthday girl (lower right) enjoys watching her friends intently engaged in the excavation process. Photo by Nancy Baum

The Museum Connections Program

For the past several years, Chicago Public Schools (CPS) has supported a program called Museum Connections. Its goal is to connect kindergarten through eighth-grade teachers with museum educators to create partnership programs for enrichment of state-mandated school curricula, especially in conjunction with the study of science and math that is emphasized at CPS Magnet Cluster Math and Science Academies. This past year Wendy Ennes became our representative to the Museum Connections program, and she used this opportunity to create a major two-part initiative for teachers and their students. Each portion of this two-part program built upon the unique resources and science-related approaches of the KADC and the Oriental Institute's Center for Ancient Middle Eastern Landscapes (CAMEL).

In order to introduce our resources to science educators at every Magnet Cluster school, Wendy organized a day-long professional-development workshop in December. Funded and publicized by the Museum Connections program, the workshop brought sixty CPS science teachers to us for a program that included a lecture on science and archaeology presented by Susan Penacho of CAMEL, an introduction and invitation to "dig" at the KADC simulated site led by Jessica Caraccci, and a Docent-led guided tour of the Museum emphasizing the role science plays in recovery and study of ancient artifacts. Workshop evaluation forms completed by these teachers, many of whom had never visited us, showed a real enthusiasm for bringing their students to take part in cross-curricular science/social-studies programming at the Oriental Institute.

The second portion of the Museum Connections initiative took place over the course of the entire 2009–2010 school year. This was a unique collaboration among the Education Department, CAMEL, and a team of teachers from Claremont Math and Science Academy, a Magnet Cluster school whose students come from an underserved community on the city's west side. Called "The Science of Archaeology: Finding the Mysterious Location of the Rare Medallion," the program provided a series of Oriental Institute workshops for the Claremont teachers on ways CAMEL uses geo-spatial technologies to reveal how Middle Eastern landscapes contain the imprint of thousands of years of human activity and how landscape research can impact and

Figure 7. Scott Branting (center), Director of CAMEL, helps Claremont Math and Science Academy students gather data for locating the "rare ancient Persian medallion" during their KADC excavation for the Museum Connections program supported by the Chicago Public Schools. Photo by Wendy Ennes

Figure 8. A Claremont Math and Science Academy student in the school's computer laboratory uses specially designed, student-friendly GIS distributional analysis worksheets to hypothesize the location of the "rare medallion" during the Museum Connections program supported by the Chicago Public Schools. Photo by Wendy Ennes

guide archaeological study of the past. This approach fit perfectly with Claremont's goal to integrate technology into their curriculum, especially for the sixth grade, where teachers had planned to introduce Geographic Information Systems (GIS) into studies of the ancient world and earth science. Their objective was to put students' interest in technology to work in ways that would inspire development of critical and intellectual skills in science, social science, math, and computing, helping prepare students for high school, college, and employment.

Led by Assistant Professor and CAMEL Director Scott Branting, CAMEL staff members Susan Penacho, Elise MacArthur, and Robert Tate created five professional-development workshops for the Claremont educators. Five teachers took part in this program — Deborah Akinwale, sixth-grade science/math teacher; Anna Johnson, Claremont technology specialist; Joy Reeves, science specialist; Kiana Shaw, sixth-grade language arts/social-studies teacher; and Mary Maloney, computer teacher. The workshops included the following:

1) a science of archaeology lecture and Museum tour at the Oriental Institute;

2) a specially developed KADC dig that placed artifact reproductions, including a "rare mystery medallion," in specific locations so that the teachers could gather data to analyze their finds using GIS;

3) an introduction to the CAMEL laboratory and the ArcGIS software program used by CAMEL;

4) distributional analysis of the simulated dig data and importing data sets into ArcGIS in order to hypothesize the location of the "rare medallion"; and

5) sharing of hypotheses on the location of the medallion and a "Big Reveal" of its location in the simulated KADC site.

Once the teachers had completed their training, they joined Wendy, Scott, and the CAMEL staff to develop a five-part program for their students that would introduce similar concepts in ways that were appropriate for sixth-grade students. Then Elise MacArthur, an experienced youth educator, visited the school and led a lively and interactive discussion on archaeology for all sixty of Claremont's sixth graders. This was followed by the students' visit to the Oriental Institute to tour the Museum and gather data on the location of the "rare medallion" during a KADC excavation (fig. 7). Returning to their school's computer lab, they used specially designed, student-friendly distributional analysis worksheets developed by intern Charlotte Simon to hypothesize the location of the medallion (fig. 8). Then they were ready for their own "Big Reveal" during another outreach visit to Claremont by Oriental Institute and CAMEL staff. We were amazed when nearly all of the students correctly concluded the location of the medallion, proving what we had hoped — that middle school students can grasp and master highly sophisticated research processes if they are presented in ways that appeal to their interests and are taught jointly by experts in science and technology, public education specialists, and middle school education professionals. We envision this pilot project as the foundation for expanded outreach programming as we seek funding to engage more educators and their students in this unique cross-curricular adventure!

Adult Education

Presenting innovative and meaningful adult-education programs to serve old friends and attract, inform, and engage new audiences has always been central to the mission of the Education Department. This past year, we collaborated with long-time associates and new partners on campus and across the community to develop a wide variety of life-long learning opportunities that included courses and events inspired by the Museum's special exhibits, Oriental Institute research, and cultural initiatives taking place throughout the city.

Courses

Many of our adult-education courses and programs are offered in partnership with the University of Chicago's Graham School of General Studies, which joins us on course development, advertising, and registration. This past year our joint multi-session courses on campus and at the university's downtown Gleacher Center included the following:

- Ancient Nubia: History, Heritage, and Salvage Archaeology, taught by Geoff Emberling;
- Cultures of Ancient Afghanistan, taught by Ilya Yakubovich;
- Digging Deeper: An Introduction to Archaeology, taught by Kate Grossman;
- The Ancient Mediterranean World: A Story of Trade, Diplomacy, War, and Migration, taught by Natasha Ayers;
- The Temples of Greco-Roman Egypt and The History of Greco-Roman Egypt, taught by Foy Scalf; and
- Women's Work, Women's Power: The Responsibilities, Actions, and Authority of Women in the Ancient Near East, taught by Ginger Emory, Katharyn Hanson, and Eudora Struble.

Our two correspondence courses offer adult-education opportunities to far-flung Oriental Institute Members and also bring us new friends from across the nation and around the world. Hieroglyphs by Mail, taught by Andrew Baumann and Mary Szabady, and Cuneiform by Mail, taught by Monica Crews and Seunghee Yie, attracted more than eighty students, whose locations ranged from New York to California and from Africa to Europe to South America.

Special Adult Education Events

In addition to formal courses, we offered a wide variety of special adult-education events throughout the year. Highlights included two major programs in conjunction with the Museum's special exhibits.

Figure 9. Speakers for the "Women in the Middle East, Past and Present" symposium listen intently to a question posed by Gil Stein (right), who served as moderator during the program's closing panel. Left to right: Orit Bashkin, Emine Evered, Janet H. Johnson, Jonathan Hall, and Jeffery Stackert. Photo by Wendy Ennes

"Women in the Middle East, Past and Present" was a public symposium that was inspired by The Life of Meresamun: A Temple Singer in Ancient Egypt, an exhibit that examined the significant social and legal rights enjoyed by ancient Egyptian women. Visitor interest in this aspect of ancient Egyptian history encouraged us to present a day-long symposium to confront the stereotypes and explore the realities of women's lives not just in ancient Egypt but also throughout the Middle East in both ancient and contemporary times.

Supported by a Norman Wait Harris Grant from the University Chicago's Center for International Studies and with additional support from the university's Centers for Gender Studies and Middle Eastern Studies, this fall event featured lectures and discussions on women in ancient times by Jonathan Hall, Phyllis H. Horton Professor in the Humanities, Chairman in the Department of Classics, and Professor in the Department of History; Janet H. Johnson, Morton D. Hull Distinguished Service Professor of Egyptology; and Jeffery Stackert, Assistant Professor of Hebrew Bible, University of Chicago Divinity School. Middle Eastern women's rights and concerns from medieval times to the present in Turkey and Iraq were discussed by Orit Bashkin, Assistant Professor of Modern Middle Eastern History, Department of Near Eastern Languages and Civilizations; and guest lecturer Emine Evered, Assistant Professor of Middle Eastern History, Department of History and the Center for Gender Studies in Global Context, Michigan State University.

Gil Stein, Director of the Oriental Institute, moderated a panel discussion featuring all the speakers (fig. 9), where questions from the audience, as well as the evaluation forms given out at the event, expressed a strong desire for the Oriental Institute to pursue this topic further. In the near future, we hope to offer another public symposium to examine women's roles in ancient Nubia, ancient and contemporary Iran, and other Near Eastern cultures not explored during this program.

In the spring we joined with the Chicago Chapter of the Archaeological Institute of America (AIA) and the Chicago Council on Global Affairs to present "Who Owns the Past?," a public forum inspired by the special exhibit Pioneers to the Past: American Archaeologists in the Middle East, 1919–1920. This exhibit raised many questions on the links between past civilizations and modern nations, the antiquities trade, and the role museums play in preserving the past. The Institute's Breasted Hall filled to near capacity as audience members from far and wide came to "Who Owns the Past?" for a discussion with Oriental Institute archaeologists and Chicago museum leaders on the ways archaeology, history, and heritage connect to political and cultural realities.

Presenters for this event included Geoff Emberling, Chief Curator of the Oriental Institute Museum and curator of the Pioneers to the Past exhibit; James Cuno, President and Director of the Art Institute of Chicago; Gil Stein, Professor of Ancient Near Eastern Archaeology and Director of the Oriental Institute; and Carlos Tortolero, President of Chicago's National Museum of Mexican Art. After discussing the issues explored by Pioneers to the Past and inviting the

Figure 10. Carlos Tortolero, President of Chicago's National Museum of Mexican Art, summarizes his views on "Who Owns the Past?" during the public forum that invited Chicago archaeologists and museum leaders to share their opinions on this issue. Photo by Wendy Ennes

Figure 11. Audience members line up to ask questions of the speakers (left to right: Carlos Tortolero, James Cuno, and Gil Stein) during the "Who Owns the Past" public forum, which filled Breasted Hall to overflowing. Photo by Wendy Ennes

other presenters to offer summations of their own views, (fig. 10) Geoff Emberling moderated an animated and occasionally heated debate among the speakers, which inspired numerous and equally animated questions from the audience (fig. 11).

This program made a strong impact on audience members, many of whom had never before visited the Oriental Institute. Evaluations showed that nearly everyone who attended felt that the forum was a success not only because it was "extremely interesting" but also because of "the exchange of varied opinions" and because "it made us more aware of such important issues."

"Who Owns the Past?" was supported in part by an Archaeological Institute of America Outreach Grant. This allowed us to offer the program free of charge and funded the videotaping of the program in its entirety, enabling us to keep discussion of these important issues alive and sustainable over time, and to share them online.

Themes in the Pioneers to the Past exhibit also encouraged us to develop "Egypt in Chicago," an Oriental Institute/Art Institute Field trip that offered an insider's view on the city's three major collections of ancient Egyptian art and artifacts. One of the goals of James Henry Breasted's 1919–1920 journey to the Middle East was to acquire ancient Egyptian artifacts for the Oriental Institute, but he also obtained ancient Egyptian objects for the Art Institute of Chicago and for the Field Museum on other expeditions. During "Egypt in Chicago," visitors gathered at the Oriental Institute, where Egyptologist Emily Teeter gave a richly illustrated lecture on Chicago's three main Egyptian collections and a tour of the Pioneers to the Past exhibit. After traveling by bus to the Art Institute, everyone enjoyed a private luncheon in the Millennium Park Room, followed by a tour of the Art Institute's Egyptian collection led by Lucas Livingston, Assistant Director of Museum Programs (fig. 12). "Egypt in Chicago" was so popular that it sold out almost immediately when first offered in winter, sold out again when offered in the spring, and appears to be on its way to another sell-out during the upcoming Summer Quarter!

Hosting jazz performances as part of the annual Hyde Park Jazz Festival continues to attract hundreds of new visitors to the Oriental Institute. This year, crowds filled Breasted Hall when Tatsu Aoki gave a concert of what critics called "an eloquent merger of ancient Japanese music and experimental American jazz" (fig. 13). Jazz violinist Samuel "Savoir Faire" Williams also

Figure 12. Visitors join Lucas Livingston, Assistant Director of Museum Programs at the Art Institute, to explore the Art Institute's collection of ancient Egyptian art, much of which was collected by James Henry Breasted. Livingston's tour was part of the highly popular "Egypt in Chicago" program offered jointly by the Oriental Institute and the Art Institute. Photo by Carole Krucoff

Figure 13. The Tatsu Aoki Ensemble filled Breasted Hall with an amazing fusion of ancient Japanese music and American jazz sounds during the Hyde Park Jazz Festival. Photo by Carole Krucoff

filled every chair in Khorsabad Court for two concerts in that magnificent and acoustically perfect setting. All told, these concerts attracted more than 500 visitors. Most asked to be signed up for the *E-Tablet* and are now regularly receiving program information, news, and membership information.

Many returning, and new, visitors came to the jazz concerts we offered in winter and spring. Supported by a grant from the Hyde Park Cultural Alliance's new Passport to Jazz program, we hosted internationally renowned ragtime keyboard artist Reginald Robinson in March and Erik Schneider's Hot Dixieland Quintet in May (fig. 14). Both presented concerts that fit perfectly with the 1919–1920 era portrayed in the Pioneers to the Past exhibit. Schneider even composed and played a special tune for the event — "The Oriental Institute Blues," now available on YouTube.com.

Figure 14. Erik Schneider's Hot Dixieland Quintet took everyone back to the 1919–1920s era of the Pioneers to the Past exhibit during a Passport to Jazz concert in Breasted Hall. Photo by Rebecca Binkley-Albright

Music of a very different sort filled Khorsabad Court when Chicago's Newberry Consort returned to the Institute for their third season with us. "Stravaganze: The Virtuoso Violinists" featured internationally acclaimed artists and Chicago celebrities Rachel Barton-Pine, David Douglass, and David Schrader. They brilliantly performed virtuosic seventeenth-century music for violin and harpsichord to a sold-out audience (fig. 15).

Another highly successful programming partnership continued this year when we presented two new dining experiences as part of the Cuisine and Cookery of the Middle East series in collaboration with the Graham School of General Studies. At Chickpea Café, Chicago

Figure 15. Concertgoers gather around David Schrader and his harpsichord during intermission at a Newberry Consort performance in Yelda Khorsabad Court. Photo by Carole Krucoff

restaurateur Jerry Suqi and his mother, master chef Amin Suqi, introduced a sold-out crowd to the uniquely flavorful dishes that are hallmarks of classic Palestinian cuisine. At "Tastes of Lebanon" at Fatoosh Restaurant, owner Samuel Elakhaoui and his wife Lina introduced us to the history and culture of southern Lebanon as they as they invited us to savor and learn how to prepare authentic dishes from their homeland.

"Dine Like an Egyptian" brought us a new Cuisine and Cookery partner — the World Kitchen Program of Chicago's Department of Cultural Affairs. Emily Teeter joined Judith Dunbar-Hines, World Kitchen Director, to create a two-part program exploring the cuisine and culinary lifestyle of the ancient Egyptians. Part I took place at the Oriental Institute, where Emily offered a lecture and then joined a team of Docents to help visitors discover all the culinary clues hidden among exhibits in the Joseph and Mary Grimshaw Egyptian Gallery. Part II, a "Dine Like an Egyptian" cooking class at the World Kitchens center in the Loop, featured Emily discussing what was being grown and eaten in ancient Egypt, followed by Judith inviting everyone to cook and enjoy a meal using those ingredients. Both sections of this event sold out almost as soon as they were announced!

Another collaboration with the city of Chicago took place when we joined with the Burnham Plan Centennial Celebration to mark the hundredth anniversary of architect and urban planner Daniel Burnham's 1909 *Plan of Chicago*. The Institute received city-wide publicity for Geoff Emberling's lecture on "The World's First Cities: Babylon and Beyond," which focused on the city as a form of settlement, how urbanization developed around cultural views of space in the absence of urban planning, and what is known about some planned ancient cities.

Partnerships with departments and organizations on campus to serve the University of Chicago and the wider community remained an important aspect of our programming this past year. During the university's annual Humanities Day in October, we hosted two discussions highlighting research at the Oriental Institute. "A Mummy Comes to Life: Science and Art Resurrect an Ancient Egyptian Priestess" featured Emily Teeter, curator of the Meresamun special exhibit; Dr. Michael Vannier, Professor in the Department of Radiology at the University of Chicago Medical Center; and Joshua Harker, a Chicago forensic artist. Their panel discussion highlighted ways in which the very latest in CT scanning enabled the Institute to discover remarkable information about the health and lifestyle of an ancient Egyptian woman and even reconstruct her physical appearance as she looked more than 3,000 years ago. During the second Humanities Day presentation, Matthew W. Stolper, John A. Wilson Professor of Assyriology, spoke on "Recording Persian Antiquities in Crisis: The Persepolis Fortification Archive Project."

During the university's Family Weekend in the fall, our Saturday Docents led "Highlights of the Collection" tours of the Oriental Institute Museum for students and their families. Also in the fall, Jessica Caracci ran a booth at the Graduate Students Resource Fair, where she introduced the cultural resources and internship opportunities available at the Oriental Institute. The Education Department also joined with Geoff Emberling and Morris Fred of the University of Chicago's

Figure 16. Filmgoers at our Sunday film series enjoyed a really old-fashioned love story when we screened Cecil B. DeMille's Samson and Delilah *on Valentine's Day*

Master of Arts in the Social Sciences (MAPSS) program to host a reception inviting MAPSS students to apply for internship opportunities at the Institute. The contributions of the students who joined us are visible throughout this year's report.

University students and staff, as well community visitors, joined us this year for the series of lunch-time gallery tours we offered each quarter in conjunction with special exhibits. Emily Teeter led a tour of Meresamun in the summer, Geoff Emberling presented a tour of Pioneers to the Past on the day after its opening in January, and Emily led a tour of the Pioneers to the Past exhibit for visitors in the spring.

Our free Sunday afternoon film showings of documentary and feature films on the ancient and contemporary Middle East continue to attract media and on-campus and community interest. This year, in conjunction with the Pioneers to the Past exhibit, we offered a special, two-part screening of *Lawrence of Arabia*. Fred Donner, Professor of Islamic History, introduced the film, which brilliantly portrays many of the World War I-era luminaries whom James Henry Breasted encountered during his historic expedition to the Middle East. And screening of two "sword and sandal" epics let us share classic 1940s–1950s Hollywood movie making at its best. *Land of the Pharaohs* starring Joan Collins was a hit in the summer. *Samson and Delilah* starring Victor Mature (fig. 16) — shown on Valentine's Day as a "really old-fashioned love story" — drew large crowds to view this Oscar winner, which we offered complete with popcorn!

Youth and Family Programming

Education offered long-time favorites as well new initiatives for youth and families this year, nearly all in collaboration with local or city-wide initiatives. Several programs used off-site formats to reach new audiences. Other events took place at the Oriental Institute to serve old friends and attract new visitors.

Outreach Programs

This past summer was our busiest outreach season. For the twelfth straight year we traveled to the Lill Street Art Center on the city's north side for "Be an Ancient Egyptian Artist," a week-long day camp for children ages eight to twelve that fills to capacity each time it's offered. Intern Lauren Wojnarowksi and teaching artist Meg Peterson took part in the two week-long sessions of the camp; each included a visit to the Oriental Institute, where the campers took part in a KADC excavation and an art-making session led by Jessica Caracci.

In August we ventured out to Millennium Park for "Labfest," a free festival of hands-on science fun and learning sponsored by Science Chicago, a city-wide initiative designed to inspire the next generation of scientists. At our booth, interns Kendra Grimmett and Lauren Wojnarowksi invited parents and children to "get up close and personal" with our replica mummy to see how the ancient Egyptians used science to preserve mummies for the afterlife (fig. 17). They also shared the ways in which today's scientists are using the latest techniques to study mummies and invited everyone to visit the Meresamun exhibit. Our Labfest activity, which was called "Meet a Mummy," enabled us to directly interact with nearly 900 parents and their children.

Also in August, Jessica Caracci and I traveled to Brookfield Zoo to meet with seventy-five suburban librarians from the Metropolitan Library System. This event launched the Macy's Pass program, an outreach campaign sponsored by the Macy's Foundation that funded suburban libraries, as well as major media throughout the city and suburbs, to publicize family programs and events taking place at participating museums and cultural institutions. At the Oriental Institute, the Education Department and the Suq are collaborating on this program. To date 121 family visitors obtained Macy's

Figure 17. At the Science Chicago "Labfest" in Millennium Park, interns Lauren Wojnarowksi (left) and Kendra Grimmett (right) invited hundreds of parents and children to "get up close and personal" with our reproduction mummy and receive information about the special exhibit Life of Meresamun. Photo by Carole Krucoff

Passes from thirty-seven different suburban libraries and redeemed them at the Suq to take the "Kids View of Ancient Egypt" audiotour at no charge. The advantages of this program are twofold. We were amazed to discover that the majority of the suburban librarians we met had never visited, and some had never even heard of, the Oriental Institute. Now they are all aware of us and providing our publicity materials to their visitors. Also most of the families coming to us with Macy's Passes are new visitors. We envision the numbers of these suburban visitors will grow when the Macy's Pass program is renewed in the coming year.

In September we took part in the 57th Street Children's Book Fair, where Kendra and Lauren invited more than 200 parents and children to "Dig into History," a simulated archaeological excavation that was one of the most popular activities at the fair. In the spring we reached our largest outreach audience when we took part in Día del Niño, an annual spring event organized by the National Museum of Mexican Art, which attracts thousands of parents and children from city's Latino community. Volunteer Programs Associate Catherine Dueñas and intern Karina Chavarria organized the activities and recruited the volunteers for our booth (fig. 18), where more than 1,000 people received samples of our bilingual activity cards and took home directions on how to find the Oriental Institute. See the Volunteer section of this report for a more complete description of Día del Niño.

Figure 18. Left to right: Volunteer Programs Associate Catherine Dueñas, volunteer Vicente Ruvalcaba, and intern Karina Chavarria introduced the Oriental Institute to more than 1,000 people at the Día del Niño family festival organized by the National Museum of Mexican Art. Photo by Randy Adamsick

Family Activities at the Oriental Institute

The KADC was the site of two family events this past year — the sold-out "Dig It" program and the very successful birthday-party pilot. And visitors at the Museum took home 11,816 of our bilingual Family Activity Cards — an increase of 9.5 percent over last year. But it was our mummies who took center stage with the family audience when we hosted Mummies Night in October. This pre-Halloween event, which was offered in collaboration with the city's celebration of "Chicagoween" and Chicago Book Month, has become an annual tradition. Mummies Night featured a showing of "Mummies Made in Egypt," an animated and live-action film from the award-winning Reading Rainbow series. Docents and interns also offered a "tomb-full" of activities than ranged from folding origami pyramids, bats, and frogs, to dressing up in costumes from "King Tut's Closet" (fig. 19) to a "Guess the Mummy Lollipops" contest. Mummies Night attracted more than 550 parents and children this year, the largest attendance ever for this highly popular event.

Figure 19. A young visitor is all smiles after dressing up in items from "King Tut's Closet" during Mummies Night, our annual pre-Halloween celebration for families. Photo by Wendy Ennes

Behind the Scenes

Taking stock of all that has been accomplished this past year, I'd like to say how much our department appreciates the expertise, support, and ongoing involvement of faculty, staff, and students, many of whom are mentioned in this report. Special thanks go to Gil Stein, Director of the Oriental Institute, and Steve Camp, Executive Director, who guided and encouraged us as we moved to become our own unit at the Oriental Institute. Grateful thanks also go to Geoff Emberling, who has inspired us, praised our successes, understood our challenges, and led us forward with tact, diplomacy, and grace.

Our sincere appreciation also goes to the family events and special programs volunteers who worked with us this past year. None of our special programs for adults, families, teachers/students, and the university community could have taken place without the time and talents of these dedicated people (fig. 20). All their names appear in the Volunteer section of this report.

Figure 20. Docent Jean Fincher (right) presents a special science-based tour for these students from Claremont Math and Science Academy as part of a new approach to integrate curriculum-related science learning into our guided-tour program. Jean was among the many volunteers who contributed their time and talents for special programs and family events this past year. Photo by Wendy Ennes

Figure 21. MAPSS intern Charlotte Simon (right) assists a Claremont Math and Science Academy student in his computer search for the "rare medallion" during the Museum Connections program. Charlotte, who designed many of the "student-friendly" materials for this program, was one of the interns who provided invaluable support for public education this past year. Photo by Wendy Ennes

This year we were fortunate to have the support and assistance of a corps of thirteen volunteer and work-study interns who aided us in countless ways. Many have already been mentioned in this report, but they also deserve recognition here as invaluable members of our team. Lauren Wojnarowski and MAPSS intern Melanna Kallionkis were central to administration and facilitation of the KADC program as well as many other aspects of our educational services for adults and families, as was MAPSS intern Kent Navelesi. Kendra Grimmet provided development and implementation services for the KADC and assisted with the NEH Teaching the Middle East initiative. MAPSS intern Charlotte Simon provided crucial support for the NEH project, the Polk Bros. Foundation bilingual project, the Museum Connections Program, and grant-writing efforts (fig. 21). MAPSS interns Sarah Brophy, Allison Drtina, Stephanie O'Brien, and Agnes Sohn did an outstanding job as KADC facilitators. Caitlin Wyler from the University of Arizona provided office management and programmatic assistance as a summer intern and joined Clare Brody and Lauren Horn in the final stages of research support for the NEH project. Karina Chavarria was central to all our programming for the Latino community. We could not have managed without each and every one of these very special interns!

Nothing would be happening without the commitment, creativity, and vision of the Education Department's staff members. The contributions of Jessica Caracci, Education Programs Associate, are visible throughout this report. Along with her outstanding leadership as coordinator of the Kipper Family Archaeology Discovery Center and supervisor this past of year of eight KADC and office and programmatic support staff interns (fig. 22), Jessica is central to all of our other programs for adults, youth, school-group visitors, and families. She administers the department's entire adult-education program and handles registrations, confirmations, and record keeping for all Museum gallery tours and public programs. Jessica also serves as our department's public-relations officer, graphic designer, and media specialist. The in-print and online publicity materials she produces have been key to this year's increase in program participation. Jessica handles the challenges of her multi-faceted position with a calm demeanor, poise, and professionalism, making it a pleasure for volunteers, staff, and faculty to work with her.

Figure 22. Left to right: Melanna Kallionakis, Jessica Caracci, Kendra Grimmett, and Sarah Brophy pose for a picture before a KADC program. Melanna, Kendra, and Sarah were among the corps of interns Jessica supervised as part of her multi-faceted public-education responsibilities, including coordination of KADC programming. Photo by Nancy Baum

Figure 23. Wendy Ennes, Associate Head of Public Education, Technology, and Innovation, assists students during the Museum Connections program, one of the many highly successful on-site and online grant-funded initiatives she has developed for teachers and schools. Photo by Carole Krucoff

Along with all of her other responsibilities, Jessica joined with Terry Friedman, Volunteer Programs Associate, to attend a five-part information and training session run by Open Doors, an organization that focuses on services to special-needs audiences. This led to a survey on ways the Museum's galleries can better meet special needs as well as the beginning of future collaborations between the Education Department and organizations that specialize in services for people with visual, hearing, physical, and developmental disabilities.

Wendy Ennes, Associate Head of Public Education, Technology, and Innovation, is key to all our grant-funded initiatives for teachers and students. She also supports a wide range of Institute and Museum initiatives, from participating on the new media committee and community focus group panel to collaborating with the university's arts initiative. Her dedication and drive, along with her grant-writing abilities, expertise in online teaching and learning, and supervisory skills make her an invaluable asset to the Education Department and the Oriental Institute as a whole.

Wendy's strong strategic-planning strengths and goal-setting abilities enable her to see the big picture and suggest approaches that can provide highly significant outcomes. A key example was her ability to leverage a modest Chicago Public Schools grant for the Museum Connections program into an initiative with great promise to become a model for ways in which the Institute's innovative approaches to archaeology can be a springboard for science-based learning and technology instruction in the nation's classrooms (fig. 23). Other examples included her contributions to the Institute's Integrated Database Project (IDB), and the successful major grant proposal for support of the IDB that she and the IDB committee crafted for submission to the national Institute of Museum and Library Services (IMLS).

Beyond the Institute, Wendy's reputation is growing as an educator with outstanding abilities to help teachers prepare children for success in this information age. This year she was invited by the Museum Education Roundtable, a national organization that provides professional development for museum practitioners, to be a presenter at "Museums and Schools: Partners in Teaching and Learning." At this day-long workshop for educators from cultural institutions throughout the Midwest, Wendy detailed the ways in which the Teacher Advisory Boards she has developed and led were central to the creation of two national outreach Web sites — the NEH Teaching the Middle East initiative described in this report, and Ancient Mesopotamia: This History, Our History, an IMLS National Leadership Grant–funded initiative available on the Oriental Institute Web site that is supporting the ancient-studies curriculum in school classrooms all across the United States.

The next section presents the many achievements of the Volunteer Program, supervised by our colleagues Catherine Deans and Terry Friedman, the extraordinarily dedicated and talented team who serve as Volunteer Programs Associates. This year our collegial relationship became even closer as we joined together with Gil Stein and Steve Camp to plan and structure our department as a new unit within the Oriental Institute. All of us are continually inspired by the creativity and commitment of our remarkable corps of volunteers. The following pages describe how the Institute and the community have benefitted from the work of our volunteers, and all that Cathy and Terry have helped them accomplish.

VOLUNTEER PROGRAM

Catherine Dueñas and Terry Friedman

Introduction

Now in its forty-fourth year, the Oriental Institute Volunteer Program continues to bring archaeology, history, and art of the ancient Near East alive to audiences of all ages. The dedication and knowledge of volunteers continue to be an invaluable asset to the Oriental Institute and the Museum. As Museum Education becomes the newly organized Public Education Department in the Oriental Institute, the Volunteer Program will continue to work and collaborate with the new unit.

Following the introduction of several key technologies this past year, we have

Figure 1. Volunteer Programs Associates Terry Friedman and Catherine Dueñas pose with former coordinators and mentors Carlotta Maher and Janet Helman. Photo by Craig Tews

begun to utilize these contemporary tools, generating a variety of options to better organize and manage the ongoing operations of the Volunteer Program. This has helped us develop innovative ways to bring the ancient Near East to new audiences in order to better engage the public with the work of the Oriental Institute in the twenty-first century.

The Volunteer Program provides opportunities for individuals to become actively involved with the Oriental Institute as Museum Docents while utilizing their many specialized skills to assist faculty and staff throughout the Institute. A thorough training program, extensive Docent library, and additional educational opportunities are offered throughout the year to support the volunteers and Docents as they pursue their own research and interests. The success and vitality of the Volunteer Program over the past forty-four years is largely due to the many unique opportunities available for Docents and volunteers to learn and expand their horizons.

Reorganization of Filing Systems and Tracking Statistics

Building on the momentum from last year's reorganization of our filing system, this year we continued compiling detailed data of our Museum visitorship, thus consolidating a more efficient system for tracking and filing statistical information of our audiences. Intern Karina Chavarria compiled past visitor statistics into detailed graphics covering the past five years. This will provide

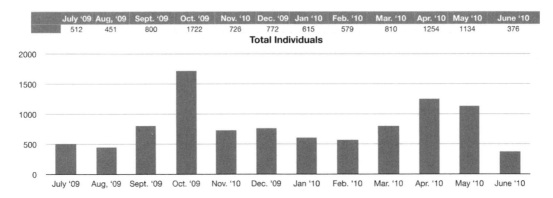

	July '09	Aug, '09	Sept. '09	Oct. '09	Nov. '10	Dec. '09	Jan '10	Feb. '10	Mar. '10	Apr. '10	May '10	June '10
	512	451	800	1722	726	772	615	579	810	1254	1134	376

Total Individuals

Figure 2. Total visitors for 2009–2010

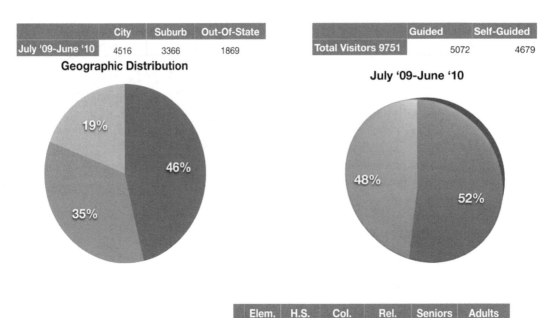

	City	Suburb	Out-Of-State
July '09-June '10	4516	3366	1869

Geographic Distribution

	Guided	Self-Guided
Total Visitors 9751	5072	4679

July '09-June '10

Elem.	H.S.	Col.	Rel.	Seniors	Adults
4192	1512	2073	427	115	1432

July '09-June '10 Group Distribution

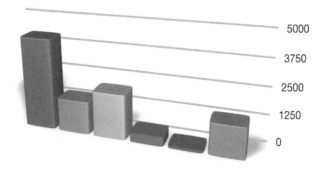

Figures 3, 4, and 5. These graphs represent the total visitors trends throughout 2009–2010

easy access to previous years' statistics, allowing for quick comparisons of demographics between years. This process was a year-long endeavor that will ensure the fluid transition into a new program for tracking and creating graphical representations of emerging visitor trends (figs. 2–5).

Tour Program

The Museum is a gem, but Docents are needed to interpret the displays, especially to younger visitors. To be sure, the artifacts are well chosen and charmingly displayed, but it is the human voice, explaining and describing, which gives emphasis to what the eyes see.

— Ida Depencier, a member of the first Docent-training class in 1966, from "Reflections of A Volunteer Docent," *Oriental Institute News & Notes*, April 1974.

Docents are the public face of the Museum and truly our goodwill ambassadors, as the above quote from the late Ida Depencier describes.

Whether with school students, religious groups, community organizations, or senior citizens, the Oriental Institute Museum Docents are eager to share their knowledge of and pride in the Museum's collection. We are pleased to announce that in the fiscal year 2009–2010, 5,072 visitors took advantage of a Docent-led tour, while 4,679 visitors chose the self-guided option.

Despite an uncertain economy, we were pleased that the numbers remained reasonably in line with last year's statistics and actually showed an increase of 7 percent over last year's overall numbers.

Opposite are the graphs that illustrate the comparisons of visitor data collected over the past year. The statistics for 2009–2010 are broken down by month, geographic distribution, group distribution, and guided versus self-guided tours. Special thanks to Karina Chavarria for her hard work in compiling these statistics, which we have found to be a useful tool in the tracking of visitor trends and demographics.

Tours in Conjunction with the KADC

This year volunteers have continued to design new and exciting ways to connect the gallery tours with the dig experience in the Kipper Family Archaeology Discovery Center (KADC). Following the incredible success of its inaugural year, this simulated dig, where participants learn about the processes of archaeological discovery, helps expose the science behind the artifacts studied in the gallery. Docents have been able to incorporate the vocabulary, concepts, and discoveries from the dig into their tours, resulting in a unique learning experience for all ages.

Special Programs and Events

The Museum Docents and volunteers continue to bring the Museum's many educational and enrichment opportunities to audiences throughout the community through outreach visits and special programs in the Museum. Volunteers have continued to enrich the experiences of visitors by offering tours of the galleries in conjunction with a variety of special events sponsored by the Education Department. These include film and music events, such as the Valentine's Day film viewing in February, the Passport to Jazz programs held in March and May, the Chicago Jazz Festival in September, and the annual Mummies Night.

On Saturday, April 17, the Oriental Institute Museum was invited, for the second year in a row, to participate in the Día del Niño festival hosted by Chicago's National Museum of Mexican Art. The festival has been a great opportunity to advance our efforts toward expanding our resources to Chicago's Spanish-speaking communities. This year's event welcomed 11,000 visitors from Chicago's Latino communities. The Oriental Institute was able to reach this year's visitors and share information regarding the new bilingual resources available in the Museum, specifically a new project that will be launched this summer, involving our gallery computer kiosks that will contain Spanish virtual interactive tours and games. At Día del Niño, Catherine Dueñas, Volunteer Programs Associate, intern Karina Chavarria, and volunteers Vicente Ruvalcaba, Eugenia Briseño, and Erica Griffin provided visitors with bilingual activity cards with images of artifacts from our collections and also helped children and youth create origami pyramids. We were able to reach over 1,000 participants, informing them about the Oriental Institute's location as well as the various resources available to the public. The majority of the visitors were unaware that the Oriental Institute Museum existed and that it is free to the public. We also had visitors who had been to our Museum and were exited to see us there. We are very hopeful that our participation in this year's festival will attract many more Spanish-speaking visitors to the Museum.

School Outreach Programs

The Volunteer Program has also continued to bring the ancient Near East to eager students through outreach programs at local schools and community groups. Now in its fourteenth year, this program continues to reach new audiences, delighting and educating students as they learn about Egypt and ancient Mesopotamia. This year, 300 participants took part in outreach programs at Millennium School in Homewood and Central Road School in Rolling Meadows. These programs are highly interactive, allowing students to learn how to write hieroglyphs, handle museum replicas, or try on costumes from ancient times. These activities bring to life the daily routines of these ancient peoples. We are delighted that the program continues to receive rave reviews and fulfill the mission of the Volunteer Program to bring the art and history of the ancient Near East alive for students of all ages.

Science Tour Program

Each year, the Volunteer Program joins Public Education to develop new tours to highlight the work of the Oriental Institute. This year, working in conjunction with the Public Education Department, CAMEL lab students, and faculty, Docents led science-oriented tours for area teachers and middle school students as part of the new "Science in Archaeology" program initiative. This important program educates teachers and students about the techniques of archaeology as well as the ways in which technology is used in archaeological research in the twenty-first century.

Volunteer Training and Management

Docent Captain System

The Docent Captain System continues to successfully link the administrative staff with Museum Docents. Each captain is responsible for scheduling a specific day of the week to supervise a group of docents, with whom they communicate via weekly e-mail reminders. Captains also mentor and guide new docents in training, giving them the support they need to become successful and confident Museum guides. The attention and vigilance of our docent captains allows the docent program to run smoothly and efficiently. We extend our thanks and appreciation to the following captains and co-captains for their hard work and dedication throughout this past year: Doug Baldwin, Noel Brusman, Myllicent Buchanan, Gabriele DaSilva, Joe Diamond, David Giba,

Figure 6. Following the volunteer recognition ceremony, docents, volunteers, faculty, and staff get a chance to mingle during the annual holiday luncheon at the Quadrangle Club. Photo by Craig Tews

Figure 7. Seated from left to right, Irene Glasner, Ray Broms, Judy Bell-Quails, Norma van der Meulen, Florence Ovadia, and Janet Calkins enjoy each other's company around the table at the annual holiday luncheon. Photo by Craig Tews

Figure 8. December Volunteer Day is a great opportunity for volunteers to reconnect and enjoy a festive holiday celebration. Seated from left to right are Nancy Baum, Michael Schaffner, Noel Brusman, Hilda Schlatter, Craig Tews, and Ira Hardman. Photo by Wendy Ennes

Teresa Hintzke, Dennis Kelley, Lo Luong Lo, Demetria Nanos, Patrick Regnery, Stephen Ritzel, Lucie Sandel, Deloris Sanders, Hilda Schlatter, and Carole Yoshida.

Throughout the year, several docent captains encouraged their groups to organize informal study sessions that focused on the development of special-interest tour topics. These sessions helped the docents enhance their own knowledge of specific areas of the collection as well as generate unique approaches for engaging audiences with interactive touring methods.

This year the Volunteer Program was sad to announce the retirement of long-time Friday captain Joe Diamond and Saturday afternoon captain Patrick Regnery. We thank them for their leadership and support throughout the years.

A special note of thanks to Education Programs Associate Jessica Caracci, whose outstanding organization and communication skills are at the very core of the tour program's success. Her patience, attention to detail, and friendly demeanor are truly appreciated by everyone with whom she works.

Volunteer Recognition and Annual Holiday Luncheon

December Volunteer Day has become an annual tradition when docents, faculty, staff, and volunteers gather to enjoy a festive holiday celebration together. This popular event includes a guest speaker, the introduction of new volunteers, and the volunteer recognition ceremony (fig. 6). The program concludes with a lovely holiday luncheon at the Quadrangle Club. This year's special event took place on Monday, December 7, and our guest speaker was Geoff Emberling, Chief Curator of the Oriental Institute Museum. He gave an outstanding PowerPoint presentation on the "State of the Museum." Volunteers were pleased to hear his annual update highlighting the Museum's future goals and projects as well as the many accomplishments during his tenure as Museum Director over these past five years.

Immediately following Geoff's presentation, the program continued with the introduction of new volunteers and the recognition awards ceremony (figs. 7, 8). We were pleased to introduce fifteen new members to the volunteer corps.

Volunteers: Class of 2009–2010

Stephanie Baness	Paul Johnson	Jane Melroy
Eugenia Briceño	Panagiotis Koutsouris	Ariel Radock
Susan Cossack	Katja Lehman	Dahlia Risk
Amanda Doren	Ann Lyden	Micheal Schaffner
Stephanie Duran	Katharine Marsden	Thiera Smith
Moriah Grooms	Sarah Means	Craig Tews

Volunteer Program MAPSS Intern, 2009–2010

Alice Brown

Returning Intern

Karina Chavarria

Recognition Awards Ceremony

This year twenty-six people were recognized for their distinguished and loyal commitment to the Oriental Institute and to the Museum (fig. 9). Their combined years of service represent 456 YEARS IN TOTAL!

Figure 9. As part of the December Volunteer Day Program, Volunteer Recognition Award recipients were honored for their years of service to the Oriental Institute. Award recipients gathered with Volunteer Programs Associates Terry Friedman and Catherine Dueñas after being recognized. From left to right are Anita Greenberg, Mary Shea, Bill Gillespie, Djanie Edwards, Mark Hirsch, Terry Gillespie, Rebecca Binkley-Albright, Mary O'Shea, Inge Winer, Shel Newman, Sandy Jacobsohn, Hazel Cramer, Janet Calkins, and Alice James (center). Photo by Craig Tews

Award recipients are recognized in two categories: active volunteers (those who participate on a routine basis) and emeritus volunteers (those who have not been as active in recent years, but who still remain involved as a part of the Oriental Institute community).

Active Volunteers

5 years	**10 years**	**15 years**	**20 years**
Djanie Edwards	Gabriele DaSilva	Janet Calkins	Sandra Jacobsohn
Mark Hirsch	Bill Gillespie	Hazel Cramer	Patrick Regnery
Mary O'Shea	Terry Gillespie	Mary Harter	
Inge Winer	Shel Newman		
Agnes Zellner			

25 years	**30 years**	**31 years**
Rebecca Binkley-Albright	Mary Shea	Anita Greenberg

Emeritus Volunteers

15 years	**25 years**	**40 years**
Barbara Storms Baird	Charlotte Collier	Muriel Nerad
	Alice James	

20 years		**30 years**
Ruth Hyman		Jane Hildebrand
Samantha Johnson		
Caryl Mikrut		
Agnethe "Neta" Rattenborg		

Figure 10. 2010 summer intern Lauren Horn worked hard to assist in the revision and completion of the 2009–2010 Annual Report. Photo by Terry Friedman

Volunteer Days

The Volunteer Program is committed to providing meaningful, ongoing educational opportunities for docents and volunteers. These events and programs provide a stimulating learning environment for volunteers to explore personal scholarly interests while also helping them develop informative and up-to-date tours. The 2009–2010 season featured many successful programs. We wish to thank Abbas Alizadeh, Susan Bazargan, Geoff Emberling, Norman Golb, W. Ray Johnson, Kathleen Mineck, and Gil Stein for contributing their time and expertise to these programs.

Fall Mini-Series

Building from the success of previous years' mini-series, we were proud to present another program to provide docents and volunteers the opportunity to examine a particular topic in greater depth. Volunteers studied the creation myths of Ancient Mesopotamia, Ancient Egypt, Anatolia, and early Christianity over the course of four Saturdays. The presentations and the discussions they precipitated helped us understand the fundamental similarities and differences among these four unique cultural mythologies. Many thanks to Foy Scalf, Andrea Seri, Theo van den Hout, and Margaret Mitchell for their participation in producing this outstanding program series. Tapes of these sessions are now available on DVD for docents and volunteers to view in the Volunteer Office.

Volunteer Training Manual

In the ongoing effort to provide the best training possible for current and future docents and volunteers, summer intern Danielle Valdez and MAPSS intern Alice Brown worked to digitize and update the volunteer training manual. Danielle scanned the 600-page document, while Alice edited the digital layout of the document; added additional images, page numbers, and tables of contents; and revised the introductory chapter. When completed, the new training manual will allow individuals to print clean copies of any chapter, or read the manual directly from the PDF files. Its format will also make it easier to update and disseminate new copies of the manual.

In the process of editing the training manual, Alice noticed sections of the Persian chapter that needed some revision. As a result of her efforts, production of a new Persian chapter began, which will be featured in the new training manual. Senior Research Associate Abbas Alizadeh, with the assistance of Susan Bazargan, substantially rewrote the chapter to present the history and artifacts of ancient Iran in a clear and concise manner. We encourage everyone, whether a veteran or new volunteer, to explore this wonderful new addition to the volunteer training manual. Thank you, Alice, Abbas, and Susan, for working so diligently on this important revision. The outcome will be a valuable educational resource for years to come.

In order to protect the integrity of the Volunteer Program and the wealth of information contained in the new volunteer training DVDs, 2010 summer intern Lauren Horn (fig. 10) worked with Tom James to transfer the contents onto an external storage space. Throughout the summer, countless hours of valuable lecture footage from the DVDs were reconverted into their early, digitized form. These precautionary measures were taken to ensure the security of the information during this period of continuous technological change and advancement.

Docent Library

Volunteers also have access to an extensive lending library of books and materials on all topics relating to the ancient Near East. Head librarian Margaret Foorman expertly oversees the collection, managing acquisitions and circulation. The Docent Library eagerly accepts donations from faculty, staff, and volunteers; Margaret highlights these new additions to the library regularly in *The Volunteer Voice*. New materials are also purchased directly for the program with funds raised at the annual book sale, held in conjunction with the December Volunteer Day. This year, the book sale raised over $150 for the Docent Library. Many thanks to Margaret for her hard work and dedication.

The Docent Library also serves as a volunteer lounge. The room bustles every day as staff and volunteers who use the space to socialize around the table, look over training materials, and get caught up on Oriental Institute Museum news. We thank all of the generous donors who have consistently replenished the sweets and goodies that so many of us enjoy regularly.

CONNECTING A COMMUNITY OF VOLUNTEERS

Volunteer Voice

The monthly newsletter, *The Volunteer Voice*, connects the many volunteers, faculty, and staff working at the Oriental Institute. The newsletter announces upcoming educational events and volunteer opportunities, chronicles important happenings from the past month, and passes on important information. Volunteers may receive *The Volunteer Voice* by e-mail or United States postal service, or read a copy in the Docent Library.

Volunteer Directory

Following her hard work updating the volunteer databases last year, Museum Docent and faculty assistant Sue Geshwender has continued to contribute many hours helping the office become more sophisticated with its use of technology. Her efforts culminated in the production of a new volunteer directory to help our dedicated volunteers connect with one another. Thank you, Sue, for your continued support and help with this ongoing project.

Interns

We were very fortunate this past year to have Alice Brown and Karina Chavarria work with us as interns in the Volunteer Office. Karina came to us as a MAPSS intern last year and continued to work with the bilingual program in the Education and Volunteer Office. She was joined by 2009–2010 MAPSS intern Alice Brown for the academic year. From administrative tasks and special projects to the maintenance of statistics databases, the contributions of these ladies helped to support and enrich the Volunteer Program's ongoing operations and new initiatives.

We were also delighted to have intern Lauren Horn from Grinnell College join us for the 2010 summer. She has been very helpful with many exciting and challenging projects over the summer months.

Museum Education Staff

We would also like to thank our Education Department colleagues for their ongoing support and astute advice throughout this past year: Jessica Caracci, Education Programs Associate; Wendy Ennes, Associate Head of Public Education, Educational Technology, and Innovation; and Carole Krucoff, Head of Public Education. In our shared office space, which is full of activity and many interruptions, their sense of humor and calm demeanor foster a congenial and productive working atmosphere.

In Memoriam

This year the Volunteer Program and Oriental Institute lost several devoted friends and supporters: Dr. George Morgan, Dorothy Mozinski, Rita Picken, David Ray, and Jo Ellen Urban. These individuals epitomized the essence of a volunteer, sharing their unique talents and skills in order to further the goals and mission of the Oriental Institute. We are so thankful for their many years of service and dedication and we will miss them greatly.

Reflection

The year 2009–2010 witnessed important changes in the Volunteer Program. We joined our colleagues in the Education Department to create a new unit within the Oriental Institute. Embracing the technological innovations introduced last year, we continued to systematically utilize our databases and track statistical trends. The revision of the docent training manual was a high priority. Improving the content and format of this important training tool will help the Volunteer Program broaden its scope and ability to integrate updates and information as needed for future training. As we further embrace this new technological mindset, we discover innovative strategies to respond to the program's administrative demands.

Even with these advances, the Volunteer Program remains committed to its primary mission established forty-four years ago: to bring the ancient Near East alive to visitors of all ages. This would not be possible without the Oriental Institute's dedicated volunteer corps. We are pleased to announce that volunteers gave 6,383 hours of volunteer service this fiscal year. With their diverse knowledge and expertise, the volunteers have helped us realize our many goals and ambitions by demonstrating their pride in and unwavering support for the Oriental Institute, and they are a treasured resource, our strongest asset, and the key to the program's historic longevity.

We wish to express our sincere gratitude to our four faithful interns this past year, Alice Brown, Karina Chavaria, Lauren Horn, and Danielle Valdez, whose collaborative spirit and fresh perspectives added so much to the production of this year's *Annual Report*.

Volunteers: Class of 2009–2010

Rebecca Bailey	Stephanie Duran	Sarah Means
Stephanie Baness	Moriah Grooms	Jane Melroy
Grace Brody	Paul Johnson	Ariel Radock
Eugenia Briceño	Panagiotis Koutsouris	Dahlia Risk
Susan Cossack	Katja Lehman	Micheal Schaffner
Amanda Doren	Ann Lyden	Thiera Smith
Robyn Dubicz	Katharine Marsden	Craig Tews

MAPSS Intern 2009–2010

Alice Brown

Administrative Assistant

Karina Chavarria

Summer Intern 2010

Lauren Horn

Advisers to the Volunteer Program

Peggy Grant Janet Helman Carlotta Maher

Docent Advisory Committee (Executive Board)

Joe Diamond Dennis Kelley Mary Shea

Museum Docents (Active)

John Aldrin	Bill Gillespie	Mary O'Connell
Dennis Bailey	Terry Gillespie	Mary O'Shea
Douglas Baldwin	Anita Greenberg	Nancy Patterson
Nancy Baum	Erica Griffin	Kitty Picken
Susan Bazargan	Moriah Grooms	Semra Prescott
Christel Betz	Debby Halpern	Patrick Regnery
Rebecca Binkley	Ira Hardman	Stephen Ritzel
Eugenia Briceño	Janet Helman	Geraldine Rowden
Noel Brusman	Lee Herbst	Lucie Sandel
Myllicent Buchanan	Teresa Hintzke	Deloris Sanders
Roberta Buchanan	Mark Hirsch	Ljubica Sarenac
Andrew Buncis	Morton Jaffee	Michael Schaffner
Gabriella Cohen	Paul Johnson	Hilda Schlatter
Susan Cossack	Dennis Kelley	Joy Schochet
Joan Curry	Stuart Kleven	Anne Schumacher
Gabriele DaSilva	Panagiotis Koutsouris	Mary Shea
John DeWerd	Katja Lehman	Daila Shefner
Joe Diamond	Larry Lissak	Mae Simon
Djanie Edwards	Lo Luong Lo	Toni Smith
Stephen Esposito	Paul Mallory	Mari Terman
Jean Fincher	Margaret Manteufel	Karen Terras
Mary Finn	Pat McLaughlin	Craig Tews
Margaret Foorman	Sherry McGuire	James Tillapaugh
Barbara Freidell	Sarah Means	Siwei Wang
Sue Geshwender	Kathy Mineck	Ronald Wideman
Dario Giacomoni	Demetria Nanos	Inge Winer
David Giba	Sean Niewoehner	Carole Yoshida
	Daniel O'Connel	

Outreach Volunteers

Andy Buncis	Bill Gillespie	Larry Lissak
Janet Calkins	Terry Gillespie	Margaret Manteufel
Joan Curry	Ira Hardman	Demetria Nanos
Joe Diamond	Panagiotis Koutsouris	Mary O'Shea
Bettie Dwinell		Carole Yoshida

Volunteers Emeritus

Debbie Aliber	Carol Green	Robert McGuiness
Muriel Brauer	Cissy Haas	Roy Miller
Charlotte Collier	Alice James	Muriel Nerad
Erl Dordal	Mary Jo Khuri	Rita Picken†
Mary D'Ouville	Betsy Kremers	David Ray†
Bettie Dwinell	Nina Longley	Janet Russell
Joan Friedmann	Jo Lucas	Elizabeth Spiegel
	Masako Matsumoto	

Affiliated Volunteers
(not active, but still part of the Oriental Institute community)

Bernadine Basile	Janet Kessler	Donald Payne
Davis Covill	Henriette Klawans	Pramerudee Townsend
Marda Gross	Alice Mulberry	Arveal Turner

Suq Volunteers

Barbara Storms-Baird	Ray Broms	Erin Mukwaya
John Baird	Peggy Grant	Jo Ellen Urban†
Judy Bell-Quails	Jane Meloy	Norma van der Meulen

CAMEL Lab

Marc Block	Alexander Elwyn	Larry Lissak
Jim Boues	Vincent van Exel	Harold Sanders
Gabriella Cohen	Devora Heard	Ron Wideman

Conservation Lab Volunteers

Claire Barker	Kristen Gillette	Lillian Rosner
	Nicole Pizzini	

Photo Database

Eric Beckman	Shaheen Gutierrez	James Pike
Michael Camp	Miranda Pettengill	Charley Spence
Allison Drtina		Lise Truex

Photography Lab Volunteers

Claire Barker	Craig Tews

Research Archives

Ray Broms	Andrea Dudek	James Tillanpaugh
Stephanie Duran	Mary Louise Jackowicz	Agnes Zellner
	George Sundell	

Diyala Project

Larry Lissak	George Sundell

Galilee Pre-History Project
Robyn Dubicz

Hacinebi Project
Irene Glasner

Nippur Project
Karen Terras

Museum
Adrienne Frie

Registration Work Study
Courtney Jacobson

Volunteers

Gretel Braidwood	Janet Helman	Toni Smith
Cassandra Calleweart	Courtney Jacobson	Junli Song
Becky Caroli	Ila Patlogan	Jim Sopranos
Joe Diamond	Andrew Rutledge	George Sundell
Maggie Geoga	Matthew Sawina	Raymond Tindel
Aleksandra Hallman	Daila Shefner	Elizabeth Wolfson

Work-study Students and Interns

Cassandra Calleweart	Maggie Geoga	Matthew Sawina
Becky Caroli	Aleksandra Hallman	Junli Song
Elizabeth Wolfson	Andrew Rutledge	

Professor Brinkman
James Torpy

Demotic Dictionary
Larry Lissak

Archives Volunteers

Jean Fincher	Daniel Kovacs	Stephanie O'Brien
Peggy Grant	Roberta Kovitz*	Robert Wagner
Sandra Jacobsohn	Manuel Alex Moya	Carole Yoshida

* indicates retirement from active service during fiscal year 2009–2010

Membership
Peggy Grant

Curatorial
Christine Efta   Adrienne Frie

Marketing

Amanda Sorensen

Tall-e Geser Project

Janet Helman

Editing Persian Training Materials

Susan Bazargan   Alice Brown

Family Events and Special Programs

John Aldrin	Mary Finn	Demetria Nanos
Rebecca Binkley-Albright	Sue Geshwender	Semra Prescott
Nancy Baum	Bill Gillespie	Patrick Regnery
Susan Bazargan	Terry Gillespie	Stephen Ritzel
Christel Betz	Erica Griffin	Vicente Ruvalcaba
Clare Brody	Mark Hirsch	Lucie Sandel
Eugenia Brisceno	Dennis Kelley	Mary Shea
Noel Brusman	Panagiotis Koutsouris	Mae Simon
Gabrielle DaSilva	Larry Lissak	Deloris Sanders
John DeWerd	Lo Luong Lo	Thiera Smith
Dario Giacomoni	Daniel O'Connell	Toni Smith
Debby Halpern	Mary O'Connell	Carole Yoshida
Jean Fincher	Kathy Mineck	

Kipper Family Archaeology Discovery Center (KADC)

Sarah Brophy   Allison Drtina   Lauren Wojnarowski
Stephanie O'Brien

Events Committee 2009–2010

Andrea Dudek   Deborah Halpern, Chair   Mari Terman
Margaret Foorman   Agnes Zellner

Strategic Planning

Shel Newman

———————

DEVELOPMENT AND MEMBERSHIP

DEVELOPMENT AND MEMBERSHIP

DEVELOPMENT

Steve Camp and Rebecca Silverman

The Development and Membership offices experienced a significant year of transition. We welcomed Maeve Reed as Membership Coordinator, Meghan Winston as Development Associate-Special Events Coordinator, and Rebecca Silverman as Development Associate. With these three new hires, the Oriental Institute now has a fully staffed Development and Membership department, able to serve the needs of our supporters as well as further the initiatives of the Institute as a whole.

Oriental Institute Donors and Members continued their generosity with another year of growth in our fund-raising totals. Fund raising increased 29 percent in 2009–2010 over the previous year. The chart below provides fund-raising totals for the past three years:

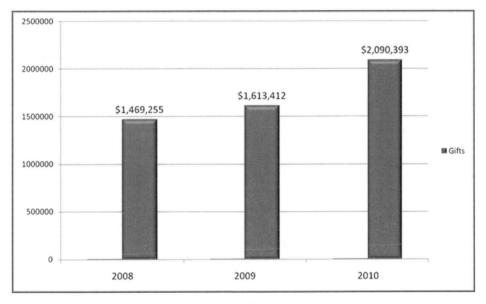

Oriental Institute fund raising 2008–2010

This increase in fund raising came at a crucial time for the Oriental Institute. While the University's support of individual departments continues to be limited by the economic downturn, our supporters have allowed us to continue programs that might have been cut or reduced while providing for continued growth in new areas, such as the launch of new field projects in the Middle East, the ongoing development of new special exhibits in the galleries, and the support of new research staff on key projects.

None of this could have been done without the support you provide to the Oriental Institute. From all of us at the Oriental Institute, thank you.

Research Endowment Campaign

In the spring of 2010, we celebrated the completion of our Research Endowment Campaign (REC), which to date has raised over $3,000,000 in critical long-term endowment support for:

- Research Archives
- Technology Initiatives
- Ancient Language Programs
- Archaeological Fieldwork Projects
- Museum Holdings and Special Collections Programs

Thanks to you, our donors and supporters, for making this campaign a resounding success.

Research Endowment Campaign Donors
Platinum Level ($100,000 or more)

The Trust Estate of Marion Cowan
Arthur & Lee Herbst
The Trust Estate of Erica Reiner
John & Jeanne Rowe
The Estate of Nancy M. Sargis

Gold Level ($50,000 to $99,999)

The Trust Estate of Alwin C. Carus
Richard & Mary Gray
Misty & Lewis Gruber
Robert & Janet Helman
Roger & Marjorie Nelson
John & Lee Ong
O. J. & Angeline Sopranos

Bronze Level ($25,000 to $49,999)

The Brookner Estate
James & Margaret Foorman
Joan Fortune
Howard G. Haas
Thomas & Linda Heagy
Neil King & Diana Hunt King
Joseph Lach
Lois Schwartz
Toni Sandor Smith
Francis & Lorna Straus
Mari Terman

$10,000 to $24,999

Alan R. Brodie
Isak & Nancy Gerson
David & Carlotta Maher
Ann Roberts
Marjorie Webster

Up to $10,000

D. M. & Mary C. Abadi

Abbas Alizadeh

Robert Andersen

Julie Antelman

Ronald R. and Marsha Baade

Laurel V. Bell-Cahill

John J. Barbie

Thomas & Francesca Bennett

Julia Beringer

Charles & Helen Bidwell

Catherine Novotny Brehm

Mary Cerven

Johna S. Compton

Brendan P. Dempsey

Andrea Dudek

Scott M. Forsythe

Gregory J. Gajda

Tawfik & Dorothy Girgis

Gene & Michele J. Gragg

David & Marsha Gratner

M. Hill & Cheryl Hammock

Robert F. Hendrickson

David C. & Betty Hess

Joan R. Hoatson

Ruth Horwich

Roger David Isaacs

Sandra Jacobsohn

Janet I. Kelly

Mark E. Lehner

Jan W. & Lois Mares

William B. McDonald & Glen A. Khant

Mila Meeker

Mariateresa Montanari

Suzanne Todd Morgan

William L. & Kate B. Morrison

Michael Nabholz

Phil & Linda Neal

Joan Hunt Parks

Rita T. Picken

Elizabeth Postell

Crennan & David Ray

Maria A. Rull

Kirk Lee Schmink

Vincent F. Seyfried

Henry & Miriam Shapiro

Patrick J. Shaugnessy

Robert M. Shelbourne

Charles M. Adelman

Mary & Stanley Allan

Thomas W. Andrews

Ardell Arthur

Miriam Reitz Baer

William M. Backs & Janet Rizner

Cynthia A. Bates & Kevin Francis Rock

Mark & Nancy Bergner

Andrea Berk

Gretel Braidwood & Raymond Tindel

Robert R. & Consuelo B. Brink

Bruce & Joyce Chelberg

Helen M. Cunningham

Ursula Digman

Ann R. Esse

Eleanor B. Frew

John R. Gardner

Frederick & Patricia Graboske

Robert & Margaret Grant

Eleanor Guralnick

H. Lawrence & Joanne S. Helfer

Reverend Richard A. Henshaw

Walter A. & Hedda Hess

Christy Hoberecht

Kamal N. & Lucy W. Ibrahim

Lise Jacobsohn

Pamela Jordan

Nicholas & Maruchi Kotcherha

Gary B. Lyall

Frank & Linda Mayer

Harriet McKay

Robert & Lois Moeller

Catherine Moore

Shirley A. Morningstar

Henry Moy

Debra Navarre

Muriel Kallis Newman

Gloria C. Phares & Richard Dannay

Harvey Plotnick

R.B. Industries, Inc.

Agnes A. Roach & Ronald Allan Ferguson

Paul Benjamin Schechter

Albert & Jane Schwuchow

Michael Sha

Patrick J. Shaugnessy

Mary G. Shea

Emma Shelton & Florence Kate Millar

Up to $10,000 (cont.)

Matthew Sideman	Dorothy J. Speidel & Irving L. Diamond
Gil J. Stein	Jerome & Hadassah Stein
Herbert A. Storck	Gerald Sufrin
Kathleen J. Sumner	George R. Sundell
Robert M. Taras	Tiffany Elizabeth Thornton
Patricia Tuchman	Marlene & Russell Tuttle
Walter H. A. & Annette A. Vandaele	Richard A. & Patty Jo Watson
Dorothy Ann Wedner	Willard E. White
Vic Whitmore	Nicole S. Williams & Lawrence Becke
Robert I. Wilson	Wendall W. Wilson
Jerome & Inge Winer	Professor Irene J. Winter
Elizabeth Wissler	Lowell T. Wynn
Mary Young	

Adopt-a-Dig Campaign

Now, with seven active digs in the Middle East, our next Development campaign aims to create stable, long-term funding for each of these archaeological excavations:

- Tell Edfu, Egypt (led by Nadine Moeller)
- The Galilee Prehistory Project: Marj Rabba, Israel (led by Yorke Rowan)
- Hamoukar, Syria (led by Clemens Reichel)
- Jericho-Mafjar, West Bank (led by Don Whitcomb)
- Kerkenes Dağ, Turkey (led by Scott Branting)
- Tell Zeidan, Syria, (led by Gil J. Stein)
- Zincirli, Turkey (led by David Schloen)

More details about Adopt-a-Dig can be found online at http://oi.uchicago.edu/getinvolved/donate/adoptadig/, or by requesting a brochure from our Development Associates.

VISITING COMMITTEE

The fall Visiting Committee meeting was held on October 21, 2009, at the Quadrangle Club, with Yorke Rowan giving a presentation on his current Galilee Prehistory Project in Israel. Cocktails and dinner followed the meeting.

The spring meeting was held on May 3, 2010, at the Fortnightly Club in downtown Chicago, thanks to our host Carlotta Maher. Two faculty guest speakers attended the meeting: Nadine Moeller presented on her excavations at Tell Edfu, Egypt, and Chris Woods provided a preview of the upcoming special exhibit on the origins of writing, which he is guest curating.

We had a number of changes to the makeup of the Visiting Committee at the end of the year. Jim Sopranos will step down as Visiting Committee Chair but remain on the Executive Committee. Throughout his tenure, Jim has provided us with the firm leadership, guidance, and support needed to successfully run the Visiting Committee and Oriental Institute programs. We look forward to continuing to rely on Jim's advice and support in the coming years.

Harvey Plotnick was appointed as a new Visiting Committee member and will serve as our new Chair. Harvey Plotnick was President and CEO of Paradigm Holdings, Inc., until his retirement in 2007. He was formerly President and CEO of Molecular Electronics Co., and previously he founded and was President and CEO of Contemporary Books, Inc., which was one of the largest publishers of adult basic-education instructional materials in the United States. A 1963 graduate in English literature from the University of Chicago, Plotnick has chaired a number of its major fund-raising campaigns, including the $650 million Campaign for the Next Century, which ended in 1996. He chaired the College and Student Activities Visiting Committee and was a member of the Alumni Association's Board of Governors and Chair of the College Visiting Committee. Plotnick has been a member of Argonne's Board of Governors since 2001. He is also a member, since 1994, of the University of Chicago's Board of Trustees. He and his wife endowed the Elizabeth and Harvey Plotnick Scholarship fund for undergraduate students, as well as a fund for graduate students in the Physical Sciences at the University. Please join us in welcoming Harvey to the Visiting Committee.

Patrick Regnery and Mary Shea will be leaving the Visiting Committee this year, and I hope you will join us in thanking them for their many contributions to the Oriental Institute.

Lastly, Janet Helman received special recognition this year as a Life Member of the Visiting Committee. This is in honor of her many years of support for the Oriental Institute both financially and in her role as Docent and volunteer. Congratulations to Janet on this wonderful honor.

The Oriental Institute Visiting Committee 2009–2010

O. J. Sopranos*, Chair

Marilynn Alsdorf	David Kipper
Kathleen G. Beavis	Daniel and Lucia Woods Lindley
Guity Nashat Becker	Jill Carlotta Maher*
Gretel Braidwood*	Janina Marks
Alan R. Brodie	John W. McCarter, Jr.
Andrea Dudek	Kathleen Picken
Emily Huggins Fine	Crennan M. Ray
Dr. Marjorie M. Fisher	Patrick Regnery
Margaret E. Foorman	John W. Rowe*
Joan Fortune	Robert G. Schloerb
Isak V. and Nancy Gerson	Lois M. Schwartz*
Margaret H. Grant	Mary Shea
Lewis and Misty Gruber	Toni Smith
Howard G. Haas	Norman Solhkhah
Deborah Halpern	Mari Terman
Thomas C. Heagy*	Walter Vandaele
Janet W. Helman*	Marjorie K. Webster*
Arthur L. Herbst*, MD	Anna M. White
Doris B. Holleb*	Nicole Williams
Neil J. King	

*denotes Life Member

Executive Committee

(through June 2010)

O. J. Sopranos, Chair

Deborah Halpern, Events
Thomas C. Heagy, Nominating and Governance

Jill Carlotta Maher
Toni Smith, Development

Nominating and Governance Subcommittee

Thomas C. Heagy, Chair

Jill Carlotta Maher   Patrick Regnery   Robert G. Schloerb

Development Subcommittee

Toni Smith, Chair

Andrea Dudek
Neil J. King
Arthur L. Herbst

Jill Carlotta Maher
O. J. Sopranos

Events Subcommittee

Deborah Halpern, Chair

Andrea Dudek
Margaret E. Foorman
Kitty Picken

Mary G. Shea
Mari Terman

Remembering Rita Picken

This year also marked the passing of Rita Picken, a true friend and generous supporter of the Oriental Institute.

Rita showed her love for the Oriental Institute not only through her involvement with the Docent program for over thirty years but also through her sponsorship of the Robert F. Picken Family Nubia Gallery and the recent special exhibit The Life of Meresamun: A Temple Singer in Ancient Egypt. At our 90th Anniversary gala in 2009, the Institute honored Rita with the James Henry Breasted Medallion — the highest honor that we give our Members and supporters to recognize their service and commitment.

Rita and her daughter, Kitty Picken, have been part of the fabric of the Institute for decades; Rita saw the people in the Oriental Institute community as a second family. She will be greatly missed.

In memory of her mother Rita, Kitty Picken and the Oriental Institute announced the endowment of the Rita T. Picken Professorship in Ancient Near Eastern Art, which will be supported by a $3.5 million gift from Kitty. The professorship will enhance the work of the Oriental Institute by adding a faculty member whose expertise in ancient art will complement the Institute's strengths in languages and archaeology. The endowment of this professorship is a fitting tribute to Rita's love of art history and will be historic, given that it is only the second endowed chair in the Oriental Institute's ninety-year history.

In closing, we at the Oriental Institute thank you all for your continued support as Donors and Members. Your contributions help keep the Oriental Institute at the forefront of research and scholarship of the ancient Middle East.

MEMBERSHIP

Maeve Reed

Publications and Marketing

With the assistance of the Publications Office, the Membership Office continues to publish *News & Notes*, the quarterly Members' magazine. The fall 2009 edition highlighted new findings at the Ubaid-period site of Tell Zeidan in Syria and the Misty and Lewis Gruber Electronic Publications Initiative, which provides free PDF downloads of all Oriental Institute publications on ancient Egypt to the public. The Winter 2010 issue introduced the special exhibit Pioneers to the Past: American Archaeologists in the Middle East, 1919–1920; provided a first look at the Oriental Institute's new excavations in Israel and Marj Rabba; and featured the Chicago House Bulletin. The spring 2010 edition took a closer look at the objects brought back to Chicago by James Henry Breasted on his 1919–1920 trip to the Middle East and introduced recent archaeological discoveries in the Persepolis Plain of Iran. The summer 2010 issue reported on the 2009 season at Tell Edfu and New Media efforts at the Oriental Institute. The Membership Office is greatly appreciative of the Publications Office for their hard work and guidance in producing *News & Notes*, as well as to all of the authors and staff contributors who provide exciting and engaging articles and program notices each quarter for our Members.

Since October of 2009, the Membership Office has been publishing the *E-Tablet*, our e-newsletter, with great success. Over 6,000 friends and supporters of the Oriental Institute receive the *E-Tablet*, which keeps them up to date with news, events, and announcements. The *E-Tablet* is published monthly, on the first Tuesday of the month, and is free to the public. To sign up for the *E-Tablet*, visit our Web site (http://oi.uchicago.edu) and click on "Subscribe to our E-Newsletter" at the bottom of the page.

In addition to the *E-Tablet*, the Membership Office has been involved in launching and maintaining several new media platforms with the assistance of the Museum and Public Education. Members are encouraged to visit the Oriental Institute page on Facebook, the Oriental Institute Twitter stream, and our Web site to interact with and learn more about the Oriental Institute and our online community.

Student Memberships

As part of the University of Chicago's Art Pass program, the Oriental Institute began offering free Membership to all university students in May of 2010. Currently, we have sixty-two new student Members. The Membership Office is partnering with Public Education to develop new outreach efforts and student-only programming for University of Chicago students. Through this effort, we aim to increase student awareness of the Oriental Institute, make the Oriental Institute an integral part of the student and campus experience at the university, and become an active participant in student events.

Events

Members enjoyed a wide variety of events in 2009–2010. On July 8, 2009, members of the James Henry Breasted Society were invited to the Research Archives for A Feast of Knowledge: Libraries and Archives, Past and Present. Attendees enjoyed a private viewing of collection highlights from the Research Archives as well as several rarely exhibited objects from the Museum. In November, our 2009 events schedule came to a close with an exceptional lecture for our Associate Members by renowned scholar Dr. Elizabeth J. Wayland Barber entitled "Women's Work, the First 20,000 Years: Women, Cloth and Society in the Ancient Near East." Dr. Barber traced the origins of cloth production in the ancient Near East and presented the audience with replica cloth samples that she recreated using ancient methods and technologies.

Our 2010 events schedule got underway early on January 11, as over 150 Members attended the Members' preview for the special exhibit Pioneers to the Past: American Archaeologists in the Middle East, 1919–1920. Members were treated to a private viewing of the exhibit a day before it opened to the public, pith-helmet–shaped souvenir cookies, catalog signing by Chief Curator Geoff Emberling, and 1920s jazz music in the Doris Holleb Family Special Exhibit Gallery. In February, Members of the James Henry Breasted Society attended Voices from the New Past, a unique evening of storytelling. Breasted Society Members were treated to a retelling of some of James Henry Breasted's adventures from his 1919–1920 journey to the Middle East by Director Gil Stein and Chief Curator Geoff Emberling, as well as personal stories from the field as told by current Oriental Institute faculty. In April, the Oriental Institute held its annual Members' event Passport to the Middle East: Check Out Our Digs! Members were invited to learn more about the Oriental Institute's seven active excavations in the Middle East by visiting with dig directors at stations distributed throughout the galleries.

In addition to Members' events, Oriental Institute Members enjoyed a comprehensive Members' lecture series in 2009–2010 with topics ranging from underwater archaeology to burial rituals and historical forgeries:

- After the Revolution: Oriental Institute Archaeology in Iran — Abbas Alizadeh (October 2009)

- The Sea of Galilee Boat — Shelley Wachsmann (November 2009); co-sponsored by the Chicago chapter of the Archaeological Institute of America

- Headless Ancestors and Ghouls: Understanding the Plastered Human Skulls of Jericho and the Origins of Agriculture — Ian Kuijt (December 2009)

- Searching for Ancient Sam'al: Four Seasons of Excavation at Zincirli in Turkey — David Schloen (January 2010)

- Death's Dominion: Chalcolithic Religion and the Ritual Economy of the Southern Levant — Yorke Rowan (February 2010)

- Biblical Archaeology, the Limits of Science, and the Borders of Belief — Nina Burleigh (March 2010)

- Tracking the Frontiers of the Hittite Empire — Ann Gunter (April 2010)

- Meluhha: The Indus Civilization and Its Contacts with Mesopotamia — Mark Kenoyer (May 2010)

- Exploring the Roots of Mesopotamian Civilization: Excavations at Tell Zeidan, Syria — Gil Stein (June 2010)

The Oriental Institute Members' lecture series aims to bring a varied selection of the most recent work and scholarship on the ancient Near East to our Members and the local community. This year, eight of these lectures were recorded with the support of Mind Online, the University of Chicago's online resource for educational video content. Video recordings from the 2009–2010 Members' lecture season as well as past seasons are available to view for free on the Oriental Institute Web site: http://oi.uchicago.edu/getinvolved/member/events/recordings.html.

Members' events would not be possible without the hard work of many dedicated Oriental Institute staff members and volunteers, and the Membership Office is thankful for all of their assistance with a very successful 2009–2010 events season.

Travel

In the past year the Oriental Institute offered two travel programs to the Middle East. In November 2009, Dr. Nadine Moeller, director of excavations at Tell Edfu, and Foy Scalf, head of the Research Archives, escorted twenty-one travelers through Egypt on the travel program Splendors of the Nile. Dr. Moeller and Scalf introduced their travelers to the wonders of ancient Egypt, took them on a seven-day cruise down the Nile, and treated them to a behind-the-scenes tour of the Oriental Institute's excavations at Tell Edfu. In April of 2010, University of Chicago Professor John E. Woods and Oriental Institute Publications editor Leslie Schramer (M.A. 2002) guided fourteen travelers on a much-anticipated Oriental Institute travel program to Iran — Iran: Persia and the Splendors of Empire. Travelers spent two weeks exploring this fascinating country and visiting past Oriental Institute excavations including Chogha Mish and Persepolis.

Plans for several future Oriental Institute travel programs are currently underway. Dr. Yorke Rowan will be escorting a small group of travelers to Israel in October of 2010 on the travel program The Holy Land: Heritage of Humanity. This travel program will provide a comprehensive look at Israel, from prehistoric burial sites to the modern-day beauty of Tel Aviv's White City, and it includes a private tour of the Oriental Institute's newest excavations in Israel, Marj Rabba. In March of 2011, Dr. Robert Ritner will lead The Wonders of Ancient Egypt, and in August/September of 2011, Dr. Theo van den Hout will lead In the Footsteps of the Hittites through Turkey and Syria. Additionally, a future travel program to Iran led by Dr. Abbas Alizadeh and a tour to Syria by Dr. Gil Stein are in the works for 2012 and 2013. Oriental Institute travel programs are unique in that our passengers experience exclusive site visits and on-site learning privileges not enjoyed by other institutions or travel groups. Our Members learn directly from some of the most eminent scholars in the world, at sites the Oriental Institute has been working on and researching for almost a century. For more information on Oriental Institute travel programs, contact the Membership Office at oi-membership@uchicago.edu, or visit our Web site at http://oi.uchicago.edu/getinvolved/member/travel.html.

Administrative Notes and Benefits

Thanks to the hard work of marketing intern Amanda Sorensen (A.M. 2010), Oriental Institute Members can now receive discounts at several Hyde Park eateries and cultural venues:

- 15% off dining and live music on Wednesday at Piccolo Mondo (1642 East 56th Street)
- 15% off dining on Tuesdays at Park 52 (5201 South Harper Avenue)
- 10% off dining Monday–Friday from noon to 5 p.m. (excludes alcoholic beverages) at Chant (1509 East 53rd Street)
- 15% off dining on Mondays at Cedars Mediterranean Kitchen (1206 East 53rd Street)
- 10% discount on theater tickets (limit four per Member) at Court Theater (5535 South Ellis Street)

To receive these discounts, a valid Oriental Institute Membership card must be presented to the establishment staff at time of purchase.

Beginning in July of 2009, the Membership Office began processing Membership renewals on a quarterly cycle. This is a departure from the previous donation-based renewal system and monthly renewal cycles employed in previous years. The renewal quarters are based on the four seasons: spring, summer, fall, and winter. All Members will receive two renewal notices by mail: one at the beginning of the quarter, and one at the middle of the quarter. The decision to move to a quarterly renewal cycle was made after analyzing and assessing past renewal practices and current industry practices, and so far has proven to be efficient and cost effective. Membership renewal rates this year have reached as high as 72 percent, almost 20 percent higher than standard projected rates for comparable cultural institutions. In addition to mailing in membership renewal forms, Members are encouraged to renew online, which is quick, easy, cost effective, and secure. An online renewal form is available on our Web site at http://oi.uchicago.edu/getinvolved/member/electronic.html.

This year, there were two staffing changes for the Membership Office. In July, Maeve Reed joined the Oriental Institute as the new Membership Coordinator, replacing Sarah Sapperstein, who left the Oriental Institute to work with the University of Chicago's Office of Alumni Relations and Development. In August of 2009, we were sad to lose Brittany Luberda (AB 2009), the Membership Programs Assistant, who graduated from the University of Chicago with a degree in art history and took up a curatorial fellowship at the Dallas Museum of Art. Following Brittany's departure, Bethany Page Bouldin (AB 2011) joined the office in September of 2009 as the new Membership Programs Assistant and has been doing an excellent job managing the Membership database, hosting events, and responding to Members' inquiries.

———————

SPECIAL EVENTS

Meghan A. Winston

The 2009–2010 event schedule was an exciting one for the Oriental Institute! We welcomed over 700 guests to the Oriental Institute during the course of the year and held events including the Pioneers to the Past Members' preview, Voices from the New Past, a Breasted Society event, and many others. In addition, we've begun the busy planning process for next year's gala, which will be held on May 2, 2011. We also said good-bye to Kaye Oberhausen, who moved on to a position at the Victory Gardens Theater, and hired a new special events coordinator, Meghan Winston, who jumped in head first and handled much of the planning for this year's events. A special thank-you goes out to the Oriental Institute Visiting Committee, Events Committee, and all others who work tirelessly to make Oriental Institute events successful.

Rita Picken Memorial

On December 10, 2009, the Oriental Institute community gathered to remember the life of Rita Tallent Picken, a true friend and generous supporter of the Oriental Institute.

Rita showed her love for the Oriental Institute not only through her involvement with the Docent program for thirty years but also through her sponsorship of the Robert F. Picken Family Nubia Gallery and the 2009 special exhibit, Meresamun: A Temple Singer in Ancient Egypt.

This past spring at the Oriental Institute 90th anniversary gala, the Institute honored Rita with the James Henry Breasted Medallion — the highest honor we give our Members and supporters to recognize their service and commitment to the Oriental Institute.

Rita and her daughter, Kitty Picken, have been part of the fabric of the Oriental Institute for decades; Rita saw the people in the Oriental Institute community as a second family. She will be greatly missed.

Members' Preview — Pioneers to the Past

On January 11, over 150 Oriental Institute Members enjoyed an exclusive preview of Pioneers to the Past: American Archaeologists in the Middle East, 1919–1920, a special exhibit showcasing antiquities that James Henry Breasted bought on his first trip to the Middle East in the early 1900s.

After Gil Stein, director of the Oriental Institute, welcomed all guests, Breasted's journey was brought to life through an address by Geoff Emberling, chief curator of the Oriental Institute Museum. During his talk, Geoff helped Members re-live this trip through many never-before-seen photographs, artifacts, and archival documents.

Figure 1. A group of women looks at a bulletin board in the Henrietta Herbolsheimer Syro-Anatolian Gallery

Following Geoff's lecture, guests were invited to tour the exhibit and enjoy a reception with food from Amazing Edibles in the Edgar and Deborah Jannotta Mesopotamian Gallery. Members enjoyed delectable hors d'oeuvres in addition to a special expansion of the Suq, which featured specially ordered merchandise and autographed copies of catalogs chronicling Breasted's excursion.

Breasted Society Event — Voices from the New Past

On February 10, forty-five Breasted Society Members enjoyed an evening of storytelling and recollection of Breasted's letters to friends and family during the Oriental Institute's first expedition to the Middle East, in 1919–1920. Breasted's letters were brought to life by Gil Stein, director of the Oriental Institute, and Geoff Emberling, chief curator of the Oriental Institute Museum, while Oriental Institute faculty members shared experiences of their own.

The night opened with a cocktail reception in the Edgar and Deborah Jannotta Mesopotamian Gallery, where guests sipped on various time-appropriate beverages made with gin and dined on food artfully presented by Jewell Events Catering. Following the cocktail reception, guests took their seats in the Yelda Khorsabad Court to hear Breasted's letters read aloud as well as other stories.

Dr. Stein opened the storytelling program by reading an excerpt from *Dead Towns and Living Men* by Sir Leonard Woolley, which tells the story of Woolley's struggle with a Turkish director

Figure 2. John Breasted, grandson of James Henry Breasted, reads a letter from his grandfather during the Voices of the New Past Breasted Society event

Figure 3. The Breasted family poses for a photo in the lobby of the Oriental Institute. From left to right: James Henry Breasted III, Barbara Breasted Whitesides, and John Breasted, grandchildren of James Henry Breasted; Dr. Gil Stein, director of the Oriental Institute; John Larson, Oriental Institute archivist; Dr. Geoff Emberling, chief curator of the Oriental Institute Museum

of antiquities to get permission to dig at a certain site in the 1920s. Following the excerpt, Dr. Emberling recounted two letters that chronicle Breasted's experience as he purchased antiquities and took aerial photos in Egypt. Afterward, Dr. Nadine Moeller shared a story about her own experience as director of excavations at Tell Edfu about how astonished Egyptian workers are to see women working in excavation sites alongside men. Dr. McGuire Gibson, Professor of Mesopotamian Archaeology, and Dr. Matthew Stolper, Director of the Persepolis Fortification Project, shared wildly entertaining stories of their mentors in the field, which included stories of getting lost in sand storms, hosting Queen Victoria's granddaughter, and a visit from the Nazis at Persepolis.

We were also honored to have several members of the Breasted family with us at the event. Members were fortunate to hear from Barbara Breasted Whitesides, granddaughter of James Henry Breasted, Sr., who noted that she "was so proud as a granddaughter" to be in attendance. To finish off the program, we heard from John Breasted, Breasted's grandson, who shared a private letter from his grandfather to his son and John's father, James Henry Breasted, Jr., about marriage, which gave us greater insight into Breasted's everyday family life.

After the storytelling concluded, guests sampled desserts from an exclusive dessert bar that featured miniature lemon meringue tarts and chocolate chip cookies, truffle lollipops and cheesecake bites.

Post-doctoral Conference — Slavery and Households in the Near East

From March 4 to 6, the Oriental Institute welcomed twelve scholars from various universities spanning North America and Europe for its annual post-doctoral conference. Participants who arrived on Thursday night were treated to a dinner at the University's Quadrangle Club.

On Friday evening, various Oriental Institute professors, in addition to conference participants, attended a small reception for our guests in the Edgar and Deborah Jannotta Mesopotamian Gallery followed by a trip to Chicago's Chinatown, where attendees dined on dumplings, wonton soup, Mongolian chicken, and other delicious dishes.

To round out the weekend, we enjoyed one last session of papers as well as a pizza lunch. A special thanks goes out to Mariana Perlinac and Laura Culbertson for all they did to ensure the weekend's success.

Research Endowment Campaign Completion Celebration

On March 27, the Oriental Institute celebrated the completion of its Research Endowment Campaign (REC). The REC, started in 2006 and expected to end in 2011, achieved its goal of reaching $3 million in just three years. All of the money raised contributed to building the endowment in the five main areas within the Oriental Institute: ancient languages, archaeological fieldwork, Research Archives, technology, and museum holdings/special exhibits.

The evening commenced with a champagne reception in the director's office for donors who had given over $10,000 to the campaign. In addition to champagne there were hors d'oeuvres, including various tartlets, bacon-wrapped scallops, and other drinks.

Following the private reception, guests heard from representatives of each of the five endowments: Dr. Geoff Emberling, chief curator of the Oriental Institute Museum; Theo van den Hout, director of the Chicago Hittite Dictionary; Foy Scalf, head of the Research Archives; John Sanders, head of technology; and Dr. Nadine Moeller, director of excavations at Tell Edfu. All five participants gave an in-depth account detailing how REC contributions have benefitted their respective projects.

Following the program, attendees enjoyed a selection of appetizers, including miniature crab cakes, three kinds of ceviche, and white-wine sangria, which were provided by Beyond Events Chicago Catering.

Annual Members' Event — Passport to the Middle East: Check Out Our Digs!

April was the highlight of the Oriental Institute event season, ending with our annual Members' event, Passport to the Middle East: Check Out Our Digs! This year our event gave guests an in-depth look at each of the seven Oriental Institute digs: the Galilee Prehistory Project, Tell Edfu, Tell Zeidan, Jericho, Zincirli, Hamoukar, and Kerkenes Dağ. Check Out Our Digs! also served as the kick-off for our new Adopt-a-Dig program, which focuses on creating a partnership of discovery between donors and field researchers.

Figure 4. Dr. Geoff Emberling, chief curator of the Oriental Institute Museum, talks to patrons at the Galilee Prehistory Project booth

The setup for this event was unique in that each of the Oriental Institute excavations had its own booth, situated at a specific place among the galleries. During the event, guests were invited to visit each of the booths and speak with the dig directors about their excavation seasons and findings. Each dig director prepared a booth with different props that helped event goers learn more about each dig.

Middle Eastern cuisine, provided by Occasions Chicago Catering, was presented in the Robert and Deborah Aliber Persian Gallery. Fare included chicken and lamb kabobs, falafel, hummus, and dolmades.

Dr. Gil Stein, director of the Oriental Institute, raffled off six custom-made pieces of artwork, commissioned from our very own artist, Angela Altenhofen. One drawing was specifically designed for each dig according to its landscape and native botanicals.

Breasted Society Event — A Sunday Garden Party at 11 Rockgate

On May 23, the Oriental Institute partnered with the Chicago Botanic Garden to present an exclusive Breasted Society and President's Circle event. About sixty-five guests attended a lecture by Judith Tankard, author of *Beatrix Farrand: Private Gardens, Public Landscapes*, which traces the life and work of one of the foremost landscape architects of the early 1900s.

Figure 5. Visiting Committee member Nicole Williams (left) with author Judith Tankard

Beatrix Farrand embarked on her career when she was in her early twenties and today is recognized as the first woman to rise above the invisible line between garden design and landscape architecture, a field that was dominated by men. She is renowned for her work on estate gardens as well as her designs for academic campuses, including the Oriental Institute courtyard.

Following the lecture, Oriental Institute Visiting Committee member Nicole Williams and her husband, Larry Becker, graciously welcomed Breasted Society and President's Circle members, as well as Oriental Institute faculty and staff, into their home and garden for a Sunday afternoon garden party.

Figure 6. Dr. Nadine Moeller (left), director of excavations at Tell Edfu, along with Lynn Abrahamson (center), director of individual giving and board relations, and James Boudreau (right), vice president of marketing and development, at the Chicago Botanic Garden

Guests were allowed to peruse the garden as they enjoyed passed hors d'oeuvres, including cucumber cups filled with chicken salad, strawberries filled with mascarpone cheese, and guava-flavored pectins, all of which were provided by Calihan Catering.

HONOR ROLL OF DONORS AND MEMBERS
* THE JAMES HENRY BREASTED SOCIETY *

Named for the founder of the Oriental Institute, the James Henry Breasted Society is an elite group of donors whose contributions are vital for the support of major research programs, as well as the day-to-day operation of the Oriental Institute. Patrons of the James Henry Breasted Society contribute $1,000–$2,499 annually, while we welcome donors of $2,500 or more into the Director's Circle.

DIRECTOR'S CIRCLE

$50,000 and Above

Trust Estate of Mr. William Rowland Boyd, New York, New York
Community Foundation for Southeast Michigan, Detroit, Michigan
The Andrew W. Mellon Foundation, New York, New York
Mr. Joseph Neubauer & Mrs. Jeanette Lerman-Neubauer, Philadelphia, Pennsylvania
Estate of Myrtle Keillor Nims, Chicago, Illinois
Miss Kathleen Picken, Chicago, Illinois
Mr. Nassef Sawiris, Cairo, Egypt
The University of Chicago Women's Board, Chicago, Illinois

$25,000–$49,999

Alwin C. Carus Mineral Trust, Dickinson, North Dakota
Mr. John W. & Jeanne Rowe, Chicago, Illinois

$10,000–$24,999

Mr. Eric & Ms. Andrea Colombel, New York, New York
Mrs. Margaret E. & Mr. James L. Foorman, Winnetka, Illinois
Professor Crawford H. Greenewalt, Jr., Wilmington, Delaware
Mr. Howard E. Hallengren, New York, New York
Mrs. Janet W. Helman & Mr. Robert A. Helman, Chicago, Illinois
Mr. David & Mrs. Barbara Kipper, Chicago, Illinois
Mrs. Marjorie Nelson & Mr. Roger R. Nelson, Chicago, Illinois
Ms. Kimberly Querrey & Mr. Louis Simpson, Chicago, Illinois
Toni Sandor Smith, Chicago, Illinois
Mrs. Lorna P. Straus & Dr. Francis H. Straus II, Chicago, Illinois

$5,000–$9,999

Ms. Deborah Aliber & Professor Robert Z. Aliber, Hanover, New Hampshire

Mr. Alan R. Brodie, Chicago, Illinois

T. Kimball Brooker Foundation, Chicago, Illinois

R. Crusoe & Son, Chicago, Illinois

Ms. Andrea M. Dudek, Orland Park, Illinois

Mr. Philip Elenko, New York, New York

Mrs. Nancy H. Gerson & Mr. Isak V. Gerson, Chicago, Illinois

Mrs. Margaret H. Grant & Mr. Robert M. Grant, Chicago, Illinois

Mr. Byron L. Gregory, Wilmette, Illinois

Mr. David P. Harris & Mrs. Judith A. Harris, Chicago, Illinois

Mr. Roger D. & Mrs. Joyce R. Isaacs, Glencoe, Illinois

Mrs. Marjorie B. Kiewit, Chestnut Hill, Massachusetts

Mrs. Lucia Woods Lindley & Mr. Daniel A. Lindley, Jr., Evanston, Illinois

Mr. & Mrs. Aldis V. Liventals, Wilton, Connecticut

Mrs. Jill Carlotta Maher & Mr. David W. Maher, Chicago, Illinois

Mrs. Barbara G. Mertz, Frederick, Maryland

Mr. James B. & Mrs. Ann V. Nicholson, Detroit, Michigan

Peerless Confection Company, Lincoln, Illinois

The Rhoades Foundation, Chicago, Illinois

Mrs. Alice E. Rubash & Mr. Norman J. Rubash, Evanston, Illinois

Mrs. Mary W. Schloerb & Mr. Robert G. Schloerb, Chicago, Illinois

Mrs. Lois B. Schwartz, Los Angeles, California

Mrs. Mary G. & Mr. Charles M. Shea, Wilmette, Illinois

Mr. & Mrs. H. Warren Siegel, San Juan Capistrano, California

Mrs. Annette A. Vandaele & Dr. Walter H. Vandaele, Washington, D.C.

Mrs. Marjorie K. Webster, Santa Barbara, California

Ms. Nicole Suzann Williams & Mr. Lawrence Becker, Glencoe, Illinois

$2,500–$4,999

Mrs. Janina Marks, Chicago, Illinois

Dr. Miriam Reitz Baer, Chicago, Illinois

Ms. Gretel Braidwood & Mr. Raymond D. Tindel, Earlysville, Virginia

Mr. Joseph M. Diamond, Hazel Crest, Illinois

Far Horizons Archaeological & Cultural Trips, Inc., San Anselmo, California

Mrs. Mary L. Gray & Mr. Richard Gray, Chicago, Illinois

Greater Kansas City Community Foundation, Kansas City, Missouri

Mr. & Mrs. Dietrich M. Gross, Wilmette, Illinois

Mrs. Misty S. Gruber & Mr. Lewis S. Gruber, Chicago, Illinois

Mr. & Mrs. Walter M. Guterbock, Hermiston, Oregon

Ms. Linda H. Heagy & Mr. Thomas C. Heagy, Chicago, Illinois

Mr. Jack A. Koefoot, Evanston, Illinois

Mr. Richard Kron & Ms. Deborah Bekken, Chicago, Illinois

Mr. & Mrs. Robert M. Levy, Chicago, Illinois

Ms. Catherine Moore, Gurnee, Illinois

Museum Tours, Inc., Littleton, Colorado

$2,500–$4,999 (cont.)

Nuveen Benevolent Trust, Chicago, Illinois

Mr. Can C. Ozbal, Maynard, Massachusetts

Ms. M. K. Pitcairn, Kempton, Pennsylvania

Dr. Audrius Vaclovas Plioplys & Dr. Sigita Plioplys, Chicago, Illinois

Mrs. Elizabeth Plotnick & Mr. Harvey B. Plotnick, Chicago, Illinois

Dr. Erl Dordal & Ms. Dorothy K. Powers, Atlanta, Georgia

Mr. & Mrs. Patrick Regnery, Burr Ridge, Illinois

Mr. Thomas F. Rosenbaum & Ms. Katherine T. Faber, Wilmette, Illinois

Saint Lucas Charitable Fund, Burr Ridge, Illinois

Mr. Thomas & Mrs. Barbara Schnitzer, Chicago, Illinois

Secchia Family Foundation, Grand Rapids, Michigan

Mrs. Angeline B. Sopranos & Mr. Orpheus J. Sopranos, Winnetka, Illinois

Mr. Oğuz Soysal, Chicago, Illinois

Ms. Anna M. White, Terra Haute, Indiana

Mrs. Elizabeth & Dr. Sharukin R. Yelda, Chicago, Illinois

Ms. Flora & Ms. Jeannette Yelda, Chicago, Illinois

$1,000–$2,499

Mr. Robert McC. Adams, La Jolla, California

Gail H. Adele, Moscow, Idaho

Mrs. Mary S. Allan & Mr. Stanley N. Allan, Chicago, Illinois

Mrs. Geraldine Smithwick Alvarez, Burr Ridge, Illinois

Archaeological Tours, New York, New York

Armstrong Foundation, Lancaster, Pennsylvania

Mr. Roger Atkinson & Ms. Janet Arey, Riverside, California

Mr. & Mrs. Ronald R. Baade, Winnetka, Illinois

Mr. John J. Barbie, Chicago, Illinois

Dr. Kathleen G. Beavis & Mr. Bruce L. Beavis, Chicago, Illinois

Mrs. Nancy D. Bergner & Mr. Mark Bergner, Chicago, Illinois

Dr. Petra M. Blix, Chicago, Illinois

Mrs. Virginia Bobins & Mr. Norman R. Bobins, Chicago, Illinois

Professor John Bonnar, Dublin, Ireland

Ms. Margaret Brandt & Mr. Albert Lyons, Eminence, Kentucky

Ms. Janice Lynn Brannon, Grayslake, Illinois

Mr. & Mrs. Cameron Brown, Lake Forest, Illinois

Mr. Steven & Ms. Heidi Camp, Winnetka, Illinois

Mr. & Mrs. Bruce S. Chelberg, Chicago, Illinois

The Chicago Community Foundation, Chicago, Illinois

Mr. & Mrs. Eric Clark, Sierra Madre, California

Mr. & Mrs. Charles F. Custer, Chicago, Illinois

Ms. Katharine P. Darrow & Mr. Peter H. Darrow, Brooklyn, New York

Ms. Margaret Hart Edwards, Lafayette, California

ExxonMobil Foundation, Houston, Texas

Mrs. Emily H. Fine, San Francisco, California

Ms. Joan S. Fortune, Santa Fe, New Mexico

$1,000–$2,499 (cont.)

Mr. Wolfgang Frye, Phoenix, Arizona

Mrs. Louise Glasser & Mr. James J. Glasser, Chicago, Illinois

Mr. Richard Cartier Godfrey & Ms. Alice Godfrey, Chicago, Illinois

Diana Grodzins & Family, Chicago, Illinois

Ms. Louise Grunwald, New York, New York

Mrs. Carolyn Werbner & Mr. Howard G. Haas, Chicago, Illinois

Estate of Jane Davis Haight, Napa, California

Mrs. Deborah & Mr. Philip Halpern, Chicago, Illinois

Mr. Graham Hamilton, Palo Alto, California

Mr. Andrew Nourse & Ms. Patty A. Hardy, Woodside, California

David & Betty Hess, Downers Grove, Illinois

Mrs. Joan L. Hoatson, Burr Ridge, Illinois

Mrs. Doris B. Holleb, Chicago, Illinois

Drs. Kamal & Lucy Ibrahim, Chicago, Illinois

Mr. Edgar & Mrs. Deborah Jannotta, Winnetka, Illinois

Dr. Rebecca Jarabak & Dr. Joseph Jarabak, Hinsdale, Illinois

Dr. Janet H. Johnson & Dr. Donald Whitcomb, Chicago, Illinois

Mr. Jack Josephson & Dr. Magda Saleh, New York, New York

Ms. Waheeb N. & Ms. Christine S. Kamil, Westfield, New Jersey

Mr. Michael & Mrs. Rosalind Keiser, Chicago, Illinois

Mr. William K. Kellogg III, Chicago, Illinois

Mrs. Diana H. King & Mr. Neil J. King, Chicago, Illinois

Mr. Frank L. Kovacs & Ms. Renee Kovacs, Corte Madera, California

Dr. Dwight R. Kulwin & Dr. Elizabeth H. Brown, Cincinnati, Ohio

Dr. Joseph T. Lach, Evanston, Illinois

Mrs. Linda Noe Laine, New York, New York

LaSalle Fund, Inc., New York, New York

Ms. Nancy Lassalle, New York, New York

Ms. Isabel Leibowitz & Mr. Marvin H. Leibowitz, Aventura, Florida

Mr. James Keith Lichtenstein, Chicago, Illinois

Mr. Michael & Mrs. Kristina Lockhart, Lancaster, Pennsylvania

Mr. & Mrs. Barry MacLean, Mundelein, Illinois

MacLean-Fogg Company, Mundelein, Illinois

Mr. Mehdi Maghsoodnia & Ms. Parisa Golestani, Menlo Park, California

Mrs. Judith W. McCarter & Mr. John W. McCarter, Jr., Northfield, Illinois

Mr. Karim Mostafa & Ms. Janet Mostafa, Philadelphia, Pennsylvania

Ms. Virginia O'Neill, Chicago, Illinois

Mr. Donald Oster, London, England

Ms. Joan Hunt Parks, Chicago, Illinois

Mr. Gaetano Fernando Perego, Chicago, Illinois

Dr. & Mrs. Harlan R. Peterjohn, Bay Village, Ohio

R. B. Industries, Inc., Niles, Illinois

Mr. Thad & Mrs. Diana Olson Rasche, Oak Park, Illinois

Mrs. Crennan Ray, Santa Fe, New Mexico

Mr. Laurance & Mrs. Annabelle Redway, Washington, D.C.

Mrs. Helga Reichel-Kessler, Bad Sackingen, Germany

Mr. Harold & Mrs. Deloris Sanders, Chicago, Illinois

$1,000–$2,499 (cont.)

The Honorable George P. Shultz & Mrs. Charlotte Mailliard Shultz, San Francisco, California

Ms. Helen L. Schumacher, Kenosha, Wisconsin

Dr. Coleman Seskind, MD, Chicago, Illinois

Mr. Matthew Sideman, Chicago, Illinois

Mr. & Mrs. Clyde Curry Smith, PhD, River Falls, Wisconsin

Ms. Lowri Lee Sprung & Mr. John Sprung, San Pedro, California

Mr. Matthew Stolper, Chicago, Illinois

Mr. David & Mrs. Jean Stremmel, Winnetka, Illinois

Ms. Jeanne Sullivan, Chicago, Illinois

Ms. Emily Teeter & Mr. Joseph Daniel Cain, Chicago, Illinois

Mrs. Mari D. Terman & Dr. David M. Terman, Wilmette, Illinois

Mrs. Sandi & Mr. Ed Thayer, Chicago, Illinois

Vanguard Charitable Endowment, Southeastern, Pennsylvania

Mrs. Rose & Mr. Robert Wagner, Chicago, Illinois

Ms. Barbara Breasted & Mr. George M. Whitesides, Newton, Massachusetts

$500–$999

Abbott Laboratories Employee Giving, Princeton, New Jersey

Academic Arrangements Abroad, Inc., New York, New York

Mr. William & Ms. Judith Alger, Santa Fe, New Mexico

Alsdorf Foundation, Chicago, Illinois

Ms. Dorothy S. Foorman & Mr. Sydney F. Anderson, Bloomington, Indiana

Mr. John & Mrs. Suzanne Batchelor, Fernandina Beach, Florida

Ms. Judith Baxter & Mr. Stephen Smith, Oak Park, Illinois

Dr. Vallo Benjamin, New York, New York

Mr. Lawrence & Mrs. Zaida Bergmann, Fairfax, Virginia

Mr. & Mrs. William Bosron, Indianapolis, Indiana

Mr. Bruce P. Burbage, Nokomis, Florida

Mr. Timothy John Crowhurst & Mrs. Cecilia Crowhurst, New York, New York

Ms. Bettie B. Dwinell, Chicago, Illinois

Mr. Richard & Ms. Delores Eckrich, Denver, Colorado

Mr. Frederick Elghanayan, New York, New York

Mr. Jeff & Mrs. Jamie Fortin, Calgary, Alberta, Canada

Mr. John & Ms. Dorothy Gardner, Chicago, Illinois

Ms. Elizabeth R. Gebhard, Washington, D.C.

Dr. Sharad & Dr. Jasleen Goel, Cincinnati, Ohio

Mr. Richard E. & Ms. Beth M. Heath, Boca Raton, Florida

Mr. John P. Henry & Ms. Jan Isaacs Henry, Colorado Springs, Colorado

Mr. Scott E. & Mrs. Carolynne A. Hertenstein, Cary, North Carolina

Mr. Stephen & Mrs. Patricia Holst, Westport, Massachusetts

Ms. Connie Howes, Lake Forest, Illinois

International Horizons, Inc., Hillsborough, North Carolina

Mr. David Isles, Concord, Vermont

Mr. John A. Kelly, Jr., & Mrs. Joyce J. Kelly, Winnetka, Illinois

Ms. Polly Kelly, Pinehurst, North Carolina

$500–$999 (cont.)

Professor Adrian Kerr & Mrs. Louise Kerr, Fort Myers, Florida
Mr. Donald Allen Link & Mrs. June Link, Princeton, New Jersey
Mr. & Mrs. Laurence Lissak, Lombard, Illinois
Mr. Donald Mayall & Ms. Carolyn Curtis, Palo Alto, California
Dr. Jack Muraskin & Ms. Annette Leavy, Philadelphia, Pennsylvania
Ms. Mary Jane Myers, Los Angeles, California
Mr. & Mrs. Phil C. Neal, Chicago, Illinois
Mr. Charles R. Nelson, Seattle, Washington
New York Times Company Foundation, Princeton, New Jersey
Mr. John & Mrs. Mary Anne Nielsen, Lombard, Illinois
Parsa Community Foundation, Redwood City, California
Mrs. Betty L. Perkins, Los Alamos, New Mexico
Dr. Gerald S. & Mrs. Joy N. Picus, Woodland Hills, California
Mr. Lawrence C. & Ms. Frances F. Rowan, Reston, Virginia
Dr. Randi Rubovits-Seitz, Washington, D.C.
Dr. Bonnie M. Sampsell, Chapel Hill, North Carolina
Nahal Iravani-Sani & Barmak Sani, San Jose, California
Mr. John Eric & Mrs. Susan Schaal, Burr Ridge, Illinois
Dr. Joseph Smolik, Switzerland
Mr. Solon & Mrs. Anita Stone, Sherwood, Oregon
Mrs. Linda C. & Mr. Harold E. Stringer, Garland, Texas
Mr. Stefano & Mrs. Mariarita Vicini, Washington, D.C.
Mr. Charles Mack Wills, Jr., East Palatka, Florida
Mr. Robert I. Wilson, Peoria, Illinois
Mr. Michael Yang, Thousand Oaks, California
Mr. Howard O. Zumsteg, Jr., & Mrs. Diane R. Zumsteg, San Francisco, California

$250–$499

3M Company, St. Paul, Minnesota
Ms. Mary C. Abadi & Mr. D. M. Abadi, Iowa City, Iowa
Mr. Gregory D. S. Anderson & Ms. Mary R. Bachvarova, Salem, Oregon
Dr. Thomas W. Andrews, Hinsdale, Illinois
AT&T Foundation, Princeton, New Jersey
Miss Janice V. Bacchi, San Diego, California
Ms. Renee Barnaby, Monroe, Washington
Ms. Barbara Bell, Cambridge, Massachusetts
Dr. & Ms. Sidney J. Blair, Oak Park, Illinois
Mr. James & Mrs. Mary Louise Bradbury, Knoxville, Tennessee
Mr. O. John Brahos, Wilmette, Illinois
Ms. Catherine Novotny Brehm, Chicago, Illinois
Mr. Bob & Ms. Pat Brier, Riverdale, New York
Mr. John A. & Ms. Judy Carmack Bross, Chicago, Illinois
Mr. Wallace Cameron, Brighton, Victoria, Australia
The Chicago Community Trust, Chicago, Illinois
Ms. Joan Cichon, West Dundee, Illinois

$250–$499 (cont.)

Mr. Steven Anthony Clark & Ms. Janet L. Raymond, Oak Lawn, Illinois

Columbia College of Art & Design, Chicago, Illinois

Ms. Johna S. Compton, Chancellor, Alabama

The Honorable Barbara F. Currie, Chicago, Illinois

Mr. Charles W. Daggs III & Mrs. Rebecca S. Daggs, Lafayette, California

Ms. Julie Derby, Algonquin, Illinois

Ms. Ann R. Esse, Sioux Falls, South Dakota

Mr. Laurence R. Evans, Moraga, California

Mrs. Ann B. Fallon, Tucson, Arizona

Mr. Barry Fitzpatrick, West Midlands, Texas

Mrs. Eleanor B. Frew, Flossmoor, Illinois

Goldman Sachs & Company, Princeton, New Jersey

Mrs. Marsha & Mr. David Gratner, Sulpher Springs, Indiana

Mr. Francis P. Green, Bloomington, Illinois

Mr. Bahador Hariri, Menlo Park, California

Mr. Richard & Mrs. Lucy Harwood, Colorado Springs, Colorado

Dr. & Mrs. H. Lawrence Helfer, Pittsford, New York

Ms. Randy Lowe Holgate, Chicago, Illinois

Mr. Arthur T. & Ms. Susan L. Hurley, Napa, California

Mr. George T. Jacobi & Mrs. Angela C. Jacobi, Milwaukee, Wisconsin

Mrs. Sandra Jacobson, Chicago, Illinois

Ms. Mary Louise Jackowicz, Chicago, Illinois

Mr. Quintin Johnstone, Hamden, Connecticut

Journeys of the Mind, Oak Park, Illinois

Mr. Robert Kao, West Linn, Oregon

Dr. Irmgard K. Koehler, Chicago, Illinois

Mr. Martin J. & Mrs. Susan B. Kozak, Wilmette, Illinois

Mr. Steven L. & Mrs. Sally Ann K. Krahn, Alexandria, Virginia

Mr. Bernard Krawczyk, Chicago, Illinois

Mr. Raju & Ms. Melanie Kucherlapati, Weston, Massachusetts

Mrs. Elisabeth F. Lanzl, Chicago, Illinois

Ms. Annette Leavy, Philadelphia, Pennsylvania

Ms. Phoebe R. Lewis & Mr. John D. Lewis, Milwaukee, Wisconsin

Lincoln Park High School, Chicago, Illinois

Dr. John & Mrs. Amy Livingood, Bethesda, Maryland

Mrs. Jadwiga Lopez-Majano, Chicago, Illinois

Mr. & Mrs. Jo Desha Lucas, Chicago, Illinois

Mr. P. E. MacAllister, Indianapolis, Indiana

Mr. Raymond McBride, Chicago, Illinois

Ms. Vivian B. Morales, Saint Paul, Minnesota

Mrs. Kate B. & Mr. William L. Morrison, Chicago, Illinois

Ms. Holly Mulvey, Evanston, Illinois

Mrs. Eileen Nash, Leicestershire, United Kingdom

Mr. Larry Paragano, Basking Ridge, New Jersey

Patterson Belknap Webb & Tyler, New York, New York

Pearson Education, Livonia, Michigan

Ms. Louise Lee Reid, Chicago, Illinois

$250–$499 (cont.)

Mrs. Lillian K. Rexford & Mr. Gary W. Rexford, Topeka, Kansas
Mrs. Marguerite Saecker, River Forest, Illinois
Mr. & Mrs. Sandbower, Baltimore, Maryland
Ms. Ljubica Sarenac & Ronald Lindenberg, Chicago, Illinois
Mr. John Shearman, Toledo, Ohio
Ms. Lois B. Siegel, Chicago, Illinois
Dr. Benjamin & Ms. Radhiah Smith-Donald, Chicago, Illinois
Mr. Kent D. Sternitzke, Fort Worth, Texas
Mr. George R. Sundell, Jr., Wheaton, Illinois
Mr. Thomas K. Tappan, Chicago, Illinois
Mr. Lester & Mrs. Sylvia Telser, Chicago, Illinois
Mr. Randolph & Mrs. Barbara Thomas, Chicago, Illinois
Mr. Alexander Weintraub, Newton Center, Massachusetts
Mr. Henry C. Wente, Toledo, Ohio
Wheaton College, Wheaton, Illinois
Mr. & Mrs. Wayne L. White, Rockport, Texas
Mr. Robert Wade Wiley, Chicago, Illinois
Ms. Debra L. Wingfield, Lenexa, Kansas
Mr. S. Courtenay Wright, Chicago, Illinois
Mr. Lowell T. Wynn III, Chicago, Illinois
Mr. Thomas Yoder, Chicago, Illinois

$100 to $249

Mr. Daniel L. Ables, Scottsdale, Arizona
Mrs. Susan M. Ables,
Ms. Sandra M. Adams, Chicago, Illinois
Mr. Charles Martin Adelman, Cedar Falls, Iowa
Mrs. Nathalie F. Alberts, Chicago, Illinois
Mrs. Sylvia K. Aldrin & Mr. John C. Aldrin, Gurnee, Illinois
Mrs. Karen B. Alexander & Mr. Walter Alexander, Geneva, Illinois
Mrs. Susan J. Allen & Mr. James P. Allen, Providence, Rhode Island
Ms. Mary Allison, Manchester, New Hampshire
Mr. Andrew C. Alt, Chicago, Illinois
Mrs. Mahvash Amir-Mokri & Dr. Ebrahim Amir-Mokri, River Forest, Illinois
Mr. Edward & Mrs. Joan F. Anders, Burlingame, California
Mr. & Mrs. Richard J. Anderson, Chicago, Illinois
Dr. James Harper Andrews & Dr. Donna Avery, Chicago, Illinois
Mrs. Julie Antelman, Santa Barbara, California
Mr. Edward H. Ashment, Manteca, California
Mrs. Melinda C. Averbeck & Dr. Richard E. Averbeck, Deerfield, Illinois
Mr. Azadeh Baderkhani, Corte Madera, California
Mr. Kian Bahr, San Mateo, California
Dr. & Mrs. Herbert R. Barghusen, Portage, Indiana
Mr. Frederick N. Bates & Dr. Ellen Benjamin, Chicago, Illinois
Mr. Douglas Baum & Ms. Lynne Wait, Homewood, Illinois
Mrs. Laurie & Mr. James Bay, Chicago, Illinois
Mr. John M. Beal, Chicago, Illinois

$100–$249 (cont.)

Mrs. Sally C. Benjamin & Dr. Richard W. Benjamin, North Augusta, South Carolina
Benjamin Foundation, Inc., Jupiter, Florida
Ms. Phoebe Bennett & Mr. Clive Davies, Arlington, Virginia
Mrs. Francesca Bennett & Mr. Thomas H. Bennett, New York, New York
Mr. Edward C. Blau, Alexandria, Virginia
Glenn F. Boas, D.D.S., Lake Forest, Illinois
Ms. Renee M. Menegaz-Bock & Professor R. D. Bock, Chicago, Illinois
Mr. Christopher Boebel & Ms. Glenna Eaves, Chicago, Illinois
Ms. Wendy M. Bradburn & Mr. Norman M. Bradburn, Arlington, Virginia
Mrs. Muriel N. Brauer, Chicago, Illinois
Mr. James Henry Breasted III, Carbondale, Colorado
Mr. Tim Brennan, Hammond, Indiana
Mr. Marcus Brewster, Cape Town, South Africa
Mr. Stephen Hayze Brown, Jr., Chicago, Illinois
Ms. Alice C. Brown, New York, New York
Mrs. Noel Brusman & Mr. Marvin Brusman, Chicago, Illinois
Ms. Myllicent Buchanan, Chicago, Illinois
Ms. Romie Bullock & Mr. T. J. Bullock, Chicago, Illinois
Ms. Bridget Burns, Brampton, Ontario, Canada
Ms. Laurel V. Bell-Cahill & Mr. Timothy F. Cahill, Sacramento, California
Miss Anne Carlisle Campbell, Chicago, Illinois
Mr. Arturo Carillo & Ms. Ivonne Carrillo, Amarillo, Texas
Mrs. Eileen Caves & Dr. Joseph A. Greene, Belmont, Massachusetts
Mr. Afsar M. Cave, San Francisco, California
Ms. Claire Chamberlain, Houston, Texas
The Children's Museum of Indianapolis, Indianapolis, Indiana
Ms. Evangeline & Mr. Martin Choate, Chandler, Arizona
Drs. Charles & Mary Chuman, Chesterton, Illinois
Mr. & Mrs. C. Daniel Clemente, McLean, Virginia
Mr. Brian L. Cochran, Tuscon, Arizona
Mrs. Lydia G. Cochrane, Chicago, Illinois
Mrs. Zdzislawa Coleman, Chicago, Illinois
Ms. Charlotte C. Collier, Springfield, Missouri
Ms. Jane Comiskey, Chicago, Illinois
Ms. Callie Conrad, Green Valley, Arizona
Ms. Susan Cossack, Arlington Heights, Illinois
Mr. & Mrs. David L. Crabb, Chicago, Illinois
Mr. Edwin L. Currey, Jr., Napa, California
Mr. & Dr. Claude Davis, Hillsborough, North Carolina
Mrs. Susan L. Dawson & Mr. Mark D. Dawson, Chicago, Illinois
Ms. Catherine Deans-Barrett, Corrales, New Mexico
Mr. & Mrs. Robert O. Delaney, Winnetka, Illinois
Mr. Brendan & Mrs. Marsha Dempsey, St. Louis, Missouri
Mr. Kevin M. Dent, White Sands Missile Range, New Mexico
Mrs. Gwendolyn P. Dhesi & Mr. Nirmal S. Dhesi, Santa Rosa, California
Michaelann Dievendorf, Hummelstown, Pennsylvania
Ms. Patricia Dihel & Mr. Glen Wilson, Grayslake, Illinois
Ms. Mary E. Dimperio, Washington, D.C.
Mr. J. McGregor Dodds & Ms. Christine Dodds, Grosse Pointe Farms, Michigan
Mr. Michael Dorner, St. Paul, Minnesota

$100–$249 (cont.)

Mrs. Rose B. Dyrud, Chicago, Illinois

Mrs. Catherine J. & Mr. Pedro A. Dueñas, Chicago, Illinois

Mr. Robert C. Eager, Washington, D.C.

Ms. Patricia Eckers, Hatley, Wisconsin

Mr. C. David Eeles, Columbus, Ohio

Mr. John Ehleiter, Chicago, Illinois

Mr. Lawrence & Mrs. Vicky C. Eicher, Charlottesville, Virginia

Mr. James Elferdink, McKinleyville, California

Mr. S. Cody Engle, Chicago, Illinois

Mr. Barton L. Faber, Paradise Valley, Arizona

Ms. Hazel S. Fackler, Chicago, Illinois

Mr. & Mrs. Eugene F. Fama, Chicago, Illinois

Mr. William A. Farone & Ms. Cynthia H. O'Douohue, Irvine, California

Drs. Martin & Janis Fee, North Tustin, California

Dr. Ronald Allan Ferguson & Ms. Anges Roach, Gurnee, Illinois

Ms. Tamara Ferrari, Antioch, California

Mr. Luis Fierro, Chicago, Illinois

Ms. Mary G. Finn, Chicago, Illinois

First Baptist Church, Elgin, Illinois

Ms. Rosanne Fitko & Mr. James L. Padgett, Lake Forest, Illinois

Dr. Michael S. Flom, Boynton Beach, Florida

Dr. Leila M. Foster, Evanston, Illinois

Dr. Samuel Ethan Fox, Chicago, Illinois

Mrs. Judy Fraas & Mr. Charles J. Fraas, Jr., Jefferson City, Missouri

Mr. Jay B. & Mrs. Marlene M. Frankel, Chicago, Illinois

Ms. Susan S. Freehling & Mr. Paul E. Freehling, Chicago, Illinois

Ms. Elisabeth R. French, Washington, D.C.

Mr. Kere Frey, Chicago, Illinois

Mrs. Barbara H. Friedell & Mr. Peter E. Friedell, Chicago, Illinois

Mr. & Mrs. Charles Friedman, Chicago, Illinois

Mr. Jared Fuller, Provo, Utah

Ms. Xue Y. Fung & Mr. David Reese, Chicago, Illinois

Mr. Gregory J. Gajda, Mount Prospect, Illinois

Mr. Ted Geiger & Ms. Hildegard Geiger, Lake Villa, Illinois

Ms. Susan Geshwender & Mr. Kevin S. Geshwender, Barrington, Illinois

Mr. Michael Gillam, Washington, D.C.

Mr. & Mrs. Thomas J. Gillespie, Chicago, Illinois

Mr. Lyle Gillman, Bloomingdale, Illinois

Mr. Jerome Godinich, Jr., Houston, Texas

Reverend Raymond Goehring, Lansing, Michigan

Mrs. Ethel & Mr. William Gofen, Chicago, Illinois

Mrs. Natalie Goldberg & Mr. Howard Goldberg, Chicago, Illinois

Mrs. Betty Goldiamond, Chicago, Illinois

Mrs. Ethel F. Goldsmith, Chicago, Illinois

Mr. John Goldstein, Chicago, Illinois

Mr. James Goosby, Hollywood, Florida

Mr. Frederick J. & Mrs. Patricia J. Graboske, Rockville, Maryland

Dr. Nathaniel & Mrs. Anita Greenberg, Wilmette, Illinois

Mr. & Mrs. Charles O. Griffin, Newburyport, Massachusetts

Mr. & Mrs. John P. Guhin, Pierre, South Dakota

$100–$249 (cont.)

Mr. & Mrs. Sidney A. Guralnick, Chicago, Illinois

Mr. Charles Scott Hamel, Chapin, South Carolina

Mr. Joel L. Handelman & Ms. Sarah R. Wolff, Chicago, Illinois

Dr. Lowell Kent Handy & Ms. Erica Lynn Treesh, Des Plaines, Illinois

Mrs. Theresa Hannah, Glenview, Illinois

Mr. Carl R. Hansen, Mount Prospect, Illinois

Dr. W. Benson Harer, Jr., Seattle, Washington

Mrs. Myra Harms & Mr. William Harms, Grayslake, Illinois

Dr. Brice Harris, Jr., & Mrs. Carolyn P. Harris, Los Angeles, California

Mr. Mitchell Harrison, Chicago, Illinois

Ms. Mary J. Hartle & Mr. James B. Hartle, Santa Barbara, California

Dr. & Mrs. Robert Haselkorn, Chicago, Illinois

Ms. Valerie H. Hatcher & Mr. Edward D. Hatcher, Morris, Illinois

Mr. Matthew Hedman, Ithaca, New York

Ms. Laura N. & Mr. Gilbert B. Heller, Denver, Colorado

Mr. Robert F. Hendrickson, Princeton, New Jersey

Ms. Hedda Hess, Chicago, Illinois

Mr. & Mrs. David C. Hilliard, Chicago, Illinois

Mrs. Mary P. Hines, Winnetka, Illinois

Mr. Fredun & Ms. Hedwig Hojabri, San Diego, California

Mr. & Mrs. Marshall P. Hoke, New London, New Hampshire

Mrs. Audrey A. Hook, Mclean, Virginia

Mrs. Leonard J. Horwich, Chicago, Illinois

Mr. & Mrs. Lawrence Howe, Evanston, Illinois

Mr. & Mrs. Richard D. Jaffe, Chicago, Illinois

Mr. Kenneth W. James, Chicago, Illinois

Ms. Caroline C. January, New York, New York

Dr. Nancy J. Skon Jedele & Mr. Thomas Jedele, Laurel, Maryland

Ms. Marie T. Jones & Mr. Richard E. Jones, Wilmette, Illinois

Mr. Richard E. & Ms. Marie Thourson Jones, Wilmette, Illinois

Ms. Ann H. Kadinsky-Cade & Mr. Michael Kadinsky-Cade, Chicago, Illinois

Mr. Stephen Katz, Chicago, Illinois

Ms. Toyoko Kawase, Naniwaku, Osaka City, Japan

Mr. & Mrs. John B. Keefe, Riverside, Illinois

Ms. Alicia Kehr, Cresskill, New Jersey

Professor Anne Draffkorn Kilmer, Tucson, Arizona

Mr. Jerome C. Kindred, Arlington, Virginia

Ms. Margaret Kingsland & Mr. John Fletcher, Missoula, Montana

Ms. Henriette Klawans, Chicago, Illinois

Mr. & Mrs. William J. Knight, South Bend, Indiana

Mr. Frank J. Kohout, Iowa City, Iowa

Mr. & Mrs. Roger Konwal, Elmhurst, Illinois

Mr. Steven Koppes, Chicago, Illinois

Mr. & Mrs. James Kulikauskas, Arlington Heights, Illinois

Mr. Peter Lacovara, Atlanta, Georgia

Lane Technical High School, Chicago, Illinois

Ms. Lynn Langton, Chicago, Illinois

Ms. Laura L. Larner-Farnum, Yorba Linda, California

Mr. William J. Lawlor III & Mrs. Blair S. Lawlor, Kenilworth, Illinois

Mr. John K. Lawrence, Ann Arbor, Michigan

$100–$249 (cont.)

Mr. Mark Leach, Cape Town, South Africa

Dr. Richard Lee, Holland, Pennsylvania

Dr. & Mrs. Leonard H. Lesko, Seekonk, Massachusetts

Mr. & Mrs. John G. Levi, Chicago, Illinois

Mr. Charlton Lewis, New York, New York

C. Likerman & A. Mavoides, Scottsdale, Arizona

Mr. Alfred R. Lipton & Ms. Kathleen Roseborough, Glencoe, Illinois

Mr. & Mrs. Richard Lo, Chicago, Illinois

Mr. & Mrs. Philip R. Luhmann, Chicago, Illinois

Mr. Elias & Mrs. Karen Lyman, Southlake, Texas

Mr. James J. Mahoney, Jr., Tallahassee, Florida

Mr. Jason Majid, Doha, Qatar

The Malcolm Gibbs Foundation, New York, New York

Mr. Daniel Malecki, Kensington, California

Ms. Maria Danae Mandis, Chicago, Illinois

Tippian I. Manske, Santa Clarita, California

Drs. Lester & Joanne Mantell, New York, New York

Ms. Glennda Susan Marsh-Letts, Springwood, Australia

Mr. Ali Mashayekhi, Homer Glen, Illinois

Ms. Susanne Mathewson, Chicago, Illinois

Ms. Masako Matsumoto, Napa, California

Ms. Josephine Maxon, Lancashire, United Kingdom

Ms. Eva C. May, New Rochelle, New York

Mr. Philip H. McCallum, Easton, Pennsylvania

Mr. William L. McCartney, Chicago, Illinois

Mrs. Judith McCue & Mr. Howard McCue III, Evanston, Illinois

McMaster-Carr Supply Company, Elmhurst, Illinois

Mr. Richard Meadow, Canton, Massachusetts

Mr. & Mrs. Bob Meier, Tampa, Florida

Ms. Sarah Meisels, Wheaton, Illinois

Dr. Ronald Michael, MD, Kankakee, Illinois

Ms. Florence Kate Millar & Ms. Emma Shelton, Bethesda, Maryland

Mr. Richard Miller, Oak Lawn, Illinois

Mr. Gene A. Miller & Dr. Jenny T. Hackforth-Jones, Madison, Wisconsin

Dr. William Miller, Duluth, Minnesota

Mr. & Mrs. Phillip L. Miller, Chicago, Illinois

Mr. Neil Miller, Trenton, New Jersey

The Honorable Martha A. Mills, Chicago, Illinois

Milwaukee Institute of Art & Design, Milwaukee, Wisconsin

Ms. Maybrit S. De Miranda, Chicago, Illinois

Mr. Robert Ralph Moeller & Ms. Lois Patricia Moeller, Evanston, Illinois

Mrs. Jane M. Moffett & Mr. D. R. Moffett, Chatham, Massachusetts

Mr. Charles H. Mottier, Chicago, Illinois

Mr. & Mrs. George Moulton, Overland Park, Kansas

Mrs. Karole Mourek & Mr. Anthony J. Mourek, Chicago, Illinois

Mr. Henry Moy, Idabel, Oklahoma

Mr. Arthur H. Muir, Jr., Thousand Oaks, California

Mr. & Mrs. Jay F. Mulberry, Chicago, Illinois

Ms. Maureen Mullen, Greenfield, Wisconsin

Ms. Kathleen B. Murphy, Deerfield, Illinois

$100–$249 (cont.)

Mr. & Mrs. Douglas G. Murray, Santa Barbara, California
Mr. David E. Muschler, Chicago, Illinois
Mr. James L. Nagle, Chicago, Illinois
Ms. Dawn Clark Netsch, Chicago, Illinois
Ms. Kate Collins & Charles Newell, Chicago, Illinois
Mr. Dale George Niewoehner, Rugby, North Dakota
Ms. Alexandra A. O'Brien & Mr. Charles E. Jones, New York, New York
Mr. Craig O'Brien, Downers Grove, Illinois
Ms. Mary O'Connell, Geneva, Illinois
Dorinda J. Oliver, New York, New York
Mr. Daniel Odisho, Saint Charles, Illinois
Ms. Linda Osman & Mr. Myras Osman, Flossmoor, Illinois
Mrs. Florence Ovadia & Dr. Jacques Ovadia, Chicago, Illinois
Mr. Clinton W. & Ms. Carol E. Owen, Chula Vista, California
Ms. Martha F. Padilla, Sunland, California
Mr. Justin Palmer, Honolulu, Hawaii
Mr. Kisoon & Mrs. Moon Young Park, Chicago, Illinois
Erika O. Parker, MD, Evanston, Illinois
Molly Patterson, Madison, Wisconsin
Pattis Family Foundation, Highland Park, Illinois
Mr. Norman & Mrs. Lorraine Perman, Chicago, Illinois
Ms. Mary Jocelyn Perry, Anchorage, Alaska
Mr. Jeffrey Peters, Saint Paul, Minnesota
Ms. Elizabeth Hopp-Peters & Mr. Kurt Peters, Evanston, Illinois
Ms. Rita Petretti, Kenosha, Illinois
Mr. Ryan Pierce, Chicago, Illinois
Ms. Joan G. Pings, Chapel Hill, North Carolina
Mr. Parto Piran-Moradi, Fremont, California
Ms. Genevieve Plamondon, Telluride, Colorado
Mr. Cameron Poulter, Chicago, Illinois
Dr. Kendall Price, St. Paul, Minnesota
Mrs. Shirin Rahimian & Mr. Soroush Rahimian, Sacramento, California
Mr. Sankar Ramachandran, Naperville, Illinois
Mr. Keith Andrew Ramsay, Denver, Colorado
Mrs. Laurie Reinstein, Highland Park, Illinois
Mr. David R. & Mrs. Pamela C. Reynolds, Oak Park, Illinois
Dr. Nancy E. Rich & Mr. Barry Rich, Madison, Wisconsin
Mr. Dean F. Richardson, Pittsburgh, Pennsylvania
Rickover Naval Academy, Chicago, Illinois
Mrs. Shirley L. Rinder & Mr. George G. Rinder, Burr Ridge, Illinois
Ms. Karen Robinson, Mahtomedi, Minnesota
Mrs. Leona Zweig Rosenberg, Chicago, Illinois
Mr. Robert & Mrs. Harriet Rosenman, Glencoe, Illinois
Mrs. Carol Rosofsky & Mr. Robert B. Lifton, Chicago, Illinois
Mr. Gregg Alan Rubinstein, Washington, D.C.
Mrs. Shirley A. Ryan & Mr. Patrick G. Ryan, Winnetka, Illinois
Mrs. Michal Safar & Mr. Mazin F. Safar, Chicago, Illinois
Mr. Dan Saltzman, Portland, Oregon
Mr. Daniel Samelson, Anchorage, Alaska
Mrs. Peggy Sanders & Mr. John Sanders, Chicago, Illinois

$100–$249 (cont.)

Ms. Roberta Schaffner, Chicago, Illinois

Ms. Lynne F. Schatz & Mr. Ralph Schatz, Chicago, Illinois

Mr. Paul Benjamin Schechter & Ms. Naomi Reshotko, Denver, Colorado

Mrs. Lawrence J. Scheff, Chicago, Illinois

Dr. & Mrs. Rolf G. Scherman, MD, Greenbrae, California

Mr. & Mrs. Timothy J. Schilling, Hammond, Indiana

Ms. Hilda Schlatter, Oak Park, Illinois

Ms. Erika L. Schmidt, Ottawa, Illinois

Mrs. Karen M. & Mr. Frank L. Schneider, Chicago, Illinois

Ms. Lillian H. Schwartz, Chicago, Illinois

Mr. & Mrs. Albert M. Schwuchow, Chicago, Illinois

Dr. Michael Sha, Carmel, Indiana

Mrs. Ruth M. Sharp & Mr. R. C. Sharp, Limestone, Tennessee

Ms. Roberta Shaw, Toronto, Ontario, Canada

Mrs. Deborah Daila Shefner, Chicago, Illinois

Mr. Robert and Mrs. Tatiana Shelbourne, Washington, D.C.

Mrs. Junia Shlaustas, Chicago, Illinois

Mr. Steve & Ms. Karen Shultz, Loma Linda, California

Ms. Mae Simon, Chicago, Illinois

Mrs. Caroline Simpson, Geneva, Illinois

Mr. Michael A. Sisinger & Ms. Judith E. Waggoner, Columbus, Ohio

Dr. Henry D. Slosser & Mrs. Jackie Slosser, Pasadena, California

Mr. Kenneth & Mrs. Adair Small, Irvine, California

Mr. Allen R. Smart, Chicago, Illinois

Mr. Robert K. Smither, Hinsdale, Illinois

Mr. Hugo F. & Mrs. Elizabeth Sonnenschein, Chicago, Illinois

Ms. Dorothy Speidel, Wilmette, Illinois

Mr. Stephen C. Sperry, Litchfield, Minnesota

Mr. David A. Spetrino, Wilmington, North Carolina

Mr. & Mrs. John Stanek, Chicago, Illinois

Ms. H. Ann Stelmach, Evanston, Illinois

Mrs. Virginia Stigler & Mr. Stephen M. Stigler, Chicago, Illinois

Ms. Patricia Stoll, Wood Dale, Illinois

Mr. Rexford K. Stone, Surprise, Arizona

Mr. Gary Strandlund & Ms. Jessica Jones, Batavia, Illinois

Mr. Darrell Sutton, Redcloud, Nebraska

Mrs. Peggy Lewis Sweesy, San Diego, California

Ms. Faye E. Takeuchi, Vancouver, British Columbia, Canada

Mrs. Dorothy L. Tatum, Oxford, Mississippi

Ms. Betsy Teeter, San Francisco, California

Mr. Gregory D. & Ms. Jane A. Thomas, Grandview, Texas

Mr. Charles E. Thonney, Torrance, California

Mr. Jim Tomes, Chicago, Illinois

Mr. & Mrs. Robert Toth, Medina, Ohio

Trans Union Corporation, Chicago, Illinois

Dr. Robert Y. Turner, Philadelphia, Pennsylvania

Mrs. Marlene Tuttle & Mr. Russell H. Tuttle, Chicago, Illinois

Mr. & Mrs. Arthur Vallette, Naperville, Illinois

Mr. & Mrs. Warren Valsa, Chicago, Illinois

Dr. Axel Vargas, Chicago, Illinois

$100–$249 (cont.)

Dr. Zsolt Vasáros, Budapest, Hungary
Mrs. Sandra Velde & Mr. Karl H. Velde, Jr., Lake Forest, Illinois
Mr. John Vinci, Chicago, Illinois
Ms. Judith Y. Wagner, Newport Beach, California
Mr. Thaddeus Walczak & Ms. Carole Lewis, Ketchum, Idaho
Mr. James A. Walters II, Irving, Texas
Ms. Marjorie H. Watkins, Glenview, Illinois
Mr. & Mrs. Richard A. Watson, Missoula, Montana
Professor Patty J. Watson & Professor Richard A. Watson, Missoula, Montana
Mr. & Mrs. Leroy Webb, Spanaway, Washington
Mr. & Mrs. Tom Wehrheim, Oak Park, Illinois
Mr. & Mrs. J. Marshall Wellborn, New York, New York
Mr. Edward F. Wente & Mrs. Leila Ibrahim Wente, Chicago, Illinois
Mr. Vic Whitmore, Boise, Idaho
Mr. Ralph E. Wiggen, Los Angeles, California
Dr. Arthur N. Wilkins, Kansas City, Missouri
Dr. Alexandra Helen Wilkinson, London, England
M. A. & R. E. Williams, Garfield Heights, Ohio
Dr. Wendall W. Wilson, Victoria, Texas
Mr. James & Mrs. Bonnie Hicks Winn, Winnetka, Illinois
Professor Irene J. Winter & Professor Robert C. Hunt, Cambridge, Massachusetts
Dr. Roxane Witke, Wilton, Connecticut
Ms. Melanie R. Wojtulewicz, Chicago, Illinois
Mrs. Grace W. Wolf, Chicago, Illinois
Mrs. Ann Wolff, Winnetka, Illinois
Ms. Cynthia Woods, Midlothian, Virginia
Ms. Debra Yates, Chicago, Illinois
Mr. & Mrs. Robert R. Yohanan, Kenilworth, Illinois
Ms. Carole Y. Yoshida, Orland Park, Illinois
Mrs. Annette Youngberg, Albany, Oregon

*We are grateful to the over 600 donors, Members, and friends
who contributed more than $30,000 in the form of gifts of up
to $100 in 2009–2010. Due to space limitations, we are unable
to list all our Friends-level donors in this volume; a special
thanks to our Members and donors for their support.*

FACULTY AND STAFF

FACULTY AND STAFF OF THE ORIENTAL INSTITUTE
July 1, 2009–June 30, 2010

EMERITUS FACULTY

Lanny Bell, Associate Professor Emeritus of Egyptology

Robert D. Biggs, Professor Emeritus of Assyriology
r-biggs@uchicago.edu, 702-9540

John A. Brinkman, Charles H. Swift Distinguished Service Professor Emeritus
of Mesopotamian History
j-brinkman@uchicago.edu, 702-9545

Miguel Civil, Professor Emeritus of Sumerology
m-civil@uchicago.edu, 702-9542

Peter F. Dorman, Professor Emeritus of Egyptology
p-dorman@uchicago.edu

Gene B. Gragg, Professor Emeritus of Near Eastern Languages
g-gragg@uchicago.edu, 702-9511

Harry A. Hoffner, Jr., John A. Wilson Professor Emeritus of Hittitology & Co-editor
of Chicago Hittite Dictionary Project
hitt@uchicago.edu, 702-9551

Wadad Kadi, Avalon Foundation Distinguished Service Professor of Islamic Studies
w-kadi@uchicago.edu, 702-2589

William M. Sumner, Professor Emeritus of Archaeology
sumner.1@osu.edu

Edward F. Wente, Professor Emeritus of Egyptology
e-wente@uchicago.edu, 702-9539

FACULTY

Scott Branting, Assistant Professor (Research Associate) & Director, Center for Ancient Middle
Eastern Landscapes (CAMEL)
branting@uchicago.edu, 834-1152

Fred M. Donner, Professor of Near Eastern History
f-donner@uchicago.edu, 702-9544

Walter T. Farber, Professor of Assyriology
w-farber@uchicago.edu, 702-9546

McGuire Gibson, Professor of Mesopotamian Archaeology
m-gibson@uchicago.edu, 702-9525

Petra Goedegebuure, Assistant Professor of Hittitology
pgoedegebuure@uchicago.edu, 702-9550

Norman Golb, Ludwig Rosenberger Professor in Jewish History and Civilization
n-golb@uchicago.edu, 702-9526

Rebecca Hasselbach, Assistant Professor of Comparative Semitics
hasselb@uchicago.edu, 834-3290

Janet H. Johnson, Morton D. Hull Distinguished Service Professor of Egyptology &
Editor of Chicago Demotic Dictionary Project
j-johnson@uchicago.edu, 702-9530

Walter E. Kaegi, Professor of Byzantine-Islamic Studies
kwal@uchicago.edu, 702-8346, 702-8397

Nadine Moeller, Assistant Professor of Egyptian Archaeology
nmoeller@uchicago.edu, 834-9761

Dennis G. Pardee, Henry Crown Professor of Hebrew Studies
d-pardee@uchicago.edu, 702-9541

Seth Richardson, Assistant Professor of Ancient Near Eastern History
seth1@uchicago.edu, 702-9552

Robert K. Ritner, Professor of Egyptology
r-ritner@uchicago.edu, 702-9547

Martha T. Roth, Chauncey S. Boucher Distinguished Service Professor of Assyriology, Director and Dean of the Division of the Humanities, & Editor-in-charge of Chicago Assyrian
Dictionary Project
mroth@uchicago.edu, 702-9551

David Schloen, Associate Professor of Syro-Palestinian Archaeology
d-schloen@uchicago.edu, 702-1382

Andrea Seri, Assistant Professor of Assyriology
aseri@uchicago.edu, 702-0131

Gil J. Stein, Professor of Near Eastern Archaeology & Director of the Oriental Institute
gstein@uchicago.edu, 702-4098

Matthew W. Stolper, John A. Wilson Professor of Assyriology, Director, Persepolis Fortification
Archive Project
m-stolper@uchicago.edu, 702-9553

Theo P. J. van den Hout, Professor of Hittite and Anatolian Languages,
Executive Editor of Chicago Hittite Dictionary Project, & Chairman of the Department of
Near Eastern Languages and Civilizations
tvdhout@uchicago.edu, 834-4688, 702-9527

Donald Whitcomb, Associate Professor (Research Associate) of Islamic and Medieval
Archaeology
d-whitcomb@uchicago.edu, 702-9530

Christopher Woods, Associate Professor of Sumerology & Editor of the *Journal of Near Eastern Studies*
woods@uchicago.edu, 834-8560

K. Aslıhan Yener, Associate Professor of Archaeology
a-yener@uchicago.edu, 702-0568

RESEARCH ASSOCIATES

Abbas Alizadeh, Senior Research Associate, Iranian Prehistoric Project
a-alizadeh@uchicago.edu, 702-9531

Annalisa Azzoni, Research Associate, Persepolis Fortification Archive Project

annalisa.azzoni@vanderbilt.net

Richard H. Beal, Senior Research Associate, Chicago Hittite Dictionary Project
r-beal@uchicago.edu, 702-3644

Stuart Creason, Research Associate, Syriac Manuscript Project
s-creason@uchicago.edu, 834-8348

Geoff Emberling, Research Associate & Chief Curator
geoffe@uchicago.edu, 702-9863

Jean Evans, Research Associate, Diyala Project

Gertrud Farber, Research Associate, Sumerian Lexicon Project
g-farber@uchicago.edu, 702-9548

John L. Foster, Research Associate, Egyptian Poetry
jlfoster@uchicago.edu, (847) 475-2613

Mark Garrison, Research Associate, Persepolis Fortification Archive Project

François Gaudard, Research Associate, Chicago Demotic Dictionary Project
fgaudard@uchicago.edu, 702-9528

Ronald Gorny, Research Associate, Alishar Regional Project
rlg2@uchicago.edu, 702-8624

Eleanor Guralnick, Research Associate, Khorsabad Project

Wouter Henkelman, Research Associate, Persepolis Fortification Archive

Thomas A. Holland, Research Associate, Tell es-Sweyhat Project
t-holland@uchicago.edu

Carrie Hritz, Research Associate, Ayvalipinar Archaeological Project

W. Raymond Johnson, Research Associate (Associate Professor) & Field Director, Epigraphic
Survey
wr-johnson@uchicago.edu, 834-4355

Charles E. Jones, Research Associate
cejo@uchicago.edu,

Morag Kersel, Research Associate, Galilee Prehistory Project

Mark Lehner, Research Associate, Giza Plateau Mapping Project
MarkLehner@aol.com

J. Brett McClain, Research Associate & Senior Epigrapher, Epigraphic Survey
jbmcclai@uchicago.edu, 702-9524

Carol Meyer, Research Associate, Bir Umm Fawakhir Project
c-meyer@uchicago.edu

Rana Özbal, Research Associate, Tell Kurdu Project

Hratch Papazian, Research Associate

Marina Pucci, Research Associate, Chatal Höyük Publication Project

Clemens D. Reichel, Senior Research Associate, Diyala Project
cdreiche@uchicago.edu, 702-1352

Yorke Rowan, Research Associate, Ancient Studies and Director, Galilee Prehistory Project
ymrowan@uchicago.edu, 702-0086

Abdul-Massih Saadi, Research Associate, Syriac Manuscript Initiative
asaadi@nd.edu, (574) 631-8419

Mohammed Moin Sadeq, Research Associate

John C. Sanders, Senior Research Associate & Head, Computer Laboratory
jc-sanders@uchicago.edu, 702-0989

Seth Sanders, Research Associate, West Semitic Political Lexicon

Oğuz Soysal, Senior Research Associate, Chicago Hittite Dictionary Project
o-soysal@uchicago.edu, 702-3644

Geoffrey Summers, Research Associate, Kerkenes Project

Emily Teeter, Research Associate & Special Exhibits Coordinator
e-teeter@uchicago.edu, 702-1062

Raymond Tindel, Research Associate
r-tindel@uchicago.edu

Magnus Widell, Research Associate
widell@uchicago.edu

Tony Wilkinson, Research Associate, MASS Project
t.j.wilkinson@durham.ac.uk

Bruce Williams, Research Associate
Bbwillia@uchicago.edu, 702-3686

Richard Zettler, Research Associate

Karen L. Wilson, Research Associate
k-wilson@uchicago.edu

STAFF

Keli Alberts, Artist, Epigraphic Survey
kelialberts@hotmail.com

Susan Allison, Assistant Registrar, Museum
    srallison@uchicago.edu, 702-9518

Amar Annus, Postdoctoral Scholar (until 08/31/09)

Alain Arnaudies, Digital Archives Database, Epigraphic Survey
    arnaudies@laposte.net

Emmanuelle Arnaudies, Digital Archives Database, Epigraphic Survey
    emmanuellearnaudies@free.fr

Denise Browning, Manager, Suq
    d-browning1@uchicago.edu, 702-9509

Marie Bryan, Librarian, Epigraphic Survey
    mebryan@usa.net, 702-9524

Steven Camp, Executive Director
    shcamp@uchicago.edu, 702-1404

Dennis Campbell, Research Project Professional, Persepolis Fortification Archive Project
    drcampbell@uchicago.edu, 702-5249

Jessica Caracci, Education Programs Assistant, Education
    j-caracci@uchicago.edu, 702-9507

D'Ann Condes, Financial Management Assistant
    dcondes@uchicago.edu, 834-0451

Laura Culbertson, Postdoctoral Scholar (from 09/01/09)
    leculber@uchicago.edu, 702-2589

Laura D'Alessandro, Head, Conservation Laboratory, Museum
    lada@uchicago.edu, 702-9519

Margaret De Jong, Artist, Epigraphic Survey
    mdejong98ch@hotmail.com, 702-9524

Christina Di Cerbo, Epigrapher, Epigraphic Survey
    tinadicerbo@hotmail.com, 702-9524

Catherine Dueñas, Volunteer Programs Associate, Volunteer Office
    c-duenas@uchicago.edu, 702-1845

Virginia Emery, Epigrapher, Epigraphic Survey
    vlemery@uchicago.edu, 702-9524

Wendy Ennes, Senior Manager, Teacher and e-Learning Programs, Museum Education
    wennes@uchicago.edu, 834-7606

Terry Friedman, Volunteer Programs Associate, Volunteer Office
    et-friedman@uchicago.edu, 702-1845

Christian Greco, Epigrapher, Epigraphic Survey
    christian.greco@usa.net

Samir Guindy, Administrator, Epigraphic Survey
    samsgu1952@hotmail.com

Lotfi Hassan, Conservator, Epigraphic Survey
hslotfi@yahoo.it, 702-9524

James B. Heidel, Architect, Epigraphic Survey

Anait Helmholz, Library Assistant, Epigraphic Survey
anaith@succeed.net

Frank Helmholz, Mason, Epigraphic Survey
frankhel@succeed.net

Carla Hosein, Financial Manager
cchosein@uchicago.edu, 834-9886

Monica Hudak, Conservator (until 09/30/09)

Thomas James, Assistant Curator of Digital Collections, Museum
trjames@uchicago.edu, 834-8950

Helen Jacquet, Egyptologist Consultant, Epigraphic Survey
jeanhelka@aol.com, 702-9524

Jean Jacquet, Architect Consultant, Epigraphic Survey
jeanhelka@aol.com, 702-9524

Hiroko Kariya, Conservator, Epigraphic Survey
hkariya@aol.com, 702-9524

Jen Kimpton, Epigrapher, Epigraphic Survey
jenkimpton@hotmail.com, 702-9524

Yarko Kobylecky, Photographer, Epigraphic Survey
museumphoto@hotmail.com, 702-9524

Carole Krucoff, Head, Public Education, Education
c-krucoff@uchicago.edu, 702-9507

John Larson, Museum Archivist, Museum
ja-larson@uchicago.edu, 702-9924

Susan Lezon, Photo Archivist and Photographer, Epigraphic Survey
suelezon@gmail.com, 702-9524

Erik Lindahl, Gallery Preparator, Museum
lindahl@uchicago.edu, 702-9516

Adam Lubin, Security and Visitor Services Supervisor
alubin@uchicago.edu, 702-5112

Jill Carlotta Maher, Assistant to the Director of the Epigraphic Survey
jillcarlottamaher@yahoo.com, 702-9524

Helen McDonald, Registrar, Museum
helenmcd@uchicago.edu, 702-9518

Kathleen R. Mineck, Research Project Professional, Chicago Hittite Dictionary Project, & Managing Editor, *Journal of Near Eastern Studies*
kmineck@uchicago.edu, 702-9592

Clinton Moyer, Research Project Professional, Persepolis Fortification Archive Project
cjm52@cornell.edu, 702-5249

Kaye Oberhausen, Development Associate (until 10/02/09)

Susan Osgood, Artist, Epigraphic Survey
sittsu@sover.net, 702-9524

Safinaz Ouri, Finance Manager, Epigraphic Survey
safinazo@hotmail.com, 702-9524

Mariana Perlinac, Assistant to the Director
oi-administration@uchicago.edu, 834-8098

Conor Power, Structural Engineer, Epigraphic Survey
conorpower@msn.com, 702-9524

Maeve Reed, Membership Coordinator (from 07/28/09)
oi-membership@uchicago.edu, 834-9777

Anna Ressman, Photographer, Museum
annaressman@uchicago.edu, 702-9517

Sarah Sapperstein, Membership Coordinator (until 07/31/09)

Foy Scalf, Head of Research Archives
scalffd@uchicago.edu, 702-9537

Sandra Schloen, Database Analyst, Chicago Hittite Dictionary Project, & Persepolis Fortification Archive Project
sschloen@uchicago.edu

Julia Schmied, Blockyard and Archives Assistant, Epigraphic Survey
julisch@citromail.hu

Leslie Schramer, Editor, Publications Office
leslie@uchicago.edu, 702-5967

Rebecca Silverman, Development Associate (from 01/04/10)
rsilverman@uchicago.edu, 702-5062

Elinor Smith, Photo Archives Registrar, Epigraphic Survey
elliesmith26@yahoo.com, 702-9524

Amir Sumaka'i Fink, Research Project Professional, Zincirli Project
asumakai@uchicago.edu

Karen Terras, Research Project Professional, Nippur Project (from 11/19/09)
kterras@uchicago.edu, 702-1352

Thomas Urban, Managing Editor, Publications Office
t-urban@uchicago.edu, 702-5967

Krisztián Vértes, Artist, Epigraphic Survey
euergetes@freemail.hu

Alison Whyte, Assistant Conservator, Conservation Laboratory, Museum
aawhyte@uchicago.edu, 702-9519

Meghan Winston, Special Events Coordinator (from 11/09/09)
meghanwinston@uchicago.edu, 834-9775

Brian Zimerle, Preparator
zimerle@uchicago.edu, 702-9516

————————————

NOTES

NOTES

NOTES

INFORMATION

The Oriental Institute
1155 East 58th Street
Chicago, Illinois 60637

Museum gallery hours:
    Tuesday and Thursday to Saturday 10:00 am–6:00 pm
    Wednesday 10:00 am–8:30 pm
    Sunday 12:00 noon–6:00 pm

Telephone Numbers (Area Code 773) and Electronic Addresses

Administrative Office, oi-administration@uchicago.edu, 702-9514
Archaeology Laboratory, 702-1407
Executive Director, 702-1404
Assyrian Dictionary Project, 702-9551
Computer Laboratory, 702-0989
Conservation Laboratory, 702-9519
Department of Near Eastern Languages and Civilizations, 702-9512
Demotic Dictionary Project, 702-9528
Development Office, 834-9775
Director's Office, 834-8098
Epigraphic Survey, 702-9524
Facsimile, 702-9853
Hittite Dictionary Project, 702-9543
Journal of Near Eastern Studies, 702-9592
Membership Office, oi-membership@uchicago.edu, 702-9513
Museum Archives, 702-9520
Museum Information, 702-9520
Museum Office, oi-museum@uchicago.edu, 702-9520
Museum Registration, 702-9518
Public Education, oi-education@uchicago.edu, 702-9507
Publications Editorial Office, oi-publications@uchicago.edu, 702-5967
Research Archives, scalffd@uchicago.edu, 702-9537
Security, 702-9522
Suq Gift and Book Shop, 702-9510
Suq Office, 702-9509
Volunteer Guides, 702-1845

World-Wide Web Address

oi.uchicago.edu
